CIVIL IDOLATRY

CIVIL IDOLATRY

Desacralizing and Monarchy in Spenser, Shakespeare, and Milton

Richard F. Hardin

DELAWARE
Newark: University of Delaware Press
London and Toronto: Associated University Presses

Associated University Presses
440 Forsgate Drive
Cranbury, NJ 08512

Associated University Presses
25 Sicilian Avenue
London WC1A 2QH, England

Associated University Presses
P.O. Box 39, Clarkson Pstl. Stn.
Mississauga, Ontario,
L5J 3X9 Canada

The paper used in this publication meets the requirements
of the American National Standard for Permanence of Paper
for Printed Library Materials Z39.48-1984.

Library of Congress Cataloging-in-Publication Data

Hardin, Richard F.
  Civil idolatry : desacralizing and monarchy in Spenser,
Shakespeare, and Milton / Richard F. Hardin.
    p. cm.
  Includes bibliographical references (p.   ) and index.
  ISBN 0-87413-426-9 (alk. paper)
  1. English literature—Early modern, 1500–1700—History and
criticism.   2. Politics and literature—Great Britain—History—16th
century.   3. Politics and literature—Great Britain—History—17th
century.   4. Spenser, Edmund, 1552?–1599—Political and social
views.   5. Spenser, William, 1564–1616—Political and social
views.   6. Milton, John, 1608–1674—Political and social views.
7. Kings and rulers in literature.   8. Church and state in
literature.   9. Monarchy in literature.   10. Religion in literature.
I. Title.
PR428.P6H34   1992
820.9'358—dc20   90-50937
                                                                            CIP

Contents

Abbreviations

Abbreviations of biblical titles and works by Shakespeare and Milton follow standard usage as given in the *MLA Handbook*, edited by Joseph Gibaldi and Walter Achert (3d edition). The bibliographic entries give full title of scholarly journals abbreviated in the notes. In the following list, see the bibliography for the full information on editions of Erasmus, Milton, and others.

Adagia	Desiderius Erasmus, *Adagia*
CPW	John Milton, *Complete Prose Works*
CWE	Erasmus, *Collected Works of Erasmus*
CWM	Thomas More, *The Yale Edition of the Complete Works of St. Thomas More*
DNB	*Dictionary of National Biography*
EETS	Early English Text Society
FQ	Edmund Spenser, *The Faerie Queene*
Laws	Richard Hooker, *Of the Laws of Ecclesiastical Polity*
LB	Erasmus, *Opera Omnia*. Leyden, 1703
MPL	J.–P. Migne, *Patrologia Latina Cursus Completus*
OED	*Oxford English Dictionary*
OO	Erasmus, *Erasmi Opera Omnia*. Amsterdam, 1969
Summa	Thomas Aquinas, *Summa Theologiae*
TLS	*Times Literary Supplement* (London)

Preface

During the 1970s, shortly before this study got under way, three books on Tudor and Stuart England appeared with the word "illusion" in the title.[1] So far as I can tell, the coincidence represented a trend, not a conspiracy. At the time, with "image-making" a subject of great political interest, scholars were recovering earlier instances of art and theater used for official propaganda. Court patronage of painting, masques, and drama existed because, in David Loades's words, "In a sixteenth-century polity so much lay in the eye of the beholder, and it was the function of the court to attract and train that eye."[2] Not every beholder took easily to this training, however. From the viewpoint of the Hebrew and Christian Scriptures, when illusion threatens to overtake the moral sense it is called idolatry. Of the many possible idolatries, that of king worship was recognized well before the period on which I write. This book studies the theme of kingly abuse of the sacral, and the critique of such idolatry implied in certain literary works from the end of the Middle Ages to Milton. *Paradise Regained*, the latest text discussed here, continues that Judaeo-Christian demythologizing of power urged in the English mystery plays, in the works of major northern humanists, in Protestant apologetical tracts like the *Vindiciae contra tyrannos*, in the Elizabethan political plays of Shakespeare, and the political episodes of *The Faerie Queene*.

A book of this kind aims, as Lauro Martines has written, "to throw light on poetry and to throw light on history—that is, to use the light of social and historical analysis to find the traces of society in poetry, and to use social literary analysis to bring the light of poetry to the mysteries of the historical world."[3] Traditionally, literary historians have staked very modest claims in the historical world, except for that tiny corner of it that is relegated to them; but the growth during the 1980s of social, cultural, and interdisciplinary history threatens to change all that. Stephen Greenblatt's idea of "self-fashioning" has shown biographers and even crusty political historians new ways to think about their subjects; Christopher Hill has moved easily between "social and historical analysis" and "social literary analysis" in his work on

9

Milton and other poets of the seventeenth century. One result has
been "new historicism" as practiced by Greenblatt, with a basis in
Foucault's ideas on the subliminal discourses of power, and by
Jonathan Dollimore, with his emphasis on the material circumstances of literature: "A play by Shakespeare is related to the
contexts of its production—to the economic and political system
of Elizabethan and Jacobean England and to the particular institutions of cultural production (the court, patronage, theatre, education, the church)."[4]

New historicism has countered a Platonizing tendency discernible in "old" historicism and criticism, castigated by Dollimore for
embracing "essentialism" or "essentialist humanism." It implicitly
denies the distinction Frye has always insisted upon between
social and literary mythology, and consequently denies that literature in some way saves us from social mythology. *War and Peace*
and a recruiting poster are equally cultural artifacts. The study of
ideas in literature is pointless because "culture does not (cannot)
transcend the material forces and relations of production," as
these writers go on to say. This means that a complex body of
ideas, feelings, or illusions like religion does not exist outside of
"the church"—not a helpful starting point, one would think, in
considering the history of the Reformation. And on the whole,
Renaissance scholars of this persuasion often dismiss religious
ideas in their considerations of the period. While discussing an
avowedly religious poem, one applauds "Empson's admirable
eighteenth-century Enlightenment hatred of religion and superstition."[5] A British scholar sniffs that "so much American criticism
has imported Christ into Shakespeare, a movement at best absurd
and at worst hideous."[6] One confesses from his *temple serena*, "To
a reader who believes, as I do, that all religious practices and
beliefs are the products of the human imagination, these charges
[by More and Tyndale] have a melancholy and desperate sound."[7]
(Is "mere" hiding somewhere behind "products of the human
imagination"?) Such criticism usually ends in privileging the present, post-Enlightenment moment, despite everything we know
about the twentieth century. Closure would seem the last possible
remaining sin in our critical antinomianism, but here one kind of
closure thrives on another: if hierophants smuggle Christ into
Shakespeare, the sons of the Enlightenment are there to drive
him out.

While invoking the intellectual situation of Reformation and
Renaissance, the method here follows that of Stevie Davies' lucid,
intelligent book on Milton.[8] Davies analyzes certain root images of

kingship in *Paradise Lost* such as the Sultan and the Father, often expounding them with the aid of Milton's other writings. I use this approach while reading the poems in dialogue with other texts and with certain Christian myths (akin to Davies' "images") that have always worked against the interests of monarchy. Like Davies, I do not read these works as polemics, nailing them to a political or religious idea; but if any text acquires meaning from ideas and from other texts, it should be worthwhile to explore this system's hidden circuits. This is not to advocate any particular set of ideas, but it does mean acknowledging that they are there. In this regard Joan S. Bennett's and John D. Cox's recent books on Milton and Shakespeare signal a meaningful turn in social-literary scholarship concerning this period.[9]

Any scholarly book is a community undertaking, and my debt to many earlier scholars will be evident in the notes. I wish also to acknowledge valuable criticism upon various parts of the book, received from Professors Frank Baron, Michael Cherniss, William Gilbert, Steve Hilliard, W. Nicholas Knight, Oliver Phillips, Manny Schonhorn, and most of all David Bergeron, who gave me a careful review of the whole manuscript. My students have also helped give shape to my ideas, especially John Kalich, Gwen Ladd Hackler, and Geraldo Sousa. My indispensable research assistant, in all the ways she knows, was my wife Virginia. The University of Kansas provided me with sabbatical leave and several periods of summer support for research and writing. The Newberry Library awarded me a summer fellowship in 1979. The staff of the Newberry, and those of the libraries of Cambridge University, the British Library, the University of Illinois, and especially the University of Kansas were most helpful. Portions of my work were given as papers at the Central Renaissance Conference in 1980 and 1985, the Congress on Medieval Studies at Kalamazoo in 1982 and 1985, and the Sixteenth-Century Studies Conference in 1982. Part of the chapter on Erasmus was published as an article in *Renaissance Quarterly* 35 (1982): 151–63, and the editors of that journal have granted permission for me to use it here.

In quoting Latin sources, I normally use published translations where available; otherwise, I have given my own translation, with the Latin text in a footnote. In all quotations, while retaining original spellings I have expanded scribal abbreviations and regularized *j, i, u,* and *v.* I provide a list of abbreviations used. Early printed books published in London are cited with year of publication only.

CIVIL IDOLATRY

Introduction: Religion and Rule

The Two Kingdoms

In a salvo against the defeated Stuart monarchy, Milton declares
that kings exist chiefly because the mass of humanity wants them.
Citing in particular the common Englishman's "besotted and degenerate baseness of spirit," he goes on to say that "the People,
exorbitant and excessive in all their motions, are prone ofttimes
not to a religious onely, but to a civil kinde of Idolatry in idolizing
thir Kings." This remark discloses an important junction between
the political and religious thought of Milton and of his age. A few
years earlier the politically moderate John Hales used similar
language in a sermon on the text, "My kingdom is not of this
world." For Hales, Christ's words refer to all kingdoms, pagan
and Christian alike: "For all this *State* and *Magnificence* used in the
managing of them is nothing else but Secular Idolatry, used to
gain veneration and reverence unto that, which in comparison of
the Kingdom we speak of its mere vanity."[1] In these words Hales
and Milton exemplify their own version of Christianity's ongoing
"sacred discontent" with society's and even its own institutions, a
feeling that originates long before the Civil War or the Reformation.[2] The two Herods, Pilate, and Caesar personified for early
Christians the diabolic power of "the world," as Nimrod, Moloch,
or Pharaoh did for the Jews. A "kingdom not of this world"
sustained in Christians a measure of alienation from the civil
government, sometimes active resistance to it. Although this book
is mostly about the theme of the two kingdoms in literature
around the time of the Reformation, it would be well to recall
certain points concerning the earlier history of this idea.

The first Christians often lived in an uneasy truce with secular
authorities, even when they submitted to St. Paul's urging that
they obey their pagan magistrates. The principle that "all power is
from God" (Rom. 13:1) may have furnished a useful guide in
simple relations with political authority, but it was inadequate
when the power of the state appeared to conflict with Christian
doctrine, as in certain requirements for public homage to the

magistrate. Tertullian, who once attempted to convince his Roman rulers that Christians should be treated as a separate nation like the Jews, wrote his *De Spectaculis, De Idolatria,* and *De Corona* to guide his fellow believers between the perilous rocks of apostasy and painful martyrdom in their dealings with the world. Yet he steadfastly believed that, as Jean Daniélou has put it, "the whole of public life in the pagan city was impregnated with the demonic."[3] Admiring Tertullian on the state's quasi-religious claims, Milton jotted in his commonplace book a statement from his *Apology* that Hooker had used a half-century before: "I will frankly call the Emperor 'Lord,' but only when I am not forced to say 'Lord' in place of 'God.' For the rest, to him I am free; my one Lord is God." (Milton adds the query, "In what sense is the father of his country Lord?")[4] If the pagan gods had originally been devils, it was of course blasphemy to worship them; but the sacrilege was almost as great if, as many believed, they had formerly been men. According to Cyprian, the gods had once been "kings, who on account of their royal memory subsequently began to be adored by their people even in death."[5] Consider, says Tertullian, "that all idolatry is worship done to men, since it is generally agreed even among their worshippers that aforetimes the gods themselves of the nations were men; and so it makes no difference whether that superstitious homage be rendered to men of a former age or of this."[6]

A later vantage point shows that the controversy over emperor-worship was historically conditioned, not part of some evolutionary process. From the seventh to fifth centuries B.C., the Greeks, even under their tyrants, had no ruler cults. These seem to have begun as a way for cities to deal with the novel situation of dependence on rulers from outside their pale.[7] Imperialism thus begot imperiolatry. The myths of Constantine show that such veneration did not automatically stop with Christianity, and it remained for Augustine to formulate the most influential statement about the relations between the two kingdoms thereafter. Because Augustine both supports the Pauline respect for civil authority and denies the claims of such authority when it has not submitted to Christ, he was frequently invoked to justify church influence upon political life. Although it is an inadequate formulation of Augustine's own political philosophy, "Augustinism," the belief that the supernatural claims of the church take priority over the natural rights of the state to govern, became a decisive force in the politics of Western Europe. Rulership deemed not "Christian," that is, pliant to church authority, suposedly had no legitimate claim. The logical extension of this idea would have been a theocratic or hierocratic state. This change from St. Paul's teaching seems in part the result of a new understanding of peace and order, the chief goods of government. Peace, defined as "the obedience to God *in faith* and under the eternal law," is the superior good. It is achieved only through perfect order ("pax omnium rerum tranquillitas ordinis"). This harmony, concealed in the divine will, is made known to man only by faith, the custodian of which is the church.[8]

Needless to say, the implications for church and state in the West were immense. If Augustinism meant churchmen's meddling in affairs of state, however, it also meant that at least occasionally the avowed Christian concern for human dignity manifested itself in political reality. Peace and order need not be on the tyrant's terms. The simple political doctrine of Gregory's *Pastoral Care*, later to be translated by Alfred the Great, might have thwarted the designs of a would-be Herod:

> And the Lord said also to Noah and his children, "Grow and multiply, and fill the earth, and your fear and terror shall be over all the beasts of the earth." He did not say over other men, but over animals, since he was forbidden to have power over men, but was allowed to have it over animals. Man is by nature superior to irrational animals, but not to other men. . . . [I]t often happens that the ruler becomes puffed up in spirit and inflated with pride when he towers so much above others that all are subject to his will, and all his commands are very quicly obeyed for his benefit. . . . But he despises his subjects and does not perceive that they are his equals in birth and virtue. . . . And so he extols himself so loftily in some respects, and yet is bound to other men by being of the same kind, although he disdains to regard them. But thus he himself is made similar to him of whom it is written that "he beholds all pride who is king of all the children of pride," Who desired a separate sovereignty, and despised the fellowship and way of life of the other angels, saying: "I will build myself a seat in the north, and be like the highest."[9]

The opening sentences of this passage bring to mind Adam's lines, in a remarkably similar context of *Paradise Lost*, concerning Nimrod:

> He gave us only over Beast, Fish, Fowl
> Dominion absolute; that right we hold
> By his donation; but Man over men
> He made not Lord; such title to himself
> Reserving, human left from human free.

But this Usurper his encroachment proud
Stays not on Man; to God his Tower intends
Siege and defiance.

(XII.67–74)

Nimrod often represents a type of civil idolatry during the Middle Ages, and Spenser puts him in the dungeon of Pride. Lucifer or Nimrod, the important difference between Milton and Gregory is not in their allusions so much as in their assumptions about the Christian implementation of peace and order. Gregory believed that people could enjoy peace only by accepting the order that came with a Christian rule shared between the ecclesiastical and secular estates. Milton, by contrast, sought to remove old priest and new presbyter alike from civil government.

My study begins at the end of the era that, in so many ways, Gregory helped to launch. Except for Octavian, the king figure in the late medieval English mystery and morality plays fully exemplifies Gregory's satanic tyrant; these plays also consciously embody the warfare between the heavenly kingdom and the proud kingship of Satan and his earthly followers. The king, a remarkably consistent type in English drama of this period, differs notably from his counterparts in the plays of other nations. Instead of wisdom he projects slyness; he expresses power through ranting and self-glorification. The English plays are peculiarly deficient in the good kings that are so much a part of other medieval lore, lacking the piety and love for their subjects found even in the Herods of Continental religious drama at this time. The dramatic origins of the king-figure are uncertain, but by the end of the fourteenth century the type was absorbed into the mythology of English society as a whole. Why this happened is difficult to say. It may be that the ranting king was just a good popular draw; it may bear out the opinion that the English never really loved monarchy as, for example, the French did.[10] Probably Herod, Pharaoh, or Caesar Augustus in all their pomp and pride were the only "kings" most townsmen ever saw. This cannot have been good for the royal image.

The dream of merging civil and religious power was never realized in the Middle Ages, and the very notion of a spiritual power analogous to that of the state came under intense scrutiny during the Reformation. Many of these critics like Erasmus, while remaining nominally faithful to Pope Gregory's successors, denied that the role of the institutional church was to enforce peace through conformity with its law. In his last extended plea for peace, Erasmus maintained, as he always had, that the church is invisible: "Only God knows the hearts of men and truly knows who belongs to Him." The earthly church, he continues, will obtain peace only by respecting the integrity of individuals. "Let us not do anything by force, and certainly do unto others what we would wish them to do unto us. Let us beseech heaven and earth but in no way force anyone into a religion that repels him."[11] This statement looks forward to Milton's ideas on inward peace and order, on rule by persuasion rather than force, brought to fruition in *Paradise Regained*.

Erasmus figures largely in this study because, of those who had any great impact on English thought and religion, he is his century's chief spokesman for the claims of inward over outward authority, whether political or religious. Although in England his influence was most felt around the time of Henry VIII's Reformation, his political and ethical opinions found a wide readership throughout the sixteenth and seventeenth centuries. Erasmus may not have been an original political thinker—many of his antityrannical arguments appear in republican works from Cicero's *De Officiis* to Boccaccio's *De Casibus Virorum Illustrium*. Yet he was highly adept at propagating his ideas, whether through his popular collections of sayings, sometimes analyzed in the longer essays of the *Adagia*, or through the *Colloquies*, imaginary meetings of minds that often aired current social issues. Erasmus believed that kings were servants of the body politic, to be kept in check by a representative assembly or council; ideally they should be elected, not born, to the office. Like Thomas More and other humanists, he was disturbed by the expansion of European monarchies in power and territory, seeing this as the real threat to order and peace in this world, and especially in his native country. For Erasmus, peace came not through an enforced harmony of ideas; it was a condition of social stability that allowed the individual to exercise his will in the pursuit of virtue. Like Milton he believed that a virtue imposed from without was a contradiction in terms. The ideal monarch was modeled on the suffering Christ, not the all-powerful Father; thus his reign would be characterized by works of charity, tolerance, and the freely won obedience of his subjects. The tyrant aimed at enslaving the common will through fear, "order" being subservience to his power.

Erasmus's political writings barely survive today, despite their careful delineation in Robert M. Adams's *The Better Part of Valor* or the books of James Tracy, Margaret Mann Phillips, and Augustin Renaudet; my chapter on his work speaks chiefly to readers

unfamiliar with these scholars and with Erasmus's political ideas.
I especially wish to consider *The Education of the Christian Prince*,
his principal work on monarchy, in the light of its formal conventions. The *Education* is a collection of aphorisms, tentative in
nature, not the discursive essay presented to us in the standard
English translation. Its very form says something about the state
of political "science" in the sixteenth century, and the author's
skepticism underlies the indirection of the form.

The last three chapters of this book hold that there is more in
common than is generally recognized in the views of Spenser,
Shakespeare, and Milton on monarchy. Peace, the quest for
Eirena, is central to Spenser's Legend of Justice, just as it was the
chief political good of medieval Augustinism. In the last half of
Book V of *The Faerie Queene*, however, both excess and defect of
monarchic power are latent threats to peace—the excess occurring
whenever the monarch lays claim to divinity. Like the other poets
considered here, Spenser neither believes in James VI of
Scotland's divine right of kings nor defends absolute rule or the
imperial concept of monarchy. With many of his literate contemporaries, he envisions the ideal civil government as a mixed
monarchy in which the aristocracy plays an active, even decisive
role. A balanced understanding of Spenser as a royal poet requires acknowledging those important passages in his work
showing that as monarchies tend toward absolutism and world
conquest, they approach the condition of Babylon.

All the texts discussed in this study concur in the monarch's
duty to keep his own humanity uppermost in mind, to avoid the
allurements of "idol ceremony," as Shakespeare's Henry V calls it.
In a sense this book is an extended commentary on the soliloquy
in which this phrase appears. More particularly, the chapter on
Shakespeare traces the contrasting movements between the second tetralogy (especially *Richard II* and *Henry V*), as it progresses
toward a renunciation of the divinity in kingship, and *Julius Caesar*,
in which a free republic degenerates into fear at the superstitious
exaltation of one man above the body politic. Although Shakespeare does not share Milton's fervent spiritual iconoclasm, he
inherits from both religious and humanistic tradition a distrust of
autocracy and democracy alike. People and autocrat feed upon
each other in giving rise to tyranny.

Milton's prose works relentlessly attack sacred kingship. If at the
beginning of the Middle Ages there had been an attempt to merge
the body politic with the mystical body of Christ, the church,
Milton ultimately took the opposing stance. The civil ruler's in-

volvement in church government matters "brings back into religion that law of terror and satisfaction, belonging now only to civil crimes; and thereby in effect abolishes the gospel by establishing again the law to a far worse yoke of servitude upon us then before."[12] Moloch, Nimrod, and even Satan in *Paradise Lost* typify this undoing of the Redemption that occurs when spiritual government is handed over to the secular ruler. For Milton, all earthly monarchs eventually aspire to compete with divine rule. With other "Puritans," Milton saw this competition on two fronts. First, the English monarchy stood for a state religion, entailing all the risks of confusion and violation of conscience that remain at issue today. Second, the Caroline monarchy itself, with all its pomp and ceremony, with far more splendor than existed at the court Spenser knew, verged on becoming a religious cult.[13] Milton says as much in *Eikonoklastes*, remarking particularly upon the "idolatrous" picture of the king at prayer that accompanied Charles's supposed book of meditations, *Eikon Basilike*. Thus the path from Milton's early antiprelatical tracts leads straight to his attacks on monarchy. The dialogue of *Paradise Regained* essentially desacralizes, even demystifies kingship by separating Christ and Christian from the wealth, power, and cultural attainment that are monarchy's chief adornments. Responding to traditional royalist arguments of sovereignty through conquest and patriarchy, Milton redefines both concepts in this poem, just as he had Christianized epic heroism in *Paradise Lost*.

A brief history of the idea of the two kingdoms emerges in the history of the distinction, inherited chiefly from St. Augustine,[14] between *dulia*, the service owed to men, and *latria*, due only to God. St. Thomas considers the subject at some length, proposing that, although we owe homage *(cultus)*[15] to God and to certain men in varying measure, there is a hierarchy of bestowing honor corresponding to a hierarchy of indebtedness. Thus, down a step from religion, the worship owed to God, stands the virtue of piety, whose object is chiefly our parents, since they are "a particular source of life as God is its universal source."[16] The virtue beneath piety is respect *(observantia)*, "through which homage and honor are shown to those in authority." Piety takes precedence over respect because it pays homage to those closer to us, who by that fact have a more pressing claim on us.[17] Subordinate to this virtue, and thus quite removed from the homage of religion, is *dulia* or "respectful service," which is "due a man because he is master." Here Thomas allows that "a man shares a limited likeness to God's control, inasmuch as he holds some particular power either over another person or over some creature."[18] Between *latria* and the other virtues a crucial difference lies in the fact that "no creature takes part in God's creative power, the reason why adoration is his due." Humans can share in the "dominion" of God, but his creative act is "uncommunicated."[19] The distinction between *dulia* and *latria* was not always observed in later theology, and in the Reformation it was often dismissed as needless hair-splitting. William Tyndale cites the use of both words in Scripture to denote the reverence owed to God.[20] Accepting the words as synonymous could lend support either to radicals, who repudiated any worshipful attitude toward the ruler, or to monarchists, who found the difference merely one of degree. Milton flatly denied the distinction. So did Thomas Hobbes, who writes that "the worship which naturally men exhibit to powers invisible . . . can be no other but such expressions of their reverence as they would use toward men."[21]

The Two Bodies

Because the monarch was both a public and a private person, one may speak of "the king's two bodies" as a useful legal notion in the sixteenth and seventeenth centuries and even beyond. Neither Shakespeare nor Spenser, however, (let alone Milton) reflects the mystical attachment to this idea that Ernst H. Kantorowicz atttributes to it in his seminal book on this subject.[22] The book has, I believe, caused some confusion by importing from the continent an idea of sacred monarchy that was foreign to English political thought during the century in which Shakespeare's kings first trod the stage.

James I may have thought of himself as like God in ruling alone and supreme, but this view was never intellectually respected under the Tudors. The English constitution always maintained that the king rules in Parliament and never granted him sovereignty alone. It is true that after the Reformation the conditions of the moment led to something like belief in absolute monarchy, chiefly induced by those who sought the monarchy's protection from the threat of Rome. This strategy underlies Tyndale's *Obedience of a Christian Man*, John Foxe's *Acts and Monuments*, and to some extent *The Mirror for Magistrates*, all of which have been cited at one time or another to support the theory of the divine right of kings as a foundation of Tudor polity. A different, and more persistent, line of thought is represented in an epigram of the young Thomas More, entitled "The Consent of the People Both Bestows and Withdraws Sovereignty": "Any one man who has command of many men owes his authority to those whom he commands; he ought to have command not one instant longer than his subjects wish. Since kings, not their own masters, rule on sufferance, why are they proud?"[23] More published this epigram throughout Europe, and yet for another two decades remained amicable with one of England's most despotic kings.

Kantorowicz's book traces a sinuous path between a twelfth-century Norman treatise on the consecration of monarchs and certain "Cryptotheological" ideas in Tudor legal thought concerning the two "bodies," natural and political, of the king. Underlying his whole book are two noteworthy assumptions. One is an evolutionist idea of history, whereby the religious structures of early medieval society are seen as gradually secularized. In modern English common law, for example, if a king is guilty of a crime before coming to the throne, his acquiring the crown "would purge the attainder *ipso facto*"; this, Kantorowicz says, illustrates "the secularization of the purging power of the sacraments" (p. 12, n. 9). If we follow this approach consistently, Bracton's legal fiction of the "immortality" of corporate bodies loses its metaphorical status, becoming a symbol—a sublimated identification of such bodies with godhead. Piercing the baseless fabric of our ancestors' vision, the anthropologist-historian discovers what was never recognized in those dim times. Yet this assumption is even more problematic than the evolutionary one, since we need look no further than Christianity for an agency committed to distinguishing between the things of Caesar and of God.

There is no denying such influences on English social mythology as the analogy with natural hierarchies, the example of the single head of the Church—"pontifex" between earth and heaven—or the Roman legal tradition of ruler as mediator between divine and human law. Such comparisons had their effect upon the political environment. Yet the very pages of *The King's Two Bodies* testify to the conscious and critical distinctions between kingship and godhead made in late medieval England. During the troubled reign of Richard II, according to Holinshed's medieval source, when the favorite John Busshy spoke for commons to the king, he "did not attribute to him titles of honour, due and accustomed, but invented *unused* terms and such *strange* names, as were rather agreeable to the divine majesty of God, than to any earthly potentate" (p. 28, italics mine). The implications of this for Shakespeare's play must wait for the appropriate chapter. Kantorowicz grants that "Bracton on the whole shows hardly a tendency to exalt the secular state in general, or to raise its immutable Time-defying essence to the quasi-holy stratum to which Frederick II and his advisers aspired" (p. 188). In other words, the numinous kingship of the Holy Roman Empire is really foreign to the main line of English political experience, notwithstanding occasional mystifiers, like John Busshy or James I, who may have attempted to introduce such ideas.

Thus *The King's Two Bodies* moves dubiously from the legal fiction of the immortality of corporate bodies to the claim that medieval and Tudor England subscribed to a sacred or mystical theory of kingship. A clue to the motive of this book on "political theology" (as the author's subtitle calls his field) is provided by Kantorowicz himself in an earlier article on his subject. After quoting the passage from Plowden's Reports that would prove the starting-point for his later book, he says: "It is from these strata of thought, I believe, that the absolutist concept 'Mysteries of State' took its origins and that, when finally the Nation stepped into the pontifical shoes of the Prince, the modern ABSOLUTE STATE, even without a Prince, was enabled to make claims like a Church." This comment (the capitals are his) emerges no doubt from the author's own bitter experience with fascism in the 1930s, when he was forced to leave his professorship of history at the University of Frankfurt, eventually reestablishing himself as a scholar at the University of California.[24] Yet his thesis bears more directly on Continental than English history—if, indeed, it may be applied at all. A peculiar religious aura was one of Nazism's more lurid aspects, but it may be doubted that there is an evolutionary continuum between the Christian idea that all power is from God and the diabolic rituals of Hitler's Germany.

The King's Two Bodies has most influenced English studies in its commentary on Shakespeare's *Henry V* and *Richard II*. Its chief fallacy, I believe, is not uncommon among intellectual-historical approaches to literature, that of assuming the point it argues, and of misrepresenting certain passages of the plays in order to secure the argument.

The treatment of Henry V's soliloquy in Act IV, scene 1 is a case in point. Kantorowicz calls this a meditation "on the godhead and manhood of a king"; yet it deals only incidentally with godhead— perhaps only in that it is spoken by a king who is, in Kantorowicz's view, by the fact of his kingship divine. The epigraph for this chapter of *The King's Two Bodies* comes from Henry's soliloquy; but what Kantorowicz omits, at the ellipsis marks, is as noteworthy as what he gives:

> Twin-born with greatness, subject to the breath
> Of every fool, whose sense no more can feel
> But his own wringing. What infinite heart's ease
> Must kings neglect that private men enjoy! . . .
> What kind of god art thou, that suff'rest more
> Of mortal griefs than do thy worshippers?

The impression here is that "thou" in the fifth line is "kings" or kingship or Henry as king. With only this epigraph a reader would never know that the "god" being addressed is not the king but Ceremony. Here are the lines that Kantorowicz omitted at the ellipsis marks:

> And what have kings, that privates have not too,
> Save ceremony, save general ceremony?
> And what art thou, thou idol Ceremony?

Quite aside from the point (with which Kantorowicz would probably agree) that these are Henry's thoughts, not necessarily Shakespeare's, we can certainly be misled by the proof-text, as given, when the author launches his discussion of Shakespeare and kingship.[25] When he calls Richard II "the kind of god that suffers more of mortal griefs than do his worshippers" (p. 26), it is already supposed that Shakespeare's equating kingship with divinity is part of the lost Elizabethan world picture. Moreover, we may surmise that Henry's godliness somehow participates in the Christian godhead, when the lines in fact refer to "god" in the sense of "idol." Had the epigraph continued,

> And what art thou, thou idol Ceremony?
> What kind of god art thou, that suffer'st more
> Of mortal griefs than do thy worshippers?

any careful reader would have been puzzled by Kantorowicz's favorable attribution of this kind of godhead to Richard. In fact Richard *does* become a peculiar mix of idol (self-idolizing) and scapegoat; but this is an effect of his mortality. The human Richard is at the center of this play. Criticism of the last decade or two increasingly reads him as a mortal who erroneously and tragically thinks himself privy to divine favor. For Ruth Nevo the divine role is just that, a role—an "inherited and as yet untried conception of himself to which he retreats at the first crisis." Richard's soliloquy in Act III, scene 2 contrasts the "illusory name of king and the real nature of man." H. A. Kelly rightly points to the evidence of the plot: Richard's expression of confidence in his safety as God's anointed (III.2.36–62) is "an absurd *Mirror for Magistrates* generality" immediately contradicted by bad news. Paul Jorgensen says that in Richard's speech "a nostalgic, almost discredited theory is voiced by a mistaken character, one who is repeatedly wrong in his point of view."[26]

The conviction that Richard is sympathetically portrayed as a sacred king so colors this chapter in *The King's Two Bodies* that Kantorowicz takes no account of evidence of earlier scholars' reading to the contrary. He does not mention Richard's characteristic heedlessness, his probable involvement in his uncle Gloucester's murder. He says nothing of the view widely held among directors and critics that Richard, through a series of misjudgments, makes himself liable to the charge of tyranny and leaves his kingdom open to opportunists like Northumberland and Bolingbroke. The line, "Down, down I come like glistering Phaeton," is said to employ the solar image to show "the splendour of the catastrophe" (p. 33); yet Phaeton was in the Renaissance an emblem of defective rule, especially rule by careless youth. Spenser associates Lucifera with Phaeton to suggest the disastrous mix of pride and wrongful government. Few would quarrel with calling the deposition scene "a scene of sacramental solemnity" (p. 35), but is this a ritual or, as Herbert Coursen has said, an antiritual? Is it Richard who is sacred or the body politic? Erasmus believed that "the office of a prince is simply to administer what belongs to all." Coursen writes:

> It is not so much that Richard *confuses* morality and divinity, history and ceremony, body natural and body politic, . . . but that he destroys their fusion so that they, like his kingdom, are inevitably in conflict. If the state is sacred, a fusion of secular with spiritual, Richard is keeper of the holy metaphor. He must preserve it, not merely use it as his license.[27]

Kantorowicz approaches the heart of the play when he says of Richard that "Over against his lost outward kingship he sets an inner kingship, makes his true kingship to retire to inner man, the soul and mind and regal thoughts" (p. 37). From this Kantorowicz does not draw the obvious conclusion that the play seems to be saying, consistent with long-established Platonic wisdom on outer and inner rule, that if Richard had set up an "inner kingship" from the beginning his "outward kingship" might have survived.

Shakespeare's English contemporaries believed that a king was sacred in so far as all authority came from God, and that the crown lived on even though the person wearing it would die. But if "sacred kingship" means that the king was, like God, above human law, there was no significant expression of this concept in Tudor political thought.[28] Even Kantorowicz admits that sacredness was often allowed to the body politic as a whole, rather than the monarch (p. 208), that Parliament was occasionally spoken of with the same "semi-theological mysticism" as the sovereign (p. 227), and that the notion of "two bodies" was often attributed to persons of high rank rather than kings (pp. 395, 434). When the earlier Stuart kings would no longer take part in public spectacles, Londoners apparently transferred their immortal longings to the Lord Mayor, whose pageants increasingly rivalled the splendor of court masques.[29] At this point, I submit that the idea has lost its definition, and that we really seem to be dealing with the universal idea that all public persons, from constables to prelates, have a public and private self. During the Roman empire any significant public service, not just rulership, could make a man a god, as instanced in the cult of Diodorus Pasparos at Pergamum, an ambassador to Rome who succeeded in getting the city's taxes lowered.[30] As a commonplace in Elizabethan thought the notion of two persons appears in Spenser's Letter to Ralegh—a passage sometimes quoted in support of Kantorowicz. "I have followed all the antique poets historical," says Spenser,

> first Homere, who in his Persons of Agamemnon and Ulysses hath ensampled a good governour and a vertuous man, the one in his Ilias, the other in his Odysseis; then Virgil, whose like intention was to do in the person of Aeneas: after him Ariosto comprised them both in his Orlando: and lately Tasso dissevered them againe, and formed both parts in two persons, namely that part which they in Philosophy call Ethice, or vertues of a private man, coloured in his Rinaldo: The other named Politice in his Godfredo.

A bit later when Spenser talks of the Queen there is no reason to say he is not still thinking of these two "parts" of any public figure: "She beareth two persons, the one of a most royall Queene or Empresse, the other of a most vertuous and beautifull Lady." This opposition between public and private person has long served as

a fruitful approach to the history plays.[31] Considering this widely
recognized pattern in Renaissance literature, it appears an unnecessary complication to identify it with a continental theory of
kingship from the earlier Middle Ages.

The Historical Moment: Desacralizing

In the literature that has been mentioned, the themes of civil
and sacred kingship take on new meaning in the context of the
post-Reformation demythologizing or desacralizing of society's
institutions.[32] The Reformation began with what Steven Ozment
has described as a "swelling popular desire to be rid of the psychological and social burdens of late medieval religion," with all
its attendant rules, rituals, and pious casuistry. Ozment shows
that in Germany and Switzerland reformers wanted "a certain
desacralizing of late medieval religious life"; they "did not set out
to regulate and sanctify society so much as to make society's
sacred institutions and religiuos doctrines social."[33] Behind the
More-Tyndale debates, Stephen Greenblatt sees "a radical and
momentous social crisis: the disintegration of the stable world
order, the desacramentalization of church and state."[34] In government this movement was nourished by the secular policies of
Thomas Cromwell and pragmatic associates like Thomas Starkey
or Richard Morison—a Calvinist who read Machiavelli to his
household while serving as English ambassador to Charles V.
Consequently, as Elton writes, "the Church found itself the servant rather than the ruler of the lay commonwealth."[35] Elizabeth's
court "was probably more secular in spirit and culture than any
which had preceded it."[36] What we call Puritanism was the social
force most concerned with desacralizing in the church itself, as is
revealed in a remark by a leader of the Presbyterian Assembly of
Divines on the "superstition" of Laudian worship: "From the Altar
to the Bell-rope, all were Sacred; no comming into the church, no
going out, without uncovering, adoration, prostration, once,
twice, thrice, forward, backward; and he that would not doe so,
was held, little better than profane. The very Churchyards were
growne so holy, that if a beast did but touch them, they were held
by some profaned."[37]

These religious developments should not be isolated from other
events in post-Reformation England. Ozment's idea of making
society's institutions social, stripping them of any mystery or

magic that prevented their working on an ordinary level, describes effectively what a sensitive and intelligent citizen would want not only for his church but for his government. It is equally what Shakespeare's Henry V seeks in divesting monarchy of "idol ceremony," and what Spenser inherits from the thought of humanist reformers of the Renaissance.

The desacralizing of monarchy might have been urged much earlier than it was, had not the Tudor throne been needed to shield England from the papacy. Tyndale and other early English reformers recognized that a protestant monarchy given full power over its subjects could deliver and defend them from Rome. When this deliverance had been accomplished, then lost, then restored, some thought miraculously, it became plausible that England was indeed an "elect nation." John Foxe's belief in this regard underlies his view of the queen as an empress, for in Roman law an *imperator* was one who answered to no higher authority, civil or religious. The image of Elizabeth as a sacred empress was validated by her own political competence. Thanks to Stuart incompetence, images notwithstanding, four decades after her reign the English would pursue their elect role without a monarchy.

Both Elizabeth and Henry VIII were unusually adept at using quasi-religious means, including the symbolism and ritual of portraiture and pageantry, to shore up their political power, a strategy that received considerable support from sympathizers with the Reformation. The successful exploiting of these visual outlets compensated for the "not very impressive" written propaganda in support of obedience, as Penry Williams describes it. Williams believes that the power of ceremony was owing to fundamental differences between that age and our own: "The mental and emotional world of the Tudor polity is not easily grasped today, when the power of religious images is seldom felt. Ritual is suspect. Political symbols, where they survive, are usually ignored. Monarchs have long tried to pretend that they are—except on special occasions—much like the rest of us."[38] Yet were our ancestors that different from us? There is, for one thing, considerable evidence that ritual was "suspect" in religion. In politics it is so conceived, for one reason or another, by all of the sixteenth-century authors discussed in this book. At several points in *The Faerie Queene*, Spenser praises the plainness of antique custom as opposed to, say, the gaudy ceremonialism of the House of Pride or the courtly showiness of the House of Busirane. Richard II's fault, in Shakespeare's play, is precisely that he *forgets* he is "much like the rest of us." Erasmus tirelessly excoriated royal pomp as empty and hypocritical, as did the younger Thomas More.

Only for a brief time could one really find a widespread cult of royalty in Tudor England, when Elizabeth became Europe's Protestant Deborah-Diana-Astraea defending Truth from the seven-headed beast. Yet despite celebrations of "Empress" Elizabeth, the awe of majesty slackens somewhat during her reign. Thanks, no doubt, to her own humanity and compassion, it was no longer true, as it had been in her father's time, that the indignation of the ruler meant death. Moreover, Parliament had considerably extended its role in government, especially the House of Commons, a much weaker body in the time of the earlier Tudors.[39] This is not to say that the monarchy did not retain some of the religious significance (aside from its function as head of the church) that is still often claimed for it.[40] Even in modern democracies the nation's leader is endowed with sufficient reverence that an attack upon him does not affect citizens in the same way that one would upon a private person.[41] What Spenser, Shakespeare, and Milton would subvert, and the focus of this study, is what Bagehot called the "mischievous sentiment" of religion whereby monarchy used its sacred role to encroach upon traditional liberties (pp. 86–87). The dangers of such encroachment had long been reocgnized in England, and the most extreme reaction might have been expected when it accelerated while the other functions of government were strong. Monarchy then became inherently blasphemous to some, Francis Osborne declaring it to be "a sacrilegious overcharging a single person with more honour and power, then so frail a creature is able to beare, without falling into the distemper of excesse."[42]

In truth, the monarch with supernatural powers had not even been a feature of medieval English political thought.[43] Error on this point has led more than one scholar to overstate the "cult" of Elizabeth and the supposed despotism of her and her family.[44] The observation that "without the Reformation there is no new nation with a deified monarch at the center for the new drama to cluster around,"[45] misrepresents, I think, both the Elizabethan monarchy and the Reformation. There was a brief time when English Protestantism clung to the monarchy as its chief protection against the tyranny of Rome; but the notion of divine or absolute kingship is quite inconsistent with the often-maintained principle that the king rules in Parliament. Well before the Tudors, the royal power—to tax, for example—was hedged by the laws and the will of the whole nation as represented in Parliament. The bare mention of "a deified monarch" invites attention to a number of discrete issues, each with its own priority in any political historian's theory of kingship: absolutism, the extraordinary or magical endowments of the crown, the rights of subjects against tyrants, the question whether the king rules as God's infalliable representative or whether only his power is derived from God, to be taken from him if he abuses it. All these issues depend on how one attributes sacredness to the crown.

The truth is that our own perceptions of Tudor monarchy have fluctuated between desacralizing and mystification in the past century. Mandell Creighton, Elizabeth's Victorian biographer, was merely amused by Christopher Hatton's passionate letters to the old queen.[46] An argument that such reverence ought to be taken more seriously was advanced in the mystical idea of kingship that found support in J. N. Figgis's *The Divine Right of Kings*. Figgis saw the Tudors as breaking sharply with the medieval past, a break that was supposed to herald the emergence of the nation-state governed by absolutist monarchs claiming divine authority. He believed that Elizabeth claimed an authority even more absolute than Frederick II's, in that there was no papal influence to mitigate her power. However, as G. R. Elton says, historians now dispute the existence of a "new monarchy" in the sixteenth century.[47]

Literary historians especially cultivate the view of Elizabeth as absolute ruler, perhaps because it adds an attractively mythic dimension to the political background of the age. A recent book on *The Faerie Queene* sees it as an "epic tribute to early absolute monarchy under Elizabeth," written "before the idea of the state had detached itself from the person of the monarch." A highly regarded article proposes an absolutist regime that prevailed from the Tudors until the Stuart collapse. In it "the king acted as the summa and symbol of this new system of power in the context of its own political theory, which argued for an incease of power not for the State but for the King."[48] It may have looked that way to James I and son, but the English polity ran on a distribution, not a concentration of power. The governments of both Elizabeth and her father managed such a splendid balancing act that, as Keir says, "Parliamentary sovereignty as well as personal autocracy could be derived from Tudor principles of government."[49] The ruler may have been "king by divine right, *dei gratia*," but "he was also a king chosen by his people, bound in a relationship of mutual duty, enjoying a power ascending to him from below."[50] This meant stress upon the "semi-divine as well as the representa-

tive character of kingship," making the crown appear "untoucha-
ble, and yet accessible."[51] No contemporary text explores the full
impact of this "and yet" quality of monarchy better than Spenser's
Mercilla episode with its peculiarly Elizabethan sense of the para-
doxes of power and mercy conjoined in one person.

The political philosophy of Richard Hooker expresses so well
the concept of limited monarchy that his work, resurrected in the
mid-seventeenth century was used vindicate the parliamentary
cause. In Hooker's politics: "The *Parlament* of *England* together
with the *Convocation* annexed thereunto is that wherupon the very
essence of all goverment within this kingdome doth depend. It is
even the bodie of the whole Realme; it consisteth of the *King* and
of all that within the *Land* are subject unto him."[52] Hooker believed in the voluntary assent of the governed in government, not
in the mysterious power of kingship to carry the day on its own.[53]
"Originall influence of power from the bodie into the *King* is cause
of the *Kings* dependencie in power upon the bodie" (3:339). In
kingdoms like England, where the people are not under "subjection" but have "willingly condescended" to the sovereign's rule,
"The King is major singulis, universis minor" (3:336–37). Yet this
latter adage, found in the controversial *Vindiciae contra Tyrannos*, is
tempered by Hooker's belief in the tradition of inherited, not
elected, monarchy. Perhaps Hooker's only real concession to divine right theorists is that "the death of the predecessor putteth
the successor by blood in seisin" (3:338).

Unlike Erasmus and Starkey, Hooker viewed law through a
historian's eyes, accepting traditional practices as right by the very
fact that they depended on the collective wisdom of generations.
In this respect he looks forward to the seventeenth-century common lawyers in Parliament.[54] This belief in gradual amelioration
toward the securing of political justice resembles Spenser's philosophy of history. Spenser's confidence in the attainment of
perfection through successive generations finds expression in the
conclusions of *Epithalamion* and the Mutability Cantos. From a
similar ameliorist perspective, Book V of *The Faerie Queene* is
rightly seen as "a brief history of the world,"[55] recounting the
progress of justice among fallen men, from the elemental chaos,
to the heroics of the lawgiver, to the establishment of peace
through order under unified rule.

As for divine kingship, Hooker believed it to be a pagan idea
(3:340–41). In ancient times the ruler was lawmaker for both state
and church; then came the one revolution Hooker would autho-
rize, Christianity. The gradual Christianizing of the secular au-

thority has made it possible for all nations to live "according to the patterne of God's own ancient elect people" (3:330). This means, for example, that like ancient Jewish kings, on occasion a Christian king must "become subject to his own subjectes," the hierarchy, in the making of ecclesiastical laws.[56] Spenser enacts this subjection of the sovereign's will to the body politic in the Temple of Isis and the Court of Mercilla, to be discussed below. On the other hand, Shakespeare's *Richard III* or Spenser's episodes of Lucifera and the Souldan illustrate the evil of truly autocratic sovereignty.

Concerning the reverence due to kings, Hooker poses a neat formula: "Unto Kings by humane right, honour by very divine right is due" (3:335). This may furnish a solution to the problem posed by the Reformation's rejecting the distinction between *dulia* and *latria*, noted earlier. Kings are fully human, both as men and kings; but because "all power is from God" they deserve our homage. Another bishop, Thomas Cooper, took greater pains to sort out this problem:

> But for as much as princes, magistrates, rulers, parents, masters and all superiors have a portion of God's authority over us, as his officers and lieutenants in their callings: therefore God doth permit unto them some part also of his honour, but so far and in such things, and such manner as before is declared, retaining unto himself our faith and religion, with all the parts of his divine worship consisting in spirit and in truth, the calling upon his blessed name, the confession of his holy truth, and the obedience of his moral law: which things he doth not make subject to any prince's authority.[57]

To attribute divinity to the *authority* invested in the sovereign allows for a sense of the sacred in monarchy or any other office, and validates the exalted, seemingly religious terms with which some writers address the ruler.

Not all religious thinkers were of Hooker's and Cooper's opinions, to digress briefly on this one point. There does seem to have been an attempt to reinstate some distinction of worship according to person, especially when the monarch offered security from Rome. Edwin Sandys, his mind on Catholic "idolatry" of the pope, writes that "it is not so great a danger to honour a prince with all humility: therein men cannot so easily exceed, because the honour is civil."[58] By the end of Elizabeth's reign, however, Puritans like William Bradshaw used this distinction between civil and religious worship to answer the charge that their liturgical singularity implied rebellion against civil authority. "As civil Cere-

monies tend to the honor of them unto whom civil worship is
due, and is a part thereof: So Religious Ceremonies tend to the
honor of him unto whom religious worship is due, and is a part
thereof." In one of several books on this subject, the exasperated
Bradshaw spread the words "Civill & Ecclesiasticall" in large type
across the page to emphasize that there must be a distinction.[59]
Hooker's Book VIII of *Ecclesiastical Polity* was unpublished until
1648, when it was used in the cause against state interference in
religion. The readers of Book I may find this paradoxical, and
indeed Book VIII was long argued as corrupt or even a forgery.
But Hooker would not have subscribed to a view of kingship that
deprived it of some share in the sacred, all power being from God.

The Monarchomachy

During this period the most intense battles on the nature and
authority of monarchs occurred not in England but in France, at a
time of bitter civil strife. The persecution of the Huguenots, especially the concurrence of the ruling monarch in the massacre of
1572, elicited many political tracts on civil government and the
duties of subjects toward kings. The influence of this "monarchomachy" on Richard Hooker goes without saying,[60] for the
news and opinion from France could not fail to interest him and
his contemporaries. The English queen and her subjects, moreover, played important roles in the French political and religious
struggles.

On the Huguenot side, the important texts in this controversy
were Francois Hotman's *Franco-gallia* (1573), written shortly after
the author's escape to Geneva; Theodore Beza's *De jure mag-
istratuum* (1576), "the first major statement of Huguenot resistance
doctrine"[61] and the more radical *Vindiciae contra tyrannos* (1579),
probably by Phillipe du Plessis-Mornay, advisor to Henry of
Navarre, a nobleman with many English associations. This last
book, published under the name of "Junius Brutus," saw English
translations in 1581 and 1589, and reappeared in England during
the critical years of 1622, 1631, 1648, 1660, and 1689.[62] On the
other side were the influential Jean Bodin's *Six livres de la republique*
(1576), Andrew Blackwood's *Apologia pro regibus* (1581), an answer
to Buchanan's *De jure regni;* Louis Le Roy's *De l'excellence du gouver-
nement royale* (1575), and other works after which King James VI's
Trew Law of Free Monarchies (1598) comes limping lightly. Bodin's

Republic was frequently reprinted and is known to have been used in lectures and libraries at Cambridge in the 1580s.[63]

In describing the king as God's "living and breathing image,"[64] Bodin must have scandalized his Protestant opponents. In this respect, as in his aversion to female rulers (IV.5), many English readers would have felt unsympathetic toward France's most able theorist of monarchy. Huguenot writers by contrast often praised English institutions and the English queen. Theodore Beza sets the "mild and beneficent government" of England under Elizabeth against "the wretched and miserable condition of so many other countries."[65] The Protestant *Reveille-Matin des Francais et leurs voisins* (1573) was dedicated to Elizabeth, and the *Vindiciae contra Tyrannos* praises the English system of government, in which "the sovereignty seems to be in the parliament"—an authority "so sacred and inviolable, that the king dare not abrogate or alter that which had been there once decreed."[66]

The *Vindiciae*, in fact, offers a most emphatic argument for separating divinity from monarchy. The first of its four sections, considering whether subjects ought to obey their ruler if his commands contradict God's, constitutes a treatise on civil idolatry, serving as the foundation for the theory of government espoused in the book as a whole. The opening page laments that

> there are many princes in these days, calling themselves Christians, which arrogantly assume an unlimited power, over which God himself has no command, . . . they have no want of flatterers, who adore them as gods upon earth, many others also, who for fear, or by constraint, either seem, or else do believe, that princes ought to be obeyed in all things and by all men. (pp. 65–66)

This section produces all the often-used examples from Scripture and ancient history of men assuming divine authority: Nebuchadnezzar, Ahab, Antiochus, Herod, Alexander, Nero— each with his inevitable fall. As in the medieval mystery plays, the words of Lucifer are put into the mouth of the self-idolizing monarch: "So often, therefore, as any prince shall so much forget himself as insolently to say in his heart, . . . I will ascend above the heights of the clouds, I will be like the Most High: then on the contrary, will the Almighty say, I will rise up more high, I will set myself against thee" (p. 78). While granting that even in pagan states the ruler's authority comes from God, the author asserts that the king's realm is inherently corporeal. Thinking of the enforcement of doctrine and worship by Catholic rulers in France and elsewhere, he accuses oppressive kings of assuming "licence to themselves to enforce the consciences, which appertain chiefly to Jesus Christ. Holding the earth not great enough for their ambition, they will climb and conquer heaven itself" (p. 66). Here, as so often in the sixteenth century, the chief sin of monarchy is described in the symbolism of Babel.

Responsibility for this sin rests partly with the "flatterers" mentioned on the first page. To believe that "the great ones of the world hold a divided empire with God himself" befits "the poet Martial, which was not ashamed to call the edicts of Domitian, the ordinances of God" (p.70). Yet, as Milton would later declare, a share of the blame also falls to the people themselves:

> The people on the other side walks after [i.e., against] the commandment, when they yield to the desires of princes, who command them that which is against the law of god, and as it were burn incense to, and adore these earthly gods, and instead of resisting them, if they have means and occasion, suffer them to usurp the place of God, making no conscience to give that to Caesar, which belongs properly and only to God. (p. 66)

With the image of burning incense before the ruler, the author draws parallels between the old and new idolatry of power.

The *Vindiciae* proceeds to build on this foundation in the next two sections, considering whether there should be resistance to the prince who violates God's law and oppresses his church, and whether the prince who oppresses a commonwealth may be resisted. Not surprisingly, in view of the aristocratic backing of the Huguenot party, the tract defines the king as one taking precedence among equals: he "holds in the place of brothers all the principal Officers of the kingdom," who in turn represent the "general estates" or the people (p. 185). The first kings, indeed, were elected (p. 124). And while God appoints kings,

> the people establish kings, puts the scepter into their hands, and with their suffrages, approves the election. God would have it done in this manner, to the end that kings should acknowledge, that after God they hold their power and sovereignty from the people, and that it might the rather induce them to apply and address the utmost of their care and thoughts for the profit of the people, without being puffed up with any vain imagination, that they were formed of any matter more excellent than other men. (p. 118)

Despite Calvin's own conservatism in these matters, his followers after 1572 were clearly moving in the direction of popular sovereignty, a belief emerging from their notion of the sovereign conscience. To assent in the worship of an alien god (or in an alien worship of God) was to surrender both personal and political liberty.

The fourth part of the *Vindiciae* bears directly on Book V of *The Faerie Queene*, handling as it does the question "Whether neighbour princes may or are bound by law to aid the subjects of other princes, persecuted for true religion or oppressed by manifest tyranny" (p. 215). The affirmative answer in this part of the *Vindiciae* would have supported fears of an international Protestant conspiracy by arguing that the first commandment not only justifies but requires intervention in countries persecuted by Catholicism. Justice requires not only avoiding injustice but defending those who suffer injustice, an obligation that especially falls to the magistrate. Religion also demands that rulers protect the church both within and beyond their territories, for the church is one, not divided by national boundaries. The *Vindiciae* supports these claims with pagan and Old Testament history, but its most compelling Christian precedent, the Crusades, endows Spenser's Saracen-battling knights with a contemporary political significance. Arthur's Souldan is a principle embodied not only in Philip of Spain, but in the Catholic League and Mary Stuart as well. "Tyranny" receives God's vengeance at the hands of the just Christian prince. Mercilla's reluctance to let "just vengeance" (ostensibly a contradiction in terms) fall on Duessa probably alludes to this famous conception of the fourth part of the *Vindiciae*. And like the *Vindiciae*, Spenser's Legend of Justice ends with a lesson in the Christian ruler's obligation to extend justice to the nations.

References to England in the fourth part leave no doubt as to who shall come to the aid of suffering Huguenots. The supposed author du Plessis-Mornay had urged as much in diplomatic communications with the English, both direct and, as in the case of his meeting with Sidney, indirect. England provided an often ineffective intrusion of small forces worrying the powers of Spain and the Catholic League throughout the last third of the century. These forays culminated in the dispatch of Essex and an army of four thousand men to fight at Rouen, long a trouble spot, where three decades earlier Protestants had ejected the Catholic administration and proclaimed that they were "the natural subjects, as we were formerly," of the Queen of England.[67]

In any attempt to understand the background of English political poetry and drama in the 1590s, the political thought of France
is almost as valuable as that of England. Evidence of this point is
in the frequency of French subjects in literature. An earlier English battle at Rouen figures largely in Shakespeare's *1 Henry VI;*
Marlowe's *Massacre at Paris* kept alive the horrors of Catholic
persecution; Daniel's *Civil Wars* presents Queen Margaret as importing French tyranny; Spenser may have thought of Essex at
Rouen in the battle with Grantorto in Book V of *The Faerie Queene.*
Spenser also tells the story of Burbon—Henry of Navarre recant-
ing his Protestantism—in Book V, an event that effectively put an
end to the monarchomachy. Ironically the greatest impact of the
Vindiciae came in the Netherlands and England, where it haunted
Elizabeth's hierarchy and increasingly became a weapon against
the state's control of worship and belief. How the book fared
under the Stuarts may be guessed in the prelate Morton's correc-
tion of *Major singulis universis minor:* rather, "Major Universis and
super omnes simul." As late as 1683 it was being publicly burnt at
Oxford, along with Buchanan's *De jure regni* and Milton's antimonarchist works.[68]

The problem of civil idolatry arises when an impulse toward
sacralizing the monarch goes awry, as it always must, since in any
human sacredness is an unstable commodity. Anthropology has
shown that divine-right sovereignty can take as much from the
monarch as it gives: "When one defers to the will of the sovereign
because he is in some sense keeper of the faith, one's deference
ceases immediately when the ruler demonstrably loses faith."[69] In
her last two decades, Queen Elizabeth's hold on her subjects'
devotion slackened. A large number of literate Englishmen, including many who had witnessed earlier government interference in religion like the ejection of Cartwright or the
sequestering of Archbishop Grindal, lost faith in the head of their
church. The metaphor of monarch as goddess has as its obverse
the monarch as idol. This is one of those "root metaphors" that
Victor Turner sees as keys to the perceptions and values of an age
(he gives the example of the seventeenth-century metaphor,
world as machine). Turner says that root metaphors "appear in the
work of exceptionally liminal thinkers—poets, writers, religious
prophets, 'the unacknowledged legislators of mankind'—just before outstanding limina of history, major crises of societal change,
since such shamanistic figures are possessed by spirits of change
before change becomes visible in public arenas."[70] Some of the

extensions of the king (queen)-idol metaphor that recur in my shamanistic texts are: the fearful and ignorant condition of the worshippers, the emphasis on grossly palpable presence, the exchange of spiritual for material benefits, the emptiness (therefore absurdity) of the idol, the exclusion of reason and moral virtue from the court-temple, and the heroism of the image-breaker.

Because of the paramount influence of religion on English culture at this time, these conditions may be described in religious terms; but they did not come into being because of religion. Ernst Kantorowicz believed that a direct route extended from the medieval consecration of the king to the modern apotheosis of the nation-state. This was very much an idea of the time in which he wrote, with Christianity often taking the blame for this state of affairs.[71] The longer view of Christianity, especially taking into account its Hebraic origins, attests otherwise. Christianity is anti-mythic; it "attacks human life at so deep a level that it disallows all existing culture."[72] No illustration of this ongoing process could be more striking in its simplicity than the English mystery plays, with their demystifying of "the world" and its kings. These early playwrights express the prerogative of religion in society: as A. E. Pollard says, "It is the essence of all religion that man's relation to God and conscience makes his relation to the state conditional and not absolute; and the absolutism of the state is a form of pagan idolatry."[73] Milton did not invent the concept of civil idolatry; he absorbed it from the English and Hebraic-Christian traditions that he considered so intently.

This book studies an issue of great significance in history as it influences the work of three major authors, each a field of study in himself. If by some chance I avoid the pitfalls inherent in writing on three such figures in one book, I still must face the fact that "thematic" criticism of this kind has taken its lumps in recent years.[74] Yet most scholars still behave as if literature mediates between the realm of pure idea and mere event. This belief should encourage study of the most sensitive, prophetic minds of the age for an understanding of ideas and events in the context of human experience. Occasionally such an understanding can even enlighten us as to the meaning of certain scenes or characters in literary works. The Renaissance is a period replete with lost learning—numerology, occult sciences, long-forgotten traditions of rhetoric and poetics, iconology, mythology, obscure philosophical traditions like neo-Platonism and Hermeticism. Still, people usually read and teach Spenser, Shakespeare, and Milton as if they bring light to a shared humanity. No small part of this humanity is grounded on political and religious ideas like those that gave impetus to the Reformation. That these ideas were (and sometimes still are) *both* political and religious is today often overlooked. Civil or secular idolatry describes a dangerous meeting point of the sacred and the profane, a point at which the necessary myth of the state is joined with an inherently demythologizing religion.

1

King of This World

Pharaoh and Herod

The literary kings of Elizabeth England descend directly from the Herods and Caesars of the Middle Ages, along with a complex of ideas that is never quite lost. An early Tudor morality play, *Mundus et Infans (The world and the child)*, opens with a boasting speech by Mundus, the World:

> For I am king and well known in these realms round.
> I have also palace ypight;
> I have steeds in stable stalwart and strong,
> Also streets and stronds fully ydight.
> For All-the-World-Wide I wot is my name;
> All richness redely it runneth in me,
> All pleasure worldly, both mirth and game.
> I am a king in every case,
> Methinketh I am a god of grace.[1]

This kind of speech has ancient roots in English drama. It appears in the earliest surviving morality plays, but originates with the bragging King Herod of the mystery and liturgical drama, the king of "towers and towns" who claims absolute dominion over his people. Literal pride of rulership merges in this figure with tropological pride of the self, allegorical pride of the world, the anagogical pride of Satan and the king of the last days. Conflicts between the world-king and the heavenly king (the child in *Mundus et Infans* replies to Mundus by invoking "Christ our King") develop the Augustinian theme of the two kingdoms, not the supposed sacredness of earthly monarchy. In this chapter, I examine the king-figure in some medieval plays in an effort to clarify the native traditions of the stage king, most of which survived into Shakespeare's and Spenser's time.[2] The figure of the world-king derives not only from dramatists' imaginations but from

41

scriptural and theological traditions well established by the time
of the earliest extant plays.

At the close of the Wakefield play *Pharaoh*, in the customary
doctrinal summing-up, Moses warns the newly liberated children
of Israel:

> Gif loving to Goddys mageste;
> His dedys ar done, his ways are trew.
> Honowred be he in Trinite;
> To him be honowre and vertew.
> Amen.[3]

The structure of this play largely depends on the conflict between
the "mageste" of God and of Pharaoh, in support of the recurrent
theme in the Bible that worship is owed to divine power alone.
The word-play in Pharaoh's first line—"Peas! of pain that no man
pas!"—establishes an ironic contrast between the tyrant's peace
and that of God's followers, who *will* "pas" from his dominion.
One sometimes hears this and similar lines described as "the
conventional call for silence" at the start of the play. In the
Wakefield plays, at least, this label is inaccurate. Only the tyrants
and their minions (Cain's boy, Pharaoh, Augustus, Herod and his
messenger, and Pilate in five plays) call for silence in this way.
When pious characters open the plays (Noah, Abraham, Jacob,
Mary, the Shepherds, Simeon, John the Baptist, and Cleophas)
they do so with prayers, not commands.

To bring out the difference between God's peace and Pharoah's,
the scene of the Wakefield play is divided in two. On one side of
the playing area or pageant wagon sits Pharaoh with his two
soldiers. On the other, Moses with two of the "pueri" or children
of Israel. On opposing sides are the throne of Egypt and the
burning bush, the seat of God. The effect of the two thrones is to
enhance Pharaoh's role as Satanic "prince of this world," consistent with allegorical readings of Exodus at that time.[4] The two
sides eventually meet, probably in the area in front of the wagon,
the "Red Sea," where the Egyptians are overcome. Pharoah's
drowning enacts the eschatalogical meaning of these events: just
as the faithful will at last pass from the bondage of this world to
heavenly peace and liberty, the "mageste" of Satan will yield to
the power of God. This "medieval" interpretation of the Pharaoh
story continues well into the age of humanism, as Thomas More,
in one of his last works, reminds readers that "the thraldome of
the chyldren of Israel under king Pharao and thegipcians sig-

nifieth the bondage of mankynde under the prynce of thys darke world, the dyvell and hys evyll spirits."[5]

We do not often think of the Corpus Christi plays as offering political commentary; no one has ever claimed that they satirize rulers or administrations. The plays do make an important statement, however, about the nature of political power. Martin Stevens sees the conflict between divine and civil law central to the Wakefield Plays, while V. A. Kolve has concluded that the author of *The Second Shepherd's Play* was committed to "a kind of Christian social reform" from his attacks on "the rich, the powerful, the fashionable."[6] Jeffrey Helterman sees Cain's "lust for mastery" in the *Mactatio Abel* as consistent with Augustine on the world's worship of power.[7] An important task of the Exodus playwright was to depict the worst, that is, the Satanic, qualities of earthly majesty so as to highlight God's benevolence. What Pharaoh manifests from the start, aside from a bullying attitude, is rivalry with God. He claims total power in a speech laced with absolutes and first-person pronouns:

> All Egypt is mine awne
> To leede aftyr my law.
> I wold my might were knawne
> And honoryd, as hit awe.
>
> (lines 9–12)

His egotism anticipates that of Herod,[8] and while not necessarily comical, his part could easily be played for laughs. Pharaoh is not a caricature of any particular king, but of kingship gone mad, swelling over its limits. His demand that his majesty be "honoryd" requires a totality of devotion that will leave no room for the God of Moses. The phrase "my law" establishes a similar opposition to the law of God. But how fully would medieval audiences allow their own rulers such a large claim to honor and the law? Certainly rulers were not regarded as absolute like Pharaoh; both their received homage and their power over the law were limited. The reverence due to kings was carefully delimited in the distinction between *dulia* and *latria*, discussed in the introduction. The proprietary tone in the phrase "my law" subverts another principle in that the medieval king was not only the father of the law, but its child as well. Even Kantorowicz admits that, particularly at the time when the York and Wakefield plays were being staged, sovereignty was never allowed to the king alone, but to the "King in Parliament."[9] But the medieval audience did not need to read political philosphy for lessons in the ideal state and the evils of absolutism. They could have learned them in rituals like the Corpus Christi procession that framed the occasion for these plays—a whole community acting with one head and heart, "an image of the ideal hierarchy a society achieves with Christ as its king."[10]

Kings may occasionally fare well in the Bible, but not in the Corpus Christi plays: as Kolve has said, "With the exception of the Chester Octavian, there are no good rulers in the cycles save the King of Kings."[11] On the other hand, Lucifer pretends to a kingly "pompe" and "pride" in the N-Town plays; in the Wakefield *Creation and Fall*, he actually sits on God's throne, foreshadowing the usurpation of God's mageste by Pharaoh, Balak (who requires diabolic assistance to rule), Caesar Augustus, Antichrist, and of course by Herod. All the cycles identify these kings with Satan, if only in their habitual swearing in his name or in the name of his handyman "Mahoun." The absurdity of their extravagant claims adds a comic tone to the plays in which they appear, so that their entries create a heightened sense of playfulness between actor and audience. This may be seen in the blustering of the customary "call for silence" which, as we have seen, seems to have been reserved chiefly for the figure of the world-king. A fragmentary early prologue preserved in the library of Cambridge University warns people to be silent, threatening punishment by "the emperor" who is about to come on stage.[12]

Like Satan, the evil king is recognized as much by his self-deification as by his arrogant, blasphemous language. The vision of worldly power competing with God is ancient in Christianity, as old as the Gospels. In tempting Christ in the desert, Satan could offer him all the kingdoms of this world, claiming, in the York verson of this scene, "all this worlde to welde, / Toure and towne, forest and felde."[13] In Luke 23, Herod and Pilate become friends at the execution of Christ, the Glossa Ordinaria observing, "The impious pact that Herod and Pilate made in murdering Christ, their successors guard by hereditary right."[14] The emblematic possibilities of this scene were not lost on early, ritual dramatists. Centuries before the Wakefield plays, in the Benediktbeuern Passion Play, the exchange of a kiss between Herod and Pilate enacts the same symbolism of this moment in Scripture.

The symbolism of the World and Satan shapes Herod's character in the mystery plays. Playwrights usually associated the ranting tyrant with Eastern, especially Moslem, autocrats. Civil idolatry had originated in the East, in Babylon, and from there would come the Antichrist of the last days. Herod's god, when it is not himself or Satan, is Mahoun or Mohammed, the all-purpose pagan deity in much medieval literature. Like the oriental despot, Herod suggests earthly power untouched by grace, cut off from divine wisdom. Scriptural commentators had always identified him with Satan,[15] contrasting his pomp with the simple humility of the true King. Rabanus Maurus's commentary on Matthew underscores the two kingships: "At the birth of the King of heaven, the king of earth is in confusion, for surely earth-bound loftiness is confounded when the towering height of the heavens is seen."[16] The theme of Fulgentius's sermon on the Epiphany is the contrast between the majesty of Christ and Herod, as the Magi "seek to adore an infant at its mother's breast, not a king ruling over people."[17] St. Peter Chrysologus, in his sermon on the Holy Innocents, depicts Herod as "blind ambition": "With an earthly fury he does not believe in the One who was heavenly born"; "Herod, occupying an earthly kingdom, fights against the heavenly one."[18] Herod thus becomes the vice of kingship, the symbol of earthly power turned in futility against its heavenly source. However, it is mainly in England that these qualities cling to Herod in religious drama. Spanish and French plays often showed Herod as a courteous, sophisticated ruler; German and Italian versions of the character seem made to show off the pomp and splendor of his court. In part, this difference appears owing to the continental playwrights' deeper appreciation of the historical King Herod as described in Josephus: "In England Herod is never the courteous host of Chantilly or Arras, nor the beloved lord and master of Arras who can turn to the people and receive enthusiastic professions of love and loyalty, and be sincerely mourned at his death."[19] Clearly, it is not the French Herod that Chaucer's Miller would have expected to see onstage.

Something of the contrast between ranting and courteous kingship is conveyed in the Wakefield *Offering of the Magi*, especially in the three kings' humble praise of Christ played off against Herod's demented self-praise and claims of power.[20] Yet little is actually said of the Magi as kings. The patristic idea of Herod as world-king helps to shape another of the Wakefield plays, *Herod the Great*. If Pharaoh is intended as a foil to divine majesty, Herod in this play is a travesty of Christ. The evil in him is absolute. The idea of killing the Innocents is Herod's own—not, as in the York cycle and most liturgical plays, that of his counselors. Herod's Nuntius, a kind of mock-angelic herald, opens the play praising

the tyrant as "the worthiest of all barnes that ar borne" (line 55).
Ironically, Herod is called by Christ's title, "king of kingys":

> Greatt dukys downe dingys for his greatt aw
> And him lowtys.
> Tuskane and Turky,
> All Inde and Italy,
> Cecyll and Surry
> Drede him and dowtys.
>
> (lines 37–45)

The theatrical purpose of the Nuntius is to build up our expectations as we await (through seventy-some lines) the entrance of the
popular ranter. The command to worship Herod must have been
delivered as it would in a modern slapstick performance:

> Downe ding of your knees,
> All that him seys!
> Displesyd he beys,
> And brykyn many bonys.
> Here he commys now . . .
>
> (lines 60–64)

Whatever reservations one may have about the irreverence of
such humor in religious drama,[21] the first three hundred lines of
Herod the Great are sheer burlesque, bearing only indirectly on its
principal subject, the murder of the Innocents. Herod is at once
elevated and deflated from his role in the Gospel. The strategy of
the humor, in fact, is like that of mock heroic poetry—to deflate *by*
elevating. Herod is king of all countries, not puppet of Galilee.
Once he gets thoroughly puffed up he is like the stupid giants of
fairy tales, full of threats to "breake ilka bone" and "clefe You
small as flesh to pott" (lines 84, 98), if his bidding is not done.

But a change comes over the ridiculous world-king in his final
scene when his speech, mostly addressed to the audience, assumes a darker, menacing edge. Herod had kept his soldiers in
tow by making empty promises; he will give us, too, a considerable reward if we will only "Wate when I come again." The
intimation here of Herod as Antichrist, parodying the second
coming of the true Christ, is borne out in the apocalyptic reference: "A hundredth thowsand, I watt, and fourty ar slain, / And
four thowsand" (lines 486–87). There is an analogue here in the
Lucerne *Passion,* where the same number of children are murdered.[22] The last stanza threatens us with broken brains if we are
disloyal to Herod before he comes again. Herod's kingly power

has been exaggerated in the play, but now he transcends history in becoming king of the last days. This role concurs with patristic sources. St. Peter Chrysologus, in one of several sermons on the Epiphany, sees the Christ-Herod opposition as foreshadowing the Second Coming.

> Why is it that God descended to earth in the time of an evil king? That he mixed his divinity with flesh? That a celestial union with an earthly body takes place? Why is it? And when will the true king not come to expel the tyrant, to vindicate the nation, restore justice to the world, return liberty? Herod, refuge of the Jewish people, has attacked the kingdom, taken away liberty, profaned the sacred, confounded order; he has destroyed learning and culture; but with justice a holy people, lacking in human things, can be aided by things divine, and God, for whom there was no man in attendance, attends upon himself. So Christ will come again to overthrow Antichrist, the world will be liberated, the homeland returned to paradise, the liberty of the world perpetuated, all the enslavement of the ages will be absolished.[23]

Of the focal points in the Corpus Christi cycle—the Nativity, the Passion, and the Last Judgment—the last held a special status in the rhythm of sacred time. The world's final days would recapitulate the central moments of history, as once again Lucifer would battle heaven, Pharaohs and Herods tyrannize over the elect, until the final victory of the Second Coming.

The Wakefield Herod's counterparts in other surviving plays similarly deify themselves. Herod makes the same claim to divinity in the opening speech of the N-Town *Adoration of the Magi:* "Ffor bothe of hevyn and of herth I am kyng sertayn."[24] The Herod of the Chester play on the Magi throws his tantrum not before the audience alone, but before the three kings when they tell him of their quest: "I am kinge of all mankynde; I byd, I beate, I loose, I bynde."[25] This blasphemous use of Christ's words to Peter and the apostles (Matt. 16:19) is accentuated by Herod's display of staff or mace and sword, the emblems of earthly rule. As the Doctor reads Herod the prophecies of Christ's kingship the sword is first cast down, then broken. In the York *Massacre of the Innocents* Herod's counselors have correctly been described as "worshipful idolaters."[26] The world-king's opening speech continues the pattern of self-exalting rhetoric:

> So bolde loke no man be
>   For to aske help ne helde
> But of mahounde and me,
>   That has this worlde in welde.[27]

Noting the "fantastic and godlike powers" that Herod claims for himself in this and other cycle plays, Rosemary Woolf has found something unique about the English conception of Herod. His rage in the York or Wakefield plays "springs not from political fear that another king will take his throne or from an overbearing response to defiance, but from the intense hatred of one who believes himself a god and now finds that the true God has come."[28]

It should be mentioned that the world-king's association with Mahoun is one of the more potent anachronisms of the mystery plays in that the perennial enemy in the East evoked the actual threat of Christ-hatred to late medieval audiences. The later Herod of the N-Town Passion Play (II) vows to force "Cristyn doggys" to accept the faith of Mohammed. "Turkish tyranny" would become a familiar symbol of civil idolatry in the next two centuries, to be used by Spenser, Shakespeare, and Milton alike. Thomas More's *Dialogue of Comfort against Tribulation* presents two Hungarian Christians facing the threat of Turkish conquest and persecution, exemplifying the widespread fear that the Turk (and by implication the new regime of heresy in England and elsewhere) was in fact Antichrist heralding the last days.

Besides Herod and Pharaoh yet another world-king could be seen in European biblical drama, though no trace of him exists in England. This is Nimrod, builder of the Tower of Babel, a chief exemplar of the Jewish contribution to the Christian tradition of desacralizing monarchy. In *Paradise Lost* Milton would make him a principal postlapsarian villain, virtually introducing a second fall with his invention of monarchy. Because Nimrod was a "mighty hunter" and "the beginning of his kingdom was Babylon" (Gen. 10:8–10), pre-Christian biblical commentary placed him at the center of a myth of power. Josephus described Nimrod as a tyrant who seduced people to live in the first city, where he set up his tower. While Augustine traced the first folly of monarchic power to Nimrod, another tradition developed that he invented idolatry, forcing people to worship his dead father or, some said, fire. The fourteenth-century *Cursor Mundi* calls him both "wrongful emperor" and founder of "maumetrie" (already Turkish tyranny looms on the horizon). He originated king worship after his father's death, commanding "alle men / As god they should that king ken." Boccaccio opens his strident attack on monarchy with an account of Nimrod which Lydgate paraphrases in his *Fall of Princes:* "summe bookis" report he was "Foundour of rihtis and off fals sacrefice," in addition to being the first king. Boccaccio's wide readership throughout Europe makes it likely that his text lies somewhere behind Nimrod's most famous pictorial representation in Brueghel's "Tower of Babel," where the king, perhaps modeled on Philip II of Spain, ironically dwarfed by his monstrous project, stands in the left foreground flanked by soldiers and venerated by kneeling workmen. The most famous French mystery cycle presents "Nembroth" as a principal figure in three plays. In "De la maledicton Cham," he refuses to serve any man and seizes the rulership; then follows the Tower of Babel play; finally, in "De l'ydolle Bellus," he allows Ninus, a prince, to make a statue of his dead father Bellus and force people to worship it. Following rabbinical tradition only one man, Abraham, stands up to the imposture. Nimrod's boasting and comic arrogrance throughout the plays establish his credentials in the world-king tradition. If anything, the Nimrod myth grows in currency during the sixteenth and seventeenth centuries, coinciding with the increase of the great monarchies. Cromwell's sympathizers knew what John Cook meant in calling Charles I a Nimrod, after "the first tyrant and conqueror that had no title," employing a symbolism that had developed and flourished during the Middle Ages.[29]

Octavian and Antichrist

Before turning to the kingship of Antichrist, it will be worthwhile to consider the one exception to the besetting royal vice of self-worship, Octavian in the Chester *Annunciation and Nativity*. As we have them, the Chester plays were almost certainly composed in the Tudor period, probably not before 1505, perhaps not earlier than 1521. The character of Octavian must have undergone revision during the history of the nativity play, for the Chester banns proclaim him a cruel tyrant like his Wakefield counterpart, not the upright ruler we actually see.[30] Thus the Chester cycle reflects different political circumstances from those of Wakefield and York, not just a different authorial viewpoint.

The Annunciation and Nativity uses the familiar divided scene of the mysteries. First, in Judea, Mary hears the angel's words and visits her cousin Elizabeth; on the other side, at Rome, the emperor boasts of his power and commands the census of his empire. Octavian's Preco or herald travels to Judea and orders Joseph and Mary to Bethlehem, where Christ is born. We finally return to Rome for the miraculous private revelation of the Nativity to Octavian.

All is well, and yet not well, in Octavian's first scene. His boasts resemble those of Herod:

> Right as I thinke, soe must all bee;
> for all the world does my willinge
> and bayne bine when I bydd bringe
> homage and fealtye.[31]

The census and tax he is about to impose are acts of sheer self-interested power. His henchman the Preco, swearing "by Mahounde" to carry out the emperor's will, is promised the best-looking lady of Judea for his services. And yet the audience knows, if only through Octavian's speech, that this is the emperor of the *pax Romana:* peace has come to all the world because "soe dreade a duke sate never on dayes / in Rome." Unlike Herod's, Octavian's claim to world rule is well-founded. His visit from the Roman senators, moreover, shows in him a measure of justice and rationality. His subjects wish to deify him out of love, not fear; yet he rejects the offer. Divinity, he says, knows neither beginning nor end; but "made I am" and "I must dye I wotte not what day." Despite initial impressions, Octavian proves to be endowed with the virtues of the ideal king—including an understanding of his place in the order of things.

The Chester cycle is rightly criticized as being short on dramatic interest, "the least imaginatively exciting" of the four complete cycles.[32] But the playwright (if there was only one) shows himself a thoughtful person, if no great dramatist. *The Annunciation and Nativity,* like other Nativity plays, contains a fairly clear structure that moves toward a resolution of the theme of power. A large part of the first scene is occupied by Mary's Magnificat, with its theme of deposing the mighty.[33] The third scene begins with Joseph's complaint to the Preco on the injustice of the imperial tax, Joseph standing in sharp contrast to Octavian; "Castle, Towre, ney riche manere / had I never in my power" (lines 401–2). He and Mary find themselves crowded out of Bethlehem by "great lordes of stowte arraye" (line 455). Even the traditional withering of the suspicious midwife's hand is made relevant to the theme of power, as a judgment upon one who "would tempt Goddes might" (line 545). As is so often true in the mysteries, the purpose of the play is not only to act out but to interpret events from Scripture.

After the midwife's scene, the Expositor interrupts to turn our thoughts back to Rome, with a lengthy account of the Temple of

Peace.[34] In legend, Rome's world supremacy had been explained by a marvelous temple containing statues of all the gods of her subject nations, a silver bell attached to each. Whenever any nation was about to revolt, the bell on the appropriate statue would ring and a brass figure of a mounted spear carrier would point the spear in the direction of the trouble. Apparently the Chester playwright chose to name it the Temple of Peace rather than the Temple of Justice or the Capitol, as it is in the sources. But in view of the warrior figure and the use of the temple a means of intelligence for making war, how can it be called the Temple of Peace? In all likelihood the playwright chose the name to enhance the symbolism of the Expositor's description. The paradox is that in a sinful world peace depends on destructive power. If anything, this suggests that the Chester dramatist was more sophisticated than his fellow cycle playwrights in his thinking about the relations between earthly and heavenly power. Rulers like Octavian are needed, we are being told, to save us from dissension and anarchy. As some political thinkers were saying, only a great world power like Rome can bring about a return to world peace.[35]

Yet the temple falls into ruin at the coming of Christ, for the prodigies no longer occur. This would seem to mean, not that power ceased to matter in the first year of grace, but that ultimately the power of kings will merge with that of heaven. The movement of the play resembles that of the entire cycle in proceeding out of history into eternity. Octavian has a vision of a "mayden bright" with the child Jesus, which is a glimpse, not of events in Bethlehem, but of the glorified madonna and child. From the Annunciation to Octavian's vision the playwright repeats this "tokeninge" of the Nativity story, hinting at especially strong spiritual resonances, as Peter Travis has explained (p. 112). This foreshadowing of the last days recalls the ancient association of the Sibylline oracles with the cult of the emperor, familiar to readers of Norman Cohn's *Pursuit of the Millennium*. Even the "Ara Coeli," the heavenly altar that will give its name to a medieval church built on the scene of this apparition, has an apocalyptic quality as a window on eternity. In the fourth and last scene, the emperor submits to the greater power revealed by this vision and welcomes the Sibyl's prophecy:

> Insense bringe, I command, in hye
> to honour this child, king of mercye.
> Should I be God? Naye, naye, witterlye!

Great wronge iwys yt were.
For this childe is more worthye
then such a thowsande as am I.
Therfore to God most mightye
insense I offer here.

(lines 659–66)

Thus a boastful emperor has been made low in keeping with the spirit of the Magnificat. The threat of civil idolatry has been removed not by eliminating earthly power, but by making it pay homage to heaven. In one source of the play, before consulting the Sibyl Octavian allowed his followers to deify him;[36] in no source is there the reasoned refutation of the senators that occurs in what I have called the second scene. Ironically, though the change in Octavian is not carried out in a psychologically realistic manner, the very offer of worship is what turns him from a self-centered monarch to a just one.

This disregard of psychology, familiar even in the next century of English drama, is thoroughly consistent with the allegorical-didactic structure of the play. The *Nativity* is a serious meditation not on the qualities of the man Octavian, but on the relation between the social order and the peace of Christ. The cycle plays had their themes just as the moralities did—themes not invented by the playwrights but existing in the theological and interpretive traditions of the age, such as the equation of Pharaoh's Egypt with the world. The meaning of Octavian's story, that the world-king must submit to the "myght of the king of kinges," parallels the version in the *Speculum Hominis Salvationis,* a popular commentary on Scripture translated into English at the time the Chester cycle was first taking shape. In this version Octavian consults with the Sibyl after being offered deification, whereupon the prophetess has a vision of the newborn Christ:

> To the Emperour Octavian / thilk Sibille shewed that thing
> And saide over his estate / yt day was borne a king
> O myght of the king of kinges / over all yt beres poustee
> Yt has delivered mankind / fro the feendis Captivitee
> Jhu gif us thi birth / til honoure with myght and mayne
> Yt in the devels thraldom / wene falle never more ageine.[37]

Turning from Chester's tory Octavian to the Wakefield Caesar Augustus we encounter a more familiar figure—the bully-king of "Castels, towers, townys, and landys," swearing by Mahound and plotting against the Christ child as he hears the prophecies. Like Herod and Pharaoh, the earthly tyrant parodies divine power:

> ffor I may bynd and lowse of band,
> Every thyng bowys unto my hand,
> I want none erthly thyng.[38]

It seems that the playwright is simply trying to capitalize on the popularity of the Herod-figure with popular audiences. Rosemary Woolf, noting the redundancy of Augustus, proposes that "the author had an indiscriminate liking for this theme and lacked an imaginative sense of when it could fittingly recur" (p. 160). It may be, however, that the figure of the world-king held a stronger attraction than we realize for people living under a monarchy. But something else saves the Wakefield *Caesar* from being just another Herod play. As Augustus rages over reports of a new king's birth, a "cosyn" named Sirinus enters to suggest that Augustus can solve his problems by launching a search for the boy, along with a new tax. The tax is tied to the theme of emperor worship, for Sirinus's scheme assumes that to pay tax is to pay homage. If everyone is forced to pay his "heede penny," the followers of the rival king will have to admit that their boy has paid homage to the emperor and is therefore inferior. Augustus sends out his messenger with the order that the people of the world must "lowtt me as thare lord alone" (line 214). Taxation becomes less an instrument of material gain than of *latria*. Although this difference between Wakefield and Chester may simply illustrate the variety of political sentiment among medieval communities, both plays oppose the world-king to the King of kings, and in both what is at stake is the reserving of worship to God alone. If only because the legend of the "good" Augustus received such currency through *The Golden Legend* and *The Mirror of Man's Salvation*, it is probable that other cycle plays on this theme would have resembled Chester more than Wakefield.

Monarchy receives equal respect in the Chester *Coming of Antichrist*, a play that Travis has called both "a brilliant comedy" and "a study in levels or degrees of power" (p. 234). Chester may be the only English cycle to possess an Antichrist play, but the subject was well established in European religious drama. Since earliest Christianity (see 2 Thess. 2), the coming of the false Messiah had been a topic of such endless speculation that the real wonder is *that* he is absent from the other cycles. Antichrist responded to the medieval notion of the symmetrical opposition between the infernal and heavenly orders, an opposition that invited comic exploitation. Just as it was customary to introduce the Nativity sequence with a pageant of Old Testament prophecies of Christ, the Chester *Antichrist* is prefaced by a briefer play on Antichrist's prophets. The author of *Antichrist* selected from the profuse lore on the subject in order to emphasize Antichrist's role as the ultimate world-king.[39] Antichrist's principal supporters are four kings, who act as a kind of chorus throughout the play. At first they make the same offer to the false Messiah that the Roman senators made to Octavian:

> Wee lyven, lord, withouten lett,
> that Cryst ys not common yett.
> Yf thou be hee, thou shalbe sett
> in temple as God alonne.[40]

All the wonders that Antichrist then works—travesties of Christ's miracles, including a staged "resurrection"—are in response to the kings' promise of worship if he can prove himself. The actual rite of idolatry, a communion feast with sacrificial lamb, is carried out after the false resurrection, with the stage direction, "Tunc transeunt [reges] ad Antichristum cum sacrificio" (line 172). Here Antichrist receives the throne in the Temple of Jerusalem, the four kings promising, "wee shall kneelinge on our kneene / worshippe thee as thy owne men" (lines 178–79). There follows a parodic Pentecost, the descent of the false spirit, and a promise to the faithful:

> You kinges, I shall advance you all,
> and, because your regions be but smale,
> citties, castells shall you befall,
> with townes and towers gaye;
> and make you lordes of lordshipp fayre,
> as well yt fall for my power.

The important point about Antichrist's promise to the kings (lines 205–44) is that it provides, in exchange for worship, exclusively earthly power for the powerful.

At this moment the Chester playwright stops short of anti-monarchism. Antichrist's opponents Enoch and Elias return to earth and bear witness to the real Christ in keeping with the ancient legends. They find the kings pliable, willing to desert Antichrist if the two witnesses can "doe him downe." As Herod in the Wakefield Master's *Herod the Great* had foreshadowed Antichrist, the false Messiah in this scene—raging at Enoch and Elias, swearing by the devil, and consulting with his Doctor—looks back to Herod. Enoch uses the same argument in refuting Antichrist's divinity—that he had a mortal beginning and will have an end—as the Chester Octavian had in dissuading his people from deifying him. The Eucharist, the sacrament in whose honor the cycle plays were performed, effects the turning point of the play. Elias blesses bread and offers it to the dead men whom Antichrist had raised up—it is unclear whether they are demons or corpses possessed by demons. Their fear of the bread proves Antichrist's falsehood. When the four kings turn against him, Antichrist slaughters them, Enoch, and Elias with his sword. Like the *Nativity*, the *Antichrist* of the Chester cycle manages to save the appearances of royalty by converting kings from the sinful worship of worldly power. The end of the play presents the overthrow by the archangel Michael and the damnation of Antichrist, as Enoch and Elias are led to blessedness.

The presence of the four kings throughout the play gives *The Coming of Antichrist* a direction that is not found in the most familiar medieval accounts of these events. Sources like the pseudo-Methodius say nothing about the Antichrist's having tributary kings:

> He will enter Jerusalem and sit in the Temple of God, thinking that he is like God. And he will be false, a deceiver, and his fraudulence will seduce many. After this the Lord will send his two most faithful servants Enoch and Elias, who in witness of him had been preserved to denounce that very enemy. And then the last will be first and the Jews will believe. Elias and Enoch will dispute with him before all the people and will show him to be a liar, false and deluding. When all the nations see him bring forth falsehood and refuted by the holy men of God, the Jews will then also believe. From the whole race of the children of Israel in those days 144,000 will be killed for Christ. Then Antichrist, full of fury, will order the holy men of God to be killed, and all who believe in them. And then will come our Lord Jesus Christ, Son of the living God, and the clouds of heaven with armies of angels and heavenly glory.[41]

The use of kings may have been suggested by the widely read "Libellus de Antichristo" of the tenth-century monk Adso, a work actually motivated by impeialist sentiments in its argument that the end of the world can only come about after the peaceful reign of a Frankish world-ruler.[42] From this tract most of the lore of

Antichrist was derived. Although Adso dwells chiefly upon the personal qualities of Antichrist, the time of his coming, and the witness of Enoch and Elias, he does mention that the first converts of Antichrist will be kings, through whom the people will be won over.[43] Adso's passing reference contrasts with the central role that the kings play in the Chester drama, however. By coincidence the much earlier Antichrist play of Tegernsee in Bavaria also uses Kings as principal figures in what seems to have been a political allegory.[44] Here the King of Babylonia's attack on Jerusalem represents Moslem opposition to the Christian presence there; the salvation of Jerusalem by the last Roman emperor, an event crucial to Adso but unmentioned in the Chester play, probably expresses the German imperialist ideals of the Tegernsee dramatist. The English play treats the political theme quite differently. When the Chester Antichrist lists the kingdoms bestowed on the tributary kings—Lombardy, Denmark, Hungary, Patmos, Italy, and Rome (lines 241–44)—it is only to convey a sense of the moment's vast importance. Far from being a commentary on specific monarchies, this play contemplates the role of all kings as imperfect but necessary mediators between the will of God and his people. With the *Nativity, Antichrist* discloses a sympathy for monarchy closer in spirit to the earlier Tudor era than any play in the other surviving cycles.

Morality Plays: The King as Self

The world-king undergoes a renovation in the English morality plays contemporary with the mysteries. To a great extent, the moralities enact histories of man the microcosm as the cycle plays represent the history of the macrocosm. The continuity between these two forms is rather like that between the moral and historical meanings in *The Faerie Queene*, where "the moral allegory is necessarily *prior;* the reader must see into himself before he is prepared to see into history."[45] We all have Herod within us. As far as can be determined from the modest corpus of extant medieval plays, the conventions of the two kinds were frequently mingled. The Digby *Mary Magdalene* offers a striking example of a labored attempt to fuse both genres. Mary is both the soul beseiged by the seven deadly sins in her castle,[46] and the historical penitent woman who in legend traveled to Europe and converted the King of Marseilles. This play is rife with idol-kings: in addition to the morality-play kings, World, Flesh, and Satan, there are the

Emperor Tiberius, Herod, the King of Marseilles, and oddly enough the characterization even extends to Mary's father Syrus. At the play's opening it is the "inperator" Tiberius who commands "silyns, in peyn of forfetur." Like the world-kings of the cycle plays, he opens with his trump card, the claim to divine prerogative:

> Of my most hyest and mytiest volunte,
> I woll it be knowyn to all the world universal
> That of heven and hell chyff rewlar am I,
> To whose magnificens none stondith egall.
>
> (lines 2–5)

The scene is brief, and except for another moment some sixty lines later, Tiberius never appears in the play again. Perhaps he is there chiefly owing to the convention that some character of his type is most effective at hushing up the audience. Only in retrospect, at the end of the play, can we understand this role as a measure of the despotism from which a Christian understanding of power has saved us. The second scene begins with a speech by Syrus to Mary, Martha, and Lazarus. At first his lines sound remarkably like the world-king's:

> Emperor, and kingges, and conquerors kene,
> Erlys, and barons, and knytes that byn bold,
> Berdes in my bower, so semely to sene,
> I commaund yow at onys my hestes to hold.
>
> (lines 49–52)

Syrus's holdings include the castle of "Maudleyn," with "all the contre, both lesse and more," the lordship of Jerusalem, and "Alle Betany." Boasting of his power and "solace," Syrus bequeathes his lands to his three children, then orders a great feast. The parallels between the speeches of Tiberius and Syrus seem deliberate, if a bit ludicrous, even taking into account Mary's reputed familial greatness in *The Golden Legend*.[47] Yet is that disparity not really the point? The power of the world, soon to conspire in the killing of Christ, is always a relative matter: compared to that of God, man's power is as paltry as Syrus's compared to Rome's.

The correspondence between Syrus and Tiberius is also owing to the dual status of the play as both mystery and morality. The irascible Tiberius and Herod are figures of the macrocosm; Syrus, basking in the comfort of family and riches, represents the concupiscible private man. (This contrast between the forward and the froward vices is common in Christian allegory, as in the characters of Cymochles and Pyrocles in *The Faerie Queene*.) One of the earliest surviving moralities, *The Pride of Life*, effects a similar migration of the world-king from the mysteries. The hero of that play is claled Rex Vivus, the King of Life, in whose first lines we recognize at once the tyrannical tones of Herod and Pharaoh:

> Pes, now, ye princes of powere so prowde,
>
> . . . .
>
> King ich am, kinde of kinges i-kore,
> al the worlde wide to welde at my wil:
> Nas ther never no man of woman i-borre
> o-gein me withstonde that I nold him spille.
>
> Lordis of lond, beith at my ledinge,
> al men schal a-bow in hal and in bowr.[48]

This play is about the pride that infects private, not public, men; yet the pride of the world-king serves as an apt metaphor for the pride of life—just as, in the old system of correspondences, the social macrocosm was a model for the life of the individual, intellect ruling as king over the subjects of body, passions, and will. In the Digby play, Syrus is the King of Life, too confident in his strength and prosperity, allowing the soul, Mary, to fall into the hands of Satan, World, and Flesh almost immediately after his death. The remainder of the play acts out the morality drama of the individual soul's salvation in the context of the larger drama of humanity's redemption.

The world-king returns later in the play as the pagan King of Marseilles:

> Avantt, avant the, onworthy wrecchesse!
> Why lowtt ye nat low to my lawdabill presens,
> Ye brawling breelles, and blabir-lippyd bicchys,
> Obedienly to obbey me without offense?
>
> (lines 925–28)

This king will undergo a conversion, however, not unlike the Chester Octavian's. By the last third of the play when Mary has witnessed the risen Christ and has taken ship to evangelize the pagans, the old idols have fallen silent. Lightning has destroyed the king's temple. Like Octavian, the king has a vision that ensures his conversion:

A fayer woman I saw in my syth;
All in white was she cladd;
Led she was with an angyll bryth;
To me she spake with wordes sad.

(lines 1623–26)

Following the tradition reported in *The Golden Legend*, the play-wright sends the king on a pilgrimage to visit St. Peter in Jerusalem. Baptized, he returns from the Holy Land as Christian king of a Christian country. As in the Chester play, the ranting world-king is transformed, and his last speech can be compared with his first as an index of this shift. He has become the saintly medieval monarch, vowing to build churches, defend the faith, punish heretics, and overthrow Mahound for Christ.

The dual genre of *Mary Magdalene* shows the reciprocal influences between private and public spheres. In a benighted world an individual soul falls into darkness. Recovering, and rejecting the pride of life, she can inspire others to follow her way. True sovereignty over self then begets legitimate rule over mankind, with Christ as the starting point of both individual and social salvation. Whatever shortcomings the Digby author may have had as a dramatic craftsman, he takes care at the end of his play to accentuate the transformation from earthly kingdoms to the kingdom of heaven. Mary has moved from castle to hermitage; the arbor where she fell, the archetypal garden of temptation, is displaced by the wilderness outside Marseilles; the physical Jerusalem gives way to the saint's vision of the heavenly Jerusalem.

The great subject of the medieval mystery play—sacred history from the Fall to Judgment Day—inevitably transcended profane history. This is a theater of types. Tyrants, unjust courts, French-speaking judges, cruel nobles and bishops, suffering and upstart commoners all occupy a place in the life of mankind as depicted on platform or pageant wagon. *Mary Magdalene* is a play of double vision, offering both this larger perspective on humanity and the mroe introspective view of the morality play. It is not the only play to do so. Other plays, like Skelton's *Magnificence*, fuse the theme of external kingship with inner sovereignty. When Skelton's hero proclaims, "I reign in my robes, I rule as me list, / I drive down these dastards with a dint of my fist,"[49] he conspicuously resembles the tyrant in the cycle plays. Magnificence suffers for his "pomp and pride" in a scene recalling the N-Town *Death of Herod* (4.26), crying out against fortune (4.28) like the "tragic" Herod of the mysteries.[50] As is well known, Skelton's play is about Henry VIII and Wolsey; a "client of Norfolks," he attacked Wolsey for removing the aristocracy from their rightful place. This does not, however, preclude what Spenser would have called a "general intention"[51] regarding the susceptibility of all self-worshipping, worldly men to folly, flattery, and hypocrisy.

The historical development of such "king of life" figures, however, is only incidental to the point of this chapter, that well before the age of Erasmus and the influence of libertarian humanist political thought there had existed the view that, if unrestrained, worldly monarchy would attempt to vie with God for human allegiance. Early Christianity—indeed, even the prophetic strain of the Old Testament—encouraged simultaneously the support and distrust of political leadership. And politics was anything but a science. At a time when the cycle plays were in their height, a condemned prisoner named Edmund Dudley offered the newly crowned Henry VIII his essay on the problems of the commonwealth. G. R. Elton has rightly described Dudley's ideas as "curiously barren," principally because the author's solution is simplistically moral: "let everyone," Dudley writes, "from the King down to the last peasant, properly fulfill his duty to god and his place in society."[52] A generation later, on the other side of the Reformation, another thinker would propose for Europe the same solution that Dudley had for England: "The fire will be extinguished," writes Erasmus, "only if we remove the fuel. The chief source of the disturbance is a breakdown of morals. . . . [E]ach individual must fulfill his proper duties. . . . Let magistrates fulfill their civil duties with good faith. . . . Let the laity keep their proper place. . . . Let each one perform his duties conscientiously before the great Knower of hearts."[53] An age of scientific solutions would expect more. But if the admirable notion that politics is an extension of ethics inspired such pallid thought, it also allowed similarly unsophisticated writers like the cycle playwrights to raise the spirits of their audience with the hope that society's problems were submissible to the simple precepts of the Gospel.

The assumptions underlying these plays are not those of the experienced political thinker. Kings were an exotic species to this audience, their power a vast but relatively abstract thing compared to that of the local nobleman and his retainers, or of the magistrates, bishop, or abbot. The authors of these plays, too—clerics most likely, schooled in Scripture, theology, and human nature as they were—[54] knew about kingship in a similarly abstract way. Scripture, not experience, had provided the raw material for their Herods and Octavians.

Yet the consequences of a social mythology may outweigh those of the most articulate philosopher. A historian of the Chester plays remarks that "the spectacle of a magnificent King, with a page-boy to hold up the trains of his robes, being dragged off to Hell" emphasizes "the equality of all men under God."[55] Two citizens of Chester who would have had a chance to see such spectacles in their youth were Christopher Goodman and William Whittingham, both to become Marian exiles. Goodman wrote, with Whittingham's introduction, the most inflammatory English political tract of the century, *How Superior Powers Oght to Be Obeyd* (Geneva, 1558). Like John Knox and John Ponet, and Milton much later, Goodman was able to build a powerful argument for civil disobedience from the writings of the Old and New Testament. Thus at the same time that monarchies were undergoing considerable expansion in territory and influence, the same Scriptures that inspired the cycle plays would provide the grounds for incisive, even radical criticism from those who had the wisdom of suffering, if not of action, under kings.

2

Erasmus: Christian Liberty and Renaissance Majesty

Christianity and Kingship

Surveying the attitudes toward monarchy in early modern England, Robert Eccleshall has traced a gradual "mystification" of politics under the Tudors, when court propaganda incrasingly hailed the sovereign as a quasi-spiritual being who "participated uniquely in the omnicompetency of the deity."[1] The same process under way in other European nations did not escape the attention—indeed, the passionate concern—of one astute observer of humanity. In a trenchant and widely read essay of his *Adagia*, first printed in 1515, Erasmus applies to kingship a favorite emblem for the contrast between appearance and reality. The "Sileni of Alcibiades" were statuettes of the homely satyr Silenus that, when opened, revealed beautiful figures of the gods. But the "reversed Silenus" could conceal something far uglier:

> When you see the sceptre, the badges of rank, the bodyguards, and when you hear those titles—"Your Serene Highness, Most Clement, Most Illustrious"—do you not revere the prince like a god on earth, and think you are looking at something more than human? But open the reversed Silenus, and you find a tyrant, sometimes the enemy of his people, a hater of public peace, a sower of discord, an oppressor of the good, a curse to the judicial system, an overturner of cities, a plunderer of the Church, given to robbery, sacrilege, incest, gambling,—in short, as the Greek proverb has it—an Iliad of evils.[2]

The remark occurs in a passage on the ordinary man's susceptibility to appearances. Its irony is doubled here in that the "god" in the Silenus is no god at all, even though he is worshipped by men. The lecher on the outside is the political rapist within. This from a man who had visited several of Europe's great courts. The

badges of rank and lofty titles are rejected not so much in themselves—they serve, after all, as amusing reminders of our folly.
More sinister are the reasons underlying our admiration of such
men and the consequences of our willingness to give them power.

As a vociferous opponent of the politics of force in his century,
Erasmus deserves more recognition than he usually receives for
shaping the ideas of the age on political and religious liberty. The
following pages will discuss some of the ways in which Erasmus
anticipates the liberalism of Milton's generation, especially in his
belief in rule by persuasion rather than force, and in a philosophy
of the state that takes into account this theme in the gospels.
Because Erasmus's political writings are not widely known, it will
be helpful to survey these works, beginning with the *Panegyric* to
Philip Archduke of Austria, proceeding to his most important
political statement, *The Education of a Christian Prince*, then to his
attempts to serve the cause of peace among the warring ide-
ologues of the Reformation. It is characteristic of Erasmus that his
main work on the craft of government should rest upon confidence in a process of education, not a system of ideas. The
theme in all his writings that is most relevant to this book is the
repeated disparagement of the linguistic and ceremonial customs
that lend themselves to king-worship. Finally, some attention is
owed to Erasmus's influence in England, where his ideas were so
widely attended, especially in religion and education, as to bear
fruit in the society for generations.

The dispraise of kings emerges from two related, and most
important, Erasmian political ideas, both of which have helped
keep his work alive for four centuries: these are his opinions on
peace and order, glanced at in the introduction. Peace, in the first
place, is to be preferred to war at any cost,[3] though it is not an end
in itself. His second ruling principle is that social concord makes
possible the exercise of that individual freedom necessary for
living a truly Christian life. None of our evil inclinations, Erasmus
held, "is so violent that it cannot be restrained by reason or
redirected toward virtue."[4] In his famous debate with Luther,
Erasmus proposed that if the human will were not free, it would
have been pointless for God to give us commandments. What
does this moral freedom mean for the body politic? As James
Tracy has said, Erasmus believed this body to be rooted "in a
shared rational agreement *(consensus)* about its ultimate moral
purpose." Because Kings serve only to administer this consensus,
"the popular notion that kings were different from ordinary mortals, that *gloria* and *maiestas* were vested in the royal person,

served no purpose, save to distract attention from the Christian principle of public *utilitas*."[5] Parallels emerge between the pomp of kingship and the ritualism of late medieval religion, so often deplored in Erasmus's theological writings. Both kinds of ceremony, political and religious, in effect override the consciousness needed to exercise Christian liberty.

The advent of the great autocrats of the sixteenth century—Francis I, Charles V, and Henry VIII—was a source of concern and perplexity to many sensitive observers in that age; but this concern was more than the mere aversion to magnificence that motivated an earlier civic humanism.[6] The sixteenth century brought with it a series of disastrous wars and an expansion of monarchies the likes of which the preceding century had not known. The Holy Roman Empire came to include, at least nominally, a vast area of Europe from Spain to Austria to the Netherlands; the ambitious Francis I had designs on Italy and the Netherlands; Henry VIII was pursuing the reconquest of France. With word play that makes the Latin worth quoting, Thomas More's epigram "De cupiditate regnandi" ("On the desire to rule") neatly captures this avaricious spirit of monarchy in the age:

> Regibus e multis regnum cui sufficit unum,
> Vix Rex unus erit, si tamen unus erit.
> Regibus e multis regnum bene qui regnat unum,
> Vix tamen unus erit, si tamen unus erit.[7]

[You will find scarcely one among the many kings for whom one kingdom is enough, if you find even one. You will find scarcely one among the many kings who rules one kingdom well, if you find even one.]

Erasmus's frequent attacks upon kings in this vein contrast, it must be granted at the outset, with his homage to particular kings during this era of growing absolutism and power-mongering. Perhaps it is this inconsistency that has led a reviewer to describe the topic of Erasmus and monarchy to be the most difficult undertaken in the book reviewed.[8] The "scourge of princes" was, after all, an "imperial councilor" to Charles V—though the pay was irregular and the duties ill-defined. Yet from one standpoint there is no real dilemma here if this topic is subsumed to the humanist's overriding concern with war as a detriment to Christian life, especially to the personal liberty required for each soul to work out its salvation. If kings caused wars, they were also in those days the only ones capable of preventing them. Furthermore, in such acts of apparent adulation as dedicating his paraphrases of the Gospels to four reigning princes (Charles V, Francis I, Henry VIII, and Ferdinand of Austria), Erasmus probably thought he could dissuade kings and their subjects from the idolatry of power. Like anyone else who believes simultaneously in original sin and the attainment of Christian ideals, Erasmus could live with the gap between expectation and performance. He would have agreed with More that "what you cannot turn to good, you may at least make less bad. For it is impossible to make all institutions good unless you make all men good, and I don't expect to see that for a long time to come."[9] Indeed, this willingness to live with imperfection gives rise to the detached wit and irony so much valued in both writers.

A second charge often brought against Erasmus's political thought, besides that of inconsistency with his actions, is that it is "primitive" and "simplistic,"—to quote Huizinga.[10] Today one source of this reluctance to accept Erasmus as a political thinker lies in his failure to extricate politics from religion. The combination, however, would seem inescapable for one who believes that "the true and only monarch of the world is Christ," and that "if our princes would agree together to obey His commands, we should truly have only one Prince, and everything would flourish under Him."[11] Erasmus's program has been described by Pierre Mesnard as "évangélisme politique." The difficulty of translating this phrase may say something about the state of both evangelizing and politics in our culture. Mesnard means by this phrase "the regeneration of man through purifying religion and baptising culture."[12] Such aims, shared by English humanists from More and Elyot to Ascham to Milton, may serve as a valid starting point for a political philosophy. Only in the context of this enterprise, moreover, can the theme of civil idolatry be thoroughly understood and appreciated in Erasmus. "Idolatry is popularly so called," he writes, "whenever incense is offered to some profane image. But true idolatry occurs whenever Christ is rejected because of a filthy pleasure, wicked lucre, desire for vengeance, or for the sake of tyranny."[13] The last category explains why the truly Christian king is so often defined by opposition to the tyrant, than whom there is "nothing more like the devil."[14]

Erasmus expresses a cardinal principle of his politics in *The Education of a Christian Prince* when he reminds the king that "if you are master of all your subjects, they must of necessity be your slaves."[15] In the years just after the defeat of Hitler's Germany,

Erasmus scholarship often stressed the dependence of the humanist's political ideals upon his New Testament concept of Christian liberty.[16] Just as nineteenth-century liberals had looked back to Erasmus for the "origins of religious toleration, of free thought, of rationalism and individualism in religion,"[17] scholars a generation ago contrasted his exaltation of human freedom with the Protestant, especially Lutheran, idea of the powerlessness of the will. This emphasis no longer prevails in Erasmus scholarship, if only because it oversimplifies both Erasmus and Lutheranism. Still, there remains a persistent libertarian spirit in Erasmus, almost alone among religious thinkers in his time, from his early pedagogical writings to his last pleas for reconciliation among Christians.

At a critical time in his life, Erasmus became friends with John Colet at Oxford. Colet's optimism, his belief that "God, made man, was the means whereby men were to be made gods,"[18] helped shape his own thoughts on human freedom for perfectibility under the rule of grace. Unlike later political thinkers, he shared Colet's belief in the changed state of man since the Incarnation, a more important fact than the presumed "state of nature" in his philosophy of man. He deeply admired Colet's ideas of peace and the body politic. In a biography of his friend written two years after Colet's death (Allen, no. 1211), he recalls a pacifist Good Friday sermon Colet preached to the king and court at Greenwich. Henry VIII, bursting with ideas of foreign conquest, was alarmed to hear that his soldiers should follow Christ as their king and imitate him rather than the Juliuses and Alexanders of this world. What kind of Christian charity is it, asked Colet, that plunges a sword into the vitals of another man?

Erasmus often objects to the way people read pagan philosohy as if Christianity had never happened. Never forget, he warns the prince regarding the study of the Classics, that "he whom you are reading is a pagan; you who are reading are a Christian. . . . Measure everything by the Christian standard."[19] Elsewhere he wrote, "That Aristotle lives today in the crowded classroom is not owing to his own followers but to Christians; even he would have perished if he had not been mixed with Christ."[20] He especially attacks those who prefer Aristotle's *Politics* to the *philosophia Christi:*

> For if Christ had said anything which is not easily fitted into our way of life, it is permitted [by such worldly thinkers] to interpret it differently; but anyone who dares to oppose the oracular pronounce-

ments of Aristotle is immediately hooted off the stage. From him we have learnt that human felicity cannot be complete without worldly goods—physical or financial. From him we have learnt that a state cannot flourish where all things are held in common. We try to combine all his doctrines with the teaching of Christ, which is like mixing water and fire.[21]

This is more than the typical humanist's antischolasticism, if only because Christ, not Plato, is proposed as the true philosopher. We are not far from the so-called rejection of learning in *Paradise Regained*. Erasmus seeks to surmount rather than accommodate pagan ideas. In political thought this aim is expressed in his publication of a Latin version of Isocrates' "To Nicocles" alongside his own Christian complement to this work, *The Education of a Christian Prince*.

Thus Erasmus's reservations about kingly pomp and power must be viewed in the context of a theology that interpreted the Christian message as simple, joyous, accessible to all without mystification or fear. This is a serious sticking point for many with Erasmus. The belief of Rudolf Otto and his disciple Mircea Eliade that any religious experience must be governed by a sense of the "mysterium tremendum"[22] resists the authority of a voice so lacking in the proper anxiety. Erasmus sees Christianity as a way of living, not only of worshipping; as for spiritual *Angst*, he believes that "fear is one of the real obstacles to the pursuit of virtue," not an incentive to ecstasy.[23] On the other hand, many readers have been drawn to the confidence in reason and in human potential that colors Erasmus's writings. Ernst Troeltsch sees the conflict between Erasmus and Luther as "not one between religious depth and moralistic superficiality; rather it was the first challenge of modern religious thought, universal and antisupernatural, to the resurgent dualism and supernaturalism of the middle ages."[24] As with the Silenus-image, Erasmus turns inside-out the model of Christ as king: it is to Christ's meekness, mercy, even suffering that the king should look for his model. Those on the crest of the "new irrationality" of the sixteenth century[25] saw quite a different God, one rather like Blake's stern geometer-creator: "God in his own nature and majesty is to be left alone; in this regard, we have nothing to do with Him, nor does He wish us to deal with Him."[26] There is no resolving this difference. Luther appeals to the transcendent God; Erasmus, like the author of the *Second Shepherd's Play*, to the incarnate God manifested in the world of men. As fear has no place in Erasmus's religion, it is antithetical to his notion of the ideal commonwealth. A central maxim of Machiavelli is that "it is safer to be feared than loved"; of Erasmus, that "Christian charity counsels people and prince alike."[27] Erasmus himself records the saying of a tyrant in Seneca—"Let them hate, if only they fear"—as controverted by the lesson of history, that in every age "fear is the poorest surety for a long duration of office."[28]

The unified religious and political sensibility is often apparent in Erasmus's condemnation of grandoise titles on spiritual grounds; the "superstition of titles" as he calls it.[29] In religion his coolness toward ceremonies, even the sacraments, is well known. Pilgrimages seemed only to distract people from Christ's teaching. He could not believe that a few pious practices could bring salvation to a cruel and tyrannical soul. When, late in life, he was coaxed into writing a liturgy for the feast of Our Lady of Loreto— whose shrine was one of the busiest places of pilgrimage in Europe—he composed a sermon that in effect undercuts the primary value of pious acts like pilgrimages. The true veneration of Mary, he says, consists of praise, honor, invocation, and imitation; but imitation is the most important of these: "those who honor her with candles, altars, temples, and shrines . . . are in danger lest they hear from their mother what the Jewish worshipper heard from his Father: 'this people honors me with their lips, but their heart is far from me.' "[30] Erasmus would have understood the Corpus Christi playwrights' use of contrasting scenes to reflect the spiritual and worldly kingdoms, as in *Pharaoh* and the Chester *Nativity*. His treatise on worship contrasts the vast liturgical machinery of pagan Rome and the simplicity of Christian practice.[31] The dismissal of religious pomp as pagan unmistakably parallels the frequent attacks on courtly splendor as inherently immoral. "What else does the prince who flaunts gems, gold, and royal purple, and all the other trappings of fortune's pomp in the eyes of his subjects, do but teach them to crave and admire the very source from which springs the foulest essence of nearly all crimes that are punishable by the law of the prince?"[32] Since the coming of Christ, whether as spiritual or political creatures, our lives are not founded on visible things.

To sum up, in a thinker who was heralded by liberals in the last century as the harbinger of intellectual freedom, the religious and political ideas are surprisingly close-knit. Whatever these ideas owe to classical antiquity has been Christianized almost beyond recognition. The ideal king, imitating Christ, leads his people freely and selflessly into the enjoyment of the fruits of peace (in part by building dikes and lowering taxes). The tyrant, modeled on Satan, if not in some sense possessed by him, makes himself the gaudy idol of the people, fastening upon their fear and greed. Yet in doing so, he unwittingly leads them to their own destruction, often in a terrible war. The paradigm is not unlike that of Shakespeare's plays of monarchy and Milton's account of man's tragic history in the last books of *Paradise Lost*. As for setting up a model government, Erasmus never bothers to do so. The reasons for this failure resemble those underlying Milton's in *The Readie and Easie Way*. If we are Christians, both men would have said, we know what it is; if not, then it doesn't make any difference. Such complacency has a long history with Christians and humanists alike. This much is clear: nowhere does Erasmus offer a portrait of a truly Christian king in history, but his pages are filled with the names of tyrants, a few (like Pope Julius II) calling themselves Christian. Readers are likely to be hard on Erasmus nowadays because this religious temper belies an unrealistic sense of political life. The "real" business of kings in the Renaissance was war and power diplomacy. In an aside that reveals how well-informed he was about these affairs, Erasmus notes a splendid irony of Renaissance warfare: the royal warmonger never really gets a large share of the fortunes of battle, the bulk of the spoils going to mercenaries and war profiteers.[33]

From the Panegyric to the Education of a Christian Prince

The dislike of ceremonies, titles, and the trappings of royalty places Erasmus in an important current of the humanist tradition.[34] With Thomas More and Lorenzo Valla, he is one of the principal thinkers engaged in the demystification of the heroic, the antichivalric enterprise of the age. Quite early in the bloody course of modern European history, he believed that the nobility and princes of the world had wasted too much life and property in the pursuit of honor. "It seems to me," he tells Francis I, "that the vast majority of wars have arisen from a few empty words, contrived as it seems to nourish human glory: as if there weren't enough ambition among mortals without feeding this illness with new titles, swelling excessively among us."[35] In the next generation of humanists, one senses the continuity of this iconoclastic temper when George Buchanan, unwittingly the tutor to England's first divine-right claimant, urges his readers to "compare some king whom you have seen decked out like a child's doll and paraded in great ceremony and with a prodigious hubbub in

order to make an empty show: compare such a one, I say, with
kings celebrated in ancient times, whose memory lives and
grows, and is honored by posterity."[36] Paradoxically, as the century progressed intellectual distaste for the gorgeousness of majesty continued alongside an increasingly elaborate ceremonialism
in the respect paid the sovereign, made possible by the vastly
increased size and influence of central governments since the
Middle Ages. It was not so much the grandeur that Erasmus and
others resented as what it signified: the concentration of ultimate
power, the power to destroy, often in the hands of a fool or an
inexperienced boy.

Before the *Panegyric* to Philip the Fair in 1504, Erasmus had
expressed few opinions on monarchy. His conventional sentiments appear in letters of 1499 to the boy princes Adolph of
Burgundy and Henry of England. This neglect of politics is surely
owing to the relatively sequestered life that he led until then, an
unkown theology student in Paris as late as 1499. There had been
firsthand experience with tyranny, though not of the political
kind. His earliest treatise attacks the stupid pride of monastic
authorities, "petty tyrants," who "want the people to be stupid,
the more easily to impose what they want and get anything
accepted, and to frighten people through superstition; for superstition is a thing from which erudition usually sets one free."[37]
The warmongering "eater of his people" was the cruel abbot writ
large.

The first serious essay in political thought, the *Panegyric*, written in an uncharacteristically Asiatic style to welcome the Archduke of Austria's visit to Brussels, has been seen as a tedious
exercise in flattery. Tedious it certainly is. But this work already
sounds the characteristic arguments for peace and freedom, the
mature *philosophia Christi*. "Many leaders," he says, seek fame in
warfare, unlike Philip, whose glory is his peacefulness. "We
would rather have you peaceful than victorious," he continues.
"In peace the arts and honest studies flourish, reverence for law
thrives, religion increases, wealth accumulates, sound morals prevail. "In war," however,

> Sacred things are profaned, divine worship neglected, and force dis-
> places law. For (as Cicero says) law is silent when armed, or if it says
> anything of benefit, it cannot be heard (as Marius aptly says) over the
> clash of arms.

In language that anticipates Colet's Good Friday sermon and
Shakespeare's dialogue between Henry V and his soldiers the

night before Agincourt, Erasmus describes the inconsistency between Christian sovereignty and warfare:

> Will the Christian prince—who ought to be most clement, who not
> only believes that he is something of a god [*numen*], just and helpful,
> but also understands that he must render a most exact accounting of
> the least small drop of human blood; to whom not only his whole
> sovereignty, not even his life should be so important that he would
> want a single person to die for his sake—will he command that some
> right or other (and here I am not, as far as that matters, speaking on
> anyone's behalf) be maintained for him with so many tears and
> bereavements, so much grief, so much blood of wretched men, so
> many human heads, so many perils and wounds, and (what is more
> damnable than all these), such calamity to public morals?[38]

The implicit question of the prince's godliness in the opening of
this long sentence is countered by the unchristian horrors of the
king's potential depredation, ending with the calamity Erasmus
most feared in war, the loss of those conditions that will permit
the individual to nourish virtue.

Attacks on war and princely courts (where "the noblemen pass
one another in order to stand the closest to Jove"[39]) continue in
The Praise of Folly (1509) and *Julius Exclusus e Caelo* (1513), the satire
on the warrior pope usually attributed to Erasmus. When this
latter work appeared, the troubles of Europe must have brought a
heightened sense of the dangers of the modern state. During the
ten years of his reign, Julius II had done as much as any secular
monarch to fan the flames of war.[40] In July 1513 the young warmonger Henry VIII sent an army of thirty thousand men to
support the Emperor Maximilian in his war against France. The
following March Erasmus wrote from England complaining about
the privations this war had brought to Henry's subjects. This
letter, to Anthony of Bergen, was expanded into one of the author's greatest adages, "Dulce bellum inexpertis [War is sweet to
those who haven't tried it]." At the same time, Erasmus thought
Maximilian's rule in the Netherlands had led to a long and messy
conflict in the Duchy of Guelders, proving again royal predilec-
tions for making unjust war at the expense of unwilling subjects.[41]

During this time of intense activity in Erasmus's life, the mid-
and later 1510s, all the principal texts on peace were written. The
1515 additions to the *Adagia* combined attacks on tyranny with
pacifist thought.[42] *The Complaint of Peace (Querela Pacis)*, translated
into English at the start of Elizabeth's reign, remains the fullest
expression of Erasmus's belief that war is totally antithetical to the
spirit of Christianity, rising to the visionary statement that "this

world of ours is the fatherland of the entire race," that divisions of
nationalities are illusory when compared to the fellowship of all
under Christ.[43] It is *The Education of a Christian Prince (Institutio
Principis Christiani)*, however, that most fully sets forth Erasmus's
ideas on the interdependence of peace and responsible kingship.

The introduction to the excellent edition of this work by Otto
Herding orients us to the nature of the *Education* more adequately
than anything available in English.[44] Erasmus first mentions the
book as under way ("in manibus") in a letter of 15 May 1515, just a
year before its first edition by Froben at Basel (Allen, no. 334). A
letter to Martin Dorp later that month helps locate the work
among Erasmus's projects up to that time. Erasmus explains that
The Praise of Folly was not a departure from the plan of his other
works, though it takes a different path:

> In the *Enchiridion* I have quite simply sketched the form of a Christian
> life. In *The Education of the Prince* I have, without pretense, drawn
> attention to those matters in which a head of state should be in-
> structed. In the *Panegyric*, under the pretext of praise, I secretly dealt
> with the theme openly developed in *The Education of the Prince*. In the
> *Folly* the same subject is treated as in the *Enchiridion*, but jokingly.[45]

Herding properly notes the opposing sets here: the obliqueness of
Folly is to the straightforward *Enchiridion* as the *Panegyric* is to the
Education. The complementarity explains why the *Panegyric* was
republished with the *Education*, both in 1516 and in the second
Froben edition of 1518, the base text for later editions. Thus the
1516 edition inlcudes the *Education*, Isocrates' "To Nicocles," the
Panegyric to Philip, as well as Plutarch's "How to Tell a Flatterer
from a Friend."

The genre of Erasmus's *Education* has few enthusiasts today.
One historian has dismissed the whole tradition of advice to
kings, from Isocrates and the pseudo-Aristotelian *Secretum Se-
cretorum* to Hoccleve's *De regimine principum*, as "dreary, cliche-
ridden books."[46] This criticism must have been as clear to Erasmus as to us, for he was disinclined to promote dreary books. It
may have suggested to him the idea of removing the clutter by
going back *ad fontes*, in true humanist fashion, to translate Isocrates' brief treatise. Thus the Froben edition represents an attempt to enclose in one volume the heart of ancient and modern,
that is, Christian, wisdom for rulers.

Yet more than one literary convention is discernible in the
Education. For one thing it represents the fusion of two medieval

literary forms that often represented opposed political views: the discursive advice to princes and the related narrative literature of the fall of princes. From the late thirteenth century on, scholars increasingly fancied themselves as royal counselors. Thomas Aquinas and his student Aegidius Romanus both wrote treatises entitled *De Regimine Principum;* the age of Erasmus also saw works on this subject by Guillaume Bude and Sir Thomas Elyot. John Skelton wrote a *Speculum Principis* for his young charge Prince Henry, including dreary cliches about marital fidelity. The monarchism of works in this class contrasts sharply with Boccaccio's *De Casibus Virorum Illustrium,* a series of tales about the fate of rulers who fail to live up to the expectations of God. Ironically *The Mirror for Magistrates* started out, in the mid-1550s, as a warning to princes continuing Lydgate's translation of Boccaccio; it evolved into a reminder to subjects that the punishment of evil princes is the perogative of God, not the public. But the two kinds, advice to princes and *de casibus* narrative, had often colored one another. Translating Boccaccio, Laurent de Premierfait converted his work into a monarchist one, while Lydgate merely softened the anti-monarchism, if only because he feared anything like popular sovereignty.[47] *The Mirror for Magistrates,* though execrating rebellion, warns against both unjust princes and unruly subjects. Erasmus's work follows the prescriptive method of the advice literature, but his examples (Alexander, Augustus, Nero, and others) recall the narratives of the *de casibus* tradition. As a rule, in his discussions of kingship Erasmus's method is to exalt the ideal sovereign's role in man's affairs by pointing out how far actual princes have fallen short.

So far as there is a common thesis between Erasmus and his avowed model Isocrates, it might be summed up in the latter's injunction, "In the worship of the gods, follow the example of your ancestors, but believe that the noblest sacrifice and the greatest devotion is to show yourself in the highest degree a good and just man."[48] Such statements accord fully with Erasmus's habitual suspicion of pomp, whether in religion or politics. Isocrates and Erasmus also share the Attic wisdom that looks beneath the surface of things: however divine kings may seem, they occupy the slipperiest rung on the social ladder. Erasmus also admits in his dedication to Charles that the aphoristic form of his *Education* was adapted from Isocrates, who had said of his essay that "in discourses of this sort we should not seek novelties, for in these discourses it is not possible to say what is paradoxical or incredible or outside the circle of accepted belief; but, rather, we should regard that man as the most accomplished in the field who can collect the greatest number of ideas scattered among the thoughts of all the rest and present them in the best form" (1:63; par. 41). In other words, even when such a work is a loosely organized collection of truisms, it is prompted by a belief in the value of collecting and scrutinizing the scattered sayings of humankind, not unlike Erasmus's own *Adagia* and *Apophthegms.*

The aphoristic nature of the *Education* should be taken into account before we dismiss the work as a bore. Because (in America, at any rate) it is usually studied in the translation of L. K. Born, it can be wrongly perceived as a rambling treatise like that of Folly, who prided herself on never organizing anything.[49] What gives a sense of aimlessness to the *Education* in this version is the translator's failure to represent faithfully that part of the author's intention which is indicated in the second half of the title: *The Education of a Christian Prince, by Erasmus of Rotterdam, Digested into Aphorisms so that Reading Will Be Less Tiresome.*[50] Born tends to combine the aphorisms (many of which are two-line sentences) into paragraphs just as was done in the eighteenth-century Leyden edition, from which he seems to have translated.[51] We have learned since Born's time to appreciate the distinct role of the aphorism in the history of prose composition, from the medical sayings of Hippocrates and Galen to the essays of Bacon.[52] It was generally accepted that only persons of authority would write in aphorisms. The Elizabethan Richard Mulcaster confessed that he had not dared to write in the form because "neither deserve I so much credit, as that my bare word may stand for a warrant." Erasmus's use of the form, then, may indicate the well-deserved confidence he had acquired since the more guarded oratory of the *Panegyric.* Writers believed with Bacon, moreover, that the aphorism was especially suited to knowledge undergoing growth. Bacon thought it especially appropriate to the human sciences, whose exact interrelations were not as yet known. Readers of Bacon's *Novum Organum* will be familiar with this aspect of Erasmus's method in the *Education.* Each aphorism is a discrete observation; there is no necessary logic to the ordering of the whole, though it is possible to detect sequences of thought here and there. It is thus a method suitable for the rough-hewn "science" of kingship in the early sixteenth century.

Aphorisms are best suited to two kinds of readers: young people who lack the patience, and political leaders who lack the time, for reading complete philosophical treatises. The point is made in Erasmus's 1531 dedication of his *Apophthegmata* (a collection of famous sayings of the ancients) to the young William Prince of Cleves:

> Accordingly I have collected from the best authors what the Greeks call Apophthegms, that is, notable sayings, because I consider no other kind of argument more befitting a Prince, especially a young one. There are indeed works very worthy of knowing which philosophers have produced concerning morals, the governing of the state, and on waging war. But how rarely does even a private man have the leisure to spend perusing in Plato the riddles and labyrinths of Socratic subtleties and Isagogian ironies? True, Aristotle wrote extensively on morals, but he seems rather to have written for philosophers, not the prince. . . . But he who is born to authority must exercise virtue readily, not dispute about it at leisure. There remains history, which, because it presents achievements, admirable or otherwise, to be viewed as if in a painting, and not without enjoyment, would seem to be more suited than philosophy for great men: but who knows how much of a Prince's limitless strength would be lost paging through these volumes? Yet just as those who wrestle have ready use of certain methods of grasping or slipping away, so those who lead in affairs of war and peace should have ready certain principles [*rationes*] by which they are advised what should be done or not done in a given situation.[53]

Those familiar with Erasmus's opinions on royalty will detect an unspoken message here: if the king has no ideas of his own, it is infinitely preferable to get them from the wisdom of the past rather than depend entirely on his counselors. Just as the *Apophthegmata* were to be studied, even memorized, the aphorisms of the *Education* were to be absorbed by the young prince, his tutors, even the wider public of cultivated citizens. Like the wisdom books of the Bible that Erasmus so much admired, like his own *Adagia*, these *rationes* compress the wide reading, reflection, and experience of a mature and cosmopolitan scholar. Opened at any point, the book was to provide food for thought. In fact it was as a book of memorabilia, rather than a continuous treatise, that Count Frederick II of Bavaria recommended the *Education* for his young nephew in 1517.[54]

One must apologize for the *Education* nowadays, however; it has not had a good press. "Erasmus," says a leading historian, "composes treatises on the proper education of rulers, liberally seasoned with flattery in hopes of making his advice more palatable to the prince to whom it is addressed." Yet in so doing, he goes on to say, Erasmus is typically ambiguous:

There is the bitter denunciation of those princes and their warlike
appetites in Erasmus' series of tracts wholly or in part devoted to the
exaltation of peace and condemnation of war. . . . Repeated again and
again without producing any effect on society and without awareness
on the part of its author that social changes more radical than any he
ever contemplated were needed to produce the effect aimed at, Erasmus' *querela pacis* begins to sound querulous indeed.[55]

This is not the place to argue Erasmus's impact on his society,
which a good many scholars (Mesnard, McConica, Quentin Skinner) think real. It has already been seen that the *Education* is not a
"treatise" in the usual sense of a composed argument. Nor is it
flattery. Consider the first aphorism in the book, a literal translation of which reads:

> Where it is accepted that a prince is to be chosen by election, the
> images of his ancestors are not to be regarded, nor the shape and
> height of his body, which was the most foolish practice (we read) of
> some barbarians in the past, but an inborn quality of mind that is
> gentle and peaceful, a temperament composed and with as little
> disposition to rashness as possible—not so vigorous a spirit that there
> would be a danger that (fortune concurring) he would erupt into a
> tyrant and not endure anyone's admonishing or advising him, nor
> again so pliant that he might allow himself to be led by the various
> whims of various people.[56]

Far from flattery, the opening of the *Education* might have made
uneasy reading for an intelligent young prince or his family.
Every Renaissance prince took a "barbarian" pride in his ancestors
and in his splendid appearance. Both Henry VIII and Francis I
had shown the characteristic penchant of the age for displays of
skill in the use of weapons; Francis's heir Henry II would die an
early death while jousting. So much for the "gentle and peaceful"
quality of mind. Moreover (and Erasmus will soon note this fact),
European princes were generally not chosen by election; the
"election" shortly after this of Charles V as Holy Roman Emperor
was anything but a function of "suffragium." Just a year earlier
Erasmus had issued a scathing statement against inherited monarchy in the adage "Aut fatuum aut regem nasci oportere [Kings
and fools are born not made]":

> You choose the man who is to have charge of a ship; but you do not
> choose the man to whom you are entrusting so many cities, so many
> human lives? But there it is, the thing is so established that it is

impossible to root it out. Kings are born, and whoever may have been picked on by chance, whether he be good or bad, stupid or wise, sane or clouded in mind, as long as he looks like a human being, he is to be trusted with supreme power in the state.[57]

Except for the unconcealed rancor, this adage restates the sense of the sixth aphorism, written to complement the first:

It is otherwise where the prince is born, not elected, which long ago was the practice among certain barbarian nations, as Aristotle says, and is almost everywhere the accepted thing in our times. In this case the chief hope of a good prince lies in correct education, which should be provided rather scrupulously, so that what has been removed from the right of election [suffragiorum iuri] may be compensated for by an application to learning.[58]

The first sentence implies that we are now, two thousand years later, more like the barbarians Aristotle spoke of so condescendingly than the Athenians for whom he wrote. It may also mischeviously suggest to complacent Aristotelians how far they are out of step with their master. The second sentence continues the sly probing at inherited monarchy: losing the right to choose the sovereign (ius suffragiorum means that only legal citizens would vote, and does not imply universal suffrage) makes education all the more necessary if civilization is not to fail completely. As Erasmus says elsewhere, careful education of the prince is not so much a civilized adornment as a desperate remedy:

The first [expedient], perhaps, will be not to receive the lion into the city. Next, by the authority of senate, magistrates, and people, to limit his power in such a way that he may not easily break out into tyranny. But the best safeguard of all is to shape his character by sacred teachings while he's still a boy and doesn't realize he's a ruler.[59]

What begins to sound like flattery in the *Education* is usually blunted at once. "Omnia debet patria bono principi": "A country owes everything to the good prince" (Herding ed., p. 138). So far, a glowing self-satisfaction in the princely breast. But this is dampened by the rest of the aphorism: "At hunc ipsum debet ei, qui rectis rationibus talem effecerit [But it owes the prince himself to the one who makes him what he is through sound principles]." The wise prince is really a creation of the teacher who instructs him in the wisdom of humanity. This is a recommendation for the new learning, certainly; but it is supported by an unyielding belief, evident throughout thousands of pages by Erasmus, in the improvement of people through such learning. Only the most cynical reading of Erasmus and similarly serious humanists would interpret this kind of statement as mere self-advertising. In the *Education*, as in the later *Apophthegmata*, the object is less to counsel princes than to show them how to be their own counselors.

A recurrent idea in the aphorisms is the inconsistency between unlimited monarchy and Christian liberty, perhaps a veiled protest against the expansionism of contemporary monarchies. If the prince meditates on his likeness to God, he will in the end be led to this conclusion: "God Himself, so that He would not rule by compulsion, gave free will to both angels and men, in order to render his empire more splendid and majestic. And can anyone seem great to himself in this name [i.e., *imperium*] because he rules over citizens who are driven with fear like cattle?"[60] As Pierre Mesnard says, Erasmus has given an entirely new meaning to the classic formula, "Princeps imago Dei." The symbol of the Christian king's rule is not the globe and crown of Byzantine emperors, but the cross.[61] In Otto Herding's words, the ancient comparison of king with deity becomes "only ethical, no longer ontic."[62] If, in the last analysis, the sovereign is really doing his job, he will resemble the suffering Christ, not the remote ruler of the heavens that monarchical propagandists had always conjured up.

The slim chance that any prince would ever take this advice makes it certain that Erasmus was directing his words to the citizen as well as the king. Throughout the *Education*, Erasmus encourages this larger audience to ponder the difference between the dismal performance of actual rulers and the exemplary behavior that people should expect from them. "Think, I ask you, how absurd it is to be seen raised to such heights, with gems, gold, purple, a court, and other ornaments of the body, with candles and things that are clearly not all yours, yet to be inferior in the true goods of the mind to many from the very dregs of the populace."[63] The imagery of this sentence attacks, in Platonic fashion, our preference for the outward over the invisible, inner realities that most count. But perhaps the monarch of pure ideas was impossible. "For my part," Erasmus says elsewhere, "I admire the pattern monarch which the philosophers skilfully paint for us, and I hardly think such princes are to be found ruling the state in the city of Plato. Certainly in the annals of history one could not find more than one or two whom one would dare compare with this model."[64] Although he never went so far as to tolerate active resistance to evil rulers, Erasmus wittily distinguished the men from the office in his annotations on Romans 13. Paul "did not say that all princes are ordained by God, but that power is: just as marriage is from God, but God does not make all marriages."[65] Many examples could be given from the *Education* of aphorisms in which a two-part, antithetical structure conveys this difference between the real thing (the ideal) and its visible sham.[66]

The aphoristic form thus indicates that Erasmus's well-known skepticism on the pretense of mankind extended to government. If we were to ask him where, in his political philosophy, true sovereignty lies, with the king or the people, he would probably accuse us of begging the question: in this world there is no such thing as true sovereignty.[67] Reviewing the atrocities of Rome's emperors, in a statement that looks forward to Richard Hooker and to Shakespeare's second tetralogy, he goes so far as to say that legitimate claim to rule by inheritance is a myth: "for authority born in force and the right of conquest, and even in crime, if it gradually wins the consent of the multitude and strikes root, can become lawful. Otherwise, if one were to trace the rise of governments from their earliest beginnings, one would find few of legitimate birth."[68] If we look back far enough, he writes, we would have to allow the people of Padua to claim the site of Troy because their progenitor, Antenor, was a Trojan; Romans might argue their rights to towns in Spain that once belonged to the empire. "What people has not, at one time or another, been driven out of its lands or driven others out?"[69] The general tenor of Erasmus's thought, however, is that there is a *ius suffragiorum* of some kind—that in important ways the ruler's authority originates in the voice of the governed: "A large part of sovereignty is the consent of the people, the thing that first brought kings into being."[70] As was noted in the preceding chapter, the same idea is the subject of one of More's epigrams.

Nevertheless, a comparison of Erasmus's and Aquinas's ideas on homage shows a surprising difference in the greater place that Erasmus concedes to the monarch—or at least to the state that may be a monarchy. Like Aquinas, he ranks *latria* (which he calls *adoratio*), the worship of God alone, as the highest kind of *pietas*. Like Tyndale and later Protestant writers, he avoids the term *dulia*, so far as I have been able to determine. And whereas Aquinas considered homage to parents (called *pietas* in his system) a higher duty than that owed the sovereign, Erasmus says that the second level of homage is that owed to our country *(patria)*,

> which gave us birth, which educated us with good laws, to which we owe even our parents themselves, and for which we must meet our death if events require it. On the other hand, what a monstrous crime it is to bring about war in one's country, or to wound it in other ways. . . .
> Something should be said of the Catholic Church here, which is not only a state but also a body. For a Christian is not only a fellow citizen with every Christian, but also a brother. Here it should be mentioned how much reverence is owed to the Church; on the other hand, how wicked it is to arouse sedition and rebellion against it. It would be well to add by way of comparison how much more binding are the ties of the Spirit than of nature.[71]

The last point about the preeminence of spiritual ties probably explains why Erasmus rearranges the Thomistic order of homage. For all his criticism of governments, he realized that a culture, especially a Christian culture, is a spiritual thing, a *communitas*, which alone can give shape and meaning to the lives of its individuals. Everywhere in Erasmus, the spiritual takes precedence over the physical. This, and the logical priority of the state to the parents in the degree of dependency, must explain the superiority of the state in Erasmus's scale of homage. However, his discussion makes it clear that the respect owed to the sovereign's person is only a part of this overall reverence for the *patria*.[72]

Despite his reservations on the exercise of kingly power, Erasmus abhorred the thought of popular rule, especially late in life when he contemplated the tragedy of the Peasants' Revolt. On Christmas Eve 1525 he grimly reports the atrocities in southern and western Germany: a hundred thousand peasants killed, daily arrests of priests, followed by torture, hanging, beheading, or burning.[73] Not only did monarchy guard against such chaos, it also ensured, as could no other form of government he knew, a measure of equity in administering the law. Throughout his life, Erasmus was influenced, like anyone who knew the legal thought of the time, by the Aristotelian notion (*Politics*, 1287b) that a king could serve as a living law, moderating the absolutism of the written law. This belief is spelled out in a letter to Sigismund I of Poland:

Indeed, it is rightly said by wise men, "The King is a living law." Law speaks in few words, but there are infinite circumstances of persons and things. In these, therefore, the king speaks for the law, pronouncing nothing more than what the law itself would say to us if it could respond on all things.[74]

Erasmus makes these remarks in the context of encouraging the king's *clementia*, not flattering him on his power. He never envisioned a government that did not locate in a single person this necessary function of equity.[75] On balance the clearest description of his ideal form of government is probably that contained in the *Education:* "a limited monarchy, checked and lessened by aristocracy and democracy."[76] As Pierre Mesnard and, most recently, James Tracy have reminded us, this was the political idea of most thoughtful Netherlanders, who submitted to emperor—so long as he let them run their internal affairs—and who rightly feared being drawn into the perennial, senseless conflicts between France and the Empire.[77]

The Language of King-Worship

Surveying history, Erasmus finds kingship always at odds with its ideal condition: enforced idolatry instead of pious homage, favoritism and self-indulgence instead of equity. The acerbic adage "Kings and fools are born not made" must have amused many a nonroyal reader with its capsule history of monarchy, beginning with the Homeric age when kings "were for the most part well-endowed with stark stupidity." The whole attack is perhaps a therapeutic exercise, compensating for the obliqueness and restraint of the *Panegyric* and the *Education*. Agamemnon is an ambitious daughter-killer; Priam, a senile fool doting on his son's girlfriend. What is more "idiotic" than Xerxes trying to terrify Mount Athos or scourging the Hellespont? "Alexander the Great showed no less kingly stupidity when he renounced his father and commanded that he should be greeted as the son of Jove."[78] In such self-idolizing, the pagan rulers offer ubiquitous instances of stupidity and vice. "And yet monsters of this kind, blackened with parricide, sacrilege, incest, in a word, with infamy of every kind, were presented with temples, altars, and divine honours by their fawning subjects."[79] A republican outburst in the adage "Ut fici oculis incumbunt [As sties stick to the eyes]" has been used to link Erasmus with the later sixteenth-century "monarchomachs": "Villages go up in flames, lands are laid waste, churches are ravaged, innocent citizens are murdered, everything is over-turned, while the prince idly plays at dice, amuses himself with dancing and players, hunts, drinks, and makes love. O extinct line of Brutus! O thunderbolt of Jove, either blunted or blind!"[80]

This chapter has been concerned with showing that there is every reason to take Erasmus's political writings seriously, es-pecially the *Education*. The subtle logic of the aphorisms, often working with that indirectness and sly association that are so characteristic of the Erasmian style, cannot have been neglected by his humanist admirers in England or elsewhere. Realizing that the *Education* is engaged in anything but flattery, we are in a better position to recognize certain consistent themes in the author's political thought at large. One such theme, simple but rich in implications for this study, is the condemnation of extravagant royal titles. It is typical of a scholar so deeply committed to the primacy of the word that political evil should be seen as rooted in an act of language.

What contributes as much as anything to the worship of mon-archy is the uncritical idiom of praise. If even the familiar titles of "lord" and "majesty" are viewed as pagan in origin, how much worse are the fantastic names given to modern kings? In his treatise on the right use of language, *Lingua* (1525), Erasmus suggests that the source of much civil idolatry lies in the unreflect-ing, irresponsible use of flattering names:

> But there is another kind of blasphemy, somewhat more concealed, but no less dangerous, whenever the people, fawning upon their princes, confer divine honors upon them, and embrace their princes gladly on account of such honor. It sometimes happens, therefore, that the prince has flatterers and scoffers instead of citizens and counsellors; that the people, on the other hand, have made tyrants instead of princes, and God is angered by the blasphemy on either side.[81]

In the *Education* the section on flatterers develops this point fur-ther. A prince's titles should "be of the sort that would remind the prince of his duties"—titles like "Most Wise" or "Most Clement"—not "Most Invincible" or "Ever August." A ruler's titles should never call to mind "sacred majesty and divinity."[82] In the casual use of such titles, especially as addressed to a young, unformed mind, blasphemy and tyranny walk hand in hand:

One of the earliest lessons [for the young prince] is pomp and pride; he is taught that whatever he wants he can have. He hears that the property of everyone belongs to the prince, that he is above the law; that the whole paraphernalia of government, laws and policies exist stored in the prince's mind. He hears the terms *sacred majesty, serene highness, divinity, god on earth,* and other such superb titles. In short, while he is yet a boy, all he learns to play at is being a tyrant.[83]

Erasmus's complaint against this mixture of slovenly education with monarchist fetishism lives on a century and a half later in Milton's scathing charge that "a king must be ador'd like a Demigod, with a dissolute and haughtie court about him," including "grooms, even of the close-stool . . . thir mindes debas'd with court opinions."[84]

Two other notable men were engaged in writing political treatises almost concurrently with the composition of the *Education.* Three months after the printing of his book, Erasmus received More's manuscript of *Utopia;* two years earlier, Machiavelli had completed *The Prince* (unpublished until 1536). In our century Machiavelli has always had the lion's share of recognition as a political thinker, and with good reason; but it is worth recalling Augustin Renaudet's strictures on the limits of his political "realism":

The Florentine is merely a technician of politics. . . . He knows politics, diplomacy, and war. He badly understands and disdains economics. Erasmus and Thomas More are better informed and more inquiring about the modest realities of which the people's existence consists. They have seen at first hand what Machiavelli had not in the course of his diplomatic missions; they are probably more human.[85]

Whether or not we agree with this—and any reader of Erasmus's colloquies and letters knows how much experience he *did* have with unscrupulous customs officers, crooked inkeepers, and the like—we must grant that the appearance of these three works at almost the same time is one of those telling coincidences in history, not unlike the simultaneous publication of *Rasselas* and *Candide.* And just as Johnson and Voltaire had their own contrasting visions of the eighteenth century, these three thinkers offered discrete visions of their world. Erasmus placed his confidence in education, in the human will rightly informed, without which it is senseless to worry over the technicalities of politics.

Erasmus's Politics in England

Modern church historians have discovered the strong impact of
Erasmus's theology on the English church, especially the decades
just after the break with Rome.[86] Interconnected as religious and
political issues then were, we should expect to find Erasmus's
ideas on kingship, war, and civil liberty represented in English
thought of the period. In fact, however, the political works seem
to have ridden into England on the coattails of those theological
and scriptural works that were in constant use and circulation
from 1520 to 1560. An English translation of "Dulce Bellum" was
published by Thomas Berthlet in 1534; *Julius Exclusus* appeared in
English twice between 1533 and 1535; *De Amabili Ecclesiae Con-
cordia* was translated in 1545, and *Querela Pacis*, in 1559. But information on English translations is not nearly so germane as the fact
that Continental editions of these and other works in Latin could
be found in hundreds of bookstalls, schools, and private libraries.
The *Enchiridion*, the central manifesto of Erasmus's *philosphia
Christi* touching every dimension of human life, was translated by
William Tyndale in 1522, surviving in ten later editions, the last in
1576. McConica and others have described the Erasmian am-
bience of Edward VI's court, and it was no doubt John Lord
Lumley's education at that court that led him to translate, at the
age of sixteen, the *Education*.

Erasmus did not exactly bring "Erasmian" political thought into
England, so much as say what was already on the minds of many.
As was seen in the previous chapter, the English already had a
well-developed nose for anything resembling absolutism; this is
demonstrated in More's account of Richard III's tyranny (in a
history begun about 1513). But Tyndale serves as a reminder that a
follower of Erasmus in religion could think quite differently from
his master on the subject of government. Tyndale was inspired to
translate the New Testament by a passage in Erasmus's *Paraclesis*
urging the benefits of reading scripture for the common man.[87]
However, no doubt fearing that the majority still sumpathized
with Rome, he gave the commons no say in the polity. A crucial
difference between him and Erasmus is his Lutheran insistence
upon the human will's powerlessness to do good. One political
consequence can be an absolute monarch ruling with the help of a
few good laymen, without any wider participation of *ius suffragiorum*. (Why have an election when virtuous choice is impossible?) Tyndale even prefers rule by a tyrant rather than an
"effeminate" king, because the tyrant will at least punish the

wrongdoers of his kingdom, whereas a weak king will extend tears and forgiveness even to the worst criminals.[88] Still, there are echoes of Erasmus in Tyndale's *Obedience of a Christian Man*, for instance the suspicion of pomp and horror of war.[89] He concurs with Erasmus's quietism as well: whoever resists kings and magistrates, he writes, "resisteth God, for they are in the room of God." Neither subscribes to "the divine right of kings," but both believe that since any king is better than none at all, it is sinful even to resist the king's officials in their line of duty.[90] The two thinkers agree here partly because they value stability and order as highly as anyone else in that age; but their underlying principles are quite different. Erasmus wants a tight social fabric so that the individual can be free to choose the path of virtue; Tyndale, so that the flow of the divine will cannot be impeded as it moves down the chain of command. If the king obstructs the flow—and this idea is perpetuated in the Elizabethan homily against rebellion—God will take care of him himself. Tyndale never mentions the danger of civil idolatry—or rather he puts it off to the supposed design of popes and bishops to usurp the place of God and the king.

With Erasmus and More, the political similarities owe less to influence than to the encounter of minds that leads readily to friendship and mutual support. They met on Erasmus's first visit to England (1499–1500), the earliest of More's surviving correspondence being a letter from Erasmus.[91] Both the *Folly* and *Utopia* were composed with the same light-handed humor, the same ingenious irony, that the two had shown in their early translation of Lucian. Nevertheless, Erasmus's effect on More's thinking has always been difficult to gauge, especially in their political ideas.

"More's thinking" is itself an elusive creature. Easy as it is to identify the liberal Christian humanist of *Utopia*, the epigrams, and the long letter to Martin Dorp defending Erasmus (Rogers, no. 15), More is also the seemingly intolerant, reactionary opponent of Tyndale—the voluminous vitriol of the *Confutations* surely owing to something more than the stylistic decorum of controversial writing. At the last, More is the unanticipated, hauntingly meditative writer of the Tower works. One index of the shift from the young humanist to the mystic and martyr is the changing sense of history and tradition. If in the *Confutations* More rises repeateldy like an embattled lawyer appealing to precedent in the matter of bishops, miracles, and relics, at an earlier date he could say even of so revered a figure St. Augustine: "He was human and could make a mistake. I trust him in most things, as much as I do anybody; but I don't trust any one man in all things."[92] Yet in the last works, especially *The Dialogue of Comfort* and the *Tristitia Christi*, he seems to rise above tradition, even time itself, into the stillness that he perceives at the center of the redemptive mystery. The early More was living in less interesting times, however, and it is fun to think how he might have influenced English politics if circumstances had continued as they were when he and Erasmus first became friends. It might as well have been Erasmus speaking his mind on kingship in *Utopia*. Kings "would never take the advice of real philosophers, drenched as they are and infected with false values from boyhood on," says Raphael Hythloday. The epigram "De cupiditate regnandi" (quoted near the beginning of this chapter) is recalled in Hythloday's observation that "most princes apply themselves to the arts of war . . . instead of to the good arts of peace. They are generally more set on acquiring new kingdoms by hook or crook than on governing well those that they already have." The king may make peace "with solemn ceremonies—which the simple-minded people will attribute to the piety of the prince and his careful compassion," when in reality his only motive is personal convenience. The Utopians delight in demystification, seeing it as "absurdity to be pleased by empty, ceremonial honors." Their kings are elected by parliament, must act with the cooperation of council and parliament, and are subject to dismissal if suspected of treason.[93]

The Utopians' dismissal of ceremony in political life seems to have caught More's fancy. Sending Erasmus a copy of his newly published *Utopia*, he can envision himself living the simple life in "Nowhere" while receiving foreign ambassadors and princes: "wretched creatures they are, in comparison with us, as they stupidly pride themselves on appearing in childish garb and feminine finery, laced with that despicable gold, and ludicrous in their purple and jewels and other empty baubles."[94] People's susceptibility to gaudy display in their rulers provided the theme of an earlier epigram, a fable, "De rege at rustico." Not unlike Erasmus's *Folly*, the poem uses the convention of the simple-minded truth-seeker:

The King and the Rustic

A country boy reared in the backwoods comes to town—more rustic than any faun or satyr. People are lined up on either side of the crowded street, and the whole town is one shout: "The king is coming!" The country boy is excited about the unusual noise and wants to see what the hubbub is all about. Suddenly the king comes into view, preceded by a great throng, a striking figure in gold on a great horse. Then "Long live the king!" redoubles everywhere, as the people look up at their king with awe-struck faces.

"Where's the king?" asks the country boy. "Where's the king?" Someone says, "There he is, the man on the tall horse there!" "He's a king?" says the country boy. "You're fooling me. Looks to me like a man in painted clothes."[95]

In *The Praise of Folly* Erasmus similarly reminds his readers of "the divine honors paid to these nobodies, and the public deification of even the most evil tyrants."[96] But the irony of regal sumptuousness can also be bitter in More's early writings. No less than twenty of the epigrams deal with kingship and tyranny. In one of these, on a picture of Herod's banquet at the beheading of John the Baptist, More evokes the mystery playwrights' world-king:

The face of the holy man is streaked with putrid gore, and the royal banquet table bears a severed head. In the same way a brother, King Atreus, presented the bodies of the two children to be eaten by their father King Thyestes. In the same way a faithful sister, a queen, gave to King Odrysius a slain son, and a faithless mother gave Itys. Such pretty mayhem adorns the banquet tables of kings. Believe me, this isn't poor man's food![97]

The epigrams and *Utopia* delighted the wits of Europe at the very time when More was beginning his own rise in the king's favor, when only the first whispers of the Reformation could be heard. Even in writing his *Richard III*, More probably had in mind the incipient tyranny of Henry VIII.[98] Throughout the 1520s, while Erasmus's voice becomes increasingly mute (though his books are selling better than ever), More tries to find a balance between the powers of monarchy and the people. Marius describes his 1523 speech, against the king's interests, defending free debate in Parliament, and his speech to the fateful 1529 Parliament contending that the king's people "make him a prince" (pp. 206, 355). Yet threatened by heretics, he also took up the defense of kingly and hierarchical prerogatives. Ultimately, even Erasmus came to accept a strong, even absolute monarchy, though he stopped short of approving massacre in the name of public order.[99] More's inconsistency as liberal humanist become zealous prosecutor of heresy did not escape notice, Tyndale reminding him of his and his "darling" Erasmus's pre-Reformation jokes at the expense of superstitious Catholics. More's answer is worth quoting because it shows how deeply he felt the change of circumstances since the days of *Folly* and *Utopia:*

> In these dayes in whyche men by theyr owne defaute mysseconstre and take harme of the very scripture of god, untyll menne better emende, yf any man wolde now translate Moria in to Englysche, or some workes eyther that I have my selfe wryten ere this, all be yt there be none harme therin / folke yet beynge (as they be) geven to take harme of that that is good / I wolde not onely my derlynges bokes but myne owne also, helpe to burne them both wyth myne owne handes, rather than folke sholde (though thorow theyr owne faute) take any harme of them, seynge that I se them likely in these dayes to do so.[100]

The pessimism refers not only to the times—"in these dayes" carefully inserted at the beginning and end of this digression. It also speaks to "men" and "folke" who seem hell-bent on misunderstanding everything. Burn the books because of bad readers, not bad texts—a novel approach to censorship! *Folly* and *Utopia* would be especially suitable for burning because their ironies place great demands on folks' minds. A trace, here, of the aging lawyer-judge's impatience with an ignorant public. More's reactionary turn a decade after *Utopia* contrasts with the relative equanimity of Erasmus's last great political-religious tract, *On Mending the Peace of the Church* (1533); but then there was always, as has been remarked, a "circumspect" quality about More, in contrast with the free-spirited Erasmus.[101] Especially on the subject of politics, it is the difference between the lawyer and the man of letters.

In English politics and political attitudes, the channels of Erasmian influence move indirectly through the terrain of religion and education. The *Colloquies,* breezy dialogues on some of the gravest topics, continued to be memorized in the schools until well into the seventeenth century. Elizabethan grammar schools far removed from St. Paul's or Westminster could be found using the *Folly.* Erasmus's influence on John Foxe has been traced as fairly typical of the Elizabethan period, and one scholar has given reasons to call Hooker's *Ecclesiastical Polity* "the synthesis of the English tradition of Erasmian humanism."[102] Elizabeth and her court were also more consistent with Erasmus's ideals of government than any of the monarchs who actually patronized the humanist. While refusing to let her court become imbroiled in religious controversy, says Loades, "Elizabeth was also the only

Tudor to share wholeheartedly the humanist horror of war and warlike displays. . . . Elizabeth's court deserved, far more than did that of Henry VIII on which it was bestowed, the accolade of Erasmus. Lord Burleigh, in caring for his wards, transformed the out of court education of the English nobility, and helped to send the sons of the gentry flocking to the universities by the end of the century."[103] Had it seen print in its time, some impact might have been made by the *Dialogue between Reginald Pole and Thomas Lupset* of Thomas Starkey, who probably began his book in 1529 to encourage Pole to enter Henry's government.[104] Like his two speakers, Starkey greatly admired Erasmus; he presents an enlightened, humane attempt at solving England's problems, on the principle that "the end of al polytyke rule ys, to enduce the multytud to vertuse lyvyng, accordyng to the dygnyte of the nature of man."[105] Like almost all Tudor political thinkers, he speaks for mixed monarchy: aristocracy tempering monarchy in the secular estate; councils hedging tyranny in the spiritual. Nothing is said about the king's *gloria* and *maiestas* in this, a cheerfully practical book concerned throughout, like More's *Utopia*, with the public good alone. Starkey's aims may not be specifically Erasmian, but are fully consistent with Erasmus's *evangelisme politique;* they further advocate the *Enchiridion* as the best available guide to living the Christian life, and the *Ecclesiastes* as the model for educating the clergy.[106]

Even more important than his educational program, which is the firmest link between Erasmus and the three authors with whom the rest of this book deals, is his reputation, to the last generation of the sixteenth century, as an "apostle of common sense"[107] before the flood. Hatred of tyranny was, as previously observed, nothing new to English society. What Erasmus added to the argument against absolute monarchy was an impassioned plea for peace and benevolence, against which later generations could measure the ferocious and pointless bloodlettings of their fathers. But pacifism was only one constituent of Erasmus's most admirable personal quality, one which still comes through today, and for which he was and at times still is damned. This is not unlike the "negative capability" that Keats imputed to Shakespeare. He is admired by everyone who must live without certainty, and is the nemesis alike of absolutists, dogmatists, and mystifiers. "If I had been able to see Erasmus in other days," writes the master ironist of the late sixteenth century, "it would have been hard for me not to take for adages and apophthegms everything he said to his valet and his hostess."[108] Of the three authors I am about to discuss, only Shakespeare offers a clear-cut case of direct contact with Erasmus's political thought; but Spenser and Milton certainly knew him, and must have sympathized with his program for the reform of rule through the assertion of Christian liberty.

3

Spenser's Anatomy of Tyranny

Literary history has portrayed Spenser as a queen-worshipper, chief propagandist for the imperial virgin's "cult." Yet Spenser's real admiration for Elizabeth did not blind him to the perils of any monarchy, including the idolatry, the confusion of priorities, implied in the casual use of the word "cult." Many of his writings, in particular the second half of Book V of *The Faerie Queene*, suggest that for all his praise of Gloriana, Spenser inclined to a belief in monarchy guided by aristocracy, the rule of an elite based on inheritance and good breeding.[1] At the center of his poem is the knight-errant, both a literary convention and a figure of some political significance. These characters inhabit a middle space as neither creatures of the monarch nor aimless road warriors. Their chief, Arthur, prince not king, the *primus inter pares* of feudal kingship, occupies the high stage. The heroic, active center of the poem is neither Gloriana nor the imperious autocrat sometimes thought of as "the" Tudor ideal.

An aristocracy, among all the available forms of government, struck the best compromise between the perceived threat of anarchy (this, to Spenser, was the tragedy of Ireland) and the entirely honorable desire for liberty. Curbing anarchy required a strong central authority, but absolute monarchy conflicted with the interests of humanism and the Reformation. If aristocracy best mediated between autocracy and anarchy, it was also most apt to succeed in overthrowing idolatry in Europe—England's task in the renewal of true religion. Yet renewal stops short of Puritan iconoclasm. The sentiment of aristocracy depended wholly on preserving the past, its customs, laws, even religious practices. On such matters Spenser would concur with Hooker: "The love of things auncient doth argue stayednes, but levitie and want of experience maketh apt unto innovations."[2] The image of the round table, a table without a head, predating the Norman Conquest like those ancient common laws that supposedly held that race of foreign kings in check, was commended precisely because of its antiquity.

Power, shared with other elements in the realm, is not exactly what invests the monarch with divinity; the monarch is God-like in being the chief source of equity and mercy. Yet he cannot exercise these qualities without power. Equity entails the ability to circumvent legal procedures and alleviate injustice directly. In the last five cantos of Book V, equity attacks the fundamental problems of international injustice in Ireland, France, and elsewhere that cause so much suffering, and submit to the authority of no court. Much of this injustice originates in the overreaching spirit of power, the subject of Spenser's meditation at the beginning of canto 12, a stanza summing up the main concerns of cantos 8 through 12:

> O Sacred hunger of ambitious mindes,
> And impotent desire of men to raine,
> Whom neither dread of God, that devils bindes,
> Nor lawes of men, that common weales containe,
> Nor bands of nature, that wilde beastes restraine,
> Can keep from outrage, and from doing wrong,
> Where they may hope a kingdome to obtaine.
> No faith so firme, no trust can be so strong,
> No love so lasting then, that may enduren long.

"Wrong" (line 6) has maintained a continual presence in these cantos. Artegall and Arthur go to Samient's aid when they see "those great wrongs" Adicia has done her (8.24). The "roiall pompe" of the Soudlan's court has been "Purchast through lawlesse powre and tortious wrong" (8.51), and the rule of the Souldan and Adicia is said to be the terrible consequence of "Wrong, when it hath arm'd it selfe with might" (9.1). Belge too has been long "overborne of wrong" by Gerioneo (11.1). Grantorto, then, the "great wrong" of the twelfth canto, draws his representational power from the accumulated wrongs of earlier cantos. The "sacred hunger" (line 1) is the desire for glory that Arthur and Gloriana's knights all share with many of the villains of the poems, especially the tyrants of Book V. If untempered, this hunger becomes (lines 1–2) sinfully "ambitious," a desire to reign that is "impotent" (from *potens*, which can mean "ruling"). Thus the paradox of unjust power: the more of it one acquires, the less "potent" he is. The next three lines assert that just power among "men" must be restrained on three fronts, each related to an emphasis in three preceding episodes. First, the Souldan with his horses and his tigress Adicia (reminiscent of Shakespeare's Queen Margaret, "a tiger's heart wrapped in a woman's hide") represents monarchial power unrestrained by "bandes of nature." Second, the foregrounding of the idol of Gerioneo suggests that this episode especially pertains to those untouched by "dread of God." Finally, Duessa's trial shows her flouting the "lawes of men." Of course in all three cases one finds elements of all three levels of violation, but the attendant symbolism of tigress, idol, and law court lays the stress upon natural, divine, and human laws, respectively. The last two lines of the stanza recall the pivotal cantos of Book V, when charity is at last joined to justice in Britomart's rescue of Artegall from the Amazons. The true love praised in the *Hymns* and *Colin Clouts Come Home Againe* can save the court from its "female" vices of idleness, vanity, and concupiscience. These lines also establish the need for faith, trust, and love in the purely natural realm if laws are to work. In the supernatural order, then, the lines suggest the theological virtues at the foundation of the Christian commonwealth.

The Spenserian Polity

So much for the ideal. The poet-civil servant and landlord, trying to squeeze slippery Irish situations into the mold of law, lets his hair down in a discourse on the actual, *A View of the Present State of Ireland.* English common law, says Irenius, matters little in a country where an Englishman can never find twelve impartial jurors or where the few honest men will likely be challenged off the juries.[3] Irish statutes, few and "slackley penned," contribute nothing to the social order, many being silly and outmoded, like the one prohibiting moustaches without beards (p. 75). Clever Irish rebels use the law to get around the law, defrauding the crown of wardships or escaping forfeitures under the treason laws (pp. 71–73). Corrupt officials disable the remaining laws: "I doe tell it and that even with greate hartes griefe and inwarde trouble of minde to see her majestie so abused by some whom they [sic] put in speciall truste of those greate affairs" (p. 143). A revealing slip, "they" for "she": it means either to identify the queen with her privy council, or to indicate her position as a corporate entity, a creation of the law. Even in Ireland she cannot do as she (or they) would like.

Both here and in Spenser's "A Brief Note of Ireland," written when Elizabeth's loyal subjects had fled Tyrone's destruction and slaughter, the queen is, if not a dupe, at least a slumbering lion, to use an image from one of Spenser's earlier poems of counsel. Cheated of her wards and lands, swindled by her corrupt administrators, insulted by an arrogant Irish aristocracy, she failed to support the one man who could have made Ireland secure, Arthur Lord Grey, in whose service Spenser had first come to Ireland. Rumor reached England of Grey's cruelty as the queen's deputy. "Eare was soon lente," to these falsehoods, says Eudoxus, using the discreet passive, and in a moment not only was "all that greate and longe chardge which she had before bene at quite loste and cancelled, but allso all that hope of good which was even at the dore put backe and cleane frustrate" (p. 160). Summing up the need for massive reforms in Ireland, Irenius criticizes the queen's council rather than the queen, but the intent and the potential danger to the author are the same (luckily for Spenser the *View* remained unpublished in his lifetime): "But as for that pourpose of the Cownsell of Englande which ye spake of that they shoulde keepe that Realme from reformacion I thinke they are moste lewdlie absued for their greate carfulnes and erneste endevours do wittnes the contrarye" (p. 211).

Essentially the *View* called for legal reform supported by restrained armed force, and supervised by a principal member of the aristocracy (p. 228). Grey had died by this time and Spenser almost certainly means (alas) Robert Earl of Essex, who three years later, having failed at the very tasks in Ireland that Spenser had in mind, would pay the charges for Spenser's burial at Westminister Abbey. Law and an executive aristocracy thus comprise the vital components of Spenser's polity, both in Ireland and in the ideal world of Book V. Astraea, Gloriana, and Eliza have become the bywords of Spenser's supposed queen-worship, but neither the *View* nor *The Faerie Queene* nor even the earlier writings will support this reductive reading of his political thought.

A feeling for law in Spenser coincides with a profound love of tradition and history. Nostalgia and sentiment aside, the law carries the influence of the past inexorably into the present. Once the law is in place not even the strongest monarch can change its course without the most strenuous effort. Past assumptions about Spenser's monarchism led some to see the poet as Bodin's disciple, endorsing such absolutist ideas as conquest theory—the belief of much concern to Milton's generation in the king's absolute right over a subject's life and property as a result of his or his ancestor's conquests. Irenius, in the *View,* seems to put it that way at first in discussing Henry II's right to rule Ireland as he wished— "ffor all is the Conquerours as *Tully* to Brutus saith." But Henry erred in allowing the Irish to acknowledge him in "Parliament," while maintaining "theire titles Tenures and seigniories" (p. 52). Eudoxus, as the naive member of the dialogue, asserts what a naive monarchist would be expected to say: "her majestie maye yeat when it shall please her alter anye thinge of those former ordinaunces or appointe other Lawes." Irenius' answer is worth quoting because it discloses much about Spenser's actual views on sovereignty under the law:

> Not soe, for it is not so easye, nowe that thinges are growen into an habit and have theire certaine Course, to change the channel and turne theire streames another waye, ffor they maye have now a colourable pretence to withstande such invocacion havinge accepted of other lawes and rules allreadye. (p. 53)[4]

What power a monarch has in theory is continually circumscribed by those effects of time and history called laws. From the very moment the king is father of the law he becomes its child. And if this cavaeat holds in a land so ruthlessly applicable to conquest theory as Ireland, how much more does it apply to England?

Ireland is a special case in the *View.* What is needed, believes Irenius, is "Reformation"—a total reconstitution of laws, a straitening of customs (the Irish should take off their noisome mantles and should drop all the O's and Mac's from their names), and a regulation of religion. Honest governors and magistrates will bring all this to pass, supported by ten thousand infantry and a thousand cavalry (p. 151) serving under experienced, incorruptible officers. At issue here is not the practicality of Spenser's plan— not unlike what was called enclave defense in the late sixties. What matters is that it was not to be enacted with that ruthless disregard for personal rights associated with autocracy. Soldiers were not to be quartered on the people and soldierly abuses not to be tolerated (132–33). Spenser's "reformation by the sword" is the most figurative of legal phrases: "by the sword I meante the Royall power of the Prince which oughte to stretche it selfe forthe in her chiefe strenghte to the redressinge and cuttinge of all those evills which I before blamed, and not of the people which are evil: for evill people by good ordinaunces and government maybe be made good / but the evill that is of it selfe will never become good"

(p. 148). Aside from the pertinence of this remark to certain fixed villains of *The Faerie Queene* (Archimago, the Blatant Beast, Braggadocchio), there is here an implicit faith in law as defining the "civility" that Irenius wants for his adopted country.[5]

From time to time Irenius and Eudoxus observe that things in England are scarcely perfect, but civility has a surer footing there largely because of the monarch herself. Spenser had helped celebrate the queen as Astraea in his first published work printed in Van der Noot's *Theatre for Worldings*.[6] The panegyric of "April" publicly registers him in Eliza's cult. Yet *The Shepheardes Calender*, like several other poems, resembles the *View* in simultaneously celebrating the queen while criticizing the effects of her government—a tactic observable in the political deliberations of *The Faerie Queene* as well.

"February" helps to measure the political distance Spenser traveled from the 1570s to the 1590s. Like the later writings, it reflects a feeling for the sacredness of the past, "holy eld" (line 206). It also condemns the new impulse to bring root-and-branch "reformation" to English religion and policies. In the fable of the oak and the briar, the husbandman represents the well-meaning but uninformed commoner too easily led by the brasher voices of press and pulpit. Some early twentieth-century commentators on the fable, rather misled by assumptions about Spenser as Puritan, could not bring themselves to perceive his sympathies with the oak.[7] Yet like the other moral eclogues of the *Calender* "February" presents the criticism of a rational conservative in religion, the sort who is far more troubled by ignorant clergy and state mismanagement than by images, incense, or holy water.[8]

A crucial line in interpreting the fable is the climactic oxymoron, "For fiercely the goodman at him did laye" (line 241). If there is any mention of Puritan iconoclasm in the *Calender* it would seem to be here in the fierce but misdirected goodness of the husbandman acting on false testimony. One thinks of the reforming zeal that had brought down ancient churches and monuments in the earlier English Reformation, and that threatened to resume in the 1570s. The husbandman is twice called "goodman" (lines 158, 214), a term suited to his lower social rank. At that time, according to the *OED*, a "goodman" referred to someone not of gentle birth, usually a yeoman or farmer. The name may also allude to Christopher Goodman, formerly chaplain to Sir Henry Sidney in Ireland, a spokesman for popular rebellion against Mary Tudor, and recipient of Leicester's patronage. The husbandman's credulous acceptance of the briar's story resembles the behavior of another naive rustic, the Red Cross Knight, who must learn that malice can subvert the best intentions. In other words, "February" deals with the threat from the simpler soul whose untutored righteousness can destroy the whole ancient fabric of religion, monarchy, aristocracy, and the cultural institutions they protect. Sacred but enfeebled antiquity comes under attack from an indignant but misguided lower class, manipulated by ambitious opportunism. The fear of the mob, or of what unscrupulous people can do with the mob, has its origins in events of the earlier sixteenth century, particularly the Peasants' Revolt and the Munster uprising—events often cited by the Elizabethan hierarchy as proving the danger of too much relgious freedom. As bad as things were in Ireland, Spenser could not put the axe to the oak even there, remarking with apparent inconsistency that "sithens we cannot now applie Lawes fitte to the people . . . we will applie the people and fitt them to the Lawes as it most convenientlye maye be" (p. 199). Wrongly read as a call for continued coercion (Brady, p. 36), this indicates a characteristically English determination to patch the existing laws rather than face the nightmare of starting over.

If laws could be criticized apart from the monarchy, so could the court. Whatever his motives, Spenser had already developed a distrust if not an aversion for that institution in its peculiar Elizabethan form. "December" records Colin's frustrating quest for preferment, encountering "loathed paddocks lording" on their "grieslie todestoole" (lines 69–70), an image that anticipates the fixed, pompous stares of Lucifera and her court when Red Cross makes his debut. The anticourt sentiment continues in *Mother Hubberds Tale* and *Colin Clouts Come Home Againe.*

The earlier of these, *Mother Hubberds Tale,* speaks most directly to the relations between the court and the monarch. Here the implications about the queen are not flattering. The ape and fox learn that the sovereign prefers "the wild beasts, that swiftest are in chase," an image that makes the courtiers into a sort of animal show. Spenser alludes, of course, to Elizabeth's well-known practice of giving pet names for her favorites. Her possessiveness toward Leicester is suggested in the "chaine and circulet of god" that she has wrapped around her "lion" (line 624), though she ironically resents the "late chayne" of the earl's 1578 marriage. It is an altogether petulant "Liege" who presides over this court of folly, readily susceptible to the ape's confidence game. In the last episode the fox and ape find the lion—now a figure of monarchy—sleeping "in secret shade." The shade is conventionally in Spenser, as in Virgil, an image of culpable inaction or sloth.[9] The tricksters catch the lion with "His crowne and scepter lying him beside/And having doft for heate his dreadfull hide" (lines 953–54). Spenser now traces the decay of monarchy into tyranny as a result of the lion's carelessness. In the previous episode the ape has distinguished himself as a false courtier. The narrative proceeds to tell what happens when such a man rises to the highest ranks. First the sly usurpers manage to win the lesser beasts, the sheep and the ass, to their cause with promises of protection from the strong (line 1078). The ape then sets himself up as sole arbiter of justice, becoming a figure of "dreadfull awe." Now an established tyrant (lines 1121, 1127), the ape surrounds himself with "forreine beasts," supporters that are neither fish nor fowl, an upstart aristocracy wholly dependent on the royal will for its validity, rather than on ancient tradition and breeding. While the tyrant's towers, like those of Lucifera, "threat the neighbor sky," the old nobility's castles crumble: "the princes pallaces fell fast/To ruine, (for what thing can ever last?)" (lines 1175–76). Here is the note of the elegy for Leicester in *The Ruines of Time*. The passing of the old nobility—"The realmes chiefe strength and girlond of the crowne" (lines 1185)—ushers in the tyrant's greatest crimes, pillaging the kingdom and allowing the wolf to devour the lambs. Seeing the ape's outlandish court dress "Alla Turchesa" (line 676), the careful observer might have forecast this Turkish tyranny, but the court was devoid of such wisdom.

The lion manages to restore order but at the expense of considerable chagrin:

> But when his crowne and scepter both he wanted,
> Lord! how he fum'd, and sweld, and rag'd, and panted, . . .
> With that in hast, disroabed as he was,
> He toward his owne pallace forth did pas.
>
> (lines 1339–44)

The image of an angry, naked lion locked out of his castle remains an emblem of royal folly, just as vivid as the "uncasing" of the fox or the cropping of the ape's ears and tail. The style of this poem may be base, but there is nothing mean about the matter, an abmonition to the monarch who had dismissed Leicester and recalled Grey: know your friends from your enemies.

Colin Clouts Come Home Againe is dedicated in a playful preface of 1591 to another aristocratic patron, Sir Walter Ralegh. Some of the poem, how much is uncertain, was written closer to 1595, the date of publication. The attack on Cynthia's court in this poem bears significantly on Elizabeth and her courtiers. As much as anything, Spenser may be registering the shock of returning to court after a long absence at a time when its mores had, at least to the unsophisticated eye, changed for the worse. The 1590s marked the beginnings of serious factionalism at court, an increased ostentatiousness of status symbols, intensified financial manipulations, and an inordinate fondness of the queen, and thus her court, for gambling. The times were ripe for court satire.[10] In this poem, then, the court is a negative image of royal generosity. Slander, envy, and pride are the sins most excoriated, as well as the falsification of love:

> love most aboundeth there.
> For all the walls and windows there are writ
> All full of love, and love, and love my deare,
> And all their talke and studie is of it.
>
> (lines 775–78)

Colin's return to Ireland need not be judged a defeat if we contrast the images of community in the proud court and the simple Irish countryside. The winter wind was not so unkind to Colin as the ungracious world of the palace.

The times conspired to fascinate Spenser with aristocracy, the source of patronage throughout his career. The visage of chilvary lived on in the pseudo-medievalism of Elizabethan tournaments and jousts. In London any quixotic horseman could tilt with the public quintain in Finsbury Fields. A wealth of popular literature in print and on the stage perpetuated the lore of medieval romance. Wharton's *Observations on the Fairy Queen* suggests, with the poem's many analogues in Malory and others, that from boyhood Spenser's mind must have been as stuffed as Don Quixote's with the paraphernalia of romance. These tales almost always center on figures of the aristocracy—melancholy barons, knights errant, lost ladies—rather than the monarch. Civilized people wanted, at times desperately, to find aristocratic antecedents for themselves; Spenser himself claimed descent from the ancient family of Despencer, despite his working-class father. By the time he came to manhood, he needed only the experience with Leicester and Grey to confirm the value of aristocracy to the social order—and, of course, to the maintenance of poetry.

This admiration separates Spenser from humanists like Erasmus, even though both men probably shared a belief in the
spiritual worth of secular life. Erasmus's colloquy "The Glory
Lover" ("Philodoxus") makes the desire for earthly honor a vice of
worldliness—"the last infirmity of noble mind," in Milton's
words. His "Ignoble Knight, or Faked Nobility" ("Hippeus anip-
pos, sive Ementita Nobilitas") presents a youth who aspires to
aristocracy because "knights do as they please and get away with
it."[11] Spenser acknowledges this side of things through characters
like Braggadocchio and Paridel, but such false knights serve
mainly to highlight the ideal ones.

Several noblemen received tributes from Spenser rivaling
Gloriana's—Leicester, first of all, in the *Calender*, praised as a
subject for epic poetry when Piers urges Cuddie to find some
great subject for his talent:

> Whither thou list in faire Eliza rest,
> Or if thee please in bigger notes to sing,
> Advaunce the worthy whom shee loveth best,
> That first the white bear to the stake did bring.
>
> (lines 45–48)

It is a "bigger" undertaking, remarkably, to praise the earl than
the queen. The first letter to Harvey in 1580 is dated from
Leicester House, and though Spenser mentions the court, the
center of his orbit was clearly the aging earl. He tells Harvey that
he is composing a *Stemmata Dudleiana*, seemingly a poem in praise
of the patron and his family. The project may survive in the tribute
to Leicester, Sidney, and their family in *The Ruines of Time* (lines
183–343), where the dead nobleman is an object lesson in mutability. Leicester's support probably enabled Spenser to marry and
gain the attention of Arthur Lord Grey, who helped set him up
comfortably in Ireland. There is no evidence that Leicester "banished" Spenser to Lord Grey; the estrangement mentioned in the
dedication of *Virgils Gnat* (c. 1580) has too readily been seen as a
permanent breach in their relations, a view that receives no support from *The Ruines of Time*.

Spenser's dedicatory poem to Grey in *The Faerie Queene*—one of
seventeen poems addressed to the foremost men and women of
the ruling class—is surely the most fulsome in its gratitude.
Spenser mentions Grey's "large bountie poured on me rife,/In the
first season of my feeble age," and his own "endlesse debt."
Although the other sonnets usually single out some achievement

of the dedicatee (Hatton's "carefull Policie," Hunsdon's pacifica-
tion of the northern rebels), the Grey sonnet ignores the public
man. Spenser presents himself as a retainer to a feudal lord in
mentioning his "vassalage," a relationship that would account for
his stubborn defense of Grey in the *View* and Book V of *The Faerie
Queene*. Although Spenser is widely remembered for his devotion
to Gloriana, nothing addressed to the queen is quite as heartfelt as
this tribute to Grey.

Grey, Leicester, and Essex may not have actual roles in *The Faerie
Queene*, but their ideal relation to the queen parallels that of
Arthur and the knights to Gloriana and Mercilla. These two royal
ladies scarcely act in the events of the poem, but they attract and
send forth heroes. They are ideal visions leading the heroes to "do
great things," consistent with the meaning of "magnificence" in
Spenser.[12] His poem, while a tribute to the queen, aims to put the
knights back on the road and liberate the melancholy barons.
Those born to lead must, in the words of one of England's first
courtesy books, endeavor "to repaire by vertue, that which by
negligence hath falen into decay, and by their noble dedes to
recover againe that which golde could not by at thandes of their
worthy predecessors."[13]

Isis, Mercilla, Equity

Historically, Elizabeth's political success begins with a religious
settlement. Spenser allegorizes this moment as he begins his own
account of national and international justice in Book V of *The Faerie
Queene*. The ordering of events—Isis before Mercilla—in this most
diachronic of Spenser's books means there must be a reconciliation between the spiritual and civil before justice can prevail in
government.

Pioneering studies by Frank Kermode and Rene Graziani have
established that the Temple of Isis in Canto 7 is built around the
theme of equity—what Hooker called the "universal power . . . to
remedie that which they [courts and judges] are not able to help
and to redress that wherein they at any time doe otherwise than
they ought to doe." It is perhaps even intended to symbolize the
equity courts adjacent to Parliament, where once a Lady chapel
had housed a statue of the Virgin crushing the serpent's head.[14]
Yet any interpreter of this episode must bear in mind that Britomart's vision prophesies a destruction and rebuilding of the
temple. Britomart dreams that the temple is threatened by storm

and fire, that the crocodile devours the flames and at first threatens to devour Isis. Subdued by Isis, he becomes her lover and causes her to give birth to a lion. The priests, who are characters *in* the allegory, not commentators *upon* it, can only interpret this in terms of Britomart's future with Artegall; but Spenser gives the reader a number of clues that encourage further investigation. We notice, for example, the heavily ritualistic, even idolatrous quality of worship in the temple. The priests wear elaborate vestments, "linen robes with silver hemd," and miters on their heds (7.4). Surely these images would remind readers of the old church, its clerical and hierarchical dress, along with its "rites and daily sacrifize." The daily sacrifice will be mentioned again at the Temple of Gerioneo, in a context clearly referring to the Catholic Mass,[15] a service that was performed daily (representing the eternal, ongoing act of Redemption), unlike the weekly communion service of the Church of England. The flames burning at the altar recall the Catholic sanctuary light, supposed to burn constantly by the tabernacle. An obvious Catholic analogy resides in the asceticism of the Priests of Isis, the merits of such an austere life being denied by Protestants of every sect.

A second motif in the dream is the purging and passing of an old order in the near-burning of the temple and the extinction of the altar fire. Surely both sets of details—the ecclesiastical symbolism and the hints of a portentous transition—would remind readers of the turbulent events of the Reformation. The ritual fire destroying the temple could refer to the self-immolation of the old church in its stubbornly maintained ceremonialism. Britomart's wearing the priestly miter and vestments thus implies the passing of eccesiastical authority to the sovereign. A new order has arisen. The crocodile represents the lower orders who in their enthusiasm for destroying the threat to true relgion swell with pride, almost managing, like the husbandman of "February," to destroy the true political authority which supports religion. Spenser indicates this meaning with his pun on the beast's "peerelesse powere" (7.15). In this state of things, the "rod of equity"—a rod that both strikes and measures—must be sternly applied to the over-powerful commons. (The rod is a paradoxical image, not unlike Elizabeth's sword in the *View* or Mercilla's sword of mercy.) The ensuing love between the subdued populace and the sovereign gives birth to great deeds, as the lion especially typifies the renewed aristocracy of the late sixteenth century, the "gentleman or noble person" whom this poem instructs "in vertuous and gentle discipline," ready to resume the quest for glory.[16]

Although idealizing the actual history, this version of the Elizabethan settlement, submitting religious differences to a benevolent monarch's guidance, is consistent with Spenser's distrust of the clergy to perform this function (see *View,* p. 222), and with his condemnation of the hierarchy in Ireland for "planting of religion . . . with terrour and sharpe penalties" rather than instruction (p. 221). Spenser may have perceived Elizabeth's diffidence toward her bishops, reflected in the fact that none of them served on her council for the two decades before Whitgift's appointment in 1586. An ecclesiastical-historical reading of the temple and dream also supports the legal theme of equity in Canto 7, for with the passing of the old order in sixteenth-century society, the responsibilty for courts of equity or chancery shifted too. The Tudor era came "at the close of the period during which the court of chancery had been presided over by ecclesiastical chancellors, and at the beginning of the period when its development was to be guided by the common lawyers."[17] The clergy is not so much purged as incorporated into the new aristocratic framework. At the end of the dream, the power of the priests is supplanted first by the unruly commons, recalling "February," then by the aristocracy, whose welfare depends on a fruitful balance between the power of the throne and the rights of the people, or at least certain people.

Here as in the *View* power alone is not what defines the sovereign in Spenser's aristocracy. The most frequently acknowledged correlative between God and the monarch was in the function of equity, in giving relief to innocent victims of the letter of the law. In England especially the crown had served to compensate for the lack in common law of a means to accommodate principles of equity or fairness. Describing this function of sovereignty, Eramus quoted from Proverbs (8:15, 16; 20:28):

> "By me kings reign and lawgivers decree just things. By me princes rule, and the mighty decree justice." Eternal wisdom, who is God's Son, said this. And what does wisdom prescribe of kings? "Mercy," he says, "and truth preserve the king, and his throne is made strong through clemency." The king shows mercy in helping the oppressed, truth in judging honestly, and clemency in tempering the severity of the law.

The idea is carried into the act repealing Henry VIII's treason statutes in 1547, which says that nothing is "more godly . . . than on the prince's part great clemency and indulgency."[18]

Undoubtedly Spenser also knew Erasmus's text from Proverbs and had it in mind when he depicted Mercilla occupying a royal throne, attended by Justice, Truth, and Peace (V.9.32). For this reason he made awe and order, allegorized as officials who manage the crowd at court, preliminary to mercy, not an end in themselves, as they might have been in an allegory of mystical kingship. The whole reason for kingship—on this point Spenser's image concurs with Erasmus's words—is mercy. Without it the throne is empty because justice, the "sacred vertue" of the poem, is defective:

> Most sacred vertue she of all the rest,
> Resembling God in his imperiall might;
> Whose soveraine powre is herein most exprest,
> That both to good and bad he dealeth right,
> And all his workes with Justice hath bedight.

> (Proem, 10)

The rhyming of "might" with "right" here answers the ancient argument from force by saying that the greatest might, God's, ultimately *does* make right. What greater power could there be, moreover, than to deal "right" to all creation, both good and evil? The stanza continues with a seeming endorsement of the divine-right theory:

> That powere [i.e., justice] he also doth to Princes lend,
> And makes them like himself in glorious sight,
> To sit in his owne seat, his cause to end,
> And rule his people right, as he doth recommend.

These are truisms of Christianity: all power is from God and reverence is due to those in authority. Yet Spenser is more definite, more limiting, in that "justice" is his operative term, not mere authority or power. Justice is earlier called a "vertue," hence a "power" like the secret virtue that was believed to inhabit plants and stones. God infuses his princes with justice exactly as the sun pours special virtues into the ruby or violet. Portia, in her famous speech on mercy in *The Merchant of Venice*, also makes the necessary distinction between justice and power:

> it [mercy] becomes
> The throned monarch better than his crown.
> His sceptre shows the force of temporal power,
> The attribute to awe and majesty,

Wherein doth sit the dread and fear of kings:
But mercy is above the sceptred sway;
It is enthroned in the hearts of kings;
It is an attribute to God himself;
And earthly power doth then show likest God's
When mercy seasons justice.

(IV.1.188–97)

Portia here echoes the theme of Proverbs: mercy sits "above the sceptred sway" in the same way that Mercilla sits above "kings and kesers." Spenser and Shakespeare are saying not merely that kings should be merciful, but that this is their chief reason for being: Mercy becomes the monarch "better than his crown."

To appreciate the richness of Mercilla's symbolism is to keep in mind Spenser's own statement that his allegory contains both general and particular intentions, allowing the possibility that Mercilla as Mercy may be every bit as important to the poem as her associations with Elizabeth. The rusty sword is a good instance. It appears that Elizabeth actually kept a rusty sword as a reminder of the peacefulness of her reign, even alluding to it in one of her poems.[19] But the sword also refers to the general theme of mercy in Book V. It is the power to punish (without which mercy cannot exist); it is also the sword of the *View* (p. 148) that can reach out beyond the law to redress especially those evils that the law unintentionally shelters.

Mercilla's palace is parodied by Lucifera's House of Pride in Book I, a comparison that helps reveal the relationship of monarch, court, law, and aristrocracy in Spenser's thought. Lucifera serves a dual role like the medieval world-kng, typifying pride of self extending into the pride of the world. Oblivious to her court, Lucifera looks into a mirror; Mercilla, by contrast, "sate on high, that she might all men see,/And might of all men royally be seene" (9.27). Lucifera stands over a "dreadfull Dragon," a self-generated evil that can quickly turn on her in her upward-looking heedlessness. At Mercilla's feet the chained lion shares in the queen's vigilance, like aristocratic power in the service of justice. Mercilla also exemplifies Christian sovereignty without need of a mystic sense of majesty or Lucifera-like theatricality. Meeting her (9.34), the knights bow to her "majesty" only to have it "tempred" with a "courteous reply." Majesty is again "abated" in the next stanza.

Lucifera's claim to absolute dominion (4.11) entails the characteristic tyrannical disregard of law, ruling instead by "pollicie"

(4.12). Spenser twice plays on the word "peerless" (Sts. 8, 11) a pun he uses elsewhere ("October," line 79, and *FQ* V.7.15, already noted), to make the point that no functioning aristocracy supports her rule. The "Lords and Ladies" around here merely "beautified" the place. Because they "frounce their curled haire" and "prancke their ruffes" (4.7, 14), they represent mere ornaments of pride, like the courtiers in *Colin Clouts Come Home Againe*. They are destined for the dungeon that Red Cross barely escapes, full of men and women who "in idle pomp, or wanton play, / Consumed had their goods, and thrifless hours" (5.51). This "idle pomp" anticipates the pun on "idol ceremony" in *Henry V,* as both words hint at the dangers of self-delusion in power. By contrast with the courtly stagnation of the House of Pride, activity at Mercilla's court is organized to mete out justice—toward rabble rousers like Malfont, toward "people mean and base" (9.23), then toward Duessa. In these three moments are represented three of the principal courts of equity as Elton presents them (*Tudor Constitution,* 179–89). Malfont's crime and punishment resemble a Star Chamber case, such as that against counterfeiting prosecuted by Coke in 1597, in which the offenders lost an ear and stood at the pillory in Cheapside wearing a paper that proclaimed their offense. The Court of Requests originated in the monarch's desire, says Elton, "to give justice to men too poor and uninfluential to secure their ends in the ordinary courts" (p. 189), that is, the "mean and base." Finally, Parliament had often been a true court in the Middle Ages and, continuing to be called "the king's High Court of Parliament" in the sixteenth century (p. 233), made a suitable forum to try public enemies like Mary Stuart or Duessa.

Duessa presents a greater threat than Radigund because she is allied with the Satanic order, thereby being impervious to any kind of law. She is the whore of Babylon who must be expelled before the victories of the last three cantos can occur. Albrecht Durer's famous woodcut showing the rulers of the world admiring the scarlet woman of Revelation is echoed in one of Tyndale's outbursts against the alliance between pope and princes: "O great whore of Babylon, how abuseth she the princes of the world! how drunk she hath made them with her wine! How shameful licenses doth she give them, to use necromancy, to hold whores, to divorce themselves, to break the faith and promises that one maketh with another!"[20] Duessa's origins lie in this early Reformation myth. Her path is strewn with broken promises because "all false faith is idolatry."[21] If in Book I she is largely a figure of idolatry in worship, signifying among other things the supposed perversion of the Mass,[22] in Book V she has come to represent a consummate false worship whose moral and political consequences are manifest. All the kinds of idolatry mentioned by Erasmus in the previous chapter (see note 13)—pleasure, wealth, vengeance, and tyranny—enter into the charges against her.

Duessa's trial represents a victory of the commonwealth as a whole, not just Mercilla's triumph. As Fletcher says, "A central purpose of Book V was to show that through her equity Elizabeth checked the tendency toward imperial absolutism. Mercilla's trial of Duessa takes place in what amounts to be a parliament, and in this framework the monarch could not, except symbolically, assume absolute right in imitation of Julius Caesar."[23] Although the poetry may not rise to the occasion,[24] there is a gathering of right forces in Canto 9, where all of the estates, common and noble, are explicitly joined against Duessa. Both parties in the church are there: "Religion" with its "holy laws" (9.49) stands for the ecclesiastical establishment; the prosecutor Zeal represents the Puritans,[25] known to be Mary's most vocal opponents. Arthur and Artegall represent the range of opinion among well-intentioned aristocrats at the time of Mary's trial. The idealized quality of Mercilla's mercy is brought out when even Arthur, predisposed to mercy because of his royal blood, is at last forced to repent his "former fancies ruth." Only Mercilla, "whose Princely breast was touched nere / With piteous ruth" remains opposed to "just vengeance." This last phrase, incidentally, echoes that in Spenser's defense of Grey, who often "suffered not just vengeance to fall" on Irish wrongdoers (*View*, p. 160). The "general intention" here has to do with the infinite mercy of God, surpassing that of even the most royal human heart, Arthur's. In the fallen world of Book V, however, the quality of mercy is subject to the higher necessity, or "strong constraint," of the sword (10.4).

Duessa's end has a fine sense of closure about it. Whore of Babylon, debutante of Lucifera's Babel-like palace, she falls to Lucifera's opposite number, whose numinous presence lends her an eschatological quality. Book IV gave us Duessa in the company of the hag Ate, whose unequal (not *isis*) feet identify her with discord. Equity now cancels inequity. In all her appearances Duessa loves to subvert aristocracy as well as law. Both are now secure, thanks not to Mercilla's power, but to her just equity.

The Souldan

One of the earliest commentators on the battles against the Souldan, Gerioneo, and Grantorto made them all represent Elizabethan conflicts with Spain, an interpretation that renders these episodes both redundant and too exclusively historical.[26] The ordering of these three events can help illuminate them. The Souldan represents a first stage, monarchy's curbing its tendency toward uncontrolled power, required before Mercilla's instruction. The Gerioneo quest extends justice beyond national boundaries; without it the universal peace desired in Grantorto's defeat cannot occur.

The conquest of the Souldan again mirrors Book I, with Arthur's first battle in *The Faerie Queene*, against Orgoglio. In both events Arthur wins because of his shield. Both are also variants of the Hercules myth: the Souldan resembles the Thracian tyrant Diomedes (8.31), whose defeat was perceived by mythographers as "victory over the tyrants of this world."[27] Orgoglio's defeat combines elements of those over the hydra and rebellious giants. During both encounters Spenser places his knight-hero inside the castle; the battle is witnessed by a virgin and her villainess-antagonist; after both victories Arthur empties the castle; both times the villainess, her hero slain, flees into the wilderness.

The differences between these battles are consistent with the personal or private emphasis in Book I as opposed to the public focus of Book V. Orgoglio, "in active, violent against the godhead and against the faith,"[28] discloses every soul's capacity for rebellion against God. The Souldan represents Nimrod-like revolt against the divine through the social order, fomented by Adicia, injustice, the lust for power that tempts anyone in public office. Spenser describes this lust for power as the Souldan's idolatry (8.19), associating the tyrant with the tigress and wild horses because "idolatrie and tyrannie resembleth more the nature of wilde beates, cruell beares, and raging lyons, then the condicion of man."[29] It is the violent principle of nature that creates Tamburlaines. With this tyrannical idolatry comes the Souldan's enslavement of Mercilla's subjects and the near bondage of Samient in dungeons that recall those of Lucifera and Orgoglio.

A comparison with Marlowe's *Tamburlaine* is informative, particularly as it shows the two poets' contrasting perceptions of power in the world. Spenser, who had establishment support for a good part of his life, is predictably more optimistic. The Souldan in *Tamburlaine* gives himself entirely to power in the world, in effect trading on his daughter Zenocrate (whose name means "rule over foreigners"). Tamburlaine's nature, which instructs humanity to "have a warring mind," finds expression in Spenser's Adicia—the same savagery that possessed the "paynim" brothers in Book I, that lawless, faithless, and joyless condition of natural men without grace. Tamburlaine's famous chariot in Part Two (IV.3) is pulled by kings rather than horses to symbolize the way the powerful can become harnessed by their lust for power. Spenser has the Souldan's chariot destroyed by the horses of power-lust for the same reason. But Spenser retains some faith in the good uses to which power can be put. In *Tamburlaine* the *contemptus mundi* degenerates into fear of the world with its relentless atrocities against the innocent (the Damascus virgins) on behalf of the evil. Suicide (Olympia) is the sole legitimate political act. Marlowe offers no Arthurs in *Tamburlaine*—or anywhere else, for that matter. Spenser finds something noble in humanity that can overcome the Adicia principle.

If the Souldan's idolatry is his lust for power, his consequent tyranny is symbolized in his being out of reach. Spenser twice mentions his standing high in the chariot (8.28,33); his loftiness, along with the blades on his wheels, makes it impossible for Arthur to draw near him (8.36). A contrast with Mercilla is again invited: her "inclyning" to meet her visitors, the "faire stoope of her high soaring thought" (9.34), differentiates her from the Souldan's "presumpteous," "sublime," and "insolent" demeanor (8.30). The whole scene, reinforced with a sense of the Souldan's grim appearance, vividly enacts Seneca's tyrant's adage, "Let them hate, if only they fear."

Arthur is more seriously threatened in this battle than in the later one with Gerioneo. The Souldan, throwing his darts as he wheels about, "made a griesly wound in his enriven side" (8.34). Not only is the wound physically harmful, it causes Arthur momentarily to lose face:

> Much was he [Arthur] grieved with that haplesse throe,
> That opened had the welspring of his blood;
> But much the more that to his hatefull foe
> He mote not come to wreake his wrathfull mood.
> That made him rave, like to a Lyon wood,
> Which being wounded of the huntsmans hand
> Can not come neare him in the covert wood,
> Where he with boughes hath built his shady stand,
> And fenst himselfe about with many a flaming brand.
>
> (8.35)

In one sense, this is the lion sprung from the union of Isis and the crocodile, the virtuous, active aristocracy that under absolute rule becomes disordered, alienated, and enfeebled by losing its share of power. As so often in Spenser's allegory, the battle is also a fight against some aspect of the hero's own self. The future holder of sovereign power must learn that he cannot rely on sheer power alone. To do so is to be reduced to a lesser role, a wounded lion "raving" in the tyrant's jungle of violence and passion (compare the repeated "rage" of Adicia in 8.46–48 just before her transformation to a tigress).

The Souldan's tactics partake of this savagery, dependent as they are on his man-eating horses. Before it occurs to Arthur to use his shield, these fierce animals "So cruelly . . . persew the chace" of Arthur's horse,

> That his good steed, all were he much renound
> For noble courage, and for hardie race,
> Durst not endure their sight, but fled from place to place.
>
> (8.36)

Like the image of the raving lion, this passage shows Arthur in a somewhat ludicrous posture. Until now, Spenser has made his hero oblivious to the power of his shield, faith, as the means by which evil will confound itself. Using it, Arthur manages to win despite his fear-struck horse (another symbol of natural passions); thus later, in the fight with Gerioneo, he can remain undaunted even when his horse is killed beneath him (11.9). At this point the victory of Arthur-Hercules merges with the traditional Hercules-Christ symbolism, just as it had in Book I during the battle with Orgoglio. The prince's entry into the castle gates and Artegall's scattering the Souldan's remaining knights "like wyld Goets" are unmistakably apocalyptic images.

So it is with Samient, the emissary from Mercilla's court. Among the possible origins of her name, is the Greek *semeion*, meaning sign or portent. The word is used in the Book of Revelation for the wonders that herald the last days:

> And there appeared a great wonder *(semeion)* in heaven: A woman clothed with the sunne, & the moone was under her feete, and upon her head a crowne of twelve starres. . . . And there appeared another wonder *(semeion)* in heaven: for beholde, a great red dragon having seven heads, and ten hornes, and seven crowns upon his head . . . (12.1,3)

Samient comes "in message," as a sign to Adicia of Mercilla's love; but just as the cruel tenants in St. Mark's parable (12.1) disregard and abuse the owner's messengers, the "sign" of mercy is rejected. In the Geneva Bible the cruel tenants represent the sinful rulers of this world.[30] Samient may thus be read as a portent of the Souldan's overthrow, as in the prophecy of Christ:

> Then said he unto them, Nacion shal rise against nacion, and king-dome against kingdome, And great earthquakes shalbe in divers places, and hunger, and pestilence, and feareful things, and gret signes *(semeia)* shal there be from heaven. (Luke 21:10–12)

Samient brings Adicia a message of "finall peace and faire attone-ment" (8.21), a sign from Mercilla. God extends mercy to the unjust even at the last. At the widest level of historical interpreta-tion Arthur's battle implies a victory over the forces of Satan, who is "prince of this worlde & almoste hathe the universal govern-ment," in the same Geneva commentary on Revelation. Finally Samient becomes a sign to lead Arthur and Artegall from the abandoned throne of the world-king to the court of Mercilla, where eschatological details, such as the subordination of "kings and kesars," are again in evidence.[31]

Gerioneo

Having overthrown the lust for power (the Souldan) and the guile and falseness that threaten the court (Duessa), Mercilla and her knights are free to undertake what are now called wars of national liberation. Spenser describes Arthur's and Artegall's vic-tories in politico-religious terms characteristic of the age, the words "idol" and "tyrant" occurring more frequently in the latter half of Book V than in all the rest of *The Faerie Queene*.[32] In the battle with Gerioneo particularly, the sacred cause of evanglizing the nations is realized in Arthur's fulfillment of God's first com-mand, the overthrow of false gods.

The Geneva Bible's notes often reflect the widespread belief that destroying "idolatry" (principally the Catholic religion and Span-ish power) was a political duty. The covenant of the Old Law meant "that both the King and the people should maintaine the true worship of God and destroy all Idolatry."[33] Like Erasmus, the annotators of this Bible did not urge the overthrow of tyrants, but they did exhort the reader not to follow unjust or irreligious commands.[34] Less conciliatory voices could be heard, though. The radical Christopher Goodman wrote that "God . . . willeth not onely the Magistrates and officers to roote out evil from amongest then, be it, idolatrie, blasphemie or open injuries, but the whole multitude are therwith charged also."[35] This policy received its fullest expression in the fourth part of the French *Vindiciae contra tyrannos,* which considers, as has been mentioned, whether princes must help Christians of other nations oppressed by tyranny or religious persecution. In his edition (p. 60), Laski finds that this chapter was published separately in England as *A Short Apologie for Christian Soldiers* (1588), supporting English aid to rebels in the Netherlands. Although Spenser would not have shared Goodman's faith in "the whole multitude," his account of the quest to rescue Belge resembles Goodman and the *Vindiciae* in proposing a Protestant foreign policy.

In Books I and V of *The Faerie Queene,* Spenser discloses the new faith in England as a principal agent doing God's work of reformation, an eschatological ideal that would continue into Milton's time. Michael Fixler contrasts Luther's "eschatology of judgment," emphasizing "the decay and collapse of the world," with the reformed version, "an eschatology of resurrection . . . with an emphasis upon the renewal of the world."[36] Both notes are sounded in Book V. Against the elegaic music of the world's decay, Spenser plays triumphant strains of renewal through virtuous action, with England at the center of the fight. These last cantos celebrate the role of heroic nobility in Spenser's time; yet the particular intention of praising Leicester in the Netherlands, Essex in France, and Grey in Ireland always serves the general intention of the allegory, to show forth the type of glorious action in the cause of truth.[37]

By describing Arthur's battle in terms of the Geryon myth, Spenser not only continues the Hercules motif of Book V, but presents an adversary with numerous implications for the historical struggle against Spain. Most obvious of these is the tradition that Geryon was a Spanish ruler. Natalis Comes, recognized as the source for much of Spenser's narrative here, summarizes the story as follows:

> Afterward Eurystheus ordered Hercules to bring him the oxen of Geryon King of Spain, those who used to devour Geryon's guests. He therefore fought and captured them. Geryon, son of Chrysaor and Callirhoe, is said to have had a triple body, and a two-headed dog captured in Erythea, and a seven-headed dragon born of Typhon and Echidna, which guarded the oxen. He also had a wicked and diligent servant to his cruelty, Eurytion. Coming to this place, after killing

Geryon, the dog Orthrus, and the fearsome Eurytion, Hercules drove the oxen from the ocean island of Gadira to Tartellum, a very famous city in Spain at that time.[38]

The main source for Comes, well known to Spenser, is Servius's commentary on the *Aeneid* (7.662), which emphasizes Geryon's kingship and military power:

> Geryon was king of Spain. He is said to have been tripled-bodied because he ruled over three islands lying off the Spanish coast, the greater and lesser Balearics and Ebusus. He is also said to have had a two-headed dog because he was very powerful in battles by sea and land.[39]

Thus far the story of Geryon supports chiefly the historical allegory of Arthur's fight with Gerioneo. Of wider significance is Geryon's being the offspring of Chrysaor, the name Spenser gives to Artegall's heaven-sent sword. It is worth looking at Landino's widely reprinted commentary on the Aeneid concerning Chrysaor (7.662):

> Hesiod also says that Medusa lay with Neptune, but when her head was cut off two sons sprang forth: Pegasus the winged horse and Crisaor, so called because he was born with a golden sword. Crisaor having left the earth went to heaven, bringing to Jove his thunder and lightning. He fathered Geryon, whom Hercules killed.[40]

The myth fits with the general allegory of Book V if we interpret Chrysaor, the divine lightning and parent of Geryon, as the divine source of all earthly power. Thundering Geryon (or Gerioneo, "new Geryon" as Hamilton notes) typifies the king who abuses his power, exercising it apart from justice. Like the other tryants of this book he has divine justice visited upon him. Spenser may also be saying that tyranny brings thunder without light. It is not important that Arthur's sword rather than Artegall's Chrysaor kills the tyrant; in using Geryon and Chrysaor as opposing symbols in Book V, Spenser's intention was to mark the absence in a tyrant of divine from earthly power.

In Belge's country Gerioneo sets up an idol-image of this tyranny, a figure that needs to be seen in its full political and religious significance. Under tyranny, a created being is raised above the level of all humanity. Gerioneo has in fact erected another Moloch,

and him his God hath named,
Offring to him in sinfull sacrifice
The flesh of men, to Gods owne likenesse framed.

(10.28)

Slavery—the "servile bond" and "yoke of inquisition" (10.27)—
unerringly follows from such tyranny, as well as the "sacrifice" of
humanity for the tyrant's ends. Spenser characterizes Gerioneo in
ways that recall the stage tyrant's alternating wrath and fear, going
back to Herod in the mystery plays. When news comes of
Arthur's victory over the seneschal, Gerioneo "gan to burne in
rage, and friese in feare, / Doubting the sad end of principle
unsound" (11.2). The slaughter of children and the exile of Belge
also suggest Herod's crimes; Gerioneo's death (he "curst, and
band, and blasphemies forth threw, Against his Gods") recalls the
customary staging of Herod at his end.

Religious idolatry contributes heavily to the political meaning of
this episode: the allusions to the Inquisition typify the politico-
religious complex of cantos 10 and 11. The Mass is a political
instrument furthering idolatry. It is the "daily sacrifice" of 11.19,
for the sake of which thousands had been sacrificed in France and
the Netherlands. The Mass is signified in Gerioneo's idol itself,
"The which this Gyant reared first on hie, / And of his owne vaine
fancies thought did frame" (11.19). This last line refers to the "will
worship" of the Mass, as Protestants called it—devising worship
after one's own fancy rather than God's explicit directions.[41] In
Belge's urging Arthur not to leave her country "Till yee have
rooted all the relickes out / Of that vilde race" (11.18), Hamilton
notes an allusion to relics in Catholic religion. Perhaps it is only
coincidental, but in his article on Geryon the Protestant my-
thographer Alexander Ross finds in the bones of Geryon, kept as
relics in Thebes, the origin of Catholic veneration of relics.[42]

A careful reading of Arthur's heroics in this episode shows him
to be once again the man of faith, not just another battling knight.
Realizing that his advantage lies with his shield, he has advanced
beyond the level of the Souldan encounter. In the fight with the
seneschal, the strength of Arthur's shield, not his spear, wins the
day by splintering the opponent's lance (10.32), while the seneschal's weak shield of faith allows "readie passage" to Arthur's
spear. The battle with the three knights also begins by reaffirming
the strength of the shield. Arthur slays the three in successively
closer stages to his ultimate objective, the idol's temple. He gradually works his way to the inner sanctum of the temple, but he

must win the castle first. Since the temple is built in front of the castle (10.28), it seems to represent a religious institution backed by a political one. The first knight is killed outside the castle; the second, at the gates, the third, by the screen in the castle hall.[43] The last detail must recall the screen separating Mercilla from those outside her audience-room.

Arthur tactics against Gerioneo are at first wholly defensive, much as they were in the fight with the three knights (10.34). Arthur allows the tyrant's force to expend itself. He takes care to "yeeld to his [Gerioneo's] despight," watching the monster's tricky moves until he has a chance to lop off a few arms. The caution persists even then:

> Nought fear'd the childe his lookes, ne yet his threats,
> But onely wexed now the more aware,
> To save him selfe from those his furious heats,
> And watch advauntage, how to worke his care.
>
> (11.13)

This is the vigilance of the true faith, in contrast, say, to the repeated rashness and imprudence of the Red Cross Knight. Arthur waits for the eventual "good Fortune" (11.13) or providential opportunity to strike. The same tactics—wariness, cutting away at the enemy piecemeal, rather than going for the kill at once—are used in the battle with Gerioneo's sphinxlike dragon. Once more the battle centers upon Arthur's shield (the dragon seemks better informed than its master on the need for taking that first), and in the struggle Arthur has a chance to cut off the creature's claws, then disjoint its tail (11.27, 29).

Spenser's handling of the Gerioneo episode calls into question any imperialist (in the modern sense) interpretation that might be put upon it. The *Vindiciae* declared that "if a prince outrageously overpass the bounds of piety and justice, a neighbour prince may justly and religiously leave his own country, not to invade and usurp another's, but to contain the other within the limits of justice and equity" (pp. 27–28). Arthur, like Leicester in 1585, rides out to kill a dragon, not to incorporated Belge into Mercilla's dominions. Historically, in a sense, the dragon was eventually killed. During the Rouen campaign in 1592, as Howell Lloyd writes (pp. 185, 191), the English army gave the Duke of Parma the wound that shortly brought him to his deathbed. With the other political cantos of Book V, this episode also upholds the Elizabethan strategy of worrying the enemy on as many fronts as possible rather than face a massive confrontation. Cantos 10 and 11 thus form an instructive contrast with an earlier version of the Geryon story that Spenser may have known (though I can find nothing to suggest he did), G. B. Giraldi Cinthio's *Dell'Hercole* (1557). This unhappy and unfinished epic that culminates in Hercules's victory over Geryon (cantos 25–26) has all the trappings of grand opera. Hercules has his own army; there is an epic council in Spain, a catalogue of Geryon's troops, and an epic sea-fight before the traditional single combat. The epic was written in honor of Cinthio's patron Ercole D'Este, recently appointed lieutenant general in the Franco-papal alliance against Spain. (The war was not seriously waged, and ended unceremoniously with a treaty a few months after the publication of *Dell'Hercole*.) The monster who rules Cinthio's Spain is an epic adversary, not the metaphysically hideous thing that Spenser presents. In Spenser's narrative the frequent echoes of Book I[44] remind us that this is not a mere chapter in the conflict of nations, but the long-awaited moment when Christianity, purged of its own inner idolatries, will be free to carry the battle into the world at large.

Grantorto

The opposition between Irena or Peace and Grantorto signifies yet another kind of tyranny. Undoubtedly the particular intention refers to Arthur Lord Grey's attempt to put down the "rebel" and Spanish threat in Ireland (anciently called Ierene or Erin).[45] Artegall typifies the chivalrous aristocrat marching on the enemy, calling for "single fight" (12.8) against its champion, just as Essex had done at Lisbon and Rouen in 1589 and 1591.[46] Yet in this canto more than any other, the aristocracy also has the role of peacekeeper. Peace, the true end of justice, properly receives the place of honor in the last canto. The total interdependence, at this time, of honoring authority and maintaining peace is felt in such contemporary statements as this apparent nonsequitur in Melanchthon's commentary on Romans 13: "Paul biddeth that we shoulde pray for the magistrate. And verily there is no greater or vehementer exercise of fayth amongst so many publique perils, than prayer for publique peace."[47] Artegall must expel the "great wrong" of civil strife that prevents the rule of peace. The principal criminals of Irena's realm, doubtless the corrupt officials of the *View* and "Brief Note," violate this peace. (12.25) Grantorto is probably less to be thought of as a single tyrant than a ruling faction, not unlike the Old English in Ireland, one that exploits the fearfulness of the people, in effect usurping sovereignty. His government through intimidation (12.15–17), unlike the devout awe of Mercilla's castle, creates a paralyzing, debilitating fear.

The eschatological symbolism already noticed in Mercilla, the Souldan, and Gerioneo persists into this canto. Grantorto is "graceless" in combat (12.18), and Irena awaits "redemption" (12.11). On the morning she is to be executed, seeing Artegall as her savior, she is compared to the flowers waiting for rain. Spenser may be thinking of the image from Ecclesiasticus: "Oh, how faire a thing is mercie in the time of anguish and trouble! It is like a cloud of raine, that cometh in the time of a drought" (35:19).

> Like as a tender Rose in open plaine,
> That with untimely drought nigh withered was,
> And hung the head, soone as few drops of raine
> Thereon distill, and deaw her daintie face,
> Gins to look up, and with fresh wonted grace
> Dispreds the glorie of her leaves gay;
> Such was *Irenas* countenance. . . .
>
> (12.13)

The "grace" and "glory" of this stanza represent the mercy shown to the just, their triumph on the day of the last battle. Locating peace at the center of this last battle, Spenser concurs with traditional Christian thinking about the last days. In the Geneva Bible note on Daniel's vision, God destroys the fourth beast "that his Church might have rest and quietnes, which thogh thei do not fully injoye here, yet thei have it in hope and by the preaching of the Gospel enjoye the beginning thereof" (Dan. 7:27). The hoped-for peace of Elizabeth's reign in history foreshadows the expected seventh day, when "all shall rest eternally / With Him that is the god of Sabbaoth hight" (VII.8.2). Yet this harmony is immediately shattered by the entry of a new cast of characters at the end of Book V. The restoration of peace hardly receives its anticipated grand final movement, for just as in the sudden, violent ending of Book II, Spenser's sense of closure remains in the service of his vision. Slander, Detraction, and the Blatant Beast mean that a sound society rests on more than political skill. "Even the returned Astraea," as Michael O'Connell says, "cannot recognize slander for what it is and reward her unjustly maligned servants."[48] All power is from God, but the wisdom to guide that power is not as freely bestowed, even on the most admirable rulers.

It has become frequent practice to read the episodes of Book V in incremental stages, each adding something to the establishment of justice. For this reason, the series of battles against the Souldan, Gerioneo, and Grantorto may be seen as progressively easier victories for the heroes. For success against the Souldan Arthur and Artegall need their joint efforts; Arthur receives his only serious wound at this time, and Samient narrowly escapes being raped. The great danger in the "Sacred hunger of ambitious mindes" (12.1) is that a lust for power will lead one man to elevate himself above the natural order, assuming "lawlesse regiment" (8.30) over others. In the final analysis, there being no incontrovertible legal basis for power, only heaven can secure us against such a breach of order. Thus the Souldan is the only tyrant to be overthrown by direct, heavenly intervention, not by the hero's might. In the battle with Gerioneo the earlier victory over lawless power enables Arthur to eliminate the idolatrous element attendant on tyranny. This accomplished, it becomes relatively easy for a fully constituted authority, having the confidence of all, to end a reign of terror where a few hold many captive. The climax of Book V, the battle with Grantorto, seems anticlimactic because it has assumed a kind of inevitability from the weight of preceding episodes. Thus it won't really do to find fault with Artegall because he has delayed completing his quest till the morning of Irena's execution. The last tyrant, who would eliminate Christian liberty by destroying peace, can be dispatched quickly only if the justiciar has support from a just, viable political institution. Irenius, in the *View*, observes that "it is but even the other daye since England grew Civill" (p. 118). The comment suggests that Spenser was not blind to the fragility of the Tudor regime. The message of Book V is that such order cannot be imposed or magically communicated by any monarch, but must come about gradually—chiefly through the educated energies of those who were born and bred to lead.

The message is not a summons to English empire. Suggestions of British imperlialism in the Legend of Justice are too easily shaped by our own historical hindsight to be fully trusted. What is more, our understanding of Spenser's politics can be more hindered than helped by the propagandizing art of his age. How much do we really know about the aims behind paintings of Elizabeth as world-queen? A reviewer has written:

Undeniably, the sumptuous fantasy of the Ditchley portrait conveys an image of Elizabeth as the ever-youthful, all-powerful Spenserian

Faerie Queene; but who was taken in by this as Gloriana increasingly came to resemble a painted doll, seeking to disguise the ravages of time so cruelly and powerfully depicted by Isaac Oliver?

Similar difficulties occur, in an even more profound form, with Van Dyck's images of Charles I. Who, if anyone, was deceived by those brilliant tableaux of a serene, dignified, elegant and triumphant monarch, the incarnation of unquestioned absolutism, which were painted at the very time when the political order they represented was on the verge of dissolution?[49]

The very allusion to Gloriana here shows how uncritical has been the general acceptance of Spenser as courtly flatterer and enthusiast for empire in the modern sense.[50] If the Ditchley portrait proves nothing about the queen's subjects' attitudes, neither should *The Faerie Queene* be regarded as a celebration of divine Astraea and her empire without accounting for what the poem really says on these subjects. I have argued that the parts of the poem most concerned with monarchy have less to say about the divine right of kings than about the idolatry of absolutism and about an aristocracy that supports mercy and peace.

It is true that in the late sixteenth century, for the first time since classical antiquity, many European poets were turning their minds to the imperial theme of national destinies. The international events of Book V would seem to find their counterpart in the epics of Camoens and Tasso, not to mention lesser poets like Trissino and Cinthio. But what a difference! Arthur and Artegall have none of the epic machinery, their battles nothing of the panorama, of Godfrey and Rinaldo; we are scarcely conscious that Artegall is accompanied by an army on the last leg of his quest to save Irena. *Tamburlaine,* in this sense, is closer to epic than anything in Book V. If Spenser wished to celebrate the Armada victory, and only that, in Arthur's battle with the Souldan he could not have concealed his purpose more completely. At least until recently, Book V has suffered too much from exclusive attention to historical identifications; it is an irresponsible interpretation that equates all the heroes with Elizabeth, all villains with Philip II—a reading not answerable to the painstaking and subtle differentiations that characteize the rest of the allegory.

Elizabeth, Mercilla, and the Sword

If Spenser belonged to Elizabeth's cult, his "Brief Note of Ireland," written on behalf of the English driven from their Irish settlements in Tyrone's rebellion, indicates that on occasion he could be quite heretical. The letter begins in the vein of a *Mirror for Magistrates* poem, the speaker appearing as a ghost complaining: "Out of the ashes of dislocation and wastnes of this your wretched Realme of Ireland. Vouchsafe most mightie Empresse our Dred soveraigne to receive the voices of a fewe moste unhappie Ghostes, of whome is nothinge but the ghost nowe left which lie buried in the bottome of oblivion" (*Prose Works*, 236). Spenser then broaches the charge that the government's neglect is due to misdirected mercy. Local administrators have been particularly irresponsible, but the queen herself must bear some share of the blame. Elizabeth allows her sunshine to spread "over Countries moste remote to the releeving of their destitute Calamaties"— France and the Netherlands, that is—"yet upon this miserable land being your owne juste and heritable dominion letteth no one little blame of your large mercie to be shed." The queen's mercy is implored for the refugees trying to stay alive in Irish port towns, "naked and comfortless lying under the towne walls and begging aboute all the streetes. . . . Could your majesties moste mercifull eyes see but some parte of the image of these our moste ruefull calamities they would melt with remorce" (p. 238). The "Note" is less a plea for personal aid than for sympathy and resolve. After again appealing to her "cairfull regard," Spenser reminds the queen less politely than he did in the *View*, of her excessive mercy toward the "rebels" in the past. The rhetoric of monarchical address being what it was, one may miss the note of resentment and accusation in these words:

> Whereas your Majestie as you have hitherto made your selfe through all the worlde a glorious example of mercie and Clemencye and even unto these vile Catifes (though most unworthie thereof) So now by extending upon them the terror of your wrath in avengement of there continuall disloyalltie and disobedinece you shall spreade the honorable fame of your Justice and redeeme both your owne honour and allso the reputacion of your people which these base raskalls through your to longe suffrance and this so late hapned reproche shaken and endangered with all moste all Christian princes besides which you shall sette a perpetuall establishment both of peace (whereby your riches shall be much increased) and allso of great strength which may from hence be drawne both to the better assurance of this your kingdome and allso to the continuall service of that your Realme of England. (p. 241)

The conclusion restates the fear "leste your Majestes wonted mercifull minde should againe be wrought to your wonted milde courses" (p. 242).

The evidence of the "Note" is that Elizabeth and Mercilla are at odds with respect to mercy and justice. Mercilla represents a mean between the excess of mercy, seen in the historical Elizabeth, and the defect of it, as seen in the tyrants of Book V. However reluctant she may be, Mercilla is willing to use the sword or unleash the lion. In Ireland—as Spenser saw it, that is— Elizabeth was not. This opposition between ideal and living exemplar resembles that in Jonsonian masques, which often seem like flattery when they match disreputable patrons with virtuous archetypes. Yet both Spenser's and Jonson's fictions exhort the real persons to acquire that ideal of excellence which belongs to their rank. If she is to prevail, Mercy must retain and display the punitive sword.

The rusty sword beneath Mercilla's throne also refers to the central role of aristocracy in Book V of *The Faerie Queene*. A well-known story of this time links the sword to that stage of "social banditry" when law and order were first imposed on the land.[51] Mercilla now holds the sword to proclaim that that time has passed. But the story I refer to touches both the theme of equity and the participation of the aristocracy in government. During the time of John de Warenne Earl of Surrey (ca. 1231–1304), Edward I ordered an inquiry into the landholdings of the aristocracy throughout his realm. Doubtful claims were to be supported with documentary proof or they would be forfeit to the crown. In Holinshed's account of the earl's stand against Edward in this matter,[52] Warenne and his rusty sword symbolize the courageous aristocrat standing guard against tyranny; Edward's order is seen as a "shift to get monie":

> Manie were thus called to answer, till at length the lord John Warren earle of Surrie, a man greatlie beloved of the people, perceiving the king to have cast his net for a preie, and that there was not one which spake against him, determined to stand against those so bitter and cruell proceedings. And therefore being called afore the justices about this matter, he appeared, and being asked "by what right he held his lands?" suddenlie drawing foorth an old rustie sword; "By this instrument (said he) doo I hold may lands, and by the same I intend to defend them. Our ancestors comming into this realme with William the Conqueror, conquered their lands with the sword, and with the same will I defend me from all those should be about to take them from me; he did not make a conquest of this realme alone, our progenitors were with him as participants and helpers."

If modern historians often see the feudal king as mitigating the power of the barons over the commons, Holinshed's story, inherited from chroniclers sympathetic with feudal aristocracy, illustrates the nobility's usefulness to the commonwealth in checking monarchy. Thus "the thing which generallie should have touched and beene hurtfull to all men," was prevented by Warenne, "who in his rare act of defending common equitie against the mightie in authoritie (who spared not to offer extreme injurie) shewed himselfe a verie true and naturall branch of nobilitie."

It is full consistent with the obvious interpretation of the rusty sword as *pax Elizabethana* that Spenser should also intend this traditional symbol of the nobleman's duty to defend "common equitie against the mightie." This defense, in fact, is accomplished in the battles of Arthur and Artegall during the last five cantos of Book V.

Another late text indicates that Spenser's belief in aristocracy was not so medieval as to exclude more recent political ideas. The Venetian Republic was widely believed the finest model of mixed government in Europe. Spenser's praise of Venice in Lewis Lewkenor's translation of Contarini reveals more sympathy with contemporary republican thought than is usually realized:[53]

> The antique Babael, empresse of the East,
> Upreard her buildings to the threatened skie:
> And second Babel, tyrant of the West,
> Her angry towers upraised much more high.
> But, with the weight of their own surquedry,
> They both are fallen, . . .
> But in their place doth now a third appeare,
> Fayre Venice, flower of the last worlds delight,
> And next to them in beuty draweth neare,
> But farre exceeds in policie of right,[54]

In his brief address to the patroness of this book, the same Countess of Warwick who was dedicatee of Spenser's *Fowre Hymns*, Lewkenor admires the "strange and unusuall forme of a most excellent Monarchie" in Venice: an elected ruler subject to laws, held in check by a council of ten and a great council of 3,000 gentlemen. Although Spenser never advocates that specific model of government, this sonnet hails a renewal of civil justice in the republic, constrasting the fallen Babel of Rome, the model of tyranny, with those towers so often praised in Contarini's book. A full-fledged republican, Milton, exploits more fully the symbolism of Babel and its founder in recounting the growth of tyranny in *Paradise Lost*.

Astraea's book does little to celebrate Astraea's reign contemporary with its publication. The religious settlement, the trial of Mary Queen of Scots, even the Armada victory would have struck readers in the later 1590s as belonging to history. Evident as was Spenser's patriotism—in, say, the prophecy of Merlin—we are hard pressed to find in Book V anything like the national elan of *Henry V* or Drayton's "Ballad of Agincourt." Instead, the allegory turns on matters of commonwealth: the obligations of governed and governors, the nature of sovereignty, the ends of government, the relation of civil and religious law. Book V is more a lawyer's than a patriot's allegory. Grantorto's very name is derived from a legal concept, and Mercilla began to be understood only when we put aside the stock historical response of generations and considered the traditions of legal thought that inform her character. The Souldan, Adicia, and Gerioneo embody the violations of natural and divine law inherent in absolute sovereignty, which Spenser, following a long tradition of humanistic and English legal thought, equates with tyranny. Finally, all the main events of these political cantos have a Christian dimension, from the Temple of Isis, with its adumbrations of the Elizabethan Church, to the eschatological symbolism of the battles. St. George's religious victory in Book I is writ large in the renewed aristocracy's political liberations, recounted in the Legend of Justice.

4

Shakespeare: Liberty and Idol Ceremony

Apologia

Arguing that in Shakespeare scholarship "the ideas of the time have become a club with which to clobber the character," Richard Levin has offered a worthy refutation of many thematic "readings" of the plays. His case against academic nonsense can make anyone think twice before producing an interpretation of a play that depends on historical and intellectual backgrounds. Such readings, says Levin, "are all based upon the contention that the real meaning of the plays is wholly or largely determined by some component of the extradramatic background and can only be apprenhended in relation to it." A good example is the old argument that King Lear commits a grievous sin against the Tudor concept of order in abdicating (once a king always a king). As Levin points out, this concept was by no means universally assumed, Charles V being a notable example of honorable abdication. Moreover, the horror of abdication is nowhere expressed in the play by the many characters who witness and comment upon Lear's giving up the throne.[1]

Two tests of thematic criticism are suggested here. One, related to studies of the "world picture," asks whether the idea being treated is truly widely held during the period in question. Another asks if the theme receives significant attention from characters and plot. Many thematic readings fail the first test rather badly. A collection of opinions from clergymen or government time-servers will be produced to make an apparently resounding case that Elizabethans believed, say, that meat was good for the liver; yet a collection just as large can be made for the opposite opinion. Did Elizabethans believe in ghosts—or, more to the point of my inquiry, did they believe in the divine right of kings or in the monarch's absolute power or in the rights of subjects to redress acts of tyranny? A wide range of contemporary opinions exists on these issues.

Theme need not be a play's raison d'etre, but in *Julius Caesar* and perhaps *Richard II* politics serve more than the nominal heroes to unify the whole.[2] When Wilbur Sanders says that "Shakespeare has pondered the unproductive violence of political controversy in his age and has seen through it to the deeper issue it evades,"[3] he means that for Shakespeare ideas, both false (the controversy) and true (the deeper issue) had consequences. It follows that the critic's task is in part to uncover that "horizon of already granted meanings and intentions"[4] lying behind the play—always acknowledging that the discovery of meaning and the act of evaluation are two different critical procedures. This horizon is not propounded, it is already there; but it may seem quite foreign to a later audience. One domain of what is sometimes disparagingly called thematic criticism, then, is simply understanding the concepts in the characters' *dianoia*, regardless of whether they are imputed to the author. Recent attention to the theatricality of life in Shakespeare, whereby kings are actors, actors are kings (Calderwood, Goldberg, Greenblatt, and others) opens up new ways to think about the plays. But in Shakespeare's political plays the theater is a model for human life, vehicle not tenor. The *dianoia* of these plays offers not imitations of ideas but true ideas. If thematic criticism sometimes makes Shakespeare sound like a political commentator, it is because he was that, among other things. He comments, through dramatic incarnation, on monarchs pretending to divinity, avaricious noblemen, hypocritical old statesmen, stupid commoners, and on all the theories that each party constructs to justify its claim to exclusivity in the power struggle. These criticisms, for the most part denials, recur so often in Shakespeare's plays, and with less regularity in those of his contemporaries, that they must be attributed to Shakespeare's mind. This mind is often ironic, iconoclastic, as Sanders says, "agnostic" (p. 158). It is a useful thing, no doubt, to analyze Shakespeare's games and plots; but it is at least as worthwhile to sort out the icons and opinions that give rise to his denials.

In fact even the most committed antithematist cannot talk for long about the plays without introducing a theme. An approach that anticipates Levin's in many ways is that of S. C. Sen Gupta in his excellent book on the histories. "If, however, the plays are considered *as* plays," he writes, "it will appear very doubtful whether Shakespeare was primarily interested in propagating any particular political or moral idea." Yet he performs a number of

historically based thematic readings, such as: "by making Richard
[II] personally responsible for his disasters, Shakespeare seems to
stress his independence of the medieval idea of tragedy, and show
in the true Renaissance spirit that man is the architect of his fate
and not a victim of the blind goddess of Fortune."[5]

Levin would agree with Sen Gupta that Shakespeare "was not a
writer of homilies or of political history" (p. 28), as would any
reasonable person. To pursue relentlessly the implications of the
homilies against rebellion could end in the view that not only
Julius Caesar and Henry IV but Dogberry and Elbow are the
unimpeachable heroes of their plays, since all power, even a
constable's, is from God. Yet against the wisdom of Ulysses on
order and degree there is also that of "a dog's obeyed in office."
What is there in the horizon of these two plays at their moment in
history that makes the words of Ulysses or Lear exactly right? Or,
to return to my own topic, why, on the night before the Battle of
Agincourt, does Henry render his memorable soliloquy on kingship and ceremony? Henry V's soliloquy is the climax of the king-
and-commoner dialectic of the Henriad—as Norman Rabkin says,
"in some respects . . . the thematic climax of the entire tetralogy."[6]
This speech bears directly on this chapter, but adequate interpretation requires searching the horizons of the speech. These contain the whole play *Henry V* and the history plays leading up to it,
especially *Richard II*, the one that most strikingly sets forth the
issues of the soliloquy. Not to be excluded is *Julius Caesar,* a play
written within a few months of *Henry V,* one that also contends
with sovereignty and ceremony. Comparing Henry V with Caesar, John Anson says that the English ruler knows his greatness to
be "an essentially social and ritualistic *persona* behind which there
stands another private, corporeal being."[7] The art of kingship lies
in distinguishing between the king's two persons and in achiev-
ing, as Anson says, "a position from which he can oversee" both
selves, private and public. Henry accomplishes this end, as Caesar does not, by liberating himself and his society from bondage
to idol (therefore idle) ceremony.

Richard II

The idea of "the king's two bodies" can become one of those
clubs to beat characters with that Levin so rightly complains of. As
was said in the introduction, it is not supported by *Richard II*, and
if it implies divine-right sovereignty of the sort that James I sup-

posed, it scarcely conforms to monarchy as practiced in sixteenth-century England. As for that period's own perspective, writes Graham Holderness, Shakespeare "would have known the Middle Ages *not* as a period dominated by order, legitimacy and the undisputed sovereignty of a monarch sanctioned by Divine Right, but as a turbulent period dominated by a great and fundamental conflict, fought out again and again and rarely suppressed, between the power of the Crown, and the power of the feudal barons."[8] Writing on this topic, an eminent English jurist has firmly, if unsubtly, called *Richard II* "a study in misgovernment, due to an over-exalted conception of the royal office by Richard, and an arbitrary disregard for the rights of subjects. The moral of it is as plain in the tragedy as in history. High-handed conduct, based on a conception of royal responsibility to God alone, is alien to the traditions of the English constitution."[9] Only add that the play is a tragedy, not just a political drama, because the "misgovernment" occurs within the person as well as the realm of Richard. This double focus, inherited from morality-play conventions of the proud soul as world-king, results in a more human king, not a more godlike one. Colet or Erasmus would say, a more human king and therefore a more Godlike one—hence the parallels with Christ's passion that seem so baffling at the end of the play.

The first act of *Richard II* belies the smooth administration of ideal monarchical justice conducted in Spenser's Mercilla episode. Duessa's trial runs on a clear division of labor, with the knight-heroes and the court in pursuit of a just verdict, and the queen in her mercy-giving capacity somewhat aloof from the proceedings. Richard, however, is hopelessly entangled in the Mowbray-Bolingbroke dispute. Family ties blur the division between peerage and royalty, the accusations reflecting gravely on the honor of both estates. Holderness accurately observes that monarchy has simply failed to balance the power between itself and aristocracy (p. 51). In the speech beginning "Mowbray, impartial are our eyes and ears" (I.1.115), Richard tries to defend himself from suspicion of partiality; but his final sentencing of the combatants satisfies no one, least of all the audience, in its apparent inequity and bias. Richard will later exemplify the defects of divine-right political thought, but the first act indicates the equal perils of mixed monarchy in which the aristocracy shares power with the king. The difference between Richard's throne room and Mercilla's is that between historical and philosophical truth.

The atmosphere of this play breathes mistrust. The formality at

Coventry implies not some golden age of well-ordered monarchy, but a guarded, apprehensive condition not unlike the fear that greets Henry V on first entering his throne room (*2H4*, V.2), fear that he must labor to dispel. At Coventry, in his increasing self-centeredness, Richard violates two principles sacred to the nobility: ceremony and time. The theme of time in the play is broached in the king's very first lines to "Old John of Gaunt, time-honored Lancaster." By the fifth act, Richard realizes his sins against time: "I wasted time, and now doth time waste me" (V.5.49). Moving toward this realization, Richard hears York warn of his offense against aristocracy when the old duke says that to deprive Bolingbroke of his inheritance is to "take from Time / His charters and his customaryrights" (II.1.195). Bolingbroke's refusal to throw down his gage lest he become "crestfallen" (I.1.188) puns on the fear that his name will fall to oblivion if he does not defend the honor of his ancient family. Manipulating time in the sentences and commutations, Richard behaves as if he transcends time like a god.

Richard is often identified with the ceremonies of monarchy, but he reserves ceremony for himself alone. His unthinking self-worship, like Lucifera's mirror-gazing, culminates in his self-identification as God's own child.[10] Later he breaks this illusion of pomp in shattering his mirror. His most serious violations of form, of course, are legal: the farming of the realm and the expropriation of Gaunt's estate. But he shows heedlessness for form in the lists when he shatters the rites of combat. The structure of the scene highlights its ceremoniousness. First comes the marshal's questioning the pair (a "mere formality," as we would say, since audience and characters alike know the points at issue). There is a taboo in the warning that no one may touch the lists, followed by a leave-taking, the herald's challenges, and a trumpet call. At this moment Richard violates the sense of flow and inevitability by throwing down his ceremonial baton. Despite its deadly implications, the ritual until now has conveyed a certain confidence that things will be settled. Richard's gesture unnerves and exasperates everyone. From the participants' viewpoint, royal arrogance has usurped the sacred life-and-death rites of the aristocracy.

If there is no clear delineation of authority in this aristocratic monarchy, there is also no clear answer to the question who brings the king to justice when he commits acts of tyranny like those envisioned in Act II. Clearly the aristocracy cannot. Just before the great deposition scene of *Richard II* the assembled nobles burst into a series of charges and counter-charges. To Bagot's claim that Aumerle collaborated in Gloucester's murder, the latter convincingly asserts his innocence (IV.1.20). No sooner has he spoken than Fitzwater throws down his guantlet in equally convincing testimony, saying Aumerle had admitted killing Gloucester, even bragged of it. Percy and another lord step in to take Fitzwater's side, whereupon the Duke of Surrey accuses Fitzwater of lying about Aumerle. Some hope of unscrambling this maze of accusations lies in Mowbray's expected return following the repeal of his exile, until we hear that Mowbray has died. No one can discern the truth. These events thrust us back to the opening scene of the play, when Bolingbroke and Mowbray contended over the same crime. Not only does the play never tell who killed Gloucester, but it leaves unresolved the quarrels over his murder, whether between Bolingbroke and Mowbray or among the assembly in Act IV. When Henry suspends the angry lords' challenges "under gage," he in effect does what Richard might have done to him and Mowbray in Act I, scene 1. For the same reason? Should Richard have done so? We do not know why either king acted as he did; we never know the truth behind the accusations.

When this scene is played—and it is often omitted in productions—the quarreling lords in Act IV must be acted as if each believes unreservedly in his own honesty, for such is the quality of their language in these impassioned denials and countercharges. The same is true of the Bolingbroke-Mowbray dispute: the audience must be utterly perplexed as to who is telling the truth. Their oaths are both sacred and serious. Bolingbroke swears by heaven,

> for what I speak
> My body shall make good upon this earth
> Or my divine soul answer it in heaven.
>
> (I.1.36–38)

as readily as Mowbray, who in the lists against Bolingbroke aims

> by the grace of God and this mine arm,
> To prove him, in defending of myself,
> A traitor to my God, my king, and me;
> And as I truly fight, defend me heaven!
>
> (I.3.21–24)

Such is the confusing stuff of *Richard II's* world, which like that of other political tragedies by Shakespeare lacks any confirming center. This is the opacity of true history: contradictions, deceptions, rumors, without the certainty that any doubts can ever be cleared up. Parents betray children; religion is at best ineffective, more often a pretext for policy; dishonor, injustice, and fear are the real ruling powers. It is as if God had abandoned the body politic to the insatiable appetites of the powerful, as if the play began and ended in the middle of *Macbeth*.

In Act I, one effect of moving from the challenge to the formal ceremoniousness of the scene at the lists must be to baffle the audience with the question of Gloucester's murder, given further exposition in the intervening scene between Gaunt and the Duchess of Gloucester. Why, if Gaunt believes that "God's substitute," Richard, "Hath caused his death" (I.2.37) does he not follow his namesake in *Woodstock* and take up his dead brother's cause, vowing revenge? More to the point, why doesn't he use his knowledge to help his son's case against Mowbray? The Duchess could be right: Gaunt counsels patience when he means despair. Alternatively the truth may lie with Gaunt's self-justification, that the quarrel is God's alone: "for I may never lift an angry arm against his minister." If so, York may act from the same motive even in the end, when he races to Henry to tell him of his son's conspiracy. Surely the sycophantic behavior of York in Act V, knowing that his son has abandoned the conspiracy, yet urging Henry not to forgive him after the plot has been defused, makes self-interest a more likely motive than patriotism. The scene anticipates another betrayal of a family member to a usurper in *King Lear*, when Edmund says that "nature thus give way to loyalty" (III.5.2). Significantly, it is when the family of York has had its bonds of love thoroughly destroyed, and when the dignity of father, mother, and son has been irrevocably compromised by their bickering and groveling before Henry, that Henry's pardon receives the Duchess of York's thanks: "A god on earth thou art" (V.3.136). Rather than take this remark as indicating Henry's newly acquired regal dignity,[11] perhaps we ought to see it as the pathetic self-abasement of an old nobility that has capitulated to usurpation, creating an idol-monarch. Does any audience see the scene with York, Aumerle, and the Duchess all cringing before Henry without at least some embarrassed laughter? The scene speaks for itself: it cannot communicate anything except complete loss of face. In the light of this scene, York's early indecision looks suspiciously like a failure of courage.[12] Possibly Gaunt is cast from the same mold, so that his caution, too, is something less than wisdom.

Gaunt may seem a choric figure in the play, the confirming center that will reassure us as to the real meaning of events.[13] The great speech on "this scept'red isle" in Act II scene I seems incontrovertible evidence of Gaunt's prophetic role. Yet other critics have seen this dying speech as a "vehement wish to dispossess Richard himself of his brithright," its patriotism quite aside.[14] In Act I when Gaunt speaks to Gloucester's widow of Richard's complicity in murdering her husband, scholars used to see Gaunt as enunciating "official Tudor doctrine" on the sacredness of kings:

> God's is the quarrel; for God's substitute,
> His deputy anointed in his sight,
> Hath caused his death; the which if wrongfully,
> Let heaven revenge; for I may never lift
> An angry arm against his minister.
>
> (I.2.37–41)

If "God's substitute" does mean "king by divine right,"[15] it does so not in the Jacobean sense, but in the general sense that legitimate power is from God. Yet religion serves politic ends admirably here, for Gaunt has done wonders with this little speech. He has guaranteed that people will know about Richard's guilt in Gloucester's murder, since Gloucester's angry widow is unlikely to keep his revelation in confidence. Appealing to heaven is also an eminently convenient way to get rid of an emotional duchess. To her anxious question, "Where then, alas, may I complain myself?" there is no safer, yet less satisfying rejoinder than, "to God, the widow's champion and defense." Gaunt will not be so quick to urge piety in the next scene, speaking to his banished son. This is not to say that Gaunt should have taken the duchess's part, only that his attitude in the scene bespeaks a cold detachment, something less than candor, and possibly an interest in using the widow's grief against the king. As for his coldness, or at least reticence, it may be relevant to add that in the entire scene Gaunt speaks sixteen lines against the duchess's fifty-eight. In summary, Gaunt's deference to "God's substitute" can be interpreted more as pretext than principle.

The world of *Richard II* resonates with deceiving voices; no one, not the king, not righteous old Gaunt, is above suspicion. Therefore, one cannot take the speeches of either as proof-texts of the play's advocating mystical kingship. As Levin tirelessly reminds us, no thematic statement should be viewed apart from the context of character and action, and context provides only limited help with Richard and Gaunt. At other moment in this play, however, an awareness of context will clarify the ethical direction of a scene. This is especially true of events that cast light on Bolingbroke's motives. What, for example, are we to think of Bolingbroke's assurances to York (II.3.113–36) that he has returned to England only to claim his inheritance, when he shortly lays claim to Richard's too?

An important instance of this kind is the trial of Bushy and Greene. Henry charges the two companions with having "misled a prince," having "Made a divorce betwixt his queen and him," and having "fed upon" Bolingbroke's own fortune by persuading the king to seize his estates (III.1.7–27). The angry peer devotes by far the greatest part of his speech to injuries against himself, leaving the strong impression that he is acting as judge and jury in his own cause. In the light of his earlier claim that Bushy and Greene are "caterpillars of the commonwealth" (II.3.166), it is surprising that he says nothing here about their supposed corruption in public office. As to the first charge, nowhere does the play support the view that Bushy and Greene have mastery over the king—in this respect the contrast with *Woodstock* could not be greater. Bolingbroke's factor Northumberland first plants this rumor in the play ("The king is not himself, but basely led / By flatterers" II.1.241). Richard makes his fatal decisions in Act I all on his own (e.g., the "farming" of the realm, which is wholly his idea, presented to Greene at I.4.42); his independence, indeed, is essential to his tragedy.

Bolingbroke's second accusation regarding the "divorce" carries a veiled reference to the homosexual reputation of Richard II as developed in *Woodstock* and the chronicles; but these implications are not in Shakespeare's play. If anything, Shakespeare's king resembles not the clothes-horse of *Woodstock* but the Richard of Drayton's *Heroical Epistles*, where his love for Isabel raises him to heroic stature. In fact the entirety of Act II, scene 2, in which Greene, Bagot, and Bushy console the queen, suggests amiable relations between the favorites and her.[16] Clearly Bolingbroke has exploited Rumor, "the common liar," who will ever be in attendance once he has taken the throne.

A seemingly straightforward scene is that in which Richard utters his famous "doctrine" of divine right; but the irony here (III.2) is indicated in the immediate entry of Salisbury with news of the Welsh defection. Thus dispirited, Richard acts out a passage from the *Vindiciae contra tyrannos*: "Let the people forsake their king, he presently falls to the ground, although before, his hearing and sight seemed most excellent, and that he was strong and in the best disposition that might be; yea, that he seemed to triumph in all magnificence, yet in an instante he will become most vile and contempible" (p. 126). Here Shakeapeare probably meant Richard to sink down, for a few moments later when he says, "For God's sake, let us sit upon the ground / And tell sad stories of the death of kings" (lines 155–56), Richard is almost certainly sitting. This emblematic use of gesture occurs frequently in the play, as in the king's descent from the battlements to meet Bolingbroke. It was very likely a gesture inherited from the mystery plays centuries earlier, when Herod held his stage tantrum on hearing the Magi had escaped, or when he was taken by death. The same enacting of a king's "fall" occurs in *The Spanish Tragedy* when the Viceroy of Portugal hears of his overthrow (I.3.10), and of course at the end of *Richard III*.

Richard II resembles *Hamlet* in its world of seeming and deception. Yet the protagonist is less equipped than Hamlet to discriminate false from true, especially as regards the "flatterers" that people his own mind. This world, where words and symbols cannot be taken at face value, has with good reason prompted interpretation of *Richard II* as a play *about* language and symbol.[17] Richard's tragedy is that he allows himself to be deluded, hence ultimately usurped, by his confidence in the lifeless symbol. What gives life to the symbol of the crown, what gives it sacredness, is the king's living up to his role. Failing that, it does no good for king or critic to invoke "the sacred, animistic bond between king and land—the corpus mysticum which includes and transcends both political kingdom and physical earth."[18] In Coursen's words, Richard fails as keeper of the holy metaphor. The bond, rendered lifeless, becomes an empty "idol," as Henry V will say in the very act of bringing the symbol of the crown back to life.

There remains the argument that Richard, for all his failures and crimes, represented the order that in Shakespeare's time "was in fact humanity's only right condition."[19] Yet it is crucial to see that order was not an end in itself. One effect of king-worship is to take both freedom and responsibility from the subject. In Eramus and Spenser the order of monarchy is an instrument of peace, and peace in turn of the personal liberty that would give each soul the fullest possible scope for working out its salvation. The tragedies of disorder in Shakespeare similarly move us not because they

violate some aesthetic or mystical status quo, but because the
liberties of good, happy people have been cut off by malice or
misfortune. Hamlet forced into the path of violence; Ophelia,
Brutus's Portia, and Lucrece[20] driven to suicide; Othello con-
strained by a different but no less devastating injustice—all exemplify the pathos of the subverted will. Cosmic or social
disorder may be the setting of tragedy, but the tragic event is
personal. Audiences feel pity for Lear in the storm, not on account of the storm itself. M. M. Reese writes that "divine right is
only a slightly elaborate way of stating the general conviction that
the gods do act through man, and that the consequences are
tragic when we try to resist their will" (p. 113). Rather, it would
seem, the tragic consequences are set in motion when human
lives are invaded by Satanic malevolence, or fortune, or perhaps
even Providence (Macduff's children must die so that James VI
may ascend the throne). Moreover, *does* God act through men,
and how do we know when he is doing so? Divine intervention
enters the plays not as assumed but as the subject of a question.

What distinguishes the history plays from the tragedies, says
Nevo, is that in the former "the protagonists are exhibited as
struggling for freedom to initiate events" (p. 60). Richard is a tragic
hero in that he is sufficiently human to make the wrong choices;
but in the early acts of the play he also makes the choice of wrong.
At least for a time he takes on the role of Spenser's Grantorto. His
haughtiness toward the dying Gaunt is offensive, but much more
destructive of Richard's "reputation" in the play is his unreflect-
ing, casual seizure of other people's land and wealth to make war
in Ireland. What stands unforgivable to Elizabethan frugality is
that the seizure is necessitated by "riot," courtly extravagance. Yet,
damning as it is, Richard's venality at least remains open for all to
see. Bolingbroke, the inscrutable usurper who so manipulates his
public image, opens the floodgates of civil war while pretending
to save his country. His pious claims of loyalty on returning from
exile do not fool Richard and serve only to confirm his hypocrisy.
Only *after* Richard has lost his kingship and liberty does he become the hero of a history play, "struggling for the freedom to
initiate events." The weariness with patience that overtakes him in
the last act leads to his one freely willed moment during the entire
play, in the sense that it emerges from the wisdom of self-knowledge. Even in the deposition his vacillating blunts the impact of a
potentially grand exit.

"Ceremony" is both the veil that conceals Richard from himself
and the cloak that Henry IV will use to hide his guilt. Although

Shakespeare may not have known the theological terms, he depicts the effects of confusing *dulia* (the honor due to authority) and *latria* (divine worship, which Richard thinks he shares). Nevo writes that in the first scenes of the tetralogy, "Feudal rituals mask the ulterior potential realities of collusion and guilt" (p. 62). Maynard Mack, Jr., detects impatience with the "cloying ceremony" of court in the early scenes of the play.[21] Whereas E. M. W. Tillyard had found in "the ritual or ceremonial element" of *Richard II* evidence that Shakespeare was consciously depicting the golden age of the old medieval order, most of the more recent critics of the play seem to agree that, far from glorifying Richard, the ceremonies of anointed kingship keep him fettered in illusion, not yet a free man.[22] At the center of the play is what Norman Rabkin calls "Richard's tragic confusion of ceremony with reality."[23] During the great speech when Richard at last recognizes his humanity, he finally sees "Tradition, form, and ceremonious duty" (III.2.173) as worthless if unreciprocated. In the same passage, "pomp" becomes an object of amusement for antic death; and later Richard will think of his wife, once "set forth in pomp" from France, now cast into widowhood and obscurity (V.1.78).

Ceremony is not redeemed until the last play of the cycle that Richard begins, when the monarch's humanity, his dependence on his fellow men as on God, is firmly established on the field at Agincourt. This does not imply a flawless unity in the entire tetralogy: the characters, especially Prince Hal, seem to shift a good deal over time.[24] Yet the four plays have a continuous vision of history, sustained by a mature, creative intelligence. Like the proud soul of the morality plays, monarchy must be purged of idolatry, an evil spirit haunting European courts during the sixteenth and seventeenth centuries. W. Gordon Zeeveld has said of Richard II that "the enormity of his offense to Shakespeare's audience lies in his presumption to sanctity, the character no English king had been allowed."[25] Richard pays for these pretensions, of course; Henry IV cannot even think of making them. Henry V, remarkably, manages to expiate both his father's sin of regicide and the blasphemy of Richard's presuming to a divine role.

Henry V and the Critics

"Without humanism, in short, there could have been no Elizabethan literature: without Erasmus, no Shakespeare."[26] Thus

Emrys Jones, in a book that faults earlier literary historians, particularly C. S. Lewis, for their neglect of Erasmus in assessing the
intellectual backgrounds of English Renaissance literature. The
criticism is accurate, though Shakespeare studies have been pay-
ing more attention to the subject. Shakespeare's first-hand knowledge of Erasmus is certain, and unquestionably both authors
shared a similar vision of human folly and a scorn for the doc-
trinaire.[27] A source in *The Praise of Folly* for one of Falstaff's
speechs[28] shows Erasmus contributing to the formation of the
character. The Fallstaff-Hal relationship also echoes the warning
against parasites in *The Education of a Christian Prince*. ("The prince
will therefore always be on the lookout to keep the proportion of
idlers down to a minimum among his courtiers, and either to
force them to be busy or else banish them from the country.")[29]
The "player king" motif in Shakespeare may well originate in one
of the *Adagia*.[30] Erasmus's hatred of war, his ideas on the humanity of kings and their responsibility to their subjects also lie nearer
the histories than does the once-assumed "Tudor doctrine" of
God-like kingship. This correspondence has led several scholars
to examine the Erasmian influence in *Henry V*, particularly J. H.
Walter, whose Arden edition lists impressive parallel passages in
Shakespeare's play and the *Education*.[31] Andrew Gurr has recently
explored the similarities between Erasmus's and Shakespeare's
emblem of the bees' commonwealth in these two works.[32] This is
not to make Shakespeare Erasmus's mouthpiece, but the humanist's influence, often unnoticed in older scholarship, may provide
an opening in the critical morass surrounding the play and its
hero, since the tacit assumption in some "divine monarch" readings of the plays is that it never would have occurred to anyone in
Shakespeare's century to say that kings were not absolute vicars of
God.

The critics' attack on Henry V as hero begins with Hazlitt's
politically charged essay in *Characters of Shakespeare's Plays*.[33]
Through the years a number of anti-Henricians have similarly
acted from their politics or moral convictions. "Purely subjective
notions paralyze their judgments," complains one scholar, "and
they write as pacifists, republicans, anti-clericals, little En-
glanders, moralists, even arbiters of etiquette, until one is as-
tounded at the prejudice Henry has managed to arouse."[34] Those
who make reasoned attempts to deal with the play fall into several
groups. Traditionalists take the playwright as endorsing both
Henry and the politics of power (e.g., E. E. Stoll, John Dover
Wilson); another group sees the play as a disguised satire on the

politics of war, with Henry as an arch-hypocrite (Gerald Gould, Harold Goddard). The latter school typifies what Richard Levin calls the "two-play" or "two-audience" approach with one *Henry V* for the thick-brained jingoist, another for the sophisticated.[35] Shaw and Mark Van Doren speak for a small party that reduces the play to an artless propaganda piece. Many recent critics (and they have my vote) see Henry as in the Kenneth Branagh film: an admirable character in a deplorable political situation (Stribrny, Reese, Jorgensen, Calderwood, Thayer).[36]

A special case is the dialectical interpretation. The title of Norman Rabkin's "Rabbits, Ducks, and *Henry V*" reflects the author's view that Shakespeare had an "intransigently multivalent perception of reality," and really wants us to buy neither a duck nor a rabbit. This interpretation raises the artist above the issues, agreeing with the ambient preference for negative capability, the sense of paradox, tension, or ambivalence. Yet Rabkin's summary of both pro- and anti-Henrician viewpoints, merely confirms the likelihood of the first. Is it really possible, for instance, that Pistol's sullen exit in Act V is supposed to evoke pathos "for the reality of the postwar world" of jobless soldiers turning to crime, of disappointed dreams of glory?[37] Related to this is Eric LaGuardia's subtle argument that, although the tetralogy traces the decline of symbolic order as language turns from poetry to policy, "we are not asked to judge whether that decline is pure gain or pure loss. It would seem wiser to think of them [the plays] as dramatizing man's continuous participation in both the mythical and historical."[38] Yet audiences *are* constantly being "asked to judge" in the political plays, this being one of their characteristics as a literary kind. "We may claim," LaGuardia writes, "that the plays dramatize the emergence of a culture purged of the nonhistorical formalism of Christian chivalry into a brighter world where the autonomous reality of nature is recognized," which means, I think, that Richard's and Hotspur's destructive egoism gives way to a recognition that time and community are real. This is unquestioned. Yet can we face the other way too? "Or, we may claim that they dramatize the tragic death of the sacramental view of nature, together with its kindred poetic sensibility, and the rise of a new order of anarchy, libertinism, and political opportunism" (pp. 70–71). The "sacramental view," by definition entailing a whole community, lies in the renewal of society that will occur in *Henry V*. As for libertinism and opportunism, these faults seem more chargeable to Richard than to Henry.

In any attempt to understand play and protagonist, the reading

of Act IV, scene 1, especially the king's one soliloquy in the play,
must be crucial. Yet Henry's speech on kingship and ceremony is
often neglected or brushed aside. A 1979 article declares, "With
the exception of his brief and relatively uninformative soliloquy
the night before Agincourt, we have no access to the private man,
and his public rhetoric is inevitably ambituous."[39] Reese (p. 331)
scarcely notices the speech in discussing the play, even though it
could be used to bolster his case that majesty depends on a
partnership between king and subject. Two studies have interpreted the speech as central to the play, but with opposite conclusions as to its meaning. These two arguments both
demonstrate, incidentally, two of the pitfalls that Levin mentions
in historical interpretation. Gordon Ross Smith has bolstered the
Gould-Goddard view with a wide array of Elizabethan writings
that condemn ceremony as the last refuge of scoundrels.[40] Yet
anyone who has read much on this subject knows that there are
impressive authorities to uphold almost any point of view. Moreover, it seems fairly clear that Henry is himself questioning ceremony in his speech, not using it as pretext, and that the action of
the whole play moves toward abandoning it as well. On the other
hand, W. Gordon Zeeveld's lengthy and informed chapter on
ceremony in Shakespeare uses Elizabethan writings to support
the pro-Henrician view. Zeeveld is more interested in sources
than plot and character development, claiming that Henry moves
toward an "acceptance of the burden of ceremony."[41] Far from it,
in fact: the last two acts of the tetralogy completely reverse
Richard's confidence in the trappings of anointed kingship, as
Henry V rectifies the earlier king's confusion of ceremony with
reality.[42]

Agincourt: Kingship without Fear

Henry's motive in going among his men before the battle is not
"to survey and view the warders," as was reported in Holinshed,
nor is it to lift his men's spirits, as the Chorus says, for he is in
disguise. His words to the troops are scarcely encouraging:

WILLIAMS. Under what captain serve you?
KING. Under Sir Thomas Erpingham.
WILLIAMS. A good old commander and a most kind gentleman.
I pray you, what thinks he of our estate?

KING. Even as men wrecked upon a sand, that look to be washed off the next tide.

(IV.1.90–95)

The most likely reason for this incognito excursion and the bleak comments is that Henry is testing his men's conviction to determine whether panic might undermine his generalship in the morning's action. He discovers fear, and at the root of his men's fear, their sense of powerlessness under the king. They have no voice in a war that may cost them their lives. As Williams says, a commoner's distrust of his king's actions is "a perilous shot out of an elder-gun. . . . You may as well go about to turn the sun to ice with fanning in his face with a peacock's feather." Williams sums up the principal arguments against war in the age, often echoing Erasmus's ideas in the *Education* and elsewhere.[43] The dialogue opens a profound examination of the nature of kingship, of the condition of men under kings.

Agincourt was an excellent proving ground for theories of monarchy because monarchy exists in its purest form in war. Sir Thomas Smith described the battlefield as the one place where the prince has truly absolute power: "This absolute power is called marciall lawe, and ever was and necessarilie must be used in all campes and hostes of men . . . that with more awe the souldier might be kept in more straight obedience, without which never captaine can doe anie thing vaileable in the warres."[44] Smith's nearest disciple in the play is Fluellen, spokesman for "the ceremonies of the wars, and the cares of it, and the forms of it, and the sobriety of it, and the modesty of it" (IV.1.70–74). But Smith's "awe," like Fluellen's ceremoniousness, if imposed too rigidly upon the army, could backfire, bringing about a spirit of craven servility rather than confidence in martial order. Henry himself believes in the "straight obedience" of his soldiers as poor Bardolph discovers and as the dialogue with Williams shows: a king is to his soldiers as a master to his servant. And yet he admits, in his soliloquy following this exchange, that such a strict bond creates a "hard condition" for king and people alike. The ardent monarchist Hobbes would later insist that if men are to lead tranquil, productive (therefore happy?) lives they must have one great power to keep them all in awe. The debate with Williams has made Henry discover the unsettling consequence of this opinion:

O Ceremony, show me but thy worth!
What is thy soul of adoration?

Art thou aught else but place, degree, and form,
Creating awe and fear in other men?
Wherein thou art less happy being fear'd
Than they in fearing.

(IV.1.230–35)

The metrical shortening of the last line places a heavy emphasis upon "fearing." Under a tyrannical rule men can fulfill themselves only through fearing or "awe." Ultimately the typical subject under such a ruler is the "wretched slave" envisioned in the last third of the soliloquy, who has traded his liberty for the security of fear.

The ironic note in Henry's portrayal of the wretched slave subverts arguments that this is firm "political doctrine." Oxymorons suggest both Henry's own divided mind and the individual's impossible straits in these circumstances. The hypothetical slave has "body fill'd and vacant mind"; in his peaceful sleep he is "cramm'd with distressful bread"; though he "sleeps in Elysium," he "sweats in the eye of Phoebus" (recalling Williams's image of fanning the sun with a peacock's feather); at the end of his life he goes "with profitable labor to his grave." This last phrase implies a contrast between the ongoing motive of honor in the Henriad and its base alternative, "profit" or private gain as a result of mere "labour," which leads only to oblivion.

At this moment, his meditation at its most intense, Henry is interrupted by Erpingham's summons. His dilemma—between his need for fearless soldiers and the apparent necessity that in a monarchy all men be subservient—is not yet explicitly solved. He can only pray for a resolution:

O God of battles! steel my soldiers' hearts.
Possess them not with fear. Take from them now
The sense of reckoning, if th' opposed numbers
Pluck their hearts from them.

(IV.1.276–79)

Henry's despondency is complicated by his sense of unworthiness before God. He has tried to make expiation for his father's crime, but recognizes that good works are vitiated by the condition of the worker:

More will I do;
Though all that I can do is nothing worth,

Since that my penitence comes after all,
Imploring pardon.

(IV.1.289–92)

Resemblances to Claudius's prayer in *Hamlet* come to mind; but like all Adam's children, Henry has inherited the consequences, not the guilt, of his father's crime.

Any interpretation of *Henry V* must take into account that the prayer is in fact answered—or least that events turn out in accordance with the prayer.[45] In his next scene Henry has solved his dilemma. If servile men cannot act with courage, then the slaves must be freed:

proclaim it Westmoreland, through my host,
That he which hath no stomach to this fight,
Let him depart; his passport shall be made,
And crowns for convoy put into his purse.
We would not die in that man's company
That fears his fellowship to die with us.

(IV.3.34–39)

The free soldiers are offered a choice: a secure life of "profitable labour" or fame, honor, remembrance—all the qualities that Falstaff and his tavern crowd have denied. In the flush of victory (IV.7) Fluellen will report that he has forgotten Falstaff's name. Henry's speech on fame is no reversion to the values of Hotspur, the chivalric anachronism so obsessed with honor and self-glorification. The difference is that Henry offers to distribute honor to the English at large, diffusing his kingly person throughout the body politic. In the first act the bishops, themselves acting selfishly, had urged Henry to act for the sake of personal and family honor ("Stand for *your* own! Unwind *your* bloody flag"; "Awake remembrance of these valiant dead / . . . *You* are their heir; *you* sit upon their throne" (I.2.101, 115). Henry now urges his army to act for collective honor: *we* shall be remembered on St. Crispian's Day:

We few, we happy few, we band of brothers.
For he today that sheds his blood with me
Shall be my brother.

(lines 60–62)

By casting off "idol ceremony" Henry has freed his men from the previous night's fear. His pun in this phrase may have been commonplace in the controversial rhetoric of Shakespeare's age, for a speech in the pre–Civil War debates attacked "idol, idle or scandlous ministers" in the Church.[46] But the pun has rich implications for the tetralogy. Richard's idleness and self-idolizing brought on England's troubles, and the "idle companions" of Prince Hal's youth seem to threaten the commonwealth. Applying the idol-idle epithet specifically to the ceremonies of coronation, Henry reflects the established thinking on these rites, for when the heir to the throne was anointed and given the scepter nothing sacramental occurred. Cranmer said that royal anointing was "but a ceremony," having "its ends and utility yet neither direct force nor necessity."[47] Edward Coke wrote that "coronation was but a royal ornament and outward solemnization of descent."[48] Even during the Civil War, both sides agreed that the king was king before his coronation.[49] Yet Shakespeare has in mind something beyond this technicality, for in existential terms even birth does not "make" a king. As Erasmus said, "for a person to be a prince it is not enought to be born, to have ancestral statutes, the sceptre and the crown. What makes a prince is a mind distinguished for its wisdom, a mind always occupied with the safety of the state, and looking to nothing but the common good."[50] Henry's soliloquy repudiates in this respect the idol-kingship of Richard, which depended on symbols to the exclusion of princely wisdom.

Fluellen gives an amusing, because distorted, reflection of such wisdom—faintly pompous and self-important, missing the sprezzatura of the real thing. He shows that formality has its uses: his attacks on the forlorn Pistol comically parody Henry's judgment of the traitors. But in the main Fluellen's eccentricity marks the limitations of ceremoniousness. When he complains that the killing of the English servant-boys is "expressly aginst the law of arms," he betrays a confusion of form and reality akin to Richard's. One wonders whether the very notion of "laws of war" did not appear contradictory if not quixotic to veterans of Europe's religious wars in Shakespeare's audience; it certainly would have to Erasmus. A similarly comic gravity undercuts Fluellen's strained analogy between Henry and Alexander the Great,[51] as misguided as his comparison of Pistol and Mark Antony in Act III, scene 6. Formality and sobriety, the qualities that Henry says separate the king from his followers, are the very attributes that determine Fluellen's comic role. His presence thus has a therapeutic purpose, to rectify these qualities through laughter.

The new fearlessness of the English allows Henry to pun on "fear" in the exchange with Mountjoy. The word-play may go unnoticed unless one recalls that in Elizabethan English the vowel in the word was still close to the sound in Middle English *fer:*

MOUNTJOY And so fare the well;
        Thou never shalt hear herald any more.
KING. I fear thou wilt once more come again for ransom.

                                                      (IV.3.126)

Spenser puns on the same word when Una approaches the disguised Archimago "with faire fearefull humblesse" (I.3.26). Shakespeare continues this word-play in the two following scenes, first when Pistol captures the French soldier Monsieur le Fer, "Master Fer" (or "master Fear" as Elizabethan audiences would have heard it). When the distraught Frenchman calls upon God, Pistol thinks the name "Signieur Dew" is meant for himself. The episode (often omitted in eighteenth-century performances, when the play seems to have been regarded as mere patriotic spectacle)[52] joins the issue of freedom and servility in fear. The comic reversal of the gentlemen serving a clown is enhanced by the Frenchman's religious awe ("je vous supplie," "Sur mes genoux"). The next scene also evokes the theme of servility, when Bourbon tries to rally his fleeing soldiers with a contempt that sharply differs from the tone of Henry's speech to his men:

> And he that will not follow Bourbon now,
> Let him go hence, and with his cap in hand
> Like a base pandar hold the chamber door
> Whilst by a slave, no gentler than my dog,
> His fairest daughter is contaminated.
>
>   (IV.5.13–17)

The Chorus had promised to show Henry "thawing cold fear" among his troops (IV. Chor. 45). By the time the battle begins, the English soldiers no longer stand as "condemned sacrifices" but free men, while the French are in the service of servile men like Pistol.

Through purging himself of the poison in kingship, the quality that sustains flattery and fear, Henry solves a problem that his father could not. Henry IV's ironic apostrophe in the soliloquy, "O, be sick great greatness, / And bid thy Ceremony give the cure!" (Part Two, IV.1.237–38), is only a breath away from the discovery of another Shakespearean king, who in the act of baring his soul finds himself. But the anagnorisis that comes with Lear's "Take Physic, pomp!" is elemental, metaphysical. Henry's aim, to reconcile the two private and public "bodies" he must wear, typifies the social action of the political plays:

> What infinite heart's-ease
> Must kings neglect, that private men enjoy!
> And what have kings, that privates have not too
> Save ceremony, save general ceremony?
>
> (IV.1.223–25)

Unlike his son, who in 3 *Henry VI* asks virtually the same question and elects to behave simply as if he were a private man, Henry manages to save the appearances of royalty. Abjuring ceremony, he ushers in a new sense of responsibility in king and subjects alike.[53] Before this night, Henry wants to unload responsibility for his actions: on the bishops for determining the justice of the war, on the conspirators for their own death sentences, on the citizens of Harfleur for the devastation should they not capitulate. Certainly by this time if not earlier, the king understands that authority must exist independently of its symbols.

Yet the final lines of the soliloquy state a problem seemingly irrelevant to the state of things at the time:

> The slave, a member of the country's peace,
> Enjoys it: but in gross brain little wots
> What watch the king keeps to maintain the peace,
> Whose hours the peasant best advantages.
>
> (lines 267–70)

First, the peace has not been maintained, second, the "slaves," or common soldiers, stay up and worry as much as the king. These lines, so much at variance with their context, appear to support an ironic reading of the speech. To be sure, "the slave" is not the common Englishman but the extreme case, the "wretched slave" envisioned in his earlier lines. Yet how can one explain Henry's claim to be maintaining the peace in the midst of an apparently unnecessary, even unjust war?

Since irony always depends on authorial intention, a prior question is whether Shakespeare believed, "No king of England if not king of France." The answer, as far as it can be given, seems to be yes—in 1415, that is. Henry V is not extending his empire but preventing the French king from doing so at England's expense. The first and second tetralogies are largely about the loss of French territories that, according to then-received history, especially in Hall,[54] had rightfully been England's. Elizabethans probably knew better than we the close blood ties of English and French ruling families in the early fifteenth century, the historical Constable of France, for instance, being half-brother to Henry V. The first tetralogy methodically plotted the decline of England's fortunes as parallel to the erosion of her French territories. Looking back over these early plays, Shakespeare can write in the epilogue to Henry V:

> Henry the Sixth, in infant bands crowned King
> Of France and England, did this king succeed;
> Whose state so many had the managing
> That they lost France and made his England bleed.

The last line has almost the force of cause and effect: to lose France is to bring disaster to England. This is in part because the loss of territory means the deprivation of the king's own honor, a connection implicit in the Daphin's insult of the tennis balls. Even Falstaff acknowledges the uses of honor when he tries to claim credit for killing Hotspur. In Henry's uncertain political circumstances, as Shakespeare would have read in the chronicles, losing France and royal honor could leave the way open to a resumption of the late civil wars. This must explain the reasoning behind the soliloquy: Henry watches on the battlefield to keep the peace at home. The condition is not unlike that in 1599, as Gary Taylor reminds us, when the monarch "had, for a generation, maintained the peace largely by fighting wars abroad" (p. 9).

Nothing in the character of Hal or Henry V supports the picture of Erasmus's land-grabbing warmonger kings. In fact, Shakespeare appears to have constructed the play so as to exonerate Henry from this charge, showing the Dauphin maneuvering him into mounting an offensive. No sack follows the seige of Harfleur, as in Holinshed and in Drayton's version of the story.[55] Moreover, Shakespeare shows the king leaving England with the memory of political conspiracy still fresh. The world of Acts I and II is not far from the deceit-charged atmosphere of *Richard II*. Yet it is too harsh to attribute Henry's motives to the politic wisdom of his father—"busy giddy minds with foreign quarrels" (*2H4*, IV.5.213). Rather, Henry finds himself confronted with a characteristically Shakespearean paradox. Peace can be attained only through war, or in the words of his own remark a little before the soliloquy: "There is some soul of goodness in this evil, / Would men observingly distill it out" (IV.1.4). That the English must fight abroad to keep from destroying each other at home is a pathetic fact of history. Like other important ideas in the main plot, this one is mirrored in the tavern scenes, as when Bardolph quells the fight between Nym and Pistol: "Come, shall I make you two friends? We must to France together; why the devil shall we keep knives to cut one another's throats?" (II.1.86). The "soul of goodness" that Henry seeks is a spirit of *discordia concors* governing the action of the play—first in the unification of the strife-torn English society, then in the concord of warring countries achieved in marriage.

The Growth of King Hal

Henry's uneasiness in the ceremonial role begins much earlier, even before the action of *Henry V*. At the instant of assuming power, the new king establishes himself as a plain man, eager to defuse the apprehensiveness, the "fear," attendant on royal solemnities.

> This new and gorgeous garment, majesty,
> Sits not so easy on me as you think.
> Brothers, you mix your sadness with some fear:
> This is the English, not the Turkish court,
> Not Amurath an Amurath succeeds,
> But Harry Harry.
>
> (2H4, V.2.44–49)

The clothes metaphor, majesty as a covering for the essential humanity shared by all people, continues into *Henry V*. Henry tells the French ambassador, "I have laid by my majesty / And plodded like a man for working days" (I.2.227), but he will soon "dazzle all the eyes of France" with his "glory." The image returns in Exeter's message to the French king: "divest yourself, and lay apart / The borrowed glories" of Henry's rightful title (II.4.78). Going into war, Henry must "put on" majesty, even though he believes that, "His ceremonies laid by," the king is but a man (IV.1.101). On his deathbed, Hal's father had promised, "a time is come to mock at form" (2H4, IV.4.118), but the prince will find it not so easy to rid himself of his costume.

An obstacle at first is the fearfulness of the court as noted above, a fear deriving partly from the Lord Chief Justice's earlier firmness with the wayward Hal. The new king will not retaliate because, recognizing that majesty is a "garment," he can understand the Justice's desire to protect the "royal image" (1.89). He sounds sincere when he claims that his wild affections have been buried with his father (1.123); but what remains behind—a person or only an image?

> The tide of blood in me
> Hath proudly flow'd in vanity till now.
> Now doth it turn and ebb back to the sea,
> Where it shall mingle with the state of floods
> And flow henceforth in formal majesty.
>
> (V.2.129–33)

Here surely the playwright looks toward themes and events of the next play in the series. The image suggests a tidal river like the Thames used in the familiar conceit of the microcosm. Until now Henry's blood has flowed inland. In the outgoing current the king will lose his self-centeredness entirely in the "state of floods," the open main of the nation. He makes good on this promise in the brotherhood of Agincourt and in his self-effacement after the victory. At the same time these lines hint at the cold formality of the king beset by enemies whom we see in the opening of *Henry V*, a play that moves us from the low ebb of Falstaff's death to the charm and warmth of the wooing scenes.

Before his triumph in France, Henry shows his cold majesty in his two encounters with the magnates of his realm—the avaricious bishops in Act 1, scene 2 and the treasonous lords in Act 2, scene 2. Both scenes are redolent with that same sense of hypocritical formality felt in the lists at Coventry in *Richard II*.

Opening the play with the bishops accomplishes two things. It clarifies their role in fomenting the war,[56] and appeals mightily to the audience's prejudice against the hierarchy of the old (and maybe new) church, especially when followed by the bishops' strident appeals for war. In the first tetralogy, at Henry V's funeral, Gloucester says that "had not churchmen prayed" against him, the heroic king might still be alive (*1H6*, I.1.33). Later the scheming Bishop of Winchester becomes a means of Gloucester's and the kingdom's downfall (*2H6*, III.1). Among the antecedents of this first scene is the mystery-play tradition that portrayed as bishops the Jewish priests scheming against Christ. So they appear in the stage directions of the N-Town or Ludus Coventriae play on the council of the Jews, where mitered bishops in red (much more obviously bishops than the two in the Branagh film) are attended by clerks and doctors in furred hoods. Erasmus's *Education of a Christian Prince* attacks bishops and priests for being "the very firebrands of war" in his day, a frequent accusation in his and like-minded humanists' writings.[57] Tyndale laments that nowadays "bishops can only minister the temporal sword," calling for their expulsion from councils of government.[58] Drayton blames an earlier civil war in England partly on the church, while the chronicler Hall dwells on Canterbury's selfish motives in urging Henry to war.[59] Dressed, probably, in the splendid robes of a medieval archbishop, Canterbury images those "devils" that Henry later describes, who

> Do botch and bungle up damnation
> With patches, colors, and with forms being fetch'd
> From glist'ring semblances of piety.
>
> (II.2.115)

Some have read the archbishop's speech on the bees' commonwealth as the consensus political philosophy in Shakespeare's time; but if there were devotees of Elizabeth as the queen bee, there were also many who had encountered the republican skepticism of Cicero's De Officiis (a text much read in Elizabethan grammar schools):

> Just as swarms of bees do not congregate in order to construct honeycombs, but devise honeycombs because they are by instinct swarming creatures, in the same way men apply their industry to actions and thought after they have formed communities according to an instinct much more powerful than that of bees. It is therefore clear that factual knowledge will be solitary and barren of results unless it is accompanied by the virtue that consists of protecting mankind, or, in other words, of promoting the social unity of the human race. The same condition holds true for courage. If courage does not function in a context of mutual benefit and human intercourse, it is hardly better than brutality and savagery. (I:57)

Oblivious to this higher sense of community, the bee-minded hierarchy do not return to the later scenes of Henry's victory and negotiations for peace. They seem put in the play to represent a dimension of self-interested hypocrisy behind the war. Henry's barely suppressed anger at this deception is apparent in his repeatedly reminding them of their sacred trust, using formal phrases invoking the deity.

Henry's coldness returns in his sentencing of the traitors, when he adopts the tone of the heavenly judge presiding over "Another fall of man" (II.2.142). It is this kind of primness that has led people to call him an "unlikeable" hero.[60] Many resent the king's deceiving the traitors in this scene (tricking them into self-condemnation by asking their advice on leniency for a drunk who reviled the king). In effect, Henry acts in conformity with Erasmus's Christian kingliness; for if the king must rule over free subjects, then ideally even the greatest criminals would freely condemn themselves. This takes a little contriving, perhaps at the expense of verisimilitude: although in 1 *Henry VI* Shakespeare indicates that the Cambridge plot is grounded in legitimate grievance, here the conspirators are merely seduced by French promises.[61] An uneasy ceremoniousness also creates a rather hollow feeling during the last fifty lines. Exeter arrests each traitor using the formulaic language of the law: "I arrest thee of high treason, by the name of. . . ." Each man in turn utters his last words and awaits the inevitable sentence. To enhance the sense of awe in these fifty lines, Shakespeare has Henry use the name of God no less than seven times—probably more reminding than necessary of the sacrilege implicit in overthrowing one's government.

These first two acts disclose a court atmosphere devoid of trust and love, an extension of the "enforced ceremony" of Brutus's famous lines on friendship (*JC*, IV.2.21). A sign of the deceit and treachery in the first half of the play, the language of ceremony remains part of Henry's mask (as in the rather bombastic speech to the people of Harfleur) until the self-examination of Act IV. It signifies less his own than his kingdom's insecurity that an open heart and free expression are impossible for him until then.[62]

This point can address two of the most frequent complaints about the king's character, even from some of his partisans—his coldness and, what perhaps is the same thing, his self-righteous piety. Almost everyone agrees that these qualities have disappeared by the last act, though Shakespeare may not make the change wholly convincing. The coldness in Acts I and II chiefly comes from seeing Henry in the company of enemies and those who would use him—the bishops, the traitors, and the French ambassador. To some extent, it is also owing to Henry's isolating himself in his "new garment." Except for Exeter, a councilor rather than a friend, the king is without companions or confidants; one feels this lack all the more severely because of Hal's fellowship in the earlier plays. Yet the histories, not unlike the tragedies, assert the dependence of even the greatest members of the commonwealth upon others.[63] Henry shows he has learned this dependency only hours before his victory, when he makes the offer to his soldiers.

Piety actually comes to Henry in this play, and it may well be that it completes a Renaissance "education of the prince." Hal

learns temperance and fortitude in Part One, justice and wisdom
in Part Two. In *Henry V*, his placing the outcome of the battle in
God's hands endows him with "religion as well as the cardinal
four [virtues], rounding out the five royal virtues listed by Elizabeth" in her first address to parliament.[64] This is not the uncritical
piety of Henry VI, so removed from the world that he cannot
discern fraudulent piety; nor is it "superstititous"[65] simply because it leads him to pray for his soldiers in battle. Yet a subtle
difference exists between Henry's formal declarations early in the
play—those associating himself with God[66]—and his insistence
after the battle that God deserves all the credit for the victory. This
humility, this acknowledgment of his humanity, accounts for his
self-conscious plainness wooing Katherine in the last act. What
some see as the unadorned brutality of warfare could equally be
the abandonment of the formalities of majesty. Now ceremony
belongs to God. Henry celebrates the victory at Agincourt with
almost obsessive self-effacement:

> O God, thy arm was here!
> And not to us, but to thy arm alone,
> Ascribe we all! . . .
> . . . Take it, God,
> For it is none but thine!
>
> (IV.8.101–7)

The Chorus reports that on his return to England Henry refused
to parade the symbols of victory, a last abjuring of ceremony,
"giving full trophy, signal, and ostent / Quite from himself to
God" (V. Chor. 21). To celebrate his victory, Henry orders not only
the traditional hymn of thanksgiving, "Te Deum," but also the
"Non nobis," Psalm 115 ("Not unto us, O Lord, not unto us, but
unto thy Name give glory."). The Geneva Bible describes this
psalm as "A praier of the faithful oppressed by idolatrous tyrants."
A marginal gloss adds, "Seeing that nether the matter nor the
forme can commend the idoles, it followeth that there is nothing
why they shulde be esteemed." As in the concluding battle of
Spenser's Legend of Justice, the same action resolves possibilities
for both tyranny and idolatry.

Liberation

In several respects the liberation in the second tetralogy resembles that in Spenser's Book V. Both undertake first to deliver the

body politic from the effects of private concupiscence, and in both a rehabilitation of honor joins with the public shaming of false knighthood. Then follows the need to deliver the state from the threat of civil discord, Duessa symbolizing the principle that is fleshed out in the rebellious Northumberland, Cambridge, Scrope, and Grey. Only in the final movement are the emphases different. Spenser shows the Christian commonwealth saved from external idolatries, Shakespeare, the self-denial that differentiates Christian king from world-king. The end of the sixteenth century brought apprehensiveness over absolutism in the state, a development that may explain Shakespeare's shift from the confident celebration of monarchy in *Henry V* to the troubled picture of the rise of tyranny in *Julius Caesar*.[67] If the Roman history play was written later, it may originate in a desire to show a purer form of autocracy, one independent of Christian virtues.

Henry several times mentions the antithesis of ideal kingship: the Turkish tyranny, the nightmare of total autocracy envisioned by Spenser, Erasmus, More, and, in their peculiar handling of Herod, the mystery playwrights. "Not Amurath an Amurath suceeds, But Harry Harry" (*2H4*, V.2.48). Henry even anticipates a son, "half French, half English, that shall go to Constantinople and take the Turk by the beard" (*H5*, V.2.202). The Turkish government proverbially stood for the difference between mixed and absolute monarchy: "Wherefore . . . if the prince of the Turkes (as it is written of him) doe repute all other his bondmen and slaves (him selfe and his sonnes onely freemen) a man may doubt whether his administration be to be accompted a common wealth or a kingdome, or rather to be reputed onely as one that hath under him an infinite number of slaves or bondmen among whom there is no right, law, nor common wealth compact, but oney the will of the Lorde and segnior."[68] Even in the conditions that most justify imposing his will on others—sedition in Act II and war in Act IV—Henry manages to keep alive the "compact" between king and subject.

Closer to events of the play, as noted in the early discussion of the French monarchomacy, the French government represented to many in Shakespeare's audience a "byword for tyranny."[69] Sir Roger Twysden observed that the French monarch "hath beene ever esteemed more absolute then the English," and Sir Thomas Smith traced the "absolute and tyrannical power and governement" there to the reign of Louis XI, whose warmaking Erasmus had deplored in the *Adagia*.[70] Whether this was an accurate assessment or not, the French monarchy was thought a virtual tyranny, and to this belief was imputed the "base and servile

behavior"[71] of the French commoners. Especially in the scene in
which Le Fer submits to Pistol, the play shows the playwright as
susceptible to this myth as anyone else. The French nobility are
every bit as devoted to honor as the English: "self-love, my liege,
is not so vile a sin as self-neglecting," says the Dauphin to his
father (II.4.75). But obsession with honor, like its neglect, brings
failure. The French nobles' self-love causes them to underestimate
the enemy and, in the scene of their rout (IV.5), leads them to
blame their own troops for their failure. Their arrogance has in it
something of Coriolanus, with his unreflecting identification of
plebians as slaves. They prove unable to lead their men back into
order, even though they still have superior numbers (lines 20–22).
The epic qualities of *Henry V* require portrayal of a worthy adversary, a requirement that Shakespeare satisfies in the French
scenes. But the great flaw of the Dauphin and his nobles is their
constitutional inability (in every sense of the phrase) to grant the
liberties that Henry allows his own troops.

The "soul of goodness in this evil" of war emerges in the
concord of the final scene. The harmony of peace—as in the
mystery plays of Pharaoh and Herod, Henry's "Peace" is the first
word in this scene—comes to the body politic with the successful
treaty, and to the private life of the king by his successful wooing
of Katherine. The cold formality of the opening acts is exchanged
for the warm rituals of peacemaking and matrimony. The French
queen voices hope for the harmony of opposites, "that this day /
Shall change all griefs and quarrels into love" (line 20). Burgundy's long speech on "mangled peace, / Dear nurse of all the
arts, plenties, and joyful births" (line 34) looks back to traditional
humanist ideas on peace, especially those found in Erasmus's
Complaint of Peace and the *Panegyric to Philip.* This play shares yet
another feature with Spenser's Book V in the eschatological un-
dertones of the ending. The imagery of Burgundy's speech serves
this purpose, partly borrowed from Isaiah's vision of a returned
golden age.[72] So does the projected marriage and the French
king's prayer for "Christian-like accord" between the two nations.
The golden age is just momentarily glimpsed, in a "Small time,"
as the Chorus says; but we see enough to realize the advantages of
brotherhood over war in helping it return.

Julius Caesar

The customary grouping of Shakespeare's plays does not
obscure the kinship between a "history" like *Henry V* and a

tragedy like *Julius Caesar*, especially since the two plays first appeared within a few months of each other. The Chorus of *Henry V* wished godspeed to "the general of our gracious empress," the Earl of Essex in Ireland. On a September afternoon, at about the time Essex was abandoning the field, a Swiss visitor named Thomas Platter saw "die Tragedy vom ersten Keyser Julio Caesare," almost certainly Shakespeare's play, in a thatch-roofed building south of the Thames. To examine these as two of Shakespeare's "political plays" (Palmer, Richmond) is to acknowledge the Renaissance habit of comparing ancient and modern. Shakespeare himself draws such a comparison when the Chorus of *Henry V* describes the king's victorious return to London:

> The mayor and all his brethren in best sort,
> Like to the senators of th'antique Rome,
> With the plebeians swarming at their heels,
> Go forth and fetch their conqu'ring Caesar in.
>
> (V. Chor. 25–28)

Here is the mythical well-ordered Rome at the height of Caesar's service to the state. Caesar's tragedy begins with the memories of these happy triumphs, much as that long saga of Henry VI's catastrophe opens with memories of the hero of Agincourt. *Julius Caesar* enacts the collapse of a republic into tyranny, an event brought on when simple adulation of the king, like that depicted in the Chorus, degenerates into king-worship. The swarming plebeians (two years later, when Essex tried to rally them, they would refuse to swarm) play a more important role in this play than in the histories, except for Cade's rebellion. They typify the "exorbitant and excessive" mob that Milton refers to in excoriating civil idolatry.

Although the play does not make Caesar alone responsible for this political tragedy, humanists before Shakespeare were more inclined to place the blame squarely with him, and it is their Caesar, in addition to Plutarch's, that guides the playwright. Much as they recognized the intelligence and wit of the author Caesar, humanists, especially in England,[73] rejected the tyrant. The result is the kind of sympathetic dispraise, not unlike his characterization by Shakespeare, that shows up in Thomas More's passing comment in a 1516 letter to Erasmus: "If Caesar in the olden days had combined this [i.e., Greek] moderate way of thinking with his lofty spirit, he would beyond doubt have won more glory by preserving the republic than he got from all the people whom he conquered and subdued."[74] Caesar's wit furnished examples for Erasmus's *Apophthegmata* and *Lingua*, but Caesar the tyrant was a thief and cutthroat. In his preface to Suetonius, Erasmus recalls how "the name of emperor . . . crept into the world from a disgraceful origin, from criminal activity in Julius first, more criminal after him in Octavius, Lepidus, and Antonius." With the Republic's demise, "Gone was the authority of the senate, gone the laws, gone the liberty of the Roman people. An emperior thus created ruled a world ensalved, and was himself the slave of creatures such as no honest man would be willing to have among the slaves in this household. The emperor was feared by the senate, and lived himself in terror of that criminal military mob. . . . A glorious monarchy indeed, such as all men might respect!"[75] Shakespeare's audiences are privileged witnesses to the awful transition that Erasmus describes.

As in *Richard II* the participants often seem not to know the consequences or meanings of acts. This failure is affirmed in symbols of misperception: at the beginning Caesar cannot hear, at the end Cassius cannot see, or interpret what he sees. In the middle a man who thinks he is to be deified becomes a "bleeding piece of earth," and what follows in the forum is an almost farcical series of misunderstandings and misinterpretations—for everyone, that is, except the theater-loving Antony. Nor is the audience any more secure in its knowledge, especially regarding the title character. As Gayle Greene has said, "our inability to know the 'real' Caesar confuses our judgment of the assassination and the assassins."[76] Greene's use of Montaigne's "Vanities of Wars" in her commentary helpfully reveals possibilities for irony and self-delusion that Shakespeare's contemporaries read in history. Boldness is a pagan virtue, even more, a Roman one. Missing from Caesar, Brutus, and the other bold men in this play is what More called a "moderate way of thinking." At a deeper level than the much-discussed irreconcilability of words and things lies a failure of *anagnorisis*, of that considered, selfless reflection upon things found in Henry's speech on ceremony.

The opening scene is the first of several that show the common people ignorantly helping to shape Rome's evil destiny. It also provides a commentary on the political situation somewhat like the gardener's scene in *Richard II*. The tribunes, vestige of now-extinct republicanism, represent that balance between monarchy and mob rule so highly prized in republican thought. Erasmus's Folly describes the spectacle of the mob and the great man, who is "to seek the applause of so many fools, to be pleased by their shouts of approval, to be led around in triumph as if he were some public spectacle for the people, and to have his statue placed in the market-place. . . . Add to this . . . the divine honors paid to these nobodies, and the public deification of even the most evil tyrant" (p. 117). Working against the tide of folly, the tribunes seek to have the "images" of Caesar "disrobed" of their "ceremonies." This language points back to the clothes and idol imagery of *Henry V*. And yet the tone of Flavius and Marullus here betokens an almost Puritanical resentment of the crowd's holiday mood in itself. It seems that the tribunes' resentment may owe less to political conviction than to envy of Caesar's elevation with their own loss of influence. Later the two officials, "for pulling scarfs off Caesar's images, are put to silence" (I.2.285). Personal jealousies aside, then, the tribunes' fears are well grounded. Working men walk idle, without their customary tradesmen's clothing, on a laboring day. The restraints required in a sound society (of the Elizabethan model) are on the point of dissolving. This early moment of conflict reveals that Rome's troubles have begun well in advance of the play. The cobbler's punning description of himself as "a mender of bad soles" betrays the serious underlying problem of irreverence to the spiritual—to Pompey's memory, to Roman authority, ultimately to the commons' own dignity as free men. The plebeians have exchanged true reverence for a kind of hollow worship (Caesar's image is twice mentioned in the closing lines of the scene) of the god who would keep all Rome "in servile fearfulness" (line 75).

Yet in the very next scene the god proves all too human: deaf in one ear, somewhat uxorious (his first word is his wife's name), meticulous in carrying out the ritual care for his wife's barrenness, undoubtedly so as to establish a dynasty once he has secured power. Caesar is a man betrayed by those he loves, but there is remarkably little to love in him. Missing are all those virtues expounded in the histories: Caesar's industry, his athletic ability (mentioned by Cassius only as an instance of Caesar's overblown reputation), and especially his learning. This first impression paves the way for Cassius's later opinion of him:

> he is superstitious grown of late,
> Quite from the main opinion he held once
> Of fantasy, of dreams, and ceremonies.

> (II.1.195–97)

The people's idolatry of Caesar finds expression a second time offstage, when the shouting crowd punctuates Brutus's and Cassius's dialogue. Casca later tells how "the rabblement hooted, and clapped their chapt hands, and threw up their sweaty nightcaps" (I.2.243), echoing the tribunes' contempt of the mob. Working the commoners, checking the nobility (Brutus and Cassius are literally outsiders in this scene), Caesar is shaping the classic tyranny portrayed in Cassius's emblem of the Colossus with "petty men" at his feet. Antony, in his peculiar role of stage manager and high priest, orchestrates this display of *latria*, as he will later manipulate the "rabblement" at Caesar's funeral. Here the ritual is baring the throat and repeatedly refusing the crown; later it will be the showing of the mantle and the bloody corpse.

The tribunes found in Caesar's influnce a "servile fearfulness," but that fear, the awe that comes with idolatry, permeates all ranks of society in these early acts of the tragedy, including the nobles:

> BRUTUS. What means this shouting? I do fear the people
>   Choose Caesar for their king.
> CASSIUS.   Ay, do you fear it?

Caesar is also a victim of this fear. Waking after the stormy night, he is moved to order a sacrifice in an effort to know the meaning of the storm. Even he surrenders to the fearfulness that the tribunes sense in Rome at large. There is no denying the power of his brief meditation on fear ("Cowards die many times . . . ," II.2.32); but does Caesar not protest too much against fear? "Would he were fatter! but I fear him not. / . . . I rather tell thee what is to fear'd / Than what I fear; for always I am Caesar" (II.2.198, 211), "Caesar should be a beast without a heart / If he should stay at home today for fear" (II.2.42). "I am constant as the northern star," but "men are flesh and blood and apprehensive" (III.1.60, 67).

The terrible storm and its portents deserve to be feared, especially in that no one understands what these signs mean. Act II, scene 2, centers on this difficulty of interpretation, as Shakespeare unhistorically compresses several omens into a single moment the morning of the assassination. Calphurnia interprets the storm as a token of Caesar's death: "When beggars die there are no comets seen; / The heavens themselves blaze forth the death of princes" (II.2.30)—a divine-right notion that might have come from Richard II. Caesar similarly constellates himself in the "northern star" image of his boastful last speech. Yet to confirm this interpretation, Caesar must order a sacrifice for augury. Back comes a new omen, a beast without a heart, prompting two contradictory interpretations. Then there is Calphurnia's dream of Caesar's bleeding statue, again receiving two possible and mutually exclusive interpretations. Caesar wavers, though willful in his wavering: "Caesar shall go forth" (lines 10, 48); "Caesar will not come" (line 68); "Give me my robe, for I will go" (line 107). A conflict between imperiousness and indecisiveness informs this scene, felt against the background of inscrutable supernatural events. It is a moment permeated with the irony of human power, especially when claiming alliance with divinity.

When Caesar contrasts himself with "flesh and blood" men in his last speech, he already thinks of himself as divine. This striking expression of the irony of his power is made all the more acute by the conspirators, who kneel (III.1.34, 75) just before closing for the kill. As they clasp his legs in apparent supplication, Caesar does not discourage their awe as Henry does when he reminds his court that they are English, not Turkish. Instead he cries, "Hence! wilt thou lift up Olympus?" disclosing his own complicity in his apotheosis. Here and throughout his last speech he differs sharply from Henry. Rather than acknowledge his humanity, he chooses to stand on ceremony, oblivious to the meaning of the assassins' genuflection. At the moment of denying his kinship with ordinary mortals, moreover, Caesar is refusing an appeal for mercy, the paramount virtue of the Christian king.[77]

The ritual tone of Caesar's killing his long been recognized, especially since Brents Stirling's well-known essay on the play.[78] For Stirling the assassination is carried out so as to satisfy Brutus's wish to depersonalize and dignify the act by making it a rite. The conspirators must be "sacrificers, but not butchers." Nothing else could explain the conspirators' grisly washing of their hands in blood. Stirling also observes, especially in the first two scenes of the play, a process of "bringing serious ritual into great prominence, and of subjecting it to satirical treatment" (p. 207). Social gestures like shaking hands or sharing wine also lose their convivial significance during the play, to be restored only at the end.[79] Yet in hiding behind ceremonies, the conspirators, especially Brutus, prove as superstitious as the man they killed.

The meanings of "ceremony" in King Henry's soliloquy apply consistently to *Julius Caesar*, even with what seem to us peculiar usages. In no other of Shakespeare's plays does the word receive such diverse treatment, as if the playwright were consciously extending it to its limits. In Calphurnia's "I never stood on ceremonies," the word refers to portents; and in the tribunes' order to remove ceremonies from Caesar's image, it means symbols of reverence—corresponding more closely to Henry's "the sword, the mace, the crown imperial." In these two sense the word does not long survive Shakespeare in English. But these special senses concur with the more familiar one in referring to an outward sign of a spiritual condition. "Ceremony" always entails placing value on externals. Ceremony becomes a cause rather than a sign in *Julius Caesar*, and the resulting superstition prevents scrutinizing the spiritual condition, the rot of Rome, for what it is. A powerful force in this tragedy is "idol ceremony," be it the vacant-minded mob's image of Caesar, or Caesar's of himself, or (as I shall shortly explain) Brutus's own idols of the mind.

Ceremony serves both the theme of civil idolatry and the critique of Stoic virtue so often noted in the play. Because ceremony enhances the dignity of power and authority, setting the great man apart from others, it is requisite in the Stoic vision of human life, which subordinates feelings to moral obligation. As a Christian Stoic, George Chapman converted Marlowe's *Hero and Leander* into an allegory of duty and pleasure, introduced by a vision of the goddess Ceremony. She symbolizes, among other things, the mystification of political power. Drawn on her gown are "The snakie paths to each observed law"; she wears a "Pentackle" or mystic star "full of circles and strange characters." "Devotion, Order, State, and Reverence / Her shadowes were; Societie, Memorie." She exists to distinguish all classes and estates of men, to prevent "Confusion" from disturbing the sacred order of society. In one hand she holds a laurel rod, symbol of learning and discipline, "To beate back *Barbarisme*, and *Avarice*."[80] To Chapman, Ceremony is an absolute, a means to ensure order in human relations, private and public, without which there is no civilization. Nothing can be more unlike the questioning of ceremony by Henry V in a play that moves beyond order to the celebration of love. When Chapman takes over Marlowe's poem, human passion must yield to Platonic love, to the Ineffable as glimpsed in the wedding of Hymen and Eucharis. Hero and Leander, in this straitened allegory, must be punished for enjoying "substance without rites" (III.147). And yet *Richard II* and *Henry V* show the illusoriness of rites without substance: a king who does not govern, an army that may lack the heart to follow its king. In the world of *Julius Caesar* and the hearts of its principal characters there is no coming to terms with ceremony. Calphurnia's famous lines, "I never stood on ceremonies, / Yet now they fright me" (II.2.13), anticipate a movement in the opposite direction from that of *Henry V*. Ceremony has acquired a strange new power over citizen and Caesar alike, symptomatic of the relapse of a free republic into fear and servitude.

Each estate of Rome attempts to cure sickness with ceremony, the consequences being exactly opposite to those intended, supporting the tragic strategy of reversal. The plebeians in Shakespeare are much more of a mob than in Plutarch's account, "less consistent, less thoughtful; they have no part in the seduction of Brutus in the conspiracy; they respond in a wholly emotional way to whoever verbally assaults them."[81] Antony in effect turns their stupidity to his own uses by appealing to their idolatry, established in the first scene of the play.

This point requires some historical context. In the display of the mantle and the corpse—both of which "speak" to the crowd more effectively than words—lies an obvious parallel with the supposed superstitious worship of images and relics by sixteenth-century Catholics. The striking effectiveness of Antony's tactics with the common people brings to mind the controversies over the use of sensory aids to religion at this time. WilliamCovell, writing against the Puritan Josias Nichols, says that "the principall excellence of our religion being spirituall, is not easily observed, of the greatest number which are carnall; and therefore we propound not naked mysteries, but clothe them; that these offering to the sences a certaine maiestie, may be received of the minde with a greater reverence."[82] But Protestants on the left insisted that vestments, gestures, and images distracted especially the plebeians from hearing the word. In the year of Covell's book a Brownist tract urged the king to destroy "all monuments of Idolatry in garments or any other things . . . Because this being done, the people are more easily perswaded & drawne to the true worship of God in spirit and truth: Whereas otherwise they are stil nourished in superstition, and have means to be intised daily to more corruption."[83] These complaints about ritual often accompany the well-known tirades against play-acting, so it is no coincidence that Antony, the most astute ritual-maker in the play, the priest and impressario who "stages" the offering of the crown, is also a lover of masques and plays.

Liturgically speaking, Brutus's mistake at Caesar's funeral lies in not recognizing the power of the image to enhance the word. Antony's response is, as Stirling says, a kind of counterceremony (pp. 211–12), but the mantle of Caesar is less a "talisman" than an object of veneration. The Roman crowd, it is true, is lured away from Brutus by Antony's rhetoric; but they are finally convinced by the visual images of the mantle and the corpse. In fact this

episode in the story of Caesar is used by the conservative Jeremy
Taylor to show how "we are more moved by material and sensible
objects than by things merely speculative and intellectual, and
generals, even in spiritual things, are less perceived and less
motive than particulars." Taylor's illustration of this point strongly
suggests that he himself had seen a performance of Shakespeare's
play:

> It was a wise design of Mark Antony when he would stir up the
> people to revenge the death of Caesar, he brought his body to the
> pleading-place, he shewed his wounds, held up the rent mantle, and
> shewed them the garment that he put on that night in which he beat
> the Nervii. . . . And thus holy meditation produces the passions and
> desires it intends; it makes the object present and almost sensible; it
> renews the first passions by a fiction of imagination.[84]

The ensuing chaos and cultural dissolution, symbolized in the
murder of the poet Cinna, are the mass effect of a "fiction of
imagination" excited and unabated by reason—the consequences
of Antony's mastery of ceremonies. In killing Cinna chiefly because he has the same name as one of the conspirators, the
commoners exemplify the ignorance and superstition of confusing the name with the thing. Idolatry does not stop with the
mob, however; the last two acts show its encroachment upon the
aristocracy, especially the seemingly impervious Brutus and Cassius.

Outwardly Cassius is as liberated spiritually as he is politically.
He refuses to stand in awe of so human a thing as Caesar, scoffs at
Caesar's new leanings toward superstition and at Casca's fear of
the portents on the night of the Lupercalia. His calling Caesar a
Colossus may echo antimonarchist writings. The *Vindiciae* says,
"Take away but the basis to this giant, and like the Rhodian
Colossus, he presently tumbles to the ground and falls to pieces."
Also Etienne de la Boétie's *Un discours de la servitude volontaire*,
often considered a monarchomach text, says of the tyrant, "I do
not advise you to shake or overturn him, forbear only to support
him, and you will see him like a great Colossus . . . fall . . . and be
broken in pieces."[85] Cassius seems as thoroughly fearless as the
republican heroic code requires. Yet his boldness does not extend
to leading the conspiracy himself, for he clearly needs Brutus and
the other nobles. His bluff Epicurean independence conceals a
certain diffidence. Behind his final conversion to belief in omens
(V.1.75—"ceremonies" in Calphurnia's sense) lie long-suppressed

doubts about his materialism. Cassius "loves no plays," Caesar reports (I.2.203), but after the killing it is Cassius who envisions the "lofty scene" being enacted on future stages (III.1.112). He eventually proves so captive to illusion that in his last battle he allows his pessimism to control his view of Titinius's foray. As though determined to fail, he perceives events through the eyes of his slave, as enslaved to sense as Antony's crowd at Rome. The final irony in his story comes with the unsought freedom that Pindarus gains through killing him. The former slave is free—but for what? There is a contrast with Henry's freeing of his own soldiers on the battlefield, the crucial difference being that here liberation comes after defeat, in a setting of despair. No sharing between leader and follower occurs, no *communitas*, on the field at Philippi. The freeing of Pindarus merely continues the dissolving social bond between classes that began in the unruly crowd of Act 1, scene 1.[86]

Brutus alone seems untouched by fear and illusion in the play, a solitary exemplar of the old Roman values. More than once his tyrant-vanquishing ancestor is mentioned. He alone of the conspirators appears moved by "general honest thought / And common good to all" (V.5.71). Yet in certain ways Brutus resembles Caesar himself, as Norman Rabkin has shown: both put country before self, yet both possess "a self-destructive vanity and a tendency to play to the galleries," and are "predictably unable to relax a self-destructive moral rigidity."[87] Such vanity might be called a form of self-idolatry, one which Brutus shares with Caesar in at least two senses. As others have observed, Brutus takes as much pride in his honor and honesty as Caesar did in his courage (recall his imperious use of the first person in the funeral oration, or such gratuitous outbursts as "I am arm'd so strong in honesty," in IV.3.67). On the other hand, such overinsistence perhaps implies secret doubts on this point, as is the case with Caesar's often maintaining his fearlessness. Brutus "has to the end . . . no insight into his own inner life"[88] because he cannot acquire the self-knowledge that comes from knowing other people. Cassius's mirror image (I.2.54–70) can mean that from Brutus's standpoint their friendship is really a form of self-worship. It is unlikely that Brutus could test his inner self by holding it up to Cassius's mirror in view of Cassius's real intent—Brutus is to be "wrought," even "seduced" (I.2.306).

Cassius can work him because he recognizes that Brutus's mind is enslaved to its own preconceptions, its own "idols" as Bacon called them. Grand conceptions determine Brutus's actions: "Did not great Julius bleed for justice' sake?" (IV.3.19); "Let's all cry, Peace, freedom, and liberty!" (III.1.110). Brutus conceives liberty and justice not according to experience and critical thought but on the basis of the linguistic, philosophical, and psychological fictions that Bacon warned against. The myth of his ancestor, the flattery of friends, the fear of what Caesar might do: these motives show all too prominently in him. Surely Cassius's mirror is a metaphor of the idolatrous solipsism ("idol" from the Greek *eidolon*, image) that is Brutus's special malady in this disordered state. During the assassination Brutus converts his own myth of justice and liberty into a ritual; but the ritual is hollow because the god to whom Caesar is sacrificed simply embodies Brutus's own prejudices.[89]

Brutus's ritualization dignifies the murder only for those inclined to accept human sacrifice as a high-minded act. It would be difficult to find a member of Shakespeare's original audience so inclined. Suppose the ritualist's reading is taken a step farther: the bloody rite is nightmarishly inconsistent with the conceptions of "peace, freedom, and liberty" that the regicides proclaim. Elizabethan presses and pulpits were arguing a similar inconsistency between spiritual freedom and the "carnal ceremonies" of Catholic worship. A few years after the writing of *Henry V* and *Julius Caesar*, a group of Puritans pleaded with the new king that "it is a special part of that *Christian libertie* which Christ hath purchased for us by his death, and which all Christians are bound to stand for: that the service wee are to doe unto God now is not mysticall, ceremoniall and carnall . . . but plaine and spirituall."[90] As with the body of Christians, so with the body politic. In point of fact the killing of Caesar and the counterceremony of Antony do not bring about true liberty, but dissolve the social matrix that makes liberty possible. If Henry V is not exactly modeled on Christ the king, he is at least the Christian king, leading his country, his army, and even his enemies into a concord that is impossible in Caesar's idolatrous Rome

The radical paganism of Caesar's and Brutus's ceremonies stands in opposition to sound ritual, creating division rather than union among its participants. In *Henry V* union finally comes about with the rites of marriage. In *Julius Caesar* it comes sadly in the closing lines, with anticipation of the "rites of burial." Whatever evils the former republic may expect, the play says, at least its fury of civil war is spent. The ruler of the state, in his desire for absolute power, indulged in a fancied apotheosis. The commons were willing to cooperate, first in erecting the idol, later in avenging its profanation. The aristocracy either contributed to the myth of Caesar for their own advantage (Antony), or indulged in iconoclasm, following an unexpressed wish to establish a competing sect (Brutus). In Act 2, scene 2, Caesar appears first in all his humanity—"Enter Julius Caesar, in his nightgown"—then leaves for the Forum having called for his official robe (1.107).[91] This is the "gorgeous garment, Majesty" that Henry V speaks of, soon to lie at the base of Pompey's statute soaked in its wearer's blood. As so often in Shakespeare, clothes symbolize the roles assumed by our essential, common humanity. The nightgown covers the private man, the toga the statesman; the mantle, at Mark Antony's urging, the mythic man, fearless hero, public benefactor. Discerning the man beneath the clothes is one of the endless challenges and delights of Shakespeare's plays, especially the plays of kingship. Henry IV, as obsessed with his public image as Caesar is, speaks of "My presence, like a robe pontifical, / Ne'er seen but wond'red at" (1H4, III.2.56), giving his son an object lession in ceremonial, not real, government. There may be a kind of magic in the garments of a king, but if so it is acquired, like that in Prospero's cloak, from the long study, energy, and wisdom of the wearer. Essential to that magic is understanding the mortality that the king shares with his subjects, as well as the briefness of his tenure in authority.

5

Milton and Civil Idolatry

"A Servile Yoke of Liturgie"

Not until Milton, in England, does a major poet make the competing claims of the state and the spirit one of his life's great themes. In a sense history propelled Milton on this course, for the debate of the century turned on the union of spiritual and civil power in the person of one monarch. The desacralizing of monarchy that would culminate in the execution of Charles I was thoroughly launched. From the viewpoint of persecuted Christian sects, the Stuarts often differed little from the imperial cults that persecuted early Christians. It is an innovation of this period that, whereas John Foxe's first readers drew comparisons between pagan and Catholic Rome, in the decades from the Laudian reforms to the Test Acts suffering believers saw their own repressive monarchy as the reincarnation of the Caesars. The trial of Faithful at Vanity Fair occurs in both the court of Pilate and the assizes of Bedford. Caesar tyrannizes over English Christians in some of the mystery plays, but not until Milton's century does Roman emperor-worship invade English soil.

For Milton the English Civil War had to do with the belief that the will of God is revealed in the individual believer's soul, not in the halls of Westminster or Canterbury. His generation's most serious political beliefs responded to a sense of the sacred, a way of looking at politics originating well before Milton. It is possible nowadays to overlook the interdependencies of civil and sacred then—to reduce the Puritan movement, for example, merely to a disguised economic revolt.[1] It seems difficult to believe that to many people then the most crucial issues of the Puritan-Anglican conflict, far more disturbing than, say, the doctrine of predestination,[2] centered on the Protestant demythologizing of liturgy. During most of the sixteenth and seventeenth centuries, English Christians were capable of violence and heroic self-sacrifice over the use of the surplice, the marriage ring, the sign of the cross, the practice of kneeling at communion—all of which came to be known in the shorthand of controversy as "the ceremonies." Thus on his way south to London the newly declared King James I was handed a petition sponsored, it was said, by over a thousand ministers of England, "all groaning as under a common burden of human rites and ceremonies." This "Millenary Petition" led to the Hampton Court Conference, where Puritans aired their differences over liturgy, the state of the clergy, and church government. There James fixed much of his attention upon the issues of the bishops', therefore the king's, authority in church government. At one point the king cut off the Puritans' debate with the declaration, "No bishop, no king!" The second day of the conference James repeated himself at his summing-up: "No bishop, no king, as before I said. Neither do I thus speak at random without ground, for I have observed since my comming to England, that some preachers before me can be content to pray for James king of England, Scotland, France and Ireland, defender of the faith, but as for supreme governor, in all causes and over all persons, (as well ecclesiastical as civil) they passe over that with silence, and what cut they have been of I after learned." Within the decade, James would be telling his Parliament that "Kings are justly called gods for that they exercise a manner or resemblance of divine power upon earth." During the ensuing years the king's "supreme governorship," not to mention his divinity, underwent a searching test in the churches and Parliament alike. By Milton's time, "No bishop, no king" would prove prophetic, Jeremy Taylor lamenting, as he quoted James's adage, "They that hate bishops have destroyed monarchy."[3]

Spenser's Legend of Justice and Shakespeare's *Julius Caesar* illustrate the danger to king and subject alike when all power is invested in the ruler. In More's epigrams and the mystery plays the figure of Herod represented worldly power corrupted by pride. It was almost inevitable that Milton should associate Charles I, claiming divine right, with "Herod . . . eat'n up of Wormes for suffering others to compare his voice to the voice of God."[4] Yet in most cases of tyranny Milton believed the people as guilty as the monarch. In this he shares with Spenser a distinct aristocratic bias. His major political writings take up the theme that people enjoy subservience—in Henry V's words, the king "is less happy being fear'd Than they in fearing." In Milton's prose tracts the common people are increasingly seen as unreliable, unprincipled, susceptible to flattering rhetoric, much like the mob in *Julius Caesar*. The popular escape from freedom translated in

Milton's mind to an escape from right reason and consciousness. This theme is already evident in his comments on "the new-vomited Paganisme of sensuall idolatry," as he calls Laudian worship in his earliest antiprelatical tract (*CPW*, 1:519). People enjoy candles, vestments, genuflection, and so forth because they can take comfortable refuge in custom and the pleasures of conforming to authority. Custom and ceremony are the enemies of consciousness. Ritualism is worship decayed to idolatry. Worship of God consists, for Milton, not of rituals but prayers, and even these must not be allowed to "harden into a crust of Formalitie" in fixed compositions. Milton differs here from the *Abridgement* of Wollebius, one of his most consistent sources for the *Christian Doctrine*. The Swiss theologian divided religion into "the Form or rite whereby God will be worshipped in his Church; and the Sanctification of his Name, all the rest of our life." Milton changes the first part of this in his version: "The parts of religion are invocation or adoration, and the sanctification of the divine name in all the circumstances of life" (*CPW*, 6:699).

Milton's antiritualism[5] is consistent with the practice of religion in his Paradise, where Adam and Eve pray, and only pray, "other Rites / Observing none, but adoration pure / Which God likes best" (*PL*, 4:736). Elsewhere in the epic when the word is used (never in the singular), "rites" refers either to idolatrous worship (as in the "wanton rites" of Peor or the rites of Hymen in the "tents of wickedness," I.144; XI.591), or to the ceremonial worship of the Jews , to be abrogated by Christ (XI.440; XII.321, 244, 534), or to the "rites of love" (IV.742; VIII.487; X.994), physical acts that are inherently shrouded in mystery, and that may be the only human acts that *do* put us in touch with the sacred.[6] There remain the "rites" of angelic worship (VII.149) in the "Temple" before the revelation of the Son. This would seem an instance of Milton's invented typology, shadowing the ceremonial worship of the Jews before Christ's coming. On the whole there is nothing in the poem that sets Milton at variance with his stated beliefs on worship in the prose works.[7]

Ritual, a social act, frees us from the limitations of self and tribe, making us aware of our role in the *communitas*, the bond of all humanity.[8] Yet in this formulation Milton would object that to leave out the self is to excise the voice of the spirit in the virtuous heart. The structure of *Paradise Regained*, it will be argued, is founded on the self-knowledge and self-sufficiency of Christ. No social force should presume to mediate between the self and God. In the chapter on the Book of Common Prayer in *Eikonoklastes*,

Milton writes, "there is no doubt but that, wholesom matter, and good desires rightly conceav'd in the heart, wholesom words will follow of themselves." As often as "the Priest puts on his Gown and Surplice, so constantly doth his praier put on a servile yoke of Liturgie." As with vestments so with prescribed or set prayers: "to imprison and confine by force, into a Pinfold of sett words, those two most unimprisonable things, our Prayers and that Divine Spirit of utterance that moves them, is a tyranny that would have longer hands then those Giants who threatn'd bondage to Heav'n." Even the Lord's Prayer is not immune to this charge in the *Christian Doctrine*, being "a pattern or model, rather than a formula to be repeated verbatim either by the apostles or by the churches today."[9] This is not to say that religion is merely intellectual for Milton. He advocates a private worship accommodating the heart and feelings as much as the mind. In spontaneous or "voluntary prayer," he says, "at least for words & matter, he who prays must consult first with his heart; which in likelyhood may stir up his affections." In set prayers, however, "having both words and matter readie made to his lips," the worshipper's "affections grow lazy, and com not up easilie at the call of words not thir own" (*CPW*, 3:506–7). In this respect, at least, Milton would have been surprised to hear that his sensibility was "dissociated," for he required the conformity of head and heart as fully as that of word and thing. The mere forms of words resemble the empty set prayer, which "also having less intercours and sympathy with a heart wherein it was not conceav'd saves it self the labour of so long a journey downward, and flying up in hast on the specious wings of formalitie, if it fall not back again headlong, in stead of a prayer which was expected, presents God with a sett of stale and empty words" (*CPW*, 3:507). The Platonic metaphor of flight was used a decade earlier in a similar context: the soul "overbodied" by liturgical trappings gives up her flight; she is said to have "bated her wings apace downeward: and finding the ease she had from her visible, and sensuous collegue the body in performance of *Religious* duties, her pineons now broken, . . . forgot her heavenly flight, and left the dull, and droyling carcas to plod on in the old rode, and drudging Trade of outward conformity" (*CPW*, 1:522).

The images of flight look back to the Neoplatonic religious poetry of the Renaissance, especially Spenser's *Hymns*. Yet with respect to the created world the philosophical grounds of *Paradise Lost* are not Platonic. The earth is real, a "shadow of heaven" only in the sense of a foreshadowing, consistent with the typological thinking behind the epic: "Milton substitutes for the ontological ascent of Neoplatonism the historical and psychological ascent of Christianity from 'shadowy Types to Truth,' the Garden to the 'Paradise within,' the Law to the Gospel, the carnal to the spiritual, outward observance to inward holiness."[10] The Platonic metaphor of flight is itself a metaphor for another kind of ascent. Since the Redemption "all corporeal resemblances of inward holiness and beauty are now past."[11] Milton dismantled the Laudian argument (which predates Laud by centuries) that people, especially the "unlearned," need a corporeal, ceremonial, outward religion. He writes that people are not so "mistaught" as the bishops think, for they often know more than their clergy (even though, he might later add, they often lack the will to act on their knowledge). "We read in our Saviours time," he says, "that the common people had a reverent esteeme of him," even though their clergy did not (CPW, 1:690). Faith does not need "the weak and fallible office of the Senses, to be either the Ushers, or Interpreters, of heavenly Mysteries, save where our Lord himselfe in his Sacraments ordain'd" (CPW, 1:519–20). The sacred is inward, spiritual, and devoid of any need for human rites, Milton believed; if anything, the hierarchy was engaged in a Satanic venture to seduce the people away from the truth through their corporeal rites, to make the inward outward. Their chief instrument to this end was monarchy, with all its own ceremonial adornments designed to dazzle and to deprive men of reason, therefore liberty. "Then you are amazed," he tells Salmasius, " 'that those who have beheld the king in Parliament seated under that canopy of silk and gold could have doubted whether majesty belonged to the king or to Parliament.' The men you speak of must have been doubters indeed not to be moved by so brilliant an argument drawn from the canopy of heaven, or even better 'the canopy of silk and gold.' " Such statements, he goes on, betray an unreasoning mind: "Against those whose hearts are clouded by superstition or whose minds are so dazzled by the very idea of gazing on the royal splendor that they can see no brillance or magnificence in honest virtue and freedom, it would be quite useless to bring the weapons of reason or argument or example" (CPW, 4:506–7). Mammon, in Paradise Lost, even before the angelic fall could not look at the glory of heaven, so fascinated was he with the gold paving stones under his feet (I.681). These complaints against custom and corporeality in religious worship are thus one with Milton's demystification of kingship in the later poetry and political writings.

Civil Idolatry in the Prose Works

Perhaps a decade before he spoke of the common people's susceptibility "not to a religious only, but to a civil kind of idolatry in idolizing their kings,"[12] Milton had begun forming his ideas on this subject. His research into English history suggested that the nation's monarchy had swollen beyond its original limits. In his commonplace book, between 1640 and 1642, he wrote: "Concerning the kings of Britain, Gildas says that they were anointed as kings, but not by God. p 199. Contrary to what the people now think, namely that all kings are anointed of God" (*CPW*, 1:474). Even earlier, in one of the few original passages in the commonplace book, Milton complains that the kings "scarcely recognize themselves as mortals," except on the day they die and the day they are crowned, when, however, "they feign humanity and gentleness, in the hope of capturing the voice of the people" (p. 431). Two entries under "King" (1637–1638) refer to the worship that the Roman emperors demanded for themselves (p. 437). This attention to the religious aspect of monarchy explains why, under the title "Subditus" (subject or citizen), Milton has made cross-references to *king, idolatry,* and *sedition.*[13] If Milton's republicanism was developing at this time, during the years just before and after the Italian journey,[14] the commonplace book shows that his political opinions were closely related to his ideas on religious worship.

The first explicitly political tract, *The Tenure of Kings and Magistrates,* appeared a few weeks after the death of King Charles. Milton cautions his readers on the potential for idolatry in kingship, using those instances of self-denying Roman emperors that had been familiar in humanist writings. Still, Milton does admit that there can be just monarchs: "Look how great a good and happiness a just King is, so great a mischiefe is a Tyrant" (*CPW*, 3:212). In earlier times flattery and ostentation were "not admitted by Emperours and Kings of best note" (*CPW*, 3:202). *Tenure* also adopts a relatively mild tone concerning "the people." The exhortation that precedes the citing of authorities is partly addressed to the people (that is, the majority), along with the presbyterians and the ministers of England. These are the nation's three erring camps in its current political confusion, though there is still hope that they will reunited for the common good: "God, as we have cause to trust, will put other thoughts into the people: (*CPW*, 3:236).

The contrast in *Eikonoklastes* is stark. If the exhortation of *Tenure* voiced at least some tentative words to the people, there were none in the work published the following October. As is well known, in his later years Milton virtually denied that the majority could ever acquire a true understanding of liberty.[15] This pessimism was fueled by the enormous popularity of *Eikon Basilike*, the book supposedly containing the last meditations of Charles I, but soon to be exposed as a piece of royalist propaganda. The opening paragraphs of Milton's long attack on this book are written with "the people" in mind: it is they "who through custom, simplicity, or want of better teaching" admire the king; theirs are "the minds of weaker men" being worked by cunning monarchists. The very name of king "needs no more among the blockish vulgar, to make it [*Eikon Basilike*] wise, and excellent, and admir'd, nay to set it next the Bible" (*CPW*, 3:339). Wave after wave of this demophobia returns in the treatise until the final paragraph, which was even more sharply barbed with the additions of 1650 (Milton added all after "rabble"): the king is accused of trying

> to catch the worthless approbation of an inconstant, irrational, and Image-doting rabble; that like a credulous and hapless herd, begott'n to servility, and inchanted with these popular institutes of Tyranny, subscrib'd with a new device of the Kings Picture at his praiers, hold out both thir eares with such delight and ravishment to be stigmatiz'd and board through in witness of thir own voluntary and beloved baseness. (p. 601)

Such delightful raillery suggests that Milton may not have been as cold to his task as either his biographer or his own opening disclaimer would indicate.[16]

The religious language in the passage just quoted (*Image doting, credulous, inchanted, ravishment*, and the allusion to the miracle of stigmata) is worth considering in the light of the subject under discussion. The sin of idolatry lies with the majority. People "are ready to fall flatt and give adoration to the Image and Memory of this man" as Catholics would to a saint (p. 344). The sin was encouraged by Charles himself and his adherents, especially the episcopal clergy. It was easy enough to construe Charles's wish for sainthood as a Caesarean craving for godhead. Cooperating in this venture were the royalist nobility and bishops, "commending and almost adoring" his book (p. 340). These, especially the clergy, are the "Deifying friends that stood about him" in his last days (p. 364), "a crew of lurking raylers, who . . . take it so currishly that I should dare tell abroad the secrets of thir *Aegyptian Apis*" (p. 363).[17] These "now mourn for him as for *Tamuz*" (p. 365).

Just as Milton has grown intolerant of the people in *Eikonoklastes*, he concedes nothing to monarchy, in contrast to *Tenure*. Now all kingship tends to devolve into the condition of civil idolatry. Milton cites the danger in royal courts "of Flatterers, and them that deifie the name of King" (p. 484). History shows kings allied to the Satanic, not the divine order:

> We may have learnt from both sacred History, and times of Reformation, that the Kings of this World have both ever hated, and instinctively fear'd the Church of God. Whether it be for that thir Doctrin seems much to favour two things to them so dreadful, Liberty and Equality, or because they [the church of God] are the Children of that Kingdom, which, as ancient Prophesies have foretold, shall in the end break to peeces and dissolve all thir great power and Dominion. (p. 509)

Erasmus had quoted from the same episode in Scripture (1 Samuel 8:11–18) in giving God's own definition of a tyrant, adding, "And do not be exercised because he calls his 'king' instead of 'tyrant,' for the old title of 'king' was as hateful as that of tyrant."[18] The course of monarchies, it seems, was inexorable. As they approach absolutism they take on the coloring of a cult. "Hee who *desires* from men as much obedience and subjection, as we may all pay to God, desires not less then to be a God" (pp. 532–33).

The title metaphor of *Eikon Basilike* and the notorious picture of the king at prayer probably stimulated Milton to assume the active role of demystifier, iconoclast. It also led him to focus his argument upon the idolatrous aspect of monarchy, as it had the author of *Eikon Alethine* (1649), the book that exposed the forgery of *Eikon Basilike*.[19] One of the authors of the commendatory verses to *Eikon Alethine*, perhaps George Wither,[20] makes the same charge against the people that Milton does:

> And let the cheated Many clearly see
> What goodly Idol 'tis they Deifie.
> And how Religiously they have bowed down
> To a square Cap in stead of Charles his Crown.

The dedication of *Eikon Alethine* attacks "those Idolators who make a King a God." The author's preface "To the Seduced People of England" wails, "o shamefull spectacle! I found an Idol-worship crept in amongst you, and saw you adoring the counterfeit Pourtraicture of one, you sometimes knew no Saint." Yet Milton deplored physical iconoclasm, unlike the author of this tract who applauds the destruction of crosses and church windows.[21] The difference is worth noting, for it underscores Milton's belief that the evil of idolatry did not reside in inanimate objects but in the willfully self-benighted majority.

Throughout the prose works that followed *Eikonoklastes*, Milton persists in arguing that monarchy not only arises from idolatrous impulses, but must, even in its best form, evolve into idolatry. In these polemics emerge the familiar patterns of humanity's fallen condition as described in the great poems. A diabolic pact is established between the king, his minions, and the majority of the people. The king insinuates himself "by subduing first the consciences of Vulgar men, with the insensible poyson of thir [the clergy's] slavish Doctrin" (p. 578). Against this pact stands the one just man: Christ, or the heroic iconoclast, or the virtuous few in Milton's audience.

Although Milton's politics during the period of the first and second Defenses (1651 and 1654) seem to imply that he believed a good monarchy possible,[22] his actual statements in these works attest the contrary. In *Tenure*, commenting on the Israelites' desire for a king (1 Sam. 7), Milton said only that God was displeased: "and though their changing displeas'd him, yet he that was himself thir King, and rejected by them, would not be a hindrance to what they intended" (*CPW*, 3:207). In the first *Defense*, Milton's comments on the same event show that his concept of civil idolatry has since crystallized: "The meaning clearly is that it is a form of idolatry to ask for a king who demands that he be worshipped and granted honors like those of a god. Indeed he who sets an earthly master over him above all the laws is near to establish a strange god for himself, one seldom reasonable, usually a brute beast who has scattered reason to the winds" (*CPW*, 4:369–70). Even more vitriolic are his words on this subject in the *Second Defense*: "The Indians indeed worship as malevolent demons whom they cannot exorcize, but this mob of ours . . . has set up as gods over it the most impotent of mortals and to its own destruction has consecrated the enemies of mankind" (*CPW*, 4:551).

Milton retains this opinion in his last prose tracts. His *Brief Notes upon a late Sermon, titl'd, The Fear of God and the King* (1660) attacks a sermon by one of the late king's chaplains Matthew Griffith. It mattered little that the fulsome Griffith was careful to acknowledge that we are forbidden to adore kings.[23] The very title of his sermon was like a red flag waved in Milton's face. Impatiently, cursorily, Milton scores the idolatry implicit in putting God and the king on the same level. His more fully developed, if hastily written, *Readie and Easie Way* (1660) recapitulates in urgent tones the theme of civil idolatry. One suspects that the deterrence of monarchy was an all-consuming aim in this eleventh-hour blue-print for the perfect government. "Can the folly be paralleld, to adore and be the slaves of a single person . . . ?" Milton asks (*CPW,* 7:448). He envisions a king who will "pageant himself up and down in progress among the perpetual bowings and cring-ings of an abject people, on either side deifying and adoring him for nothing don that can deserve it" (p. 426). He compares the English, on the eve of betraying "the good old Cause" to those Jews who preferred "to returne back to *Egypt* and to the worship of their idol queen" (p. 462). If Milton had ever seen the Pharaoh of the mystery plays, he would have known at once what he represented. It was his single-minded, uncritical antimonarchism that prompted the author of *The Censure of the Rota* (a searching analysis of *The Readie and Easie Way*) to exclaim,

you admire Commonwealths in generall, and cry down Kingship as much at large, without any regard to the particular Constitutions which onely make either the one or the other good or bad, vainly supposing all slavery to be in the Government of a single Person, and nothing but liberty in that of many, which is so false that some Kingdoms have had the most perfect form of Common wealths as ours had, and some Republiques have proved the greatest Tirannies, as all have done at one time or another.[24]

It would be difficult to say what Milton's ideal government would be, to judge from the sketchy proposals so accurately criticized in the Rota's pamphlet. There should be no king, but the nation should elect a governing grand council whose membership would remain perpetual. Everyone in the nation would mind his own business and be reasonable. There would be as little room as possible for the voice of the perfidious majority. Perhaps Milton's ideal government at this time in his life could be described as an aristocracy of merit, though exactly how "merit" would be deter-mined is not specified. The energy that went into destroying myths in Milton's political thought seemingly equaled the creative energy being poured into his poetry at this time. He destroyed the myth of monarchy, but this may have been supplanted in his own mind by a myth of antimonarchy.

It is perhaps now more apparent why Milton enters a cross reference to "idolatry" under "subject" in his commonplace book. Although they may be led astray now and then by their priests or rulers, the people are ultimately responsible for the sin of idolatry, as Christopher Goodman had urged they were a century earlier. The difference in Milton is his virtual certainty that under a monarchy the subject will become abject. Milton's conviction on this point may have been tentative and private in the late 1630s and even as late as the writing of *Tenure;* it was confirmed, however, by the popular reaction to the king's book and the rising clamor for the return of a king, as Milton put it, "to go a whooring after."[25]

Monarchy in Hell

Milton was not an original political philosopher. In the prose works his ideas were so often shaped by the ideology of his opposition that one cannot discover much that truly advances the debate. Even when, as in *The Readie and Easie Way,* he tried to come up with a political system of his own, it proved ill thought-out and vulnerable to attack. If he brought one role from the prose works to the poems, especially *Paradise Lost* and *Paradise Regained,* it must be that of the author as demystifier or demythologizer, a role Milton had explicitly assumed in choosing the title for *Eikonoklastes.* In *Paradise Lost* hell especially offers repeated instances of Milton's using myths to demythologize, as with the series of allusions to the pagan gods as fallen angels who "durst fix / Thir Seats long after next the Seat of God" (I.382). This line refers both to the historical building of pagan shrines near the Temple of Jerusalem and to the absolutist drives of monarchs throughout history, aspiring to the condition of gods.

Of these demon gods, the one that best conveys the royal power-lust in its disregard for the sacredness of human life is "*Moloch,* horrid King besmear'd with blood" (I.392). In Moloch civil idolatry proves to be among the foremost human abominations.[26] The derivation of Moloch's name from "king" was well known in biblical scholarship, so that in the above phrasing, unfixed by any definite article, "King" seems to denote the very essence of kingship. That even Solomon, the model of the godly king in Renaissance minds, should lapse into worshipping Moloch shows how susceptible monarchy is to corruption.[27] On the next two occasions when Moloch appears the name is also in apposition with "king." In the battle in heaven he is "*Moloch* furious King" (VI.357). (Is his being split in two on the battlefield Milton's prophetic joke on the "king's two bodies"?) In the council scene Milton calls our attention especially to Moloch's kingship and his intense desire to be like god:

> Moloch, Scepter'd King
> Stood up, the strongest and the fiercest Spirit
> That fought in Heav'n; now fiercer by despair;
> His trust was with th'Eternal to be deem'd
> Equal in strength, and rather than be less
> Car'd not to be at all.
>
> (II.43)

Steadman rightly observes that Moloch's speech at this point "disguises despair as courage;"[28] it can be added that this self-deception is a consequence of the idolatrous element in monarchy. Moloch personifies, as John Peter says, "the recklessness already seen in Satan."[29] The well-known bravura of Satan in Book I abounds with sentiments of courage in despair, and is what attracts our fallen fancies to Satan. In his pursuit of total power, vying with the Eternal, the only end for Satan, and therefore Moloch, must be annihilation. The complex metaphor of the sun in eclipse carries this point with great force (I.597): the eclipse "disastrous twilight sheds / On half the Nations, and with fear of change / Perplexes Monarchs." Notions of immortal monarchy flatter both king and subject with illusions of earthly permanence. The monarch is, via conventional imagery, the sun, now in eclipse. In the tenor of the metaphor, he is the tyrant puzzled by the mysterious force of the greater King, recalling the celestial wonders that confounded Pharaoh and Herod. The lines also recall Milton's sonnet to the political iconoclast Fairfax, who is said to fill Europe's "jealous monarchs with amaze / And rumors loud, that daunt remotest kings" (lines 3–4). In *Eikonoklastes* Milton calls it "an honour belonging to [God's] Saints . . . to overcome those European Kings, which receive their power not from God, but from the beast" (*CPW*, 3:598).

The city of Pandemonium is an appropriately diabolic fusion of the civil and religious. Although a place of state business, it is "built like a temple" (I.713); it resembles the monumental buildings of Babylon, Egypt, and Assyria, where the pagan confusion of the civil and sacred first occurred. Milton continues the tradition (noted in the mystery plays, *The Faerie Queene*, and *Henry V*) of associating civil idolatry with the orient. His contemporary Francis Osborne believed the very notion of the divine right of kings to have been "borrowed from the Easterne Idolaters."[30] Yet what makes hell especially ripe for idolatry is the attitude of the majority, symbolically shrunken as they enter the city gates. Here is the prototype of "the rage and torrent of that boisterous folly and superstition that possesses and hurries on the vulgar sort," as Milton writes in *Eikonoklastes* (p. 348). In hell, "the hasty multitude Admiring enter'd" (I.730)—their mindless busyness being conveyed in the imagery of insects: "Thick swarm'd," "the hiss of rustling wings," and of course the simile of the bees (I.768).[31] Later, after Mammon's speech, the applause, likened to the wind in hollow rocks (II.285), suggests the emptiness and hardness of heart in both idol and idolaters; the "blust'ring wind," as with Spenser's Orgoglio, is a foil to the true breath or spirit of God. The idolatrous triad—leader, minions, and people—appears in its totality in hell. The hasty multitude's "admiring" connotes the unreflective gawking of the common people, whom Milton ridiculed for venerating Charles's portrait in *Eikon Basilike*. To appreciate the fullness of beauty, the viewer must have a full intellect, but here the emptiness of the idol is matched by the vacuity of the admirers. In *Paradise Regained*, Christ will define the multitude partly in terms of such admiration:

> And what the people but a herd confus'd,
> A miscellaneous rabble, who extol
> Things vulgar, and well weigh'd, scarce worth the praise?
> They praise and they admire they know not what.
>
> (III.49)

In addition to Moloch and Pandemonium, a most memorable image of civil idolatry in *Paradise Lost* is the picture of Satan in the opening lines of Book II, seated on the throne of an oriental despot. The imagery, probably influenced by Spenser's portrait of Lucifera, connotes despotic elevation: Satan "aspires," is "exalted," "rais'd," "uplifted." The appeal to "just right, and the fixt Laws of Heav'n" echoes that of his divine-right successors on earth. Indeed, Joan S. Bennett and Christopher Hill have provided an impressive collection of parallels between the monarchies of Satan and Charles I.[32] Such historical readings, however, should not lead to the mistake that early historicists made with Spenser, in emphasizing the "Charlesness" of Satan to the neglect of the underlying complex of ideas that both he and Charles exemplify. Satan's triumphal march after the council furnishes the climactic image of civil idolatry in Book II: Satan "seem'd"

> Alone th'Antagonist of Heav'n, nor less
> Than Hell's dread Emperor with pomp Supreme
> And God-like imitated State.
>
> (II.508–11)

"State" means "condition" here, but carries with it the sense of polity. Hell is the pattern of all the pseudo-divine states that will come into being on earth; at their head marches the founder of monarchy. The point is almost, but not quite made by John Steadman: "Satan's followers both honour him as monarch and worship his as a god."[33] More precisely, taking into account Milton's position that kingship is by its very nature a form of idolatry, the fallen angels worship Satan as a god *because* they honor him as a monarch.

Infernal monarchy has its human manifestations. Satan's and Moloch's earthly counterpart, the founder of monarchy, is Nimrod, whose story is told in Book XII. We have already seen (pp. 48-49) that in earlier centuries he was identified as the founder of both monarchy and idolatry. The brief description in Genesis ("a mighty hunter before the Lord") Milton interprets as meaning "in despite of Heav'n / Or from Heav'n claiming second Sovranty" (XII.34): the first earthly king is also the first to claim divine right. An excellent contemporary instance of Nimrod's place in the popular antimonarchist mythology appears in the capsule history of world monarchy provided by the Hertfordshire minister Edward Harrison, an obscure man who describes himself as "Sometimes Preacher to Col: Harrisons Regiment":

> The first breach upon right Government that I read of, was made by *Nimrod*, Chams Nephew, of whom we read in *Gen.* 10. 10. whom Historians report was the first that brought men into *subjection* by *force* and *violence*, establishing his Principality in the Kingdom of *Assyria;* which *Tyranny* of his was *successively* exercised upon the *People,* and submitted unto for a long time in the days of succeeding *Tyrants,* during continuance of the *Assyrian, Mede, Persian, Grecian* and *Roman Monarchies,* till the *People* of *Rome* coming to the knowledge of their own *Power* and *Liberty,* threw the *Tyrant Kings* out of their saddles; then succeeded the Government by *Consuls, Decem Viri,* and Tribunes, all which lasted 1084 years, till at last *Cesar* taking advantage by their manifold divisions, first got the office of *perpetual Dictator,* and afterwards the *Title* and *Power* of an absolute *Emperor, Et nunquam postea nisi de principatu quaesitum,* saith *Tacitus,* that is, *Then came no other question to be debated, but who should be the Soveraign Prince of the State;* which was the condition of the generallity of the World, especially since the *Civil*

and *Ecclesiastical State* were by *Antichrist* jumbled together to enslave both *Souls* and *Bodies* of the *People;* which *Mystery of Iniquity* hath been fully discovered in these times of *Light,* wherein God hath begun to *stain the pride of glory,* especially in *England.*[34]

There was, then, a direct line of succession from the "mighty hunter" to Charles I. Stevie Davies has explored the literary embodiment of this succession in *Paradise Lost.* "Once Satan has been established as the archetype of a vitiated kingship, which displays itself in overpowering but tawdry magnificence while it feeds on unnatural, predatory cruelty, the image is extended through a kind of family or chain of subsidiary kings invading all time and space, from Moloch to Pharaoh to Charles I."[35] In an early work— his tone would change after the Peasants' Revolt—Luther asserted that "the money and property of princes is seldom worthy of being put to Christian uses, just as it is rarely acquired otherwise than in the manner in which Nimrod gained his property and money."[36] The implications of this contrast between the kingdoms of God and Nimrod evolve more fully in *Paradise Regained.*

Not to be overlooked are the parallels between Pandemonium and Nimrod's city of Babel, most of which have been noted by Steadman and Knott.[37] Both cities are built on a plain (I.700, XII.41), and as the gold bricks of hell are refined from the lake of liquid fire (I.701), Babel's bricks are mortared with a "black bituminous gurge" that boils up from "the mouth of Hell" (XII.42). The fatal tower of Babel recalls the high towers that Mammon or Mulciber enjoyed building, first in heaven, then in hell (I.733, 749). Again, however, the primary fault for the idolatry of Nimrod lies with the majority. As the individual is too readily subject to the tyranny of the passions, the society of man is excessively "subject from without to violent Lords" (XII.86–93).[38] Adam is naive, as Michael intimates, "to think that Nimrod is the real source of the problem: a man whose passions rule his reason is already a slave; unable to rule himself, he will inevitably become a subject, and in his external servitude make his inner subjection visible."[39] The political fallacy of monarchy ("Man over men / He made not Lord; such titles to himself / Reserving" XII.69) leads to the theological folly of the Tower of Babel.

The first section of this chapter proposed that Milton's assertion of liberty as the condition of right reason excluded any element of the irrational in divine worship. Neither "shadowy" typology in Scripture nor shadowy rites in prayer were to be tolerated. Also, as has been seen (p. 22), Milton rejected the ancient distinction between *latria,* the worship owed to God, and *dulia,* the reverence owed to earthly authority. Both words refer to the worship of god alone. To Milton the veneration of kings, attended by the customary sense of awe and majesty, betokened the misplaced values consequent upon idolizing a man. In his economy of emotions fear was useful only as a beginning of wisdom. Words pertaining to fear, like "awe" and "awful" belong to that part of the Miltonic vocabulary which ought, in Stanley Fish's words, to act upon us like litmus paper.[40] Such words "test the acidity (sin) by taking on the hue of the consciousness that appropriates them." Fear is the litmus test of both civil and religious idolatry. In his first prose tract Milton looks back to the bad old days of Catholicism, when "the Seale of filiall grace became the Subject of horror, and glouting adoration, pageanted about, like a dreadfull Idol" (*CPW,* 1:523). In the divorce tracts he finds the Church of England investing marriage with "an awfull sanctity . . . as if it were to be worshipt like some *Indian* deity"; and the marriage law is "a daring phantasm, a meer toy of terror awing weak senses" (*CPW* 2:277, 667). In the *History of Britain* Milton praises Ida King of Kent for "tempring the aw of Magistracy, with a natural mildness," and approves Gildas's attacking the early English clergy who sought to "keep in aw the superstitious multitude" with their rituals (*CPW,* 5:172, 175).[41]

Fear is the dominant chord in the first two books of *Paradise Lost.* Milton designed hell as a gigantic emblem of the evil state, imbued with what he calls in the *Treatise of Civil Power* "the spirit of bondage to fear," as opposed to "the spirit of adoption to freedom" (*CPW,* 7:265). All the atavistic fears of humanity permeate the language and imagery of fire and darkness, hugeness, heights and depths, wandering, dislocation, dissonance—all the terrors of the night, in fact, that Milton had catalogued in his first prolusion, "Whether Day or Night is More Excellent."[42] If there are moments in the "awful Ceremony" of hell (1:753) when we are put in mind of the effects of civil idolatry in our own century, it must be because the poet had a prophetic insight—an intuitive, yet fully conscious grasp of the psychology of epidemic fear. Milton also exploits the emotive value in the mere use of words pertaining to unreasoning fear in Books I and II. "Dread," with its derivatives, appears more than a dozen times in the first two books; "terror," "terrible," and "horrid," are also frequent. Although Shakespeare is the first to use "horrid" (Latin *horridus,* "bristling") in this sense, Milton exploits the word with a special eye to the awesome, bristling appearance of an ancient army on line—the "horrid Front" of the devils passing in review (I.563), the "horrid crew" of the fallen army at the outset (I.51), the "horrid arms" of Moloch's speech (II.63). Thus the phrase "Moloch horrid King" becomes a formula for a whole complex of meaning in Milton: the idolatry of kingship, the fearfulness of subjects under monarchy, the terrible destructive power that subjects are willing to yield to the hands of their rulers.

The Father of His Country

Milton banished monarchy to hell in a century that published an unprecedented number of writings defending it as God's preferred method of government. He particularly undercut two myths of royalty that are not widely known today. One, the justification of monarchy by ancient conquest, is especially singled out in *Paradise Regained*. Another, with ramifications in all three poems, is the patriarchal theory, they view that fatherhood was the origin and even the model of good government. Just as Adam and all succeeding fathers are sole rulers of their families, so the father-king rules the collection of families known as the state. Monarchists took pleasure in associating the fatherly role of the king with the first person of the Trinity as well as the ordinary human father, and in the whirl of analogy the purely metaphorical status of the argument could get lost. The patriarchal theory of kingship occurs in Aristotle, Plato, and in Christian authors of later ages, but it was most fully developed in England by Milton's contemporary Sir Robert Filmer, who believed it to be historically, not just metaphorically, valid.[43]

Filmer pursued his simple idea with a rare single-mindedness. The mere fact of divine approbation in Eden canceled the need for any other evidence to justify kingly rule. Milton probably never saw Filmer's best known book, *Patriarcha* (published in 1680, twenty-seven years after the author's death), but he could have known of this quiet country gentleman's tardy reply to Philip Hunton's *Treatise of Monarchy* (1643), called *The Anarchy of a Limited or Mixed Monarchy* (1648). Not until his three books published in 1652, however, did Filmer offer his extensive biblical evidence for patriarchalism. *Observations concerning the Originall of Government* specifically attacks Milton's first *Defensio*, along with Hobbes and Grotius. *Observations upon Aristotles Politiques* offered as a principal thesis "that the people are not born free by nature" (p. 115), because all children are subject to their parents. Adam was "the

Father, King and Lord over his family: . . . a son, a subject, and a servant or slave were all one and the same at first" (p. 148). The third tract of Filmer's annus mirabilis, *Directions for Obedience to Governors in Dangerous or Doubtful Times,* uses some predictable shuffling to disallow the fatherhood of the current Protector. In this book Filmer's version of biblical history contrasts markedly with Milton's in *Paradise Lost.* Noah is distinguished not as the "one just man" but as the restorer of paternal monarchy after the flood. At the fall of Babel mankind was divided into seventy-two "distinct families, which had fathers for rulers over them" (p. 141). After Moses, Hebrew rulers held power as "reputed" heirs of earlier father-kings. Filmer has an answer to the obvious argument that children grow up and are no longer subject to their fathers: this process is not by decree of nature but by the laws of society, enacted by "the fatherly power of princes" (p. 149). The existence of tyrants poses no problem either. "There is, and always shall be continued to the end of the world, a natural right of a supreme Father over every multitude, although, by the secret will of God, many at first do most unjustly obtain the exercise of it" (p. 151).

Through the century Filmer's theory remained alive, provoking the notable opposition of John Locke. Although Milton never spoke of Filmer directly, he attacked patriarchalism in the opening chapter of the first *Defensio;* and it was perhaps this conspicuous discussion that led Filmer to print his reply. Milton tells Salmasius:

> Indeed, you are wholly in the dark in failing to distinguish the rights of a father from those of a king; by calling kings fathers of their country, you think this metaphor has forced me to apply right off to kings whatever I might admit of fathers. Fathers and kings are very different things: Our father begot us, but our kings did not, and it is we, rather, who created the king. It is nature who gave the people fathers, and the people who gave themselves a king; the people do not exist for the king, but the king for the people. We endure a father though he be harsh and strict, and we endure such a king too; but we do not endure even a father who is tyrannical.[44]

The attention here given to the phrase "fathers of their country" bears noting. We have already seen Milton's interest in the implications of this phrase as early as his Commonplace Book (*CPW,* 1:433). As late as *Tenure* he was willing to admit the possibility of a just king who could be called "the public father of his Countrie" (*CPW,* 3:212). By the 1650s, however, he saw the title as one to be

earned through virtue, not inherited. Thus in the *Defensio Secunda*
Cicero is "father of his Country" though he never ruled it (*CPW,*
4:446), Cromwell is praised because in rejecting the title of king
for protector, "you assumed a certain title very like that of father of
your country" (*CPW,* 4:672). Milton firmly deprives the phrase of
any numinous content it might receive because of the ruler's
presumed status in nature.

The concept of fatherhood behind the political theory of Filmer
and many other patriarchalists was narrowly centered on the
father's power, not unlike Freud's patriarch of the primal horde.
Filmer went so far as to say that in primitive times a father had life-
and-death power over his son, for "where there are only Fathers
and Sons, no sons can question the Father for the death of their
brother."[45] It may well be, as historians tell us, that "affective
family relationships" had scarcely begun to exist during this period. If so, Milton is ahead of his time, first in the affection shown
for his own father in "Ad Patrem" and *The Reason of Church Government*, secondly in his portrayal of Adam, the anguished parent
watching his children and their children suffer and die—quite
unlike the dour patriarch that Filmer gives us. In *Paradise Lost*
relationships defined by mere power belong to the Satanic order.
King Nimrod enslaves his subjects, King Moloch devours them.

A knowledge of the patriarchalist controversy contributes to the
whole mosaic of the kingship-theme in the major poems, to begin
with in the way it influences the characterization of Adam. The
relations between Adam and Eve, for one thing, are anything but
monarchical in Filmer's absolute sense. It has long been recognized that if Adam held dominion over Eve's will the consequences for Milton's cherished voluntarism, not to mention his
poem, would have been harsh. Adam and Eve are not "unequals"
(8:383), but they are conceived more as complementary than
equal beings. Milton's language in their presence often challenges
us to understand the politics between them. Eve's beauty

> implied
> Subjection but required with gentle sway,
> And by her yielded, by him best receiv'd,
> Yielded with coy submission, modest pride,
> And sweet reluctant amorous delay.

> (IV.307–11)

The challenge to the paraphraser here is quite deliberate. Subjection is "required"—"but." (And required by whom?) Can a
subject "delay" what is required of her? Here it seems she must—

she is required not to be required. The "gentle sway" may be the rule of Adam (over or by Eve?), but it is also the old lovers' dance to and fro, the frustration of desire to prolong desire. The oxymorons "coy submission" and "modest pride" characterize the lovers' relation in this poem much more faithfully than the much-quoted "He for God only, she for God in him." Also deliberately equivocal is the moment after the quarrel in the garden, when Eve "persisted, yet submiss, though last" (that is, though she had the last word). Paradise is less a monarchy than an aristocracy of two with Adam as the *primus inter pares.*

From our first glimpse of Paradise, Adam is consistently presented as the father of the race. Both in Book V, line 506 and Book IX, line 376, he is "the Patriarch of mankind"; but in both cases this phrase comes in the context of God's commanded obedience. In the first, Raphael has reminded Adam of the rewards in store "if ye be found obedient"; in the second, at the parting in the garden, "patriarch" takes on a shade of irony. Had he been obedient, Adam would have been an honored patriarch. But after the fall Michael shows how impotent Adam is to prevent one of his sons from murdering the other, let alone keep his later descendants from suffering. All that remains of the patriarchal virtues are the love and care that Adam shows during these revelations. Milton depicts this powerless love with great feeling in the elegiac comparison of Adam's penitent tears with Noah's flood:

> How didst thou grieve then, Adam, to behold
> The end of all thy Offspring, end so sad,
> Depopulation; thee another Flood,
> Of tears and sorrow a Flood thee also drown'd,
> And sunk thee as thy Sons; till gently rear'd
> By th'Angel, on thy feet thou stood'st at last,
> Though comfortless, as when a Father mourns
> His Children, all in view destroy'd at once.
>
> (XI.754–61)

This image of the Job-like father, loving, patient, comfortless, returns with Manoa in *Samson Agonistes.* In both cases it contrasts with the patriarchalists' concept of fatherhood as defined exclusively by power and authority.

In Book XII the patriarchal myth of kingship receives another shock. Adam sees the generations after him living in "Families and Tribes / Under paternal rule," which Milton also describes as "fair equality, fraternal state" (XII.24–26). The sight of Nimrod grasping the first kingship provokes Adam, "fatherly displeas'd," to see the usurper as an "execrable Son so to aspire / Above his Bretheren" (XII.63–64). In both these passages Milton's joining of filial with brotherly relations reminds us of the larger human brotherhood or *communitas*, the sonship of all Adam's children ("When Adam delved and Eve spann . . .") that effectively limits the power of any single father. Later events of Genesis continue to subvert the patriarchalist idea. Ham, "th' irreverent Son" of Noah, dishonors his father; men forsake God "While yet the Patriarch liv'd, who scap'd the Flood" (XII.101, 117). On the other hand there are virtuous sons who reject their fathers' ways. Abraham departs "from his Fathers house, / His kindred and false Gods" (XII.121–22). Joseph, explicitly "a younger Son" rather than the eldest son of patriarchal favor, becomes "a Son whose worthy deeds / Raise him to be the second in that Realm / Of Pharaoh" (XII.160–63). Neither lineage nor race determines just authority, but virtuous action alone. Similarly David's fatherhood of Christ ("of Kings, the last") is set against that of Solomon "for Wealth and Wisdom fam'd." In effect Solomon's idolatries bring on the dispersal of the tribes and the later age of factious priests who "regard not David's Sons," handing their people over to strangers (XII.329–58). Milton's recurring description of Jewish history in terms of sonship and fatherhood accords with Jewish patriarchal custom, of course, but at every chance it undercuts the supposed correspondence between patriarchal relationship and the ways of God. After all, had Milton's own father pursued this course, the poet would have been born into idolatry.

In short, kingship has nothing to do with fatherhood, except in that kings should love and care for their people as fathers do. Nor is fatherhood itself any guarantee of the moral virtue and wisdom that human authority requires.

Having seen this history, Adam is in a better position to appreciate what Michael told him at the outset. If he had not sinned, Adam would indeed have been the object of patriarchal veneration. Michael's hypothetical account presents something very much like a world emperor cult, though empire is of course irrelevant to an unfallen world. Eden might have been "thy Capital Seat," says Michael, where people would have come "to celebrate / And reverence thir great Progenitor":

> But this preeminence thou has lost, brought down
> To dwell on even ground now with thy Sons.
>
> (XI.347–48)

As in XII.24–26, "paternal rule" in the fallen world yields to "fraternal state."

In *Paradise Regained* Satan appeals to Christ's patriarchal right to power as David's son, often setting the human against the divine sonship. Christ's two fathers thus come to epitomize the demands of the two kingdoms.

In amplifying the second temptation, Book III bears most fully on the patriarchal issue. Satan repeatedly invokes Christ's earthly lineage:

> But to a Kingdom thou art born, ordain'd
> To sit upon thy Father David's throne;
> By Mother's side thy Father, . . .
>
> (lines 151–53)

> They [duty and zeal] themselves rather are occasions best:
> Zeal of they Father's house, Duty to free
> Thy country from her Heathen servitude.
>
> (lines 174–76)

> [Babylon is] rebuilt by him who twice
> Judah and all thy Father David's house
> Led captive and Jerusalem laid waste.
>
> (lines 281–83)

>   thy Kingdom though foretold
> By Prophet or by Angel, unless thou
> Endeavor, as thy Father David did,
> Thou never shalt obtain.
>
> (lines 351–54)

Satan, of course, knows that "father David" is not the whole truth; already in I.93 he says that God is in some sense Christ's father. Shortly before the first quoted passage, in fact, in the speech beginning "Think not so slight of glory: therein least / Resembling thy great Father" (III.109), Satan admits this point to Christ. Only when he slips into his "temptation mode" (as opposed to his "anguish mode"—the two alternate fairly regularly in Book III) does Satan forget the other side of things and insinuate the purely worldly arguments of patriarchalism. Christ draws Satan's attention back to his heavenly father in response to Satan's speech containing the first two of the above quotations:

> If of my reign Prophetic Writ hath told
> That it shall never end, so when begin
> The Father in his purpose hath decreed.
>
> (III.184–86)

To this Satan replies in anguish envisioning "thy Father's ire" (III.219)—only to resume his temptation and the invoking of father David in the speech beginning at line 267, the most elaborate of those in Book III, culminating in the promise that

> Thou on the throne of *David* in full glory,
> From *Egypt* to *Euphrates* and beyond
> Shalt reign, and *Rome* or *Caesar* not need fear.
>
> (III.383–85)

Christ's reply firmly quashes the David argument—even though the indefatigable adversary will return to it in Book IV. For one thing, he asks, where was your zeal "For *Israel*, or for *David*, or his Throne, / When thou stood'st up his Tempter . . .?" (IV.409). Moreover, he says, "if I mean to reign David's true heir," you say I must regain the ten lost tribes, who chose to live in sin among idolaters. Yet if they were returned to "their ancient Patrimony," they would most likely remain "Unhumbl'd, unrepentant, unreform'd" (III.428). Patriarchalism would of course require that these tribes be "regained" (III.371), whether they are worthy subjects or not.

Each instance of Satan's naming "thy Father David" connotes not the holy David of Scripture but the mythic king presiding over a worldly Jewish nation. Satan inadvertently grants as much when he later upbraids Christ for refusing "David's throne, or Throne of all the world" (IV.379). A scholar has noted as puzzling the absence of explicit references to David in the panoply of scriptural allusions during Christ's victory in Book IV of *Paradise Lost*, especially in view of "the dozen messianic references to the throne of David in *Paradise Regained*."[46] Very likely Milton did not want to associate Christ's victory with that of any earthly king, even David. References to David in *Paradise Regained* almost all come from the mouth of Satan, or Satan elicits them from Christ. Satan distorts the story of David from its biblical context much as royalists and propagandists for monarchy did with Charles I and Charles II. Laud's posthumously published sermon before the first Charles, *A Commemoration of King Charles His Inauguration* (1645), compares the newly born Prince Charles and his father to

Solomon and David—the first tract, perhaps, but hardly the last, to employ this conceit. In *Eikon Basilike* this sort of aggrandizement provoked Milton to describe the king's execution as partly "a warning to all Kings hereafter how they use presumptuously the words and protestations of *David*, without the spirit and conscience of *David*" (*CPW*, 3:381–82).

Satan's stress on the human paternity of Christ contributes to his principal aim of making Christ forget his spiritual for his worldly kingdom. But in the end Satan is in every sense of the word confounded: "O Son of *David*, Virgin born; / For Son of God to me is yet in doubt" (IV.500). His ensuing analysis and probing of the phrase "Son of God" in this speech betrays a last, frantic attempt at rationalization closing in skepticism:

> The Son of God . . . bears no single sense;
> The Son of God I also am, or was,
> And if I was I am; relation stands;
> All men are Sons of God.
>
> (IV.517–20)

Understanding the full implications of Son in this poem—spiritual or physical offspring and heir, patriarchal continuer, descendant—we can better appreciate the angelic hymn at the end of the poem, praising Christ for victory "against th' Attempter of thy Father's Throne" (IV.603). Instead of regaining "Father David's throne," all the while "Israel's true king" (III.441) has been defending the city of God and the rich resources of the inner life. Christ is finally "heir of both worlds" (IV.634) because of a victory won wholly in the kingdom of the spirit.

It is possible that the patriarchal myth was under attack in Milton's third major poem, *Samson Agonistes*, chiefly in his handling of the character Manoa. Why is Manoa here at all? In the biblical story, of course, he seems to have died before the events of Milton's poem. One writer has proposed that "by keeping Manoa very much alive, by having him partake as a human father in the suprahuman feats and regeneration of his son, Milton ties the drama together and relates the eternal visionary experience to the humdrum world of everyday life."[47] Manoa is an all-too-human father with a heroic, mythic son. His characterization can also be seen in the light of the political theory I have been discussing, for his presence in the play directly reverses the patriarchalists' assumed qualities of the all-powerful father and the servile son. Being one of Samson's two fathers, Manoa inadvertently confuses, as Satan intentionally does in *Paradise Regained*, the worldly and the providential roles of the hero. This is not to say that the chief reason for his presence in the play is to debunk Filmer. Epideictic rhetoric in the Renaissance always took into account parentage and ancestry as one of the required topics of celebrating a person's life. Thus we need Manoa to know the full greatness of Samson. There is evidence, however, that Milton used Manoa to measure the presuppositions of patriarchalism.

Manoa's qualities as a father, the "pater carus" of Milton's "Ad Patrem," resemble those of Adam pitying his children; he is not the awesome archetype of patriarchal lore. Throughout the poem, however mistaken his perceptions, he is anxious not to "omit a Father's timely care" (line 602). At the end, when he describes his tireless petitions on his son's behalf to the Philistine lords, "with supplication prone and Father's tears" (line 1459), the reader is struck by the pathos in this well-meaning if benighted old man. His presence during the offstage catastrophe and his blind confidence in his vision of his son's future underscore his humanity and, by contrast, his son's spiritual heroism.

A patriarchalist image that Milton uses often in the poem to suggest the ironies of Samson's condition is that of the house. The regal sense (as in "the house of Stuart") is often opposed to the religious one (as in "in my father's house there are many mansions"). When Manoa tells Samson of the shame that has "befall'n thee and thy Father's house" (line 447), he betrays the narrowness of his, unlike his son's, horizons. He wants God to find a way, he tells Samson, "to return thee / Home to thy country and his sacred house" (line 518), but in the end Manoa simply wants Samson to adorn his own house: the old man hopes to "view him sitting in the house ennobl'd / With all those high exploits by him achiev'd" (lines 1491–92). Samson will become a living scutcheon for the house of Manoa, and idol of fame for future generations. This is the meaning, surely, behind Manoa's affirming at the last that Samson has bequeathed "to himself and Father's house eternal fame" (line 1717). The words are exactly right, though the sense is wrong: Samson has won heavenly fame chiefly for his heavenly father's house. The destruction of the worldly kingdom, like Christ's rejection of the world, is required for admission into the kingdom of God. When Christ "home to his Mother's house private return'd" in the last line of *Paradise Regained*, Milton gave the final answer to those who wanted the Messiah to act as a public man for the house of David. (The Mother's house never figures into patriarchalist speculation.) A similar intention lies behind the similar phrasing of Manoa's vow to take Samson's body "with silent obsequy and funeral train / Home to his Father's house" (lines 1732–33). In the Bible the burial is in fact said to have been performed by "the house of his father."

Manoa's presence effectively undercuts the assumptions of patriarchal politics: Samson's virtues are supremely irrelevant to his father. As in *Paradise Regained* the idea of the powerful father passing on his gifts to his son is an exploded myth. In the kingdoms of this world, whether among generations or citizens, original sin is the great equalizer.

"Conquest Fraudulent": Inward Kingship in Paradise Regained

> Divine right is latent in kingship; but only the king too weakly human to rule by his own right, and too inhumanly sophisticated to rule by popular assent, will try to make it explicit. As soon as he does this, divinity will be dulled by the light of mundane arguments. This happened in Milton's lifetime. Like Shakespeare's kings, Satan is subject to undesirable foreign affections, and treats his people as puppets, but the conflict is not between him and his peers or subjects, or within himself between man and king, but between himself and God as rival kings.[48]

J. B. Broadbent here correctly states the difference between Shakespeare and Milton on kingship. Milton seeks to expose the lie of divine right in kingship. Unlike Shakespeare he is impatient with surfaces; his conflicts are metaphysical, as Broadbent implies, not limited to the struggles of the mind or the body politic. Still, the conflict must be imaged, as it was in the battle of heaven in *Paradise Lost*. There, as in *Paradise Regained*, God meets and defeats Satan through his Son. In both encounters, too, readers are sometimes distressed to find that there *is* no conflict—that for the Son to meet Satan is to defeat him. Ultimately it is a "conflict" only from Satan's point of view, and this is chiefly because, "self-tempted, self-deprav'd," Satan is oblivious to the "mundane arguments" that certify the illusoriness of his kingship.

Of Milton's poems *Paradise Regained* is the most relevant to the seventeenth-century critique of civil idolatry. In a sense it constitutes the real answer to Matthew Griffith's sermon, rather than the cursory *Brief Notes*. The conflict between Satan and Christ really amounts to a dialectical opposition between true and false monarchy, as Milton works toward a definition of that mysterious

Christian concept "the kingdom of God" as opposed to conventional, and therefore Satanic, notions of kingdom.[49] Reading
this poem we can see how thoroughly Milton's thinking about
politics has influenced his conception of the debate between Satan
and Christ.[50] *Paradise Regained* is a political poem, exemplifying as
sharply as any work of seventeenth-century England the interdependence of politics and Christianity.

One of the much-debated issues concerning sovereignty at this
time, one that at different times had powerful claims on both
royalist and parliamentarian allegiances, is disclosed at the outset
of Satan's first speech to his council, in the allusion to "This our
old Conquest" and "this fair Empire won of Earth and Air" (I.46,
63). The right of Charles I to rule "by conquest"—that is, by the
victory of his ancestor William the Conqueror—was one of the
common arguments used in support of the royalists during the
Civil War era, declining only when the Parliamentary forces could
make the same claim. In *Paradise Regained* Milton offers a powerfully reductive counterargument to the assumptions of conquest
theory: if we owe our loyalties to the one who conquered and
maintained his rule, and if the first and most lasting conquest in
human history was by Satan, our first allegiance must be to hell.

A succinct account of conquest theory in the seventeenth century by John M. Wallace traces the argument from Hugo Grotius
at the beginning of the century to the Whig attacks on the theory
during the 1680s and 1690s.[51] Perhaps one reason why modern
political historians have not taken the theory seriously, despite
Locke's attention to it in *The Second Treatise of Government* (chap.
16), is the pointless debates that it could lead to, such as whether
or not Roman conquest meant that Pontius Pilate had his power
from God. More significant was the royalist belief that the king,
ruling by divine right inherited from his conquering ancestors,
did not need the consent of his subjects. In the opinion of Philip
Hunton, even "the Bodies and lives of the Conquered are at the
Will and Pleasure of the Conquerour." Necessarily the claims of
inheritance were tied to those of conquest, as in John Bramhall's
statement that Charles I's title rested on "a Multitude of conquests, the very last of whereof is confirmed by a long Succession
of foure and twenty royall Progenitors and Predecessors."[52] This
myth of conquest (often linked to the myth of Nimrod), along
with the countermyth of the "Norman yoke,"[53] has its roots in the
ancient idea of sovereignty from power, the argument of
Thrasymachus in the *Republic*. Like Erasmus, Milton believed that
only Christianity could furnish a satisfactory answer to this posi-

tion. In this he differs from Hobbes, who sought to incorporate Christianity into the power theory of sovereignty.

Paradise Regained does not dismiss conquest but redefines it, much as *Paradise Lost* had epic heroism. It is one of those concepts like "Son of David," and "kingdom of God," whose meaning is deferred until the end of the poem. Satan views conquest with what Arnold Stein calls his "familiar mastery of small denominations of time."[54] He sacrifices the vision of eternity for the petty triumphs of history. At the end of the poem the heavenly chorus salutes Christ as the true "vanquisher," exposing the false conquest of Satan:

> now thou has aveng'd
> Supplanted Adam, and by vanquishing
> Temptation, hast regain'd lost Paradise,
> And frustrated the conquest fraudulent.
>
> (IV.606–9)

Just as true conquest transcends history, it has nothing to do with outward power. Christ's conquest, like his kingdom, is inward. As Satan begins the temptation, Christ presents an image of human nature at its most vulnerable physically. Christ is enfeebled from a long fast, exposed to the dangers of isolation and the fears of the night. Thus when the Father predicts his Son's "winning by Conquest what the first man lost" (I.154), he offers a paradox: "His weakness shall o'ercome Satanic strength" (I.161). This can mean that the divine nature at its weakest is stronger than Satan's strength, but it also refers to the traditional Christian irony: as worldly wisdom is folly, as worldly riches mean poverty, so "God hath chosen the weak things of the world to confound the things which are mighty."[55] Milton renews the *deposuit potentes* theme of the mystery plays (see above, p. 50, n.33). The idea of conquest through weakness manifests the "one great central paradox which virtually transmutes activity and passivity into one another."[56] The strategy of Christ's new conquest of human hearts, conceived at the same moment in history when the old strategy is abolished, aims first "to vanquish by wisdom hellish wiles" (I.175), then "by winning words to conquer willing hearts, / And make persuasion do the work of fear."[57] In *Eikonoklastes* Milton attacked the institution of monarchy for its tyrannizing over the people, and the people for their faintheartedness in clinging to monarchy. In this poem Satan typifies both kinds of error. From God's point of view he is the subject who lacks the "willing heart" to receive the truth, so that debate with Christ is repeatedly shown as futile. For the reader he is the conqueror who rules by force and fraud. As God Christ confounds the first Satan; as man, the second.

When in Book III, Satan tempts Christ to seize control of the earthly kingdom that is "rightfully" the inheritance of David's offspring, it has been stated that "to this seemingly altruistic proposal in itself there is no objection."[58] Nothing could be more out of line with *Paradise Regained*, however. To "seize control" is simply to continue in the Satanic way of conquest, to use the adversary's means to attain the end. Christ has just refuted these methods a few lines earlier in the temptation:

> They err who count it glorious to subdue
> By Conquest far and wide, to overrun
> Large Countries, and in field great Battles win,
> Great Cities by assault: what do these Worthies,
> But rob and spoil, burn, slaughter, and enslave
> Peaceable Nations. . . .
>
> (III.71–76)

The "Worthies" are the conventional objects of medieval and Renaissance hero-worship—usually the "Nine Worthies," all military figures, yet most of them (like Joshua, Charlemagne, Arthur) woven into the mythology of European Christianity. This repudiation of conquest looks back to the demystifying of epic heroism in *Paradise Lost*. Christ continues the speech by describing the hero's inevitable regress from conqueror to king to idol:

> neighboring or remote,
> Made Captive, yet deserving freedom more
> Than those thir Conquerors, who leave behind
> Nothing but ruin whereso'er they rove,
> And all the flourishing works of peace destroy,
> Then swell with pride and must be titl'd Gods,
> Great Benefactors of mankind, Deliverers
> Worship't with Temple, Priest and Sacrifice?
> One is the Son of *Jove*, or *Mars* the other,
> Till Conqueror Death discovers them scarce men,
> Rolling in brutish vices, and deform'd,
> Violent or shameful death thir due reward.
>
> (III.76–88)

The irony of conquest theory is nicely framed in the cycle suggested here, from "Conquerors" on the battlefield to "Conqueror Death."

This passage also shows that conquest is a condition of civil idolatry, one of the principal stipulations underlying Satan's notion of power and glory. Satan's followers become gods on earth, as anticipated in the opening books of *Paradise Lost*, and become "Kings" as well, for after the fall Satan led them

> From Hell's deep vaulted Den to dwell in light,
> Regents and Potentates, and Kings, yea gods
> Of many a pleasant Realm and Province wide.
>
> (I.116–18)

The fraudulent conqueror's obsession with outward power and authority remains consistent with his characterization in *Paradise Lost*, finding expression in his repeated attempts to ferret out the secret of Christ's kingship. Of the triple roles of Christ—prophet, priest, and king—he seems to understand only the last.[59] When this voyeur of monarchies approaches Christ with the question, "Has thou not right to all Created things?" McKellar aptly reminds us that "the matter of first importance to Eve and to Christ is not their *right* to all created things but their *duty* to trust and obey God."[60] As is usual in those with fixations, Satan does not realize he is being irrelevant. His language often supports this fixated characterization—an infatuation with lofty titles and the first-person pronoun, an almost comic way of revealing his obsession through repetition:

> Think not so slight of glory: therein least
> Resembling thy great Father; he seeks glory,
> And for his glory all things made, all things
> Orders and governs, nor content in Heaven
> By all his Angels glorified, requires
> Glory from men, from all men good or bad,
> Wise or unwise, no difference, no exemption;
> Above all Sacrifice, or hallowed gift
> Glory he requires, and glory he receives
> Promiscuous from all Nations, Jew or Greek,
> Or Barbarous, nor exception hath declar'd;
> From us his foes pronounc't glory he exacts.
>
> (III.110–20)

A few lines later Satan is said to be "insatiable of glory" (line 148), suggesting a Tantalus-like figure whose gains are all losses. These anxious repetitions not only signal that the breakdown is near; they also provide a clue to the distemper, a megalomaniac obses-

sion with absolutes: "all" is repeated almost as much as "glory";
there is "no difference, no exemption," "nor exception." The
words betray the conqueror's knowledge that his victory has been
temporary, a sham—especially the deft "exacts," denoting the
compulsion of an unwilling subordinate by his powerful superior.

When Satan offers to furnish Christ with the "regal Arts, And
regal Mysteries" of state, he insinuates the old royalist argument
that only the initiate can sustain sovereignty. John Ware argued
against this view in 1649, declaring that "Kings have always been
jealous of the people, and have held forth their own interest, as a
Mystery or *Riddle,* not to be pried into by ordinary understand-
ings."[61] The true mystery of kingship that Milton aims to disclose
resembles the Platonic idea that outward depends upon inner
rule. In the *Treatise of Civil Power,* written early in 1659, he believed
that Christ had come "to demonstrate the capacity of His spiritual
kingdom to subdue all the powers of this world by its inward
authority alone," assuming that "if the state were allowed any
initiative in religion it would exercise it repressively."[62]

To accentuate the importance of inward government, Milton
portrays the temptation of Christ as progressing from a private
emphasis in Books I and II to a public perspective in Books III
and IV.[63] Through the treatment of Christ's reflections in Book I,
and through Mary's reminiscences and the banquet of sense in
Book II, the first half of the poem brings out the humanity of
Christ. Pursued in infancy by the archetypal world-king, "the
Murd'rous King" Herod, Christ is now "Private, unactive, con-
templative, / Little suspicious to any King" (II.76–82). The contrast
between Christ and Satan is enhanced by that between "righteous
Job" (I.426), the model of the private man's patience, and the
unjust King Ahab (through whose prophets' "four hundred
mouths" God had deceived him). Ahab's story affirms that truth
must come to humanity not from prophets and oracles but from
the inside, from "the Spirit of Truth henceforth . . . an inward
Oracle" (i.462). It is not exactly that Satan has learned, by the time
he returns to his council in Book II, that Christ is impervious to
the lures of the private man, but that, knowing his messianic role,
he wants to believe that he is dealing with someone of the Alexandrian or Caesarian dimension.

The banquet beginning the second temptation, then, serves to
bridge the private and public themes of Books II and III. Book II
chiefly pertains to Christ's display of "that kingship over the self
which in Milton's view constitutes the basis for any kind of public
rule."[64] It has long been recognized that "Splendor" (II.366), not

hunger, is the operative force in the banquet temptation.[65] Satan recreates the earthly pomp of Caroline and Restoration—perhaps even Cromwellian—courtly fetes (lines 350–65).[66] The theme of splendor leads naturally to that of wealth, both of which Christ rejects citing the plainness of republican Rome as proof that, even among pagans, opulence is irrelevant to statecraft. Christ's closing lines (457–86) serve as a climax to the theme of inwardness, anticipating his reply to the offers of worldly glory in Books III and IV: "Yet he who reigns within himself, and rules / Passions, Desires, and Fears, is more a King" than any earthly ruler (lines 466–67). The entire speech looks back to Shakespeare's second tetralogy: kingly power brings with it "sleepless nights": the "chief Praise" of kingship lies, or ought to lie, in the ruler's troubles and cares on behalf of his people; the person who lacks inner control "ill aspires to rule / Cities of men."

Book III opens the perspective of the poem onto the world of public conquests, though Christ sustains the praise of private virtue as a minor theme throughout Satan's gaudy projects and heady lists of place-names. Smuggled into Satan's geography lesson is the suggestion that his power has always counted for more than God's. The "first golden Monarchy" of Babylon hints at a rivalry with "golden age" justice. "*Israel* in captivity still mourns" the success of the Babylonian conquest of the ten tribes; the Israelites would have remained captive had not the Persian "Cyrus set them free" (III.270–84). Satan's offer of the kingdom of Parthia's support, with his enthusiastic account of warfare, insidious diplomacy, and renewed warfare, is dismissed by Christ as "Much ostentation vain" (III.387). The "cumbersome Luggage of war" (III.400) recalls the "tedious havoc" of epic heroism abjured in *Paradise Lost*.

Yet Parthia and the earlier monarchies are dwarfed beside the great empire of Rome that Satan conjures up in Book IV. In magnificent proportions, Rome incorporates all the splendor, wealth, and military strength Satan has praised until now. Surprisingly, even Satan professes indignation at the "horrid lusts" of the reigning emperor and the debauchery of Rome's government. Here is ostensibly Satan's most diabolic temptation: that Christ should use his power for good to overthrow the greatest force for evil in his world. Throughout, Satan is confident that his means must inevitably be used to achieve God's end in the world. Yet he has missed the point of Christ's doctrine of the inner self. Earlier Christ refused consideration for the ten lost tribes because they had "wrought their own captivity" through sin (III.415). Now he

refuses to intervene with the lustful emperor: "Let his tormentor
Conscience find him out" (IV.130). As for the Roman people, they
are "degenerate, by themselves enslav'd"; who could "of inward
slaves make outward free?" (IV.132–45). When His time comes,
says Christ, He will destroy not only Rome but "all Monarchies
beside throughout the world: (line 151). This whole episode on
worldly kingdoms leads to Christ's rejecting Satan's offer, which
entails his concept, of civil power with the commandment against
idolatry:

> It is written
> The first of all Commandments, Thou shalt worship
> The Lord thy God, and only him shalt serve; . . .
> The Kingdoms of the world to thee were giv'n,
> Permitted rather, and by thee usurp't,
> Other donation none thou canst produce:
> If given, by whom but by the King of Kings,
> God over all supreme?
>
> (lines 175–86)

Implicitly the Christian principle that all power is from God is
here used to invalidate conquest theory. Those who conquer by
force and fraud are really usurpers of divine order.

As in *Paradise Lost*, Satan's temptations inadvertently advance
the very cause they seek to frustrate. The second temptation ends
with Satan himself revealing the kingdom of God, though it is a
realm that neither he nor we are yet fully able to grasp:

> A Kingdom they [the stars] portend thee, but what Kingdom,
> Real or Allegoric I discern not,
> Nor when, eternal sure, as without end,
> Without beginning.
>
> (IV.389–92)

One purpose of the "rejection of humane learning" in the last
phase of the second temptation is to advocate the wisdom of
Hebrew "political science" over that of pagan antiquity.[67] We are
reminded that the Athenian school produced as its most famous
graduate "Great *Alexander* to subdue the world" (IV.252). Christ's
praise of Jewish philosophy, the climax of his survey of ancient
wisdom, leaves Satan as usual shuffling for a new point of attack.
The Old Testament prophets, "men divinely taught," gave us

> The solid rules of Civil Government
> In thir majestic unaffected style. . . .

> In them is plainest taught, and easiest learnt
> What makes a Nation happy, and keeps it so,
> What ruins Kingdoms, and lays Cities flat;
> These only, with our Law, best form a King.

The prophetic and historical books of Scripture, Milton's frequent source for illustrations in his political writings, teach better than anything from Greece or Rome that in civil life monarchic power and splendor must be subdued by "Law" and divine guidance.

The third temptation marks Satan's one and only attempt to use the tyrant's ultimate weapon, force, upon Christ's person. It is the moment that would be most fearful to any of us, but it seems to affect Christ the least, so impervious is he to outward things. In expanding Luke's version of this event, Milton's image of the Temple evokes details of the earthly kingdoms in the previous temptation. Jerusalem

> lifted high her Towers,
> And higher yet the glorious Temple rear'd
> Her pile, far off appearing like a Mount
> Of Alabaster, with golden Spires.
>
> (IV.545–48)

The emphasis on height in this account ("in scorn" Satan says that Christ is now "highest plac't, highest is best" line 553) draws together a number of scenes in the second temptation, beginning with the "pleasant Grove . . . High roof't" of the banquet scene (II.293). There is the scene of "Huge Cities and high tow'r'd" that Satan shows Christ in Book III (line 261); there is Rome "With Towers and Temples proudly elevate" (IV.34), and

> Th' Imperial Palace, compass huge, and high
> The Structure, skill of noblest Architects,
> With gilded battlements, conspicuous far,
> Turrets and terraces, and glittering Spires.
>
> (IV.51–54)

The language is of course Satan's, and reopens the obsessive tone noted earlier. The elaboration of grandeur, especially the words pertaining to height, show his own fixation with place—both in the sense of rank and "place" as opposed to time, which he would rather forget about. Spenser had used the same symbolism of height in describing Lucifera and the House of Pride. Satan's scornful "highest is best" contradicts everything Christ will teach about the life well lived, revealing the sickness in his envy of the

Son of God's preferred place in heaven. It may be that the height of the Temple is intended to connote spiritual as opposed to mere physical heights of profane "Towers and Temples." More likely, though, it is a reminder that Christ has come to level the high places: even the Temple must at last fall to the Miltonic God of inward, not outward, spaces.[68] Inwardness is as much the mark of true government as of true religion, the outwardness necessary to monarchy being a sign of its ultimately un-Christian character. Regarding Romans 13, Milton agreed that the civil magistrate could use force in governing the outward man. The spiritual side, however, is the exclusive province of religion: only religion "deals with the inward man and his actions, which are all spiritual and to outward force not lyable" (*CPW*, 7:524). When Satan entered, the inward world became subordinated to outward government, as in the Erastian system of the Laudian church, and as is attempted in Satan's assault upon Christ's will.[69] Matthew Griffith, in dedicating his objectionable sermon to General Monck, had written that "it is a greater honour to make a king than to be one."[70] Milton has Christ reply in terms more consistent with the gospel precepts on humility:

> to give a Kingdom hath been thought
> Greater and nobler done, and to lay down
> Far more magnanimous than to assume.
>
> (II.481–83)

The magnanimity and sovereignty of Christ will be proved in giving rather than in conquest. Frye has remarked, concerning the vision of earthly monarchies in *Paradise Lost*, "The reason why kingship on earth is so apt to become idolatrous is precisely that it is the external projection of the inner sovereignty of God."[71] Nothing outward happens in *Paradise Regained*, that is, no public miracle, no visible change in the protagonist. Artistically it was a singular challenge to write a long narrative poem in which nothing happens; perhaps this explains why in his last years Milton could not endure to hear *Paradise Lost* preferred to *Paradise Regained*.[72] The only external event, as we have seen, the one most likely to stir the emotions of ordinary mortals, is treated with what must have been a calculated off-handedness.

Every stage of *Paradise Regained* contributes to an inward development, whether of Christ's consciousness or, as I am more inclined to believe, the reader's own understanding of the son of God and the kingdom of God. Michael Fixler has traced Milton's concept of the kingdom from his earlier notion of a society perfected by reform to his later belief, beginning in the mid 1640s, in the kingdom as conscience, the kingdom within.[73] In the *Treatise of Civil Power* Milton says that Christ rejected outward government in his church "to shew us the divine excellence of his spiritual kingdom, able without worldly force to subdue all the powers and kingdoms of this world, which are upheld by outward force only" (*CPW*, 7:256). Later he adds a comment most relevant to the debate between Christ and Satan (the "adversarie"): "Then surely he hath not chosen the force of this world to subdue conscience and conscientious men, who in this world are counted weakest; but rather conscience, as being weakest, to subdue and regulate force, his adversarie, not his aide or instrument in governing the church" (p. 257). Here the kingdom seems to mean both church and conscience, or rather, perhaps, an invisible church of "conscientious men," entirely without external government. On one central problem of church government, that of maintaining the clergy, Milton declared in *The Likeliest Means to Remove Hirelings* that the clergy should trust in God for their maintenance, like the apostles. At any rate, "certainly it is not necessarie to the attainment of Christian knowledge that men should sit all thir life long at the feet of a pulpited divine" (*CPW*, 7:302). In *Paradise Regained* and the late prose works, Christ's kingdom must finally be treated as a divine mystery whose existence may be recognized in its attributes and effects—especially in what it is *not*—though the human intellect cannot fully comprehend what it is. It is inward and invisible, established by Christ, governed by conscience, observable in the lives of the just, and has nothing to do with worldly force or fear. Milton's understanding of the kingdom as inward may not be fully consistent with modern biblical scholarship on the subject; but he presents a Christ very similar to that of modern scholars—distinctive not in prophesying the kingdom but in realizing that it is being ushered in by himself.[74]

In their search for the kingdom of God, seventeenth-century readers would associate themselves most fully with the disciples in this poem. For one thing the prayer of Christ's followers would be familiar to many who had been persecuted for religion's sake during the first decade of the Restoration:

> Behold the Kings of th'Earth how they oppress
> Thy chosen, to what height thir pow'r unjust
> They have exalted, and behind them cast
> All fear of thee; arise and vindicate
> Thy Glory, free thy people from thir yoke!

(II.44–48)

At the climax of the second temptation, Christ responds by casting Satan "behind" him (IV.193), showing the readers by example how they may remain private yet still impervious to public threats. The modern reader's attitude on first taking up *Paradise Regained* is not unlike the disciples' feeling during their anxious prayer: we expect, and they assume, that "something will happen." Neither they nor we realize, on first impression, that everything is changed from this time on in the logic of power, glory, and kingly office, even though "nothing happens."

Murderous Herod, conquering Alexander, and depraved Tiberius all earn the appropriate ignominy in *Paradise Regained*, but if anyone is guilty of civil idolatry it is the people, the "miscellaneous rabble" of Christ's speech to Satan. In *Samson Agonistes* there is no Moloch-serving king at the spectacle, only Dagon, the Philistine nobility, and "the people . . . . / Impetuous, insolent, unquenchable" (line 1421). Samson, like patient Job and the few just men commemorated in *Paradise Lost,* stands outside the idolatrous triad of king, priest, and people. In place of a king in this poem stands the mere unresponsive idol that kingship, for Milton, really is. In contrast to the people Milton offers the Chorus, the rational minority and chosen few who yet stand in need of resolve, not unlike the audience for whom Milton wrote both prose and poetry. The Chorus is educated in the process of Samson's self-discovery, as Mary Radzinowicz has shown; but it is important to keep in mind her point that the occasion for this tragedy was "the failure of the English people to respond to the offer of liberty" made by their leaders in the Interregnum.[75] Accordingly, the Chorus ought not to be seen as representing "everyman" in the play, let alone the people of England.

If, as many critics now believe, the Chorus is educated along with Samson during his last hours,[76] we may take as a viable response to the mystery of evil the passage in the second stasimon beginning "God of our Fathers, what is man." Here the common people are conspicuously excluded from providential care:

> Nor do I name of men the common rout,
> That wand'ring loose about
> Grow up and perish, as the summer fly,
> But such as thou hast solemnly elected.

> (lines 674–77)

Earlier in his political writing Milton had been hopeful, or at least ambivalent, about "the people." Now they are quite cut off from a part in divine history. They do not even share in the punishment that god inflicts through Samson's last heroic act, for the Messenger reports afterward that "The vulgar only scap'd who stood without" (line 1659).

The feast of Dagon typifies the great idolatrous civic spectacles that Tertullian had condemned. Its participants, the luxurious lords and muddled masses, will reap the wages of false worship. But set apart from the profane spectacle is the inward drama of Samson's last hours, exemplifying that "sacred" tragedy that Milton had sought to exclude from Tertullian's blanket condemnation of drama.[77] The elect audience at this godly spectacle can depart with "calm of mind," having understood more fully the "highest wisdom" of the hidden God.

For those who, like Owen Barfield or Walter Ong, can speak of an "evolution of consciousness,"[78] Milton represents a watershed in the history of English literature and culture alike. The appeal to right reason colors all his prose works; and in the genre of epic, which in many respects had been ruled by the unconscious, Father Ong writes, "Milton's strong infusion of logic" represents the "expropriation of parts of the unconscious by consciousness."[79] In politics, through the efforts of Milton's fellow rationalists, the whole people had been offered the opportunity for a new life. They could have both a politics and a religion deprived of ritual and man-made symbol, the clouds of superstitious awe. Never mind that the Commonwealth government was on the verge of a number of self-made crises: Milton saw in the popular outcry over the king's death and the success of *Eikon Basilike* confirmation of his worst suspicions about the common man. The multitude proved what the prelates had always claimed about their need for outward shows; they chose ignorance, and even the true God worshipped in ignorance was worshipped as an idol.[80] The popular retreat into king worship led not only to Milton's hell but to the more sustained attack on the kingdoms of this world in *Paradise Regained*.

Epilogue: No Ceremony No Bishop, No Bishop No King

Milton had been released from arrest by parliamentary order for some six months when, on 22 and 23 April 1661, the coronation festivities for Charles II were held. *Paradise Regained,* if we may believe Thomas Ellwood, was still five years away. The new monarch was showered with the enthusiasm of thousands who had remained faithful to his cause, and other thousands simply hoping for a stability and prosperity that had never come under Cromwell. As was the custom, the king was also showered with hyperbole. James Heath, soon to become martyrologist of royalism, was moved to compare the unusual star that supposedly shone at Charles's birth to the star of Bethlehem. In the official coronation sermon, Bishop George Morley drew parallels between Charles and Christ in their rebuilding of their kingdoms. Later, he likened the thunder that occurred after the coronation to the thunderous voice of God in heaven at the time of John's baptism of Christ. (Antimonarchists drew other conclusions.) Festive symbolism in the procession depicted Charles in terms of Isaiah's Messiah bringing in the Golden Age.[1] Milton's response to these events is readily imagined. All the delusions of monarchy and monarchical religion had returned: the sacred king, fawning bishops, and blasphemous ceremonies that he had helped drive from England twenty years earlier.

Had he lived to see the event, Milton might have taken some consolation in the coronation of William and Mary in 1689. For one thing, it featured a more temperate sermon by Bishop Gilbert Burnet, sometime chaplain to Charles II and expelled from that position for upbraiding the king on his morals. The text for the occasion of installing England's new parliamentary sovereign was 2 Samuel 23:3, 4:

> *The Rock of Israel spoke to me: He that ruleth over men must be just, ruling in the fear of the Lord.* Here are the true measures of Government; it is a *Rule,* and not an *Absolute Dominion;* it is a *Rule over men,* and not a

Power, like that which we have over Beasts. In a word, it is the conduct of free and reasonable beings, who need indeed to be governed, but ought not to be broken by the force and might of Power.[2]

Whereas Morley had seen fit to compare the king to Christ, following the tone of many earlier court-churchmen, Burnet stresses the ruler's humanity, his limitations. Though princes "look *like Gods*, yet they must *die like Men*" (p. 15). Milton's adversary Griffith had spoken of the fear of God and the king; Burnet accentuates the fear of God *by* the king:

> This will accustom Princes to consider, that how much soever they may be raised above their Subjects, yet they are as nothing before God, who as he set them up by Providence, so he can pull them down at his pleasure. *He poureth contempt upon Princes* [Ps. 107:4]; and when he blasts the Counsels, and intends to defeat the Designs of the Greatest and Loftiest Monarchs, how easily do Crowns fall, and Thrones shake? (p. 14)

"Providence" might at one time have meant "the Design of the Greatest and Loftiest Monarchs"; now it refers to the will of Parliament, especially the House of Commons, very much present that day at Westminster Abbey.[3] Burnet touches a chord that echoes back through Milton to Erasmus and earlier humanist libertarians when he contrasts the "oppressed Subjects" under the Roman emperors with their flattering courtiers and their "Rites of Divine Adoration" (p. 3). A younger minister published a poem on the occasion, celebrating the new limited monarchy with a fleeting glance back at the Stuart king:

> Monarchs that grasp at too much pow'r and might,
> Look small when rais'd above their lawful height,
> And mounting higher vanish out of sight.[4]

This new theme of moderation in kingship is more significantly reflected in the new coronation oath (essentially the same oath still in use), placing two new requirements on the sovereign: to rule by the statutes of Parliament, and to uphold the "Protestant Reformed Religion established by law." From this point on, the king "was no more than one of the essential elements in the legislature. His monarchy was hereditary, but also parliamentary."[5] Ironically, conquest theory could now support the revolution. Charles Blount set forth the idea in *King William and Queen Mary Conquerors* (1693), though for his pains Parliament ordered the book burned by the common hangman.[6] Whatever belief in the divine right of kings lingered into the last decade of the seventeenth century was severely shaken by the accomplished fact. Parliament had established that its prerogative to make and unmake kings took precedence over hereditary claims to the throne.

The ceremonies of kingship remained more or less intact at William's and Mary's coronations, but perhaps for the first time the ruling monarch was out of sympathy with the event. William refused to perform the traditional coronation activities of washing the feet of the poor and touching for the King's Evil. Later he told a visitor from Amsterdam that he thought the whole "comedy" at the Abbey a collection of "foolish old Popish ceremonies."[7] In this case, at least, the coronation ceremony had contributed more to the well-being of the body politic than to its head of state. Especially in view of the conspicuous presence of the House of Commons, it was a celebration of the achievements of England's revolution, unwilling though the new king might prove to follow in step with the ascendant philosophy of the Whig party. Bishops, ceremonies, and kings had remained in spite of the clamorous Commonwealth; yet the names scarcely matched up with the things they had been at the start of the century. Then it had been axiomatic for the likes of Bishop Bancroft to maintain that no one could be a loyal Englishman who did not consent to the ministerial surplice and kneeling at communion. According to the Puritan William Bradshaw, the bishops had formulated their own maxim, "No ceremonie, no bishop," to go along with James I's "No bishop, no King."[8] In time the logic of this sequence would prove impeccable. Milton belongs to a later generation of Puritans who were antiritualistic, antiprelatical, *and* antimonarchical, just as Bancroft held Puritans to be circa 1600. It is certain, however, that in Bancroft's own time there was no thought by the vast majority of Puritans whose writings survive that completing the religious reformation would require a political revolution. History has tended to blame the Stuarts themselves for this state of affairs. Whereas for the Tudors the royal prerogative entailed "a right to dispense with the law if equity required it," for James I and his successors it meant "freedom to disregard the law because that was under the king," which meant "true absolutism." Under James and his son, too, the court ceased to function as a viable point of contact in government: the early Stuarts failed, accordingly, "progressively isolating themselves, first by corruption bordering on the grotesque, and later by a refinement and sophistication which made Charles I inaccessible and incomprehensible to all but a chosen few. As a result, political opposition went 'out of court' in the 1630s, . . . with consequences which provided the measure of the Tudor achievement."[9]

There have always been those who see no real connection between England's political and ecclesiastical conflicts in the seventeenth century. Clarendon reports that the lawyers' refusal to take the bishops' cause seriously led to an estrangement between the church and legal profession during the Commonwealth period and after.[10] Others, including the poets discussed in the foregoing pages, understood more fully that sacred symbolism could be used as a powerful support for wrong. Behind several of Henry V's speeches lies an awareness that fear is the consequence of an excessive reverence for monarchs. Fear is also the concomitant of ritualistic religion: Spenser's Abessa and her mother are "full of ghastly feare" and "Nigh dead with feare" in their superstitious practices (*FQ*, I.3.12–13). Cranmer complained that Catholic rites served only to "darken and confound" the hearts of worshippers; Milton would compare the Catholic eucharist to "a dreadful idol."[11] The political consequences of reverential fear are threatening in Henry V's soliloquy, but salutary and stabilizing in Matthew Wren's 1627 sermon on the same text that Griffith would later use: "Fear God, my son, and the king." Standing before King Charles, Wren could say without criticism from anyone who mattered that "*God* is not *feared*, if the *King* be not."[12] Among Laudian bishops with whom such thinking later became identified, Wren was perhaps the most hated by the Puritans. Yet Laudianism served mainly to whet the reaction of the opposition in church and state: as awe and fear were consequent to kingship, so were they to idolatry.

In this one respect, though surely others might be added, Shakespeare's history plays were prophetic. England's bitter harvest of royalty's aggrandizement would be reaped a half-century later. By then the notion that monarchy entailed a kind of idolatry had taken root in many minds. John Hales, in deploring "secular idolatry," defines "outward pomp and shew" as "one of the greatest stays of the kingdom of this world: some thing there must be to amaze the people, and strike them into wonderment, or else majesty would quickly be contemned."[13] John Ware anticipates the theme of *Paradise Regained* in declaring, "True *Majesty* is in the spirit and consists in the Divine *Image* of *God*, in the *minde*, which the Princes of the World comming short of, have supplied its defect with *outward* [here, for once, the italics are mine] badges of

Fleshly honour; which are but *Empty shews* and *carnall appearances,* when void of the *substance.*"[14] Mindful that Christ expressly forbade such pomp in his own kingdom, at least one great sect, the Quakers, came into being partly in reaction against the rituals of the law and state as they were then perceived. One of Milton's ruling ideas, as we have seen, is the necessity of political freedom in the spiritual war of which man is the center. The transitory nature of ceremonies, mere *significantia,* renders them futile obstacles in our passage to the *significata* of Truth and Spirit. If the idols will not less us pass, then they must be broken.

In his masterful history of iconoclasm during the Tudor Reformation, James Phillips has concluded that this activity was "a highly developed order of daring philosophical violence," because the images destroyed were seen to evoke the authority of the old church and therefore, in a very real sense, to have power over people.[15] There was power, too, in the ceremonies of church and state, and especially in the splendid figure of a king—more power, Milton believed, than was owing even to the best of the kind. If we think today that such symbolism cannot have had much to do with people's lives and with the political turbulence of the seventeenth century, then it may be that we have been thoroughly conditioned to that rationalistic way of thinking that followed hard upon Milton's generation.[16] Awful ceremony is for many of us not only a sign of ignorance, a lapse into barbarism, but it is the mark of simple-mindedness. The prevailing religious climate allows even a Jesuit liturgist to say of current trends in worship that "His childish enthusiasm behind him, modern man has learned through some painful experience to become a realist."[17] At least in the English-speaking world, such voices seem to be drowning out the sentiments exemplified in a French clergyman's lament that the vanishing of the custom of blessing the marriage bed is "the sign of a desacralization of everyday life, and of that boundary that is accentuated between the sacred rituals of the church and the activities of profane life, which the Middle Ages never separated."[18] In an academic, inoffensive way, it is the anthropologists who have become the new Laudians, the preservers of cult and symbol. The evidence shows that they have escaped the rationalism of the post-Reformation West more completely than, say, economic historians. Victor Turner and Mircea Eliade, in very different ways, have reminded us of the inevitability of ritual, of some testimony of the sacred, in any viable society.[19] Concerning the easy dismissal of such practices by modern thinkers, Anthony Storr has written,

It is redolent of nineteenth-century armchair anthropology which assumed that the rituals and ceremonies of cultures other than our own were childish practices which civilized man had outgrown. Indeed, one of the principal objections to the old-fashioned Freudian and Kleinian interpretations of ritual, art, and literature is that they make the sublime appear trivial by their implicit assumptions that the irrational, emotional, and imaginative aspects of human nature are infantile modes which ought to have been superseded by the light of clear reason.[20]

Yet for the opposite view it is unlikely that Milton wanted to "make the sublime appear trivial" in his loathing of church and state rituals. It may be that for every Malvolio (or Freudian) who lacks the sense of play to participate in the celebration of human life, there are also the occasional emancipated Puritans capable of an *Arcades* or *Comus*. Donald Davie has observed that 'to minds of a certain temper ceremony, whether in worship or in art" or, Milton would add, in politics, "is more meaningful and momentous according as it is more austere."[21] Sitting at communion service, though a more "natural" posture than kneeling, might thus be seen as a ritual gesture in itself; as the Quakers recognized, even coming together to church on a particular day of the week constitutes a ceremonial act. The ceremonies of English life at the end of the seventeenth century grew relatively more austere as the *significantia* were brought into fuller correspondence with what they signified. The lengthy process whereby the illusions of monarchy were at first protected out of national interest, then tolerated, then abhorred speaks more to the difference than the likeness between art and ritual. We have the "observation," as William Carlos Williams would call it,[22] of the greatest poets of that age to attest that the authoritarian symbols of the past were inadequate, in the national consciousness, to the quest for true order and peace.

Notes

Preface

1. Roy Strong, *Splendour at Court: Renaissance Spectacle and Illusion* (London: Weidenfeld and Nicolson, 1973); Stephen Orgel, *The Illusion of Power: Political Theater in the English Renaissance* (Berkeley and Los Angeles: University of California Press, 1975); Joel Hurstfield, *The Illusion of Power in Tudor Politics* (London: Athlone Press, 1979). The last of these, the 1978 Creighton lecture in History, shows that the semidivine attributes of earlier Tudor monarchy began to disappear with the coming of Elizabeth.

2. David Loades, *The Tudor Court* (London: B. T. Batsford, 1986), 8.

3. Lauro Martines, *Society and History in English Renaissance Verse* (Oxford: Basil Blackwell, 1985), 4.

4. Alan Sinfield and Jonathan Dollimore, eds., *Political Shakespeare* (Ithaca: Cornell University Press, 1985), viii. Insofar as new historicism can be defined, a convenient definition is the introduction to Heather Dubrow and Richard Strier, eds., *The Historical Renaissance: New Essays on Tudor and Stuart Literature and Culture* (Chicago: University of Chicago Press, 1988), 1–12.

5. Frederic Jameson, "Religion and Ideology: A Political Reading of *Paradise Lost*," in Francis Barker et al. eds., *Literature, Politics and Theory* (London: Methuen, 1986), 48.

6. R. V. Holdsworth et al., "Shakespeare," *Year's Work in English Studies* 65 (1984): 210.

7. Stephen Greenblatt, *Renaissance Self-Fashioning from More to Shakespeare* (Chicago: University of Chicago Press, 1980), 113.

8. Stevie Davies, *Images of Kingship in* Paradise Lost: *Milton's Politics and Christian Liberty* (Columbia: University of Missouri Press, 1983). I came to this book after writing part of my own and found a number of correspondences between them, including the title of my second and her first chapters.

9. Joan S. Bennett, *Reviving Liberty: Radical Christian Humanism in Milton's Great Poems* (Cambridge: Harvard University Press, 1989); John D. Cox, *Shakespeare and the Dramaturgy of Power* (Princeton: Princeton University Press, 1989). Their points of departure are, respectively, Hooker and Augustine, while mine is Erasmus, but our conclusions, apparently drawn independently of one another, are similar.

Introduction: Religion and Rule

1. Milton, *Eikonoklastes*, in *Complete Prose Works of John Milton*, ed. Don M. Wolfe (New Haven: Yale University Press, 1953–82), 3:343 (all citations from the prose of Milton are from this edition, abbreviated as *CPW*); Hales, *Golden Re-*

mains (1673), 157–58. Hales's sermon must be dated before 1645: see Pierre Desmaizeaux, *A Historical and Critical Account of the Life and Writings of the Ever-memorable John Hales* (London, 1719), 68. David Norbrook, *Poetry and Politics in the English Renaissance* (London: Routledge and Kegan Paul, 1984), discusses Puritan aversion to Elizabeth's cult and Fulke Greville's "sweeping denunciation of all secular honour as idolatry" pp. 157–94. For other references to civil idolatry, see those on "King Worship" provided in William Lamont and Sybil Oldfield, eds., *Politics, Religion and Literature in the Seventeenth Century* (London: Dent, 1975), 1–28.

2. Herbert N. Schneidau, *Sacred Discontent: The Bible and Western Tradition* (Baton Rouge: Louisiana State University Press, 1976).

3. *A History of the Early Christian Doctrine before the Council of Nicaea*, vol. 3 of *The Origins of Latin Christianity*, trans. David Smith and John Austin Baker (London: Darton, Longman and Todd, 1977), 412.

4. *CPW*, 1:433. Cf. Richard Hooker, *Of the Laws of Ecclesiastical Polity*, in *Works*, ed. W. Speed Hill (Cambridge: Harvard University Press, 1977–82), 3:359 (*Laws* VIII.4.3).

5. "On the Vanity of Idols," in *Writings of Cyprian*, trans. Robert Ernest Wallis, Ante-Nicene Christian Library, vol. 8 (Edinburgh, 1876), 443–44.

6. *On Idolatry*, trans. S. Thelwall. Ante-Nicene Christian Library, vol. 11 (Edinburgh: T. & T. Clark, 1872), 163 (chap. 15).

7. S. R. F. Price, *Rituals and Power: The Roman Imperial Cult in Asia Minor* (Cambridge: Cambridge University Press, 1984), 25, 29–30. For a readable if colored account of the conflict between faith in Christ and in the emperor, see Ethelbert Stauffer, *Christ and the Caesars* (London: SCM Press, 1955).

8. H. X. Arquillière, *L'Augustinisme politique: Essai sur la formation des théories politiques du Moyen-Age*, 2d ed. (Paris: J. Vrin, 1955), 51–67, especially 54, 60, 62–63. The phrase is from Augustine, *De Civitate Dei*, 19:13.

9. Trans. Henry Sweet, *EETS*, o.s. 45 (London, 1871), 108–11.

10. J. H. Grainger, "The Activity of Monarchy," *Cambridge Quarterly* 7 (1977): 297–313.

11. "On Mending the Peace of the Church," in *The Essential Erasmus*, trans. John P. Dolan (New York: Mentor, 1964), 343–44, 386.

12. *A Treatise of Civil Power in Ecclesiastical Causes* (1659), *CPW*, 7:265.

13. Valuable evidence for this is Stephen Kogan, *The Hieroglyphic King: Wisdom and Idolatry in the Seventeenth-Century Masque* (Rutherford, N.J.: Fairleigh Dickinson University Press, 1986).

14. *De Civitate Dei*, X.1.

15. See *Summa Theologiae* (New York and London: McGraw Hill and Eyre and Spottiswoodie, 1964), vol. 41, trans. and ed. T. C. O'Brien, p. 5, note h. References to the *Summa* are to this ed.

16. IIa IIae, 102.1 Resp. (p. 23).

17. IIa IIae, 102.3 Resp. (pp. 27–31).

18. IIa IIae, 103.3 Resp. (p. 41).

19. Loc. cit., Resp. ad 1 (p. 41).

20. *An Answer to Sir Thomas More's Dialogue, The Supper of the Lord*. Parker Society (Cambridge: Cambridge University Press, 1850), 57 and n. Cf. John Jewel, *Reply to Harding's Answer*. Parker Society (Cambridge: Cambridge University Press, 1847), 666.

21. Milton, *CPW*, 6:666. Hobbes, *Leviathan Parts I and II*, ed. Michael Oakeshott (Oxford: Basil Blackwell, 1957), 72 (I.12); the distinction is specifically

observed, however, in what appears to be a contradictory statement on p. 425 (IV.45).

22. Ernst H. Kantorowicz, *The King's Two Bodies: A Study in Mediaeval Political Theology* (Princeton: Princeton University Press, 1957).

23. More, *History of King Richard III and Selections from the English and Latin Poems*, ed. R. S. Sylvester (New Haven: Yale University Press, 1976), trans. L. Bradner and C. A. Lynch, pp. 142–43.

24. "Mysteries of State: An Absolutist Concept and Its Late Mediaeval Sources," *Harvard Theological Review* 48 (1955): 65–91. For a valuable account of Kantorowicz, see *On Four Modern Humanists*, ed. Arthur Evans (Princeton: Princeton University Press, 1970), 146–219.

25. Marie Axton, *The Queen's Two Bodies: Drama and the Elizabethan Succession* (London: Royal Historical Society, 1977), 115, follows Kantorowicz's reading, and conceives of her book as extending his observations on Tudor culture. Although this book is impressively documented, I disagree with many of the author's interpretations of the evidence—e.g., that Lyly's *Endimion* uses myth to "explore the discrepancy between the two bodies of the monarch" (p. 71). This is true only in that, say, a masque often uses myth to idealize its honoree, who may as easily be a member of the peerage as the monarch. The flattery of such entertainments was, of course, widely recognized.

26. Ruth Nevo, *Tragic Form in Shakespeare* (Princeton: Princeton University Press, 1972), 75–76, 78; Henry A. Kelly, *Divine Providence in the England of Shakespeare's Histories* (Cambridge: Harvard University Prerss, 1970), 207; Paul Jorgensen, "A Formative Shakespearean Legacy: Elizabethan Views of God, Fortune, and War," *PMLA* 90 (1975): 222–23 (p. 229).

27. Herbert Coursen, *Christian Ritual and the World of Shakespeare's Tragedies* (Lewisburg, Pa.: Bucknell University Press, 1976), p. 56.

28. Christopher Morris, *Political Thought in England: Tyndale to Hooker* (London: Oxford University Press, 1953), 83.

29. David Bergeron, rev. of Roy Strong, "Art and Power: Renaissance Festivals 1450–1650," *Renaissance Quarterly* 39 (1986): 791.

30. Price, *Rituals and Power,* 48.

31. See, e.g., Una Ellis Fermor, *The Frontiers of Drama* (London: Methuen, 1945), 34–55; John Palmer, *Political Characters of Shakespeare* (1945; rpt. London: Macmillan, 1961), 39.

32. *Demythologizing,* the theological term proposed by Rudolf Butlmann, is "an attempt to separate the essential message from the cosmological 'mythology' which no modern man can believe," according to Richard E. Palmer, *Hermeneutics* (Evanston, Ill.: Northwestern University Press, 1969), 28. It must be distinguished from *demystification* as propounded by Marx, Nietzsche, and Freud, which treats such symbols "as a false reality which must be shattered" rather than as a "window to reality" (p. 44). *Desacralizing,* I hope, avoids the theological, political, or psychological associations that the other two words have acquired, though it can embrace both activities. Erasmus demythologized kingship but demystified the Shrine of Walsingham; in both cases he sought to remove these subjects from the realm of the sacred into which they had been transferred by the culture. See below, n. 72.

33. *The Reformation in the Cities: The Appeal of Protestantism to Sixteenth-Century Germany and Switzerland* (New Haven: Yale University Press, 1975), 8–9, 119.

34. Greenblatt, *Renaissance Self-Fashioning,* 113, though I prefer Ozment's

analysis to the Foucault-like claim that at the root of this crisis lay the "subversive perception" of imagination's role in creating oppressive institutions.

35. G. R. Elton, *The Tudor Constitution*, 2d ed. (Cambridge: Cambridge University Press, 1982), 345.

36. David Loades, *The Tudor Court*, 183.

37. Daniel Cawdry, *Superstitio Superstes: or The Reliques of Superstition Newly Revived* (1644), fol. Alv. On political consequences of the reformation of worship, see Carlos M. N. Eire, *War against the Idols* (Cambridge University Press, 1986), 276–310.

38. *The Tudor Regime* (Oxford: Clarendon Press, 1979), 359, 360.

39. S. T. Bindoff, *Tudor England* (1950; rpt. Harmondsworth: Penguin, 1966), 214–23.

40. Cf. Walter Bagehot, *The English Constitution* (1867; rpt. London: C. A. Watts, 1964), 86–90; J. G. Blumler et al., "Attitudes to the Monarchy: Their Structure and Development during a Ceremonial Occasion," *Political Studies* 19 (1971): 149–71, though in the latter, "religion" seems too reductively identified with "the affirmation of the moral values by which a society lives" (p. 152).

41. Sidney Verba, "The Kennedy Assassination and the Nature of Political Commitment," in *The Kennedy Assassination and the American Public*, ed. Bradley S. Greenberg and Edwin B. Parker (Standord, Calif.: Stanford University Press, 1965), 348–60 (especially 353–54).

42. *A Perswasive to Mutuall Compliance under the Present Government* (Oxford, 1652), 24.

43. Christopher Morris, *Political Thought in England: Tyndale to Hooker* (London: Oxford University Press, 1953), 7.

44. I share Gordon Ross Smith's concern that in the interpretation of Elizabethan literature, "Recent literary criticism has had a tendency to suppose a widespread acceptance of authoritarian governments, but that is probably an error of emphasis." "A Rabble of Princes: Considerations touching Shakespeare's Political Orthodoxy in the Second Tetralogy," *JHI* 41 (1980): 29–48 (p. 33). Smith goes on to regret the neglect of Erasmus among critics of Shakespeare's histories, a problem which my chapter on him addresses.

45. Philip Edwards, *Threshold of a Nation: A Study of English and Irish Drama* (Cambridge: Cambridge University Press, 1979), 3. Cf. a similar overstatement on "the divinity of a king," p. 39. Robin Headlam Wells, *Spenser's* Faerie Queene *and the Cult of Elizabeth* (London: Croom Helm, 1983), in his elucidation of the Marian cult underlying that of Elizabeth, at times represents Spenser as an uncritical worshipper.

46. *Queen Elizabeth* (London: Longmans Green, 1899), 151–52.

47. G. R. Elton, "The Divine Right of Kings," intro. to J. N. Figgis, *The Divine Right of Kings*, rpt. Elton, *Studies in Tudor and Stuart Politics and Government* (Cambridge: Cambridge University Press, 1974–81, 2:207. For recent assessment of divine right theory see David Wootton's introduction to his ed., *Divine Right and Democracy: An Anthology of Political Writings in Stuart England* (Harmondsworth: Penguin, 1986), with bibliography.

48. David Lee Miller, *The Poem's Two Bodies: The Poetics of the 1590* Faerie Queene (Princeton: Princeton University Press, 1988), 69, 17. Franco Moretti, " 'A Huge Eclipse': Tragic Form and the Deconsecration of Sovereignty," trans. D. A. Miller, *Genre* 15 (1982), 7–40. Moretti's view that the monarchy is self-determined, "having its origins in itself" (p. 9), like Miller's numinous body, sharply

differs from the only "bodie" Hooker proposes, the body politic in which the monarch originates (see below). Moretti's is the lead article in a special collection on the subject of power and Renaissance literature.

49. Sir David Lindsay Keir, *The Constitutional History of Modern Britain, Since 1485*, 8th ed. (London: A. and C. Black, 1966), 135.

50. G. R. Elton, "The Divine Right of Kings," 210. Cf. similar comments in Baumer, *Early Tudor Theory of Kingship*, 18; Morris, *Political Thought in England*, 83; George L. Mosse, *The Struggle for Sovereignty in England* (East Lansing: Michigan State College Press, 1950), 6.

51. Elton, *The Tudor Constitution*, 12. Note also that statute and common law took precedence over royal proclamation (p. 22).

52. Hooker, *Works*, 3:401 (*Laws* VIII.6.11). Most of my discussion of Hooker concerns Book VIII, edited in this edition by P. G. Stanwood. At the end of this paragraph, however, I substitute for Stanwood's "scism" the reading "seisin" in Raymond Houk's earlier edition (New York: Columbia University Press, 1931), p. 241.

53. Claire Cross, *The Royal Supremacy in the Elizabethan Church* (London: George Allen Unwin; New York: Barnes and Noble, 1969), 36.

54. Robert Eccleshall, *Order and Reason in Politics*, 145; the point is made earlier by H. C. Porter, "Hooker, the Tudor Constitution and the *Via Media*," in *Studies in Richard Hooker*, ed. W. Speed Hill (Cleveland: Case Western Reserve, 1972), 89.

55. Fletcher, *Prophetic Moment*, 149.

56. "As now the state of the *Church* doth stand, *Kinges* being not then [in the primitive Church] that which now they are and the Clergie not now that which then they were" the "consent of the highest power" as well as of the laity and clergy is required to make church law (3:393). "For wheras in *Regall States*, the *King* or supreme *Head of* the *Commonwealth* had before *Christianitie* a supreme stroke in the making of lawes for religion, he must by embracing *Christian* religion utterly thereof deprive himself and in such causes become a subject to his own subjectes" (3:408).

57. *Admonition to the People of England* (1589), p. 214, in Cross, *The Royal Supremacy*, 146. Joan S. Bennett, *Reviving Liberty*, traces the line of political thought from Aquinas to Hooker to Milton as "humanist antinomianism" (pp. 97–109), a tradition to which I believe Erasmus also belongs.

58. *Sermons* (Sermon on Acts 10.34) (Cambridge, Eng.: Parker Society, 1841), p. 272.

59. Bradshaw, *A Treatise of Divine Worship* (1604), fol. C1; *Twelve Generall Arguments* (1605), fol. B6.

60. F. J. Shirley, *Richard Hooker and Contemporary Political Ideas* (London: SPCK, 1949).

61. Julian H. Franklin, ed. and trans., *Constitutionalism and Resistance in the Sixteenth Century: Three Treatises by Hotman, Beza, & Mornay* (New York: Pegasus, 1969), 30. A lineage of this controversy, from Martin Bucer through Ponet, Knox, and Goodman, is on pp. 30–31. On resistance see also Donald Kelley, "Ideas of Resistance before Elizabeth," in Dubrow and Strier, *The Historical Renaissance*, pp. 48–76, and below, pp. 111–16.

62. Harold J. Laski, intro., *A Defence of Liberty against Tyrants* (New York: Harcourt Brace, [1924]), 60.

63. Shirley, *Richard Hooker*, 185.

64. Quoted by Shirley, *Richard Hooker*, 190.

65. Beza, *The Right of Magistrates*, trans. Franklin, p. 118.

66. In quoting the *Vindiciae*, I use the 1689 translation edited by Laski (here, p. 134), correcting a few errors that have entered into his text. Franklin's text is severely abridged. Richard C. McCoy, *The Rites of Knighthood* (Berkeley: University of California Press, 1989), observes that the *Vindiciae*, besides justifying rebellion, aimed to supplant feudal with constitutional institutions of government (p. 26).

67. Howell A. Lloyd, *The Rouen Campaign 1590–1592* (Oxford: Clarendon Press, 1973), 5.

68. Thomas Morton, *Christus Dei, The Lords Anoynted* (Oxford, 1643), 12; J. W. Allen, *A History of Political Thought in the Sixteenth Century* (1928; rev. rpt. London: Methuen, 1957), 331.

69. Robert E. Goodin, "Rites of Rulers," *British Journal of Sociology* 29 (1978): 281–99 (p. 294).

70. Victor Turner, *Dramas, Fields and Metaphors* (Ithaca: Cornell University Press, 1974), 28.

71. Cf. George LaPiana, "Theology of History," in *The Interpretation of History*, ed. Joseph Strayer (1943; rpt. New York: Peter Smith, 1950), 151–86 (especially 183–84); more recently, Gary Lease, "The Origins of National Socialism: Some Fruits of Religion and Nationalism," in *Religion and Politics in the Modern World*, eds. Peter H. Merkl and Ninian Smart (New York: New York University Press, 1983), 63–88. Contrast Leonardo Boff, *Jesus Christ Liberator*, trans. Patrick Hughes (New York: Orbis, 1978), and see Joan S. Bennett's comparison of Milton's radical Christianity with that of liberation theologians, *Reviving Liberty*, pp. 200–202.

72. Amos N. Wilder, *Theology and Modern Literature* (Cambridge: Harvard University Press, 1958), 70, quoted in Schneidau, *Sacred Discontent*, 3. Marcel Gauchet goes so far as to say that Christianity leads to the disappearance of religion in *Le desenchantement du monde: Une histoire politique de la religion* (Paris: Gallimard, 1985), a book touching many of the issues discussed here, such as the Reformation, absolute monarchy, and divine right.

73. A. E. Pollard, *The Evolution of Parliament*, 345, quoted in J. W. Allen, *Political Thought in the Sixteenth Century*, p. 230.

74. See below, pp. 124–26.

Chapter 1. King of This World

1. Edgar T. Schell and J. D. Schuchter, eds., *English Morality Plays and Moral Interludes* (New York: Holt, Rinehard, 1969), 169.

2. Although the king figure in medieval drama seems to have received no book-length scholarly treatment, it is an important concern in Robert Potter, *The English Morality Play: Origins, History, and Influence of a Dramatic Tradition* (London: Routledge and Kegan Paul, 1975), e.g., 67–69.

3. Quotations from this and other medieval plays, unless otherwise indicated, are from the edition by David Bevington, *Medieval Drama* (Boston: Houghton Mifflin, 1975). Middle English in other texts is regularized following Bevington's practice.

4. Nicolaus of Lyra's comment on Exodus I:1: "Per filios autem Israel manentes cum egyptiis intelligi possunt virtuosi manentes cum vitiosis: per regem autem egypti diabolus: qui est princeps huius mundi." Bible, 6 vols. (Lyons, "1508," i.e., 1520), 1:123. The association was commonplace: cf. St. Bernard of

Clairvaux' 39th Sermon on the Song of Songs, "De curribus Pharaonis, id est diaboli." Rosemary Woolf, *The English Mystery Plays* (London: Routledge and Kegan Paul, 1972), notes stylistic parallels between the speeches of Pharaoh and the devil of *Harrowing of Hell* in the York cycle, as well as between the Pharaoh-Moses and Satan-Christ dialogues (p. 154).

5. *A Treatice upon the Passion*, ed. Gary E. Haupt, in More, *Complete Works* (New Haven: Yale University Press, 1976), 8:58.

6. Martin Stevens, *Four Middle English Mystery Cycles* (Princeton: Princeton University Press, 1987), 169; V. A. Kolve, *The Play Called Corpus Christi* (Stanford, Calif.: Stanford University Press, 1966), 167.

7. Jeffrey Helterman, *Symbolic Action in the Plays of the Wakefield Master* (Athens: University of Georgia Press, 1981), 29–30.

8. Just as the character of Lucifer in the Wakefield *Creation* is modeled on Herod, that of Pharaoh was too, especially on account of traditional parallels between Pharaoh's killing of the first-born males and Herod's slaughter of the Innocents. See *Speculum hominis salvationis*, chap. 9.

9. Ernst Kantorowicz, *The King's Two Bodies*, 155, 20, 225. On medieval kingship's actual limitations, see the essays in Joel Rosenthal, ed., *Kings and Kingship*. Acta 11 (Binghamton, N.Y.: Center for Medieval and Early Renaissance Studies, 1986).

10. Peter W. Travis, *Dramatic Design in the Chester Cycle* (Chicago: University of Chicago Press, 1982), 10.

11. *The Play Called Corpus Christi*, 143.

12. "The Cambridge Prologue," in *Non-Cycle Plays and Fragments*, ed. Norman Davis, EETS supplem. ser. 1 (London, 1970), 115.

13. *York Plays*, lines 145–46 (p. 182).

14. Bible, ed. cit., 5:179v. The entire passage, the latter part referring more specifically to pagan and Jewish persecutors, reads: "Nefandum foedus quod herodes et pilatus in occidendo Christum pepigerunt / successores eorum hereditario iure costodiunt: dum iudei et gentiles: sicut genere et religione / ita mente quam dissidentes: in christianis tamen prosequendis / et fide Christi perimenda consentiunt. [. . . While the Jews and pagans, as different in race and religion as they are in mind, agree that Christians must be attacked and their faith destroyed.]"

15. For Herod as Satan, see Isidore of Seville: Herod "diaboli formam expressit, vel gentium, qui, cupientes exstinguere nomen Christi de mundo, in caede martyrum saevierunt." *Allegoriae quaedam Scripturae Sacrae*, MPL, 83:118. The Glossa Ordinaria on Matthew 2:1 states: "Herodes diabolum qui cognita divinitate Christi prosequitur eum in membris suis." Bible, ed. cit., 5:12.

16. "Coeli Rege nato, rex terrae turbatus est, quia nimirum terrena altitudo, confunditur cum celsitudo coelestis aperitur." *MPL*, 107:757.

17. "Quid est hoc, delectissimi fratres, ut isti Magi regem Iudaeorum adorandum quaererent, cum ipsi Iudaei non essent? Et quem regem? Utique non Herodem sed Christum. Volunt adorare regem nuper natum nec adorant regem ante annos aliquot ordinatum. Adorare cupiunt infantem lactantem nec adorant regem populis imperantem." Sermo IV, in *Sancti Fulgentii Episcopi Ruspensis Opera*, ed. J. Fraipont, Corpus Christianorum Series Latina, XCIA (1968), 912.

18. Sermo 152, *MPL*, 52:605. Cf. *The Golden Legend* on the Feast of the Epiphany, where Gregory is quoted as saying that "an earthly king cannot help being troubled in the presence of the King of Heaven." Trans. Granger Ryan and Helmut Ripperger, 2 vols. (London: Longmans, 1941), 1:86.

19. Miriam Anne Skey, "Herod the Great in Medieval European Drama," *CompD* 13 (1979): 330–61 (p. 353). Stephen May, "Good Kings and Tyrants: A Re-Assessment of the Royal Figure on the Medieval Stage," *Medieval English Theatre* 5 (1983): 87–102, warns against hasty labeling of all kings as tyrants, but admits, "a splendid monarch . . . must appear guilty until proven innocent, as in the case of the exceptional [Chester] Octavian" (p. 96).

20. David Staines, "To Out-Herod Herod: The Development of a Dramatic Character," *CompD* (1976): 29–53 (p. 45). See n. 1, p. 51 for a summary of earlier work on the character. Staines traces the twofold course of Herod as comic braggart and tragic figure. Both roles, I believe, are consequences of the absurdity and frustration of the claims of the world-king.

21. For contrasting opinions see Eleanor Prosser, *Drama and Religion in the English Mystery Play* (Stanford, Calif.: Stanford University Press, 1961), and Rose A. Zimbardo, "Comic Mockery of the Sacred: *The Frogs* and *The Second Shepherds' Play*," *ETJ* 30 (1978): 398–406.

22. Skey, "Herod the Great," 356. On Herod and Antichrist, see Helterman, *Symbolic Action*, 115–38.

23. "Quid est quod tempore regis nefandi Deus descendit ad terras? Miscetur divinitas carni? fit terreno corpori coeleste commercium? Quid est? etquando non verus rex expulsurus tyrannum, vindicaturus patriam, instauraturus orbem, libertatem redditurus adventat? Herodes refuga gentis Judaicae invasit regnum, libertatem sustulit, profanavit sancta, confudit ordinem; quidquid disciplinae, quidquid cultus est, abolevit; merito ergo genti sanctae, qui humana desunt, divina succurrunt, et adest Deus ipsi, cui homo non erat qui adesset. Sic iterum Christus veniet, ut Antichristus subruat, liberetur orbis, paradisi patria reddatur, mundi perpetuetur libertas, saeculi servitus tota tollatur." Serm. 156, *MPL*, 52:613.

24. *Ludus Coventriae*, ed. K. S. Block, *EETS*, e. s. 120 (1922), 1.8.

25. *The Chester Mystery Cycle*, eds. R. M. Lumiansky and David Mills, *EETS*, supplem. ser. 3 (1974), lines 117–18 (p. 164).

26. Noted by Staines, "To Out-Herod Herod," 45.

27. *York Plays*, ed. Lucy Toulmin Smith (1885; rpt. New York: Russell and Russell, 1963), 147 (lines 17–20).

28. *English Mystery Plays*, 203.

29. Josephus, *Jewish Antiquities*, 1.4; Augustine, *City of God*, 16.3–5; Peter Comestor records the idolatry motif in *Historia Scholastica* (*MPL*, 198:1088–89); *Cursor Mundi*, ed. Richard Morris (*EETS*, o.s. 57), lines 2289–92; Lydgate, *Fall of Princes*, ed. Henry Bergen (Washington, D.C.: Carnegie Institute, 1923), 1:1260; on Brueghel, see S. A. Mansbach, "Pieter Brueghel's Towers of Babel," *Zeitschrift fur Kunstgeschichte* 45 (1982): 43–56, also the general history of Babel-iconology in Helmut Minkowski, *Aus dem Nebel der Vergangenheit steigt der Turm zu Babel* (Berlin: Rembrandt Verlag, 1960); *Le Mistere du Viel Testament*, ed. Baron James de Rothchild. Societe des Anciennes Textes Francais, vol. 13 (rpt. 1966), containing the Nimrod plays, was first printed ca. 1500; John Cook, *King Charles His Case*, quoted in Stevie Davies, *Images of Kingship in Paradise Lost*, 34.

30. Lawrence M. Clopper, "The History and Development of the Chester Cycle," *MP* 75 (1978): 219–46. R. M. Lumiansky and David Mills, *The Chester Mystery Cycle: Essays and Documents* (Chapel Hill: University of North Carolina Press, 1983), believe the cycle took its present shape in the fifteenth century. Ruth M. Keane, "Kingship in the Chester Nativity Play," *Leeds Studies in English* 13 (1982): 74–84, thinks Octavian was changed to conform to "Reformation

theology," but one wonders why the Golden Legend material could have survived a Reformer.

31. *Chester Mystery Cycle*, 106 (lines 229–32). On the possibility that this is a composite of two plays, the first originally ending when Joseph falls asleep at line 116, see D. S. Bland, "The Chester 'Nativity': One Play or Two?" *N&Q* 208 (1963): 134–35.

32. Rosemary Woolf, *The English Mystery Plays*, 306. Peter W. Travis, *Dramatic Design in the Chester Cycle* (Chicago: University of Chicago Press, 1982), sees the plays as "the most conservative, the least realistic, the most reminiscent of Latin liturgical drama" (p. 27).

33. On the theme of deposing the powerful, see Kolve, *Play*, 157.

34. An accessible source is *The Golden Legend*, chap. 5, though others were used too. Samuel B. Hemingway, ed., *The English Nativity Plays* (1909; rpt. New York: Russell and Russell, 1964), 227–32, cites Neckham's *De Naturis Rerum*, chap. 174; Higden's *Polychronicon*, 3.44; Martinus Polonus, *Supputationes*, and the twelfth-century *Mirabilia Romae*.

35. The classic statement is Dante's *De Monarchia*. On its late medieval English analogues, see Ruth Mohl, "Monarchy in 'Mum and the Sothsegger,' " in her *Studies in Spenser, Milton, and the Theory of Monarchy* (New York: Frederick Ungar, 1962), 42–65.

36. See Hemingway on the *Mistere du Viel Testament*, 223.

37. *The Mirroure of Mans Salvacionne*, Roxburghe Club, no. 118 (London, 1888), chap. 8, p. 37.

38. *Cesar Augustus*, in *The Towneley Plays*, eds. George England and Alfred W. Pollard. *EETS*, e.s. 71 (London, 1897), lines 13–15.

39. On Antichrist as ruler of the world see W. Bousset, *The Antichrist Legend: A Chapter in Christian and Jewish Folklore*, trans. A. M. Keane (London: Hutchinson, 1896), 191–94.

40. *Chester Mystery Cycle*, p. 410 (lines 61–64).

41. Quoted in W. W. Greg, ed., *The Play of Antichrist from the Chester Cycle* (Oxford: Clarendon Press, 1935), x–xi: "Ingredietur autem in Ierusalem et sedebit in templo dei putans se quasi sit deus. Et erit fallax [et mendax] et fraudulentia eius seducet multos. Post hoc mittet dominus duos famulos sincerissimos, Enoch et Heliam, qui in eius testimonio reservati fuerant ad arguendum ipsum inimicum. Et tunc erunt novissimi primi et erunt credituri Iudei. Helias autem et Enoch arguent ipsum coram omni populo et ostendent eum mendacem esse et fallacem et confusum. Videntes autem cuncte gentes mendacium ipsum proferentem et a sanctis dei confusum et tunc erunt Iudei credituri. Ex omni tribu filiorum Israel erunt interfecti pro Christo.c.xliiii milia in diebus illis. Tunc Antichristus furore repletus iubebit sanctos dei interfici et qui eis sunt credituri. Et tunc veniet dominus noster Iesus Christus filius dei vivi in nubibus celi cum agminibus angelorum et gloria celesti."

42. Frank Kermode, *The Sense of an Ending* (Oxford: Oxford University Press, 1966), 10.

43. "Reges autem et principes primum ad se convertet et deinde per illos ceteros populos." Adso, rpt. in Karl Young, *The Drama of the Medieval Church* (Oxford: Clarendon Press, 1933), 2:498 (text of "Libellus," pp. 496–500).

44. See Young, 2:390–93 (text of Tegernsee *Ludus de Antichristo*, pp. 371–87). This play and Adso's "Libellus de Antichristo" are translated by John Wright, *The Play of Antichrist* (Toronto: Pontifical Institute of Medieval Studies, 1967).

45. Michael O'Connell, *Mirror and Veil: The Historical Dimension of Spenser's Faerie Queene* (Chapel Hill: University of North Carolina Press, 1977), 68.

46. The *psychomachia* is sufficiently conventional, though it has been noted that, owing to the Vulgate translation of the Greek *koma* (village) as *castellum* in Luke 10:38, some believed that Mary had actually lived in a castle. See Clifford Davidson, "The Digby *Mary Magdalene* and the Magdalene Cult of the Middle Ages," *Annuale Medievale* 13 (1972): 70–87.

47. "Together with her brother Lazarus and her sister Martha, she was the possessor of the fortified town of Magdala near Genezareth, of Bethany close by Jerusalem, and of a large section of Jerusalem itself." *The Golden Legend*, 2:355–56.

48. Text in *Tudor Interludes,* ed. Peter Happe (Harmondsworth: Penguin, 1972), 11.113, 121–126. W. A. Davenport, *Fifteenth Century English Drama* (Cambridge, Eng.: D. S. Brewer, 1982), 26–29, discusses Herod's similarity to later morality "kings" from a moral rather than political viewpoint.

49. Stage 3, scene 21, in *The Complete Poems of John Skelton Laureate*, ed. Philip Henderson (London: J. M. Dent & Sons, 1959), 211. The entire speech may be consulted in support of my point.

50. David Staines, "To Out-Herod Herod."

51. Letter to Ralegh: "In that Faery Queene I meane glory in my generall intention, but in my particular I conceive the most excellent and glorious person of our soveraine the Queene, and her kingdome in Faery land." The relation of the political to the psychological king-figure is not inconsistent with the view that, as Masao Yamaguchi says in an essay influenced by Kenneth Burke, kingship is "the dramatic space which is capable of being stabilised in the imagination of peoples as a symbolic universe symbolising the inner life of the individual." "Kingship as a System of Myth: An Essay in Synthesis," trans. Simon Pleasance, *Diogenes* 77 (1972): 43–70 (p. 68). On Skelton, see J. H. Scarisbrick, *Henry VII* (1968); rpt. Harmondsworth: Penguin, 1972), 302.

52. *Reform and Reformation: England, 1509–1558* (Cambridge: Harvard University Press, 1977), 1–2, discussing *The Tree of Commonwealth* (1510). Morris, *Political Thought in England,* 17, observes that the concept of order and degree in this work is used to support the aristocracy, not the crown.

53. "On Mending the Peace of the Church," in *Essential Erasmus,* trans. Dolan, 378.

54. Kolve, *Play,* 277, n. 14.

55. F. M. Salter, *Medieval Drama in Chester* (Toronto: University of Toronto Press, 1955), 89.

Chapter 2. Erasmus: Christian Liberty and Renaissance Majesty

1. *Order and Reason in Politics,* 76–96 (p. 77).

2. "Sileni Alcibiadis," in *Erasmus on His Times: A Shortened Version of the Adages of Erasmus,* trans. Margaret Mann Phillips (Cambridge: Cambridge University Press, 1967), 83 (hereafter cited as *Adagia*). The essay was frequently published separately, translations appearing in Spanish, German, Dutch, and (ca. 1543) English (p. 77, n.).

3. Robert P. Adams, *The Better Part of Valor: More, Erasmus, Colet, and Vives on*

Humanism, War, and Peace, 1496–1535 (Seattle: University of Washington Press, 1962), 106–8. Contrast the argument of Jose A. Fernandez, "Erasmus on the Just War," *JHI* 34 (1973): 209–26, which seems narrowly dependent on the *De Bello Turcico*. The view of Erasmus as an absolute pacifist (cf. Ferdinand Geldner, *Die Staatsauffassung und Fürstenlehre des Erasmus von Rotterdam* [Berlin: E. Ebering, 1930]) is qualified by later scholarship, e.g., Eberhard von Koerber's thesis, *Die Staatstheorie des Erasmus von Rotterdam* (Berlin: Duncker & Humbolt, 1967), in which Erasmus is seen as a prophet of such modern instruments of peace as international arbitration, fixed national boundaries, and the world court. See also John C. Olin, "The Pacifism of Erasmus," *Thought* 50 (1975): 418–31, in part a reply to Fernandez, as is John Mulryan, "Erasmus and War," *Moreana* 23 (1986): 15–28.

4. *Enchiridion (Handbook of the Militant Christian)*, in *The Essential Erasmus*, trans. John P. Dolan (New York: Mentor, 1964), 45.

5. *The Politics of Erasmus: A Pacifist Intellectual and His Political Milieu* (Toronto: University of Toronto Press, 1978), 46–47.

6. Hans Baron, "Franciscan Poverty and Civic Wealth as Factors in the Rise of Humanistic Thought," *Speculum* 13 (1938): 1–37 (p. 15).

7. *Epigrammata* (Basel, 1518), 262–63.

8. Eli Sobel, rev. of Otto Herding and Robert Stupperich, eds., *Die Humanisten in ihrer politischen und sozialen Umwelt* (Boppard: Boldt, 1976), in *RenQ* 31 (1978): 197. See, in the collection reviewed, Leon Halkin, "Erasme et la politique des rois," 109–18.

9. *Utopia*, trans. Robert M. Adams (New York: Norton, 1975), 29.

10. Johan Huizinga, *Erasmus and the Age of the Reformation*, trans. F. Hopman (1924; rpt. New York: Harper and Row, 1957), 153.

11. Preface to Suetonius, SWE, 4:383.

12. *L'essor de la philosophie politique au XVIe siècle*, 3d ed., *De Petrarque à Descartes* 19 (1969): 87.

13. *Ratio Verae Theologiae* (1518), *LB*, 5:120: "Idolatria vulgo dicitur, quoties thus incenditur signo cuipiam profano: vera idolatria est, quoties ob foedam voluptatem, ob turpe lucrum, ob vindictae cupiditatem, ob tyrannidem contemnitur Christus."

14. "Aut fatuum aut regem nasci opportere," *Adagia*, ed. cit., 40.

15. Trans. Lester K. Born (New York: Columbia University Press, 1936), 177.

16. E.g., Albert Salomon, "Democracy and Religion in the Works of Erasmus," *Review of Religion* 14 (1950): 227–49; Albert Hyma, "Erasmus and the Reformation in Germany," *Medievalia et Humanistica* 8 (1954): 99–104.

17. Bruce E. Mansfield, "Erasmus in the Nineteenth Century: The Liberal Tradition," *Studies in the Renaissance* 15 (1968): 193–219 (p. 218).

18. Colet, *De Corpore Christi Mystico*, quoted in Catherine A. L. Jarrott, "Erasmus's Annotations and Colet's Commentaries on Paul: A Comparison of Some Theological Themes," in *Essays on the Works of Erasmus*, ed. Richard L. DeMolen (New Haven: Yale University Press, 1978), 125–44 (p. 136).

19. *Education of a Christian Prince*, trans. Born, 199.

20. Dedication to Henry VIII of the *Paraphrase on St. Luke's Gospel*, Allen, no. 1381: "Nam quod Aristoteles hodie celebris est in scholis, non suis debet, sed Christianis: perisset et ille, nisi Christo fuisset admixtus."

21. "Dulce bellum inexpertis," *Adagia*, trans. cit., 123–24.

22. Rudolf Otto, *The Idea of the Holy*, trans. John W. Harvey (London: Oxford University Press, 1923), 12–24; Eliade, *Myths, Dreams and Mysteries*, trans. Philip

Mairet (1960; rpt. London: Fontana, 974), 123 (where "the God of Erasmus" is called "the God of philosophers, . . . an idea, an abstract notion").

23. *Enchiridion*, trans. Dolan, 56.

24. Cited in Mansfield, "Erasmus in the Nineteenth century," 217. This reductive characterization of the Middle Ages is, of course, in the benighted tradition of the nineteenth century.

25. Paul Sellin, "The Hidden God: Reformation Awe in Renaissance English Literature," in *The Darker Vision of the Renaissance: Beyond the Fields of Reason.* UCLA Center for Medieval and Renaissance Studies Contributions, 6 (Berkeley and Los Angeles: University of California Press, 1974), 153.

26. *Martin Luther: Selections from His Writings,* ed. John Dillenberger (Chicago: Quadrangle Books, 1961), 191, cited by Sellin, p. 154.

27. Otto Herding, "Isokrates, Erasmus, und die Institutio principis christiani," in *Dauer und Wandel der Geschichte: Aspekte Europäische Vergangenheit. Festgabe für Kurt von Raumer,* eds. Rudolf Vierhaus and Manfred Botzenhart (Munster: Verlag Aschendorff, 1966), 136.

28. *Education*, trans. Born, 190. The tyrant's saying also conflicts with Cicero's republican sentiment on fear: "To arouse fear in others is a bad guarantee of longevity, while on the other hand good will is faithful unto eternity." (The observation is made concerning the "tyrant" Julius Caesar.) *De Officiis* (II.23), trans. Harry D. Edinger (Indianapolis: Bobbs Merrill, 1974), 85.

29. From *De Conscribendis Epistolis,* quoted in Tracy, *Politics,* 152, n. 134 (my trans.). For an excellent discussion of Erasmus's linking ritualism to tyranny, see Tracy's *Erasmus: The Growth of a Mind.* Travaux d'Humanisme et Renaissance, 121 (1972), 144–51.

30. *Virginis Matris apud Lauretum Cultae Liturgia* (1523), *00* 5, no. 1 (ed. Leon Halkin), 100: "qui cereis, qui donariis, qui templis ac delubris illam honorant . . . in periculum veniunt ne audiant a Matre, quod Iudaicus cultor apud Prophetam audit a Patre: Hic populus labiis me honorat, cor autem eorum procul abest a me." On Erasmus's association of the Jews with religious ceremonialism, see John B. Payne, "Erasmus: Interpreter of Romans," *Sixteenth Century Essays and Studies,* ed. Carl S. Meyer (St. Louis: Foundation for Reformation Research, 1971), 2:17.

31. *Modus Orandi Deum* (1524), *00* 5, no. 1 (ed. J. N. Bakhuizen van den Brink), 137: "Pro triumphorum, ovationum, et supplicationum inanibus pompis habemus hymnos et gratiarum actiones [Instead of the futile pomp of triumphal processions, spectacles, and public solemnities, we have hymns and prayers]".

32. *Education*, trans. Born, 151.

33. "Dulce bellum inexpertis," *Adagia,* ed cit., 137.

34. Though not the only current, for as Paul Kristeller reminds us, the more familiar "civic humanism" of Hans Baron can be countered by instances of a "despotic humanism," even in fifteenth-century Italy. "The Moral Thought of Renaissance Humanism," *Renaissance Thought II: Papers on Humanism and the Arts* (New York: Harper and Row, 1965), 47.

35. Preface to paraphrase of Mark (1523), Allen, no. 1400: "Mihi videtur maxima bellorum pars ex inanibus aliquot vocabulis, velut in alimoniam humanae gloriae excogitatis, oriri: quasi parum fuerit ambitionis inter mortales, nisi novis titulis aleremus hoc malum, ex sese nimium gliscens in nobis." Quentin Skinner, *The Foundations of Modern Political Thought* (Cambridge: Cambridge University Press, 1978) takes J. H. Hexter to task for saying that More and Erasmus opposed the pursuit of honor, citing such remarks as (in the *Enchiridion*) that the

prince should follow "the path of right and honor" (1:234). Clearly Skinner's proof-texts refer to honor as moral virtue, while Hexter is talking about honor as worldly glory (cf. the colloquy "Philodoxus," "The Lover of Glory," 1531). The ambiguity is familiar in Shakespeare.

36. *The Powers of the Crown in Scotland,* trans. Charles F. Arrowood (Austin: University of Texas Press, 1949), 59; cf. p. 94. On the Erasmian "denigration of the honour cult," in the later sixteenth century, see Mervyn James, "English Politics and the Concept of Honour," in *Society, Politics and Culture* (Cambridge: Cambridge University Press, 1986), 320–21.

37. *The Antibarbarians,* trans. Margaret Mann Phillips, CWE, 28:80.

38. *Panegyricus ad Philippum, OO* 4, no. 1 (ed. Otto Herding): 72–75: "Pacificum, inquam, te malumus quam victorem, ac tanto prorsus malumus, quanto modis omnibus pax bello praestantior. In pace calent artes, florent honesta studia, viget legum reverentia, augescit religio, crescunt opes, pollet morum disciplina. In bello collabuntur defluunt commiscentur haec omnia et simul cum omni genere calamitatum nulla non lues morum ingruit. Sacra prophanantur, cultus divinus neglectui habetur, in iuris locum vis succedit. Silent enim (ut ait Cicero) leges inter arma, ut si quid loquuntur salutare, non queunt (ut aeleganter dixit Marius) ob armorum strepitum exaudiri" (lines 500–508). "Num Christianus dux, quem oportet esse clementissimum, quo non modo *numen* aliquod esse *iustumque memorque* credit, verum etiam mox illi de minutissima quoque guttula sanguinis humani exactissimam rationem esse redendam intelligit, cui non totum imperium, non etiam vita sua tanti debet esse, ut quemquam innocentem sua causa velit perire, postulabit, ut ius illud nescio quod suum (neque enim hic laboro, quanti referat, hic an ille potiatur) tot lachrymis tot orbitatibus tanto luctu tam multo cruore miserorum tot mortalium capitibus tot periculis tot vulneribus et (quod his omnibus damnosius) tanta morum pernicie sibi constet?" (lines 569–76).

39. *Praise of Folly,* in *Essential Erasmus,* trans. Dolan, 156. On the theme of war in *Folly,* see Adams, *Better Part,* 44–54.

40. See "Spartam nactus es hanc orna," *Adagia,* ed. cit., 103–4, where Julius is listed among rulers whose wars have brought a variety of human miseries. Tracy, *Politics,* 30–32, says Erasmus's attacks on Julius are motivated largely by partisanship.

41. Tracy, *Politics,* 71–107.

42. With "Dulce Bellum," cf. "Aut fatuum aut regem nasci oportere," Scarabeus aquilam quaerit," "Sileni Alcibiadis," and "Spartam nactus es hanc orna."

43. *Essential Erasmus,* trans. Dolan, 197.

44. *OO* 4, no. 1 (1974): 97–130. My summary in this paragraph refers especially to pp. 97–107 and 118–30. The introduction in Born's translation (pp. 3–130) chiefly concerns sources and analogues.

45. Allen, no. 337: "In Enchiridio simpliciter Christianae vitae formam tradidimus. In libello De principis institutione palam admonemus quibus rebus principem oporteat esse instructum. In Panegyrico sub laudis praetextu hoc ipsum tamen agimus oblique quod illic egimus aperta fronte. Nec aliud agitur in Moria sub specie lusus quam actum est in Enchiridio."

46. J. H. Hexter, *The Vision of Politics on the Eve of the Reformation* (New York: Basic Books, 1973), 215. On the history of the genre, see Allan Gilbert, *Machiavelli's "Prince" and Its Forerunners* (Durham: Duke University Press, 1948).

47. Henry Bergen, ed. *Fall of Princes*, *EETS*, e.s. 121–24 (London, 1923–27), 121, xx.

49. *Isocrates*, Loeb ed., trans. George Norlin (1928; rpt. London: Heinemann, 1966), 1:151 (par. 20).

49. *Praise of Folly* in *Essential Erasmus*, trans. Dolan, 102.

50. Herding ed., 136: "Institutio Principis Christiani per Erasmum Roterodamum aphorismis digesta quo minus onerosa sit lectio." Inexplicably, Born translates the subtitle, "separated into pertinent chapters" (p. 137).

51. *LB* at least tried to preserve the separateness of the aphorisms by extending the white space between them, within the "paragraphs." Although Born does not, he does seek to improve the logic of *LB*'s paragraphing. E.g., he begins his fourth paragraph ("Where there is no opportunity to choose the prince . . .") with an aphorism that marks a clear change of direction, whereas in *LB* this aphorism is buried in the midst of a long paragraph. Born reveals his insensitivity to the aphoristic nature of the work when he says, "Furthermore, the *Institutio* is full of platitudes, repetitions, and miscellanies that at first seem to detract" (p. 30). Detract from what? one might ask, in a work that has no whole to detract from.

52. See Brian Vickers, *Francis Bacon and Renaissance Prose* (Cambridge: Cambridge University Press, 1968), pp. 60–95, the source of the remarks on the form in this paragraph.

53. *LB*, 4:87: "Proin ex optimis quibusque auctoribus collegi: quae Graeci vocant Apophthegmatas, hoc est, egregie dicta, quod viderem non aliud argumenti genus Principi, praesertim juveni, magis accommodum. Sunt illa quidem scitu dignissima, quae Philosophi de moribus, de Republica administranda, deque bello gerendo literis prodiderunt. Sed quoto cuique vel privato tantum est otii, ut apud Platonem Socraticarum argutationum, ironiarum & Isagogarum ambages ac labyrinthos evolvere vacet? Aristoteles autem copiose quidem scripsit de moribus, sed Philosophis scripsisse videtur, non Principi. . . . At ei qui ditioni nascitur, statim expedienda virtus est, non per otium disputanda. Restat Historia, quae quoniam res praeclare secusve gestas velut in tabula spectandas repraesentat, nec id absque voluptate, magnatibus viris aptior esse videtur: sed hic ut infinitam voluminum vim Principi vacet evolvere, quis possit meminisse? Atqui quemadmodum ii qui certant in palaestra, certos quosdam prehendendi elabendique modos ad manum habent: ita qui in pacis bellique negotiis versantur certas rationes in promptu habere convenit, quibus admoneantur, quid pro re nata sit facto opus, quid non."

54. Prince Philip was to read the book, "explaining and translating it" three hours a day. Born, trans., *Education*, 28–29, and n. 17.

55. Hexter, *The Vision of Politics*, 84–85.

56. Herding ed., *Institutio*, 136: "Ubi receptum est suffragiis ascisci principem, illic non perinde spectandae sunt maiorum imagines, sive species corporis aut proceritas, quod a barbaris nonnullis olim ineptissime factitatum legimus atque indoles animi mansueta placidaque, sedatum ac minime praeceps ingenium nec ita concitatum, ut periculum sit, ne accedente fortunae licentia erumpat in tyrannidem et admonentem aut consulentem non ferat, nec rursus ita lentum, ut cuiuslibet arbitrio quovis duci sese patiatur." For all its cumbersomeness, I prefer my version to Born's, which translates "ubi" as temporal, loses the "not so much . . . as" sense of "non perinde . . . atque," and reads "indoles animi mansueta placidaque" as referring to the barbarian practice:

"When a prince is to be chosen by election it is not at all appropriate to look to the images of his forefathers, to consider his physical appearance, his height of stature (which we read that some barbarians once most stupidly did) and to seek a quiet and placid trend of spirit. Seek rather a nature staid, in no way rash, and not so excitable that there is a danger of his developing into a tyrant under the license of good fortune and casting aside all regard for advisors and counselors. Yet have a care that he be not so weak as to be turned now this way and that by whomever he meets" (p. 139). I wish to acknowledge Professor Oliver Phillips's grammatical assistance on this point.

57. *Adagia*, ed. cit., 40.

58. Herding, ed., *Institutio*, 136. "Caeterum ubi nascitur princeps, non eligitur, quod et olim apud barbaros aliquot nationes fieri solitum testatur Aristoteles et nostris temporibus ubique fere receptum est, ibi praecipua boni principis spes a recta pendet institutione, quam hoc diligentiorem etiam adhiberi conveniet, ut quod suffragiorum iuri detractum est, id educandi studio pensetur."

59. "The Godly Feast," in *The Colloquies of Erasmus*, trans. Craig R. Thompson (Chicago: University of Chicago Press, 1965), 58 (Eusebius speaking).

60. Herding, ed., *Institution*, 166: "Deus ipse, ne coactis imperaret, et angelis et hominibus liberum dedit arbitrium, quo splendidius et angustius redderet imperium suum. Et quisquam hoc nomine sibi magnus videtur, quod metu adactis civibus ceu pecudibus imperet?"

61. *L'essor de la philosophie politique*, 96.

62. Herding, "Isokrates, Erasmus, und die Institutio," 132.

63. Herding, ed., *Institutio*, 145: "Cogita, queso, quam sit absurdum gemmis auro purpura satellitio reliquisque corporis ornamentis, ceris et imaginibus planeque bonis non tuis omneis tanto intervallo superare, veris animi bonis multis e media fece plebis inferiorem conspici."

64. "Scarabeus aquilam quaerit," *Adagia*, ed. cit., 50–51.

65. *LB*, 6:635 (Rom. 13:1): "non dixit, omnes Principes ordinatos a Deo, sed Potestatem: quemadmodum matrimonium est a Deo, sed non omnes conjuges jungit Deus."

66. See Herding ed., *Institutio*, "Ne putaris te Christum . . ." (147–48); "Nullius pestilentiae . . ." (149); "Hoc interest inter principem ac tyrannum" (152–53); "Deus ipse . . ." (166).

67. Mesnard, *L'essor de la philosophie politique:* "Erasme rejette precisement l'idée d'une souveraineté véritable" (p. 124), referring especially to the aphorism: "Cogitato semper dominum imperium regnum maiestatem potentiam ethnicorum esse vocabula, non Christianorum; Christianum imperium nihil aliud esse quam administrationem quam beneficentiam quam custodiam" (Herding ed., *Institutio*, 164). ("Know always that *lord, sovereignty, kingdom, majesty,* and *power* are pagan, not Christian words. Christian sovereignty is nothing else than helping, than kindness, than protecting.")

68. Preface to Suetonius, *CWE*, 4:381. Cf. Richard Hooker's point that occasionally "they whose ancient predecessours were by violence and force made subject doe growe even by little and little into that most sweete forme of kingly government" (3:340). The idea of gradually validated usurped sovereignty may owe something to Aristotle, *Politics*, 3.10.

69. "Dulce Bellum inexpertis," *Adagia*, 131.

70. Herding ed., *Institutio*, 216: "Bona pars imperii consensus est populi, ea res primo reges peperit."

71. *Ecclesiastae, sive de Ratione Concionandi* (1535), *LB* 5:1081: "Ad secundam

speciem [pietatis] pertinet, quam multa debeamus patriae, quae genuit, quae bonis legibus educavit, cui & ipsos parentes debemus, pro qua mors oppetenda sit si res postulet. Ex adverso, quam immane scelus sit, patriae bellum inferre, aut aliis rationibus laedere. . . .

"Huic adhaeret locus de Ecclesia Catholica, quae non solum est una civitas, verum etiam unum corpus. Christianus enim omni Christiano non tantum civis est, verum etiam frater. Hic tractabitur quanta reverentia debeatur Ecclesiae; contra, quanta sit impietas, adversus eam rebellionem ac seditionem excitare. Adhibebitur amplificatio per comparationem, quanto arctiora sint vincula Spiritus quam naturae."

72. Ibid. 5:1081: "Congruit his, quid honoris debeatur Regibus ac Magistratibus, & quanto plus iis qui muneribus Ecclesiasticis funguntur. [It follows from these remarks what honor is owed to kings and magistrates, and how much more to those who are concerned with ecclesiastical duties.]" Thomas was more consistently dedicated to mixed monarchy: see James M. Blythe, "The Mixed Constitution and the Distinction between Regal and Political Power in the Works of Thomas Aquinas," *Journal of the History of Ideas* 47 (1986): 547–65.

73. Allen, no. 1653, quoted in Augustin Renaudet, *Etudes Erasmiennes* 1521–29 (Paris: E. Droz, 1939), 120; cf. Mesnard, p. 127. Erasmus's "contempt for the common people" is compared, rather one-sidedly, I think, with Zwingli's fuller sense of the public man in G. W. Locher, "Zwingli und Erasmus," in *Scrinium Erasmianum*, ed. J. Coppens (Leyden: Brill), 2:235–50 (trans. Isbell, Shaw, and Rummel, *Erasmus in English* 10 [1979–80]: 2–11).

74. Allen, no. 2034: "Siquidem recte dictum est a sapientibus viris, Regem esse vivam legem. Lex pauciloqua est, at infinitae sunt rerum et personarum circunstantiae. In his igitur rex pro lege loquitur, nec aliud tamen pronuncians quam lex ipsa diceret si nobis ad omnia respondere posset."

75. Cf. *Panegyric*, ed. Herding, 63, the passage beginning, "Tu major legibus."

76. Born trans. *Education*, p. 173; Herding ed. *Institutio*, p. 163, lines 85–87.

77. Mesnard, *L'essor*, 131–35; Tracy, *Politics*, 17–22, 103–7; Renaudet, *Etudes* 107. Like Renaudet, Mesnard points out (citing Henri Pirenne, *Histoirie de Belgique*, 3:137) that Charles V himself considered the Low Countries as quasi-autonomous (*L'essor*, 131).

78. *Adagia*, ed. cit., 36–37.

79. Preface to Suetonius, *CEW* 4:377; cf. Born trans. *Education*, 162.

80. *Adagia*, ed. cit., 145; cf. Ferdinand Geldner, *Die Staatsauffassung*, 141, cited in Tracy, *Politics*, 105.

81. *OO* 5, no. 1 (ed. Herding): 306: "Verum est aliud blasphemiae genus, aliquanto quidem tectius, sed haud ita multa minus perniciosum, quoties populus, adulans suis principibus defert eis honores divinos, et principes hoc honoris libenter amplectuntur. Itaque fit interdum ut princeps pro civibus et consiliariis habeat palpones et irrisores, populus vice principum habeat dementes tyrannos, et utrinque blasphemia provocatur deus." Erasmus's marginal note here reads, "idolatria."

82. Herding ed., *Institutio*, 178.

83. "Aut fatuum aut regem," *Adagia*, ed. cit., 42.

84. *The Ready and Easy Way*, *CPW* 7:425–26.

85. *Etudes Erasmiennes*, 85. On Erasmus and economics, see p. 76 and Renaudet, "Erasme économiste," in *Mélanges offerts à m. Abel Lefranc*, n. ed. (Paris: E. Droz, 1936), 130–41.

86. James Kelsey McConica, *English Humanists and Reformation Politics under Henry VIII and Edward VI* (Oxford: Clarendon Press, 1965); cf. anon. review, "A Fine Fellow Erasmus," *TLS*, 3 June 1965, p. 454. A dissenting view that finds Erasmus's influence overstated and "a certain hollowness" in Erasmus's spirituality is J. T. Rhodes, "Erasmus and English Readers of the 1530's," *Durham University Journal*, n.s. 40 (1978), 17–25. Theology in this period cannot be separated from education, Erasmus's influence on which is discussed in Jean Simon, *Education and Society in Tudor England* (Cambridge: Cambridge University Press, 1966).

87. C. H. Williams, *William Tyndale* (London: Thomas Nelson, 1969), 4. On Tyndale and the *Enchiridion*, see pp. 10–12. Tyndale was also moved to translate Erasmus's life of Colet, including (ironically) the account of the Good Friday sermon on kingship (see notes to Allen, no. 1211).

88. *Obedience of a Christian Man*, in *Doctrinal Treatises*, ed. Henry Walter (Parker Society, 1848), 180. Henry VIII was delighted with this book: see Scarisbrick, *Henry VIII*, 325.

89. "Let kings defend their subjects from the wrongs of other nations, but pick no quarrels for every trifle: no, let not our most holy fathers make them no more drunk with vain names, with caps of maintenance, and like baubles, as it were puppetry for children, to beggar their realms, and to murder their people, for defending of our holy father's tyranny" (pp. 204–5).

90. *Obedience*, 175, 177, 179. Cf. Erasmus, *Paraphrase of St. Paul's Epistle to the Romans* (1517): "Proinde qui Principi aut Magistratui etiam impio & Ethnico, suo fungenti officio resistit, is non resistit homini fungenti, sed Deo, a quo proficiscitur omnis auctoritas" (*LB* 7:820). ["Therefore he who resists a prince or magistrate, even a wicked and pagan one, in the performance of his office, does not resist the man in office, but God, from whom all authority proceeds."] On Tyndale's differences with divine right theory, see Williams, *William Tyndale*, 140–41, and below, chap. 3, notes 35 and 47 on Melanchthon.

91. Elizabeth F. Rogers, ed., *The Correspondence of Sir Thomas More* (Princeton: Princeton University Press, 1947), 3. More convenient for More-Erasmus correspondence are the representative translations in her *Selected Letters* (New Haven: Yale University Press, 1961). The *Correspondence* always refers the reader to Allen for these letters. Richard Marius, *Thomas More: A Biography* (New York: Knopf, 1984), contains a valuable discussion of the Erasmus-More friendship.

92. *Selected Letters*, 37 (Rogers, no. 15).

93. *Utopia*, trans. Adams, 22–23, 10, 25, 57, 39.

94. *Selected Letters*, 85 (Rogers, no. 29).

95.

> Rusticus in sylvis nutritus venit in urbem,
> Rusticior Fauno, rusticior Satyro.
> En populus plena stetit hinc, stetit inde platea,
> Unaque vox tota, Rex venit, urbe fuit.
> Rusticus insolita vocis novitate movetur,
> Quidnam ita respectet turba, videre cupit.
> Rex subito invehitur, celebre praeeunte caterva,
> Aureus, excelso conspiciendus equo.
> Tum vero ingeminant, vivat rex. undique regem
> Attonito populus suspicit ore suum.
> Ruisticus, o ubi rex? ubi rext est? clamat. at unus,
> Ille, ait, est illo qui sedet altus equo.

Hiccine rex? puto me derides, rusticus inquit.
Ille mihi picta veste videtur homo.

(Epigrammata, ed. cit., 249)

96. *The Essential Erasmus,* trans. Dolan, p. 117.
97.

In eandem picturam
Ora viri foedo sancti fluitantia tabo,
Decussumque gerit regia mensa caput.
Corpora sic regi rex Atreus ambo Thyesti
Natorum apposuit frater edena patri.
Sic regi Odrysio natum regina peremptum
Fida soror, genetrix perfida ponit Itim,
Talia regales ornant bellaria mensas.
Crede mihi non est pauperis iste cibus.

(Epigrammata, ed. cit., 259)

See Uwe Baumann, "Thomas More and the Classical Tyrant," *Moreana* 86 (1985): 108–27.
98. Richard Sylvester, *CWM* 2:cii–ciii. More's view of kingship is ably outlined in Alistair Fox, *Thomas More: History and Providence* (New Haven: Yale University Press, 1983), 162–66.
99. Renaudet, *Etudes,* 117, citing in contrast Luther's *Wider die rauberischen und morderischen Rotten der Bauern* (1525). J. Lindenboom states that Erasmus came to approve the execution of heretics: *Erasmus: Onderzoek naar zijne theologie en zijn godsdienstig gemoedbestaan* (Leyden, 1909), 92–103, cited in Albert Hyma, "Erasmus and the Sacrament of Matrimony," *Archiv für Reformations Geschichte* 48 (1957): 163. See also Karl Heinz Oelrich, *Der späte Erasmus und die Reformation.* Reformations-geschichtliche Studien und Texte, 86 (Münster/Westfallen, 1961). A more humane late Erasmus is argued in Roland H. Bainton, "Erasmus and the Persecuted," *Scrinium Erasmianum* 2:197–202.
100. *Confutation of Tyndale's Answer* (1532), ed. Louis A. Schuster, Richard Marius, James P. Lusardi, and Richard J. Schoeck, *CWM* 8 (1973): 179.
101. M. Nedoncelle, "L'Humour d'Erasme et l'humour de Thomas More," *Scrinium Erasmianum* 2:567.
102. Joan Simon, *Education,* 380; Bruce Mansfield, *Phoenix of His Age: Interpretations of Erasmus c 1550–1750* (Toronto: University of Toronto Press, 1979), 110–14 on Foxe; Marco Orru, "Anomy and Reason in the English Renaissance," *JHI* 47 (1986): 177–96, on Hooker (p. 186).
103. David Loades, *The Tudor Court,* 125–26.
104. For the date and politics of the *Dialogue,* see Thomas F. Mayer, "Faction and Ideology: Thomas Starkey's *Dialogue,*" *Historical Journal* 28 (1985): 1–25; also his "Thomas Starkey: An Unknown Conciliarist at the Court of Henry VIII," *JHI* (1988): 207–27.
105. *Dialogue,* ed. T. F. Mayer, Camden ser. 4, vol. 37 (London, 1989), 36.
106. *Dialogue,* 139–40. Mayer, "Faction," notes that "instructyon of a chrystun man" may not mean the *Enchiridion,* but the *Christiani Hominis Institutum* or the *Education.* Tyndale's English *Enchiridion* had already appeared, and Starkey implies that the "instructyon" is not yet translated.
107. Phrase from Margaret Mann Phillips, *Erasmus and the Northern Renaissance* (New York: Macmillan, 1950), 226–27.

108. Montaigne, "Of Repentance," *Complete Essays*, trans. Donald M. Frame (Stanford: Stanford University Press, 1958), 615.

Chapter 3. Spenser's Anatomy of Tyranny

1. H. S. V. Jones *(Spenser Handbook)* attributes Spenser's belief in aristocracy to Aristotle (Variorum ed., Book V, 293–94).

2. Hooker, *Works*, 2:37 (V.7.3).

3. *A View of the Present State of Ireland*, ed. R. Gottfried, in *Works of Edmund Spenser: A Variorum Edition* (Baltimore: Johns Hopkins University Press, 1949), 10:66, 69. Most recent attention to the *View* has addressed its moral implications: foremost, I think, is the close reading by Sheila Cavanagh, who sees Spenser as a moderate on Ireland in " 'Such Was Irena's Countenance: Ireland in Spenser's Prose and Poetry," *Texas Studies in Literature and Language* 28 (1986): 24–50. Brendan Bradshaw, "The Elizabethans and the Irish: A Muddled Model," *Studies* 20 (1981): 233–44, attributes Spenser's Irish attitudes to supposed Calvinism; Nicholas Canny, "Edmund Spenser and the Development of an Anglo-Irish Identity," *Yearbook of English Studies* 12 (1983): 1–19, says Spenser spoke for the New English against the Old, seeking to promote "individualism and self–sufficiency" (p. 5). David J. Baker, " 'Some Quirk, Some Subtle Evasion': Legal Subversion in Spenser's *A Vewe of the Present State of Ireland*," *Spenser Studies* 6 (1985): 147–63, rightly says Spenser aimed to expose the susceptibility of English law to corruption, thereby arguing the need for the queen's exercise of her prerogative in direct rule; Kenneth Gross, *Spenserian Poetics: Idolatry, Iconoclasm, and Magic* (Ithaca: Cornell University Press, 1985), 78–109, finds in the tract Spenser's recognition that both law and myth are of limited value. Finally, see the all-out attack, claiming that Spenser wanted "total and immediate war" and a "scorched-earth policy" by Ciaran Brady, "Spenser's Irish Crisis," *Past and Present* 111 (1986): 17–49. My object is not to justify Spenser on Ireland but to examine his ideas on law and government; still, I believe that Brady overstates somewhat, and misrepresents Spenser's use of the word "sword" (note, e.g., the part of the text missing at the ellipses in his quotation on p. 39).

4. For clarity's sake I have inserted the first two commas here and deleted a superfluous "to" in the second sentence. Later scholars' readiness to identify Spenser with Bodin's absolutist theory is exemplified in H. S. V. Jones, "Spenser's Defense of Lord Grey," *University of Illinois Studies in Language and Literature* 5 (1919): 196–97, which omits notice of this ensuing passage (also without comment in the *Variorum*).

5. For "civility" as a principal effect of good government, see, e.g., *View*, pp. 43, 49, 54, 96, 106, 113, 115, 157, 209, 218, 225. Cf. the many instances of the theme in Starkey, *Dialogue*, index p. 146.

6. *Theatre for Worldlings* (1569; rpt. New York: Scholars' Facsimiles, 1939), fol. A6.

7. See comments of Higginson, Padelford, Greenlaw, and others in *Variorum*, 7:254, 261, 602–9. Recently scholars have resumed the historical and topical approach to Spenser's pastorals: see the discussion in David Norbrook, *Poetry and Politics in the English Renaissance* (London: Routledge and Kegan Paul, 1984), which does not, however, examine "February." Ronald Bond sees the poem as reflecting Spenser's warning to Elizabeth about the need to protect the

old aristocracy from the envy of arrivistes: "Supplantation in the Elizabethan Court: The Theme of Spenser's February Eclogue," *Spenser Studies* 2 (1981): 55–65; Louis Montrose replies in "Interpreting Spenser's February Eclogue: Some Contexts and Implications," 67–74, arguing for Spenser's "ambivalent engagement" with all his characters and their positions in the *Calendar.* Historians still occasionally speak of Spenser as a "Puritan": e.g., Horton Davies, *Worship and Theology in England* (Princeton; Princeton University Press, 1975), 2:254. On the varieties of Elizabethan Puritanism, see H. C. Porter, intro., *Puritanism in Tudor England* (London: Macmillan, 1971), 9–11. For a discussion of the elusive meaning of "Puritanism" see Michael G. Finlayson, *Historians, Puritanism, and the English Revolution* (Toronto: University of Toronto Press, 1983), 3–8, 42–76. John N. King, "Was Spenser a Puritan?" *Spenser Studies* 6 (1985): 1–31, also objects to the label. Spenser is still "Puritan" in Norbrook (e.g., p. 61).

8. Both E. K. and the age of Greenlaw believed holy water revealed the oak's benightedness; but see *FQ* I.ll.36 and 12.37 for instances favoring it. Oaks are of course sacred in their association with the Golden Age and druidical religion.

9. See Richard F. Hardin, "The Resolved Debate of Spenser's 'October,' " *MP* 73 (1976): 257–63.

10. See David Loades, *The Tudor Court* (London: B. T. Batsford, 1986), 163, 190–91.

11. *Colloquies,* trans. Thompson, 432.

12. Hugh Maclachlan, "In the Person of Prince Arthur: Spenserian *Magnificence* and the Ciceronian Tradition," *UTQ* 46 (1976/7): 125–46 (p. 141).

13. Anon., *The Institucion of a Gentleman* (1555), fols. 3–3v. Richard C. McCoy, *The Rites of Knighthood,* provides an informed account of the Elizabethan "chivalric compromise" (pp. 9–27) between monarchy and aristocracy, and of Essex's maneuverings to assert aristocracy, pp. 79–102.

14. Graziani, "Elizabeth at Isis Church," *PMLA* 79 (1964): 376–89. Kermode, " 'The Faerie Queene', I and V." *Shakespeare, Spenser, Donne* (London: Routledge and Kegan Paul, 1971), 58, 56. Hooker, *Works,* 3:424. Donald V. Stump, "Isis versus Mercilla: The Allegorical Shrines in Spenser's Legend of Justice," *Spenser Studies* 3 (1982): 87–98, sees the Temple as an emblem of defective justice, equity in a vacuum, in contrast to the perfect justice of Mercilla's Palace. Although I don't think Spenser separates mercy from equity, I agree that "Spenser designed his allegorical shrines so as to contrast the early years of Elizabeth when she was weak and vulnerable, with the height of her reign, when she had defeated all her enemies" (pp. 91–92). On equity, see W. Nicholas Knight, "The Narrative Unity of Book V of *The Faerie Queene:* 'That Part of Justice which is Equity,' " *RES* 21 (1970): 267–94: "In Spenser mercy bears the same relationship to divine justice (or clemency to the rigour of the law), as equity bears to justice" (p. 291). On common law and equity see Sir William Holdsworth, *A History of English Law* (London: Methuen, Sweet and Maxwell, 1924), 5:215–18.

15. On Gerioneo's temple, see Hamilton's notes, also Stump, "Isis," 92, and D. Douglas Waters, "Spenser and the 'Mas' at the Temple of Isis," *SEL* 19 (1979): 43–53.

16. Cf. Fletcher, *The Prophetic Moment:* "to the extent that Gloriana sends her knights on good quests, she has sons, many lions to serve her Court of Maidenhead" (p. 275). The lion symbolizes both monarchy and the nobility also in *Mother Hubberds Tale.*

17. Holdworth, *History of English Law,* 5:268.

18. Erasmus: " 'Per me reges regnant et legum conditores iusta decernunt; per me principes imperant et potentes decernunt iustitiam.' Dixit autem hoc aeterna sapientia, qui est Filius Dei. Quid autem praescribit sapientia regibus? 'Misericordia,' inquit, 'et veritas custodiunt regem, et roboratur clementia thronus eius.' Misericordiam praestat in sublevandis oppressis, veritatem in integre iudicando, clementiam in temperanda legum severitate." Letter to Sigismund I (Allen, 2034); act of 1547 in Elton, *Tudor Constitution,* 64.

19. William Nelson, "Queen Elizabeth, Spenser's Mercilla, and a Rusty Sword," *RN* 18 (1965): 113–17. Note that Elizabeth's poem (ca. 1570) refers to the troublesome Mary Stuart as a Duessa-like figure:

> The daughter of debate that discord aye doth sow
> Shall reap no gain where former rule still peace hath taught to know.
> No foreign banished wight shall anchor in this port;
> Our realm brooks not seditious sects, let them elsewhere resort.
> My rusty sword through rest shall first his edge employ
> To poll their tops that seek such change or gape for future joy.

20. *Obedience of a Christian Man,* 188.

21. Nohrnberg, *Analogy,* p. 223.

22. See D. Douglas Waters, *Duessa As Theological Satire* (Columbia: University of Missouri Press, 1970).

23. *The Prophetic Moment,* 208.

24. The argument over the artistic weaknesses of Book V is perhaps out of place in this discussion. Still, too many good readers have found a decided thinness in Book V, including canto 9. Cf. Graham Hough, *A Preface to* The Faerie Queene (New York: Norton, 1963), 200: "As if half-aware of this [decline in the poem's quality] Spenser introduces Mercilla's house in ix, as another attempt at an allegorical core. Mercilla is of course Queen Elizabeth in the aspect of a just and merciful ruler; but Spenser brings very little imaginative conviction to his task." O'Connell, *Mirror and Veil,* 126, attributes the slackening to Spenser's inability "to make his poem an authentic vehicle of prophecy, to judge history in sufficiently moral terms." The prophetic voice does not seem to have failed in Book I, however.

25. The attribution of zeal to Protestant hard-liners was already proverbial. More uses the word often to characterize the reformers' attitude in *Apology,* e.g., chap. 21 (*CWM,* 9:76). Cf. Jonson's Zeal-of-the-Land Busy in *Bartholomew Fair,* and Hooker's discussion of the extremes of zeal and superstition in religion, *Works,* 2:27–29 (V.3).

26. See John Upton's commentary, *Variorum,* 227, 301.

27. Dunseath, *Spenser's Allegory,* 193, quoting Pierre Bersuire.

28. Patrick Cullen, *Infernal Triad: The Flesh, the World, and the Devil in Spenser and Milton* (Princeton: Princeton University Press, 1974), 54.

29. Christopher Goodman, *How Superior Powers Oght to be Obeyd,* (1558; rpt. New York: Facsimile Text Society, 1931), 143.

30. *The Geneva Bible,* intro. Lloyd Berry (Madison: University of Wisconsin Press, 1969), note on Mark 12:9 ("He will come and destroy these housband men and give the vineyard to others."): "He sheweth the plague that shal befale these ambitious and covetous rulers," whose hearts are hardened against Christ." The type of the ruler who "hardens his heart" is of course Pharaoh (Ex. 4:21). Further biblical quotations in this book are from this version.

31. This reading of "Samient" need not conflict with Hamilton (p. 584), who traces it to Middle English *sam*, "together." The *-ent* may be by analogy with *sapient*, or may be the Latin participial ending (hence "signing" or "portending") on the Greek noun. On Spenser's apocalyptic sense, and Erasmian influence, in Book I, see Florence Sandler, "*The Faerie Queene:* An Elizabethan Apocalypse," in C. A. Patrides and Joseph Wittreich, eds., *The Apocalypse in English Renaissance Thought and Literature* (Ithaca: Cornell University Press, 1984), 148–74.

32. In Book V "idol" occurs at 7.6, 7.8, 7.15, 8.19, 10.8, 10.13, 10.27, 10.28, 10.29, 11.19, 11.20, 11.21, 11.33. For "tyrant," see 10.8, 10.12, 10.18, 11.2, 11.38 (twice), 11.50, 12.3, 12.8, 12.13, 12.17, 12.19.

33. Note on 2 Kings 11:17.

34. Richard L. Greaves, "The Nature and Intellectual Milieu of the Political Principles in the Geneva Bible Marginalia," *Journal of Church and State* 22 (1980): 233–49.

35. *How Superior Powers Oght to be Obeyd*, p. 180. Qualified support for killing "tyrants, that is cruell officers" existed in Lutheran writings like Philip Melancthon, *A Civile Nosgay*, trans. John Goodale (ca. 1550), fols. D4v–D7. See also Eire, pp. 284–87, on Lutheran roots of Calvinist resistance theories, and David H. Wollman, "The Biblical Justification for Resistance to Authority in Ponet's and Goodman's Polemics," *Sixteenth Century Journal* 13 (1982): 29–41, which shows the two finding authority for resistance even in Romans 13:1–7. See also above, chap. 1, n. 61.

36. *Milton and the Kingdoms of God* (London: Faber and Faber, 1964), 39, quoting T. F. Torrance, "The Eschatology of the Reformation," *Scottish Journal of Theology*, Occasional Papers, no. 2 (1952), 40.

37. Cf. Maurice Evans, *Spenser's Anatomy of Heroism* (Cambridge: Cambridge University Press, 1970), 200: "The poet must have realized how little the episodes of Belge and Gerioneo resembled the English exploits in the Low Countries."

38. "Postea vero iussit Eurystheus ut puniceos Geryonis Hispaniae Regis boves, qui hospites vorarent, ad se adduceret, quare ad illos opprimendos contendit. Dicitur Geryon Chrysaoris & Callirrhoes filius triplex corpus habuisse, canemque duorum capitum in Erythea, ac septem capitum draconem ex Typhone & Echidna genitum, qui boves ipsos custodiret. Habuit vero suae crudelitatis ministrum impigrum ac diligentem Eurytionem. Huc profectus Hercules Geryone, caneque Orthro, & pastore Eurytione interemptis boves ex Oceani insula Gadira ad Tartellum per id temporis [sic] celeberrimam Iberiae civitatem abigebat, . . ." *Mythologiae* (1567; rpt. New York: Garland, 1976), 205–5v.

39. G. Thilo ed., *Servii Grammatici . . . Commentarii* (Leipzig: Teubner, 1887), 2:178: "Geryones rex fuit Hispaniae. qui ideo trimembris fingitur, quia tribus insulis praefuit, quae adiacent Hispaniae: Baliaricae minori et maiori et Ebuso. fingitur etiam bicipitem canem habuisse, quia et terrestri et navali certamine plurimum potuit. hunc Hercules vicit." Cf. Comes, *Mythologiae*, 210v.

40. *Publii Virgilii Maronis Opera* (Strasbourg, 1502), fol. CCCV2: "Hesiodus etiam ait. Medusa cum Neptuno concubuit: vero cum illi caput abscissum est: ex utero duo filii emicuerunt: Pegasus equus alatus: & Crisaor: sic dictus: quia cum aureo ense natus est. Crysaor: relicta terra ad coelum accessit: Iovi tonitrum: et fulmen ferens. Hic autem genuit Geryonem. quem Hercules interemit." See Hesid, *Theogony*, 11.280–94. A traditional etymology of Geryon is the Greek *geruein*, cry or roar (Comes, *Mythologiae*, 212), hence the connection with thunder. Cf. Nohrnberg, *Analogy*, 401, n. 242. Comes says that Geryon was the

child of Callirhoe and Chrysaor or Pegasus.

41. According to William Perkins, idolatry can occur "when God is worshipped otherwise and by other means than he hath revealed in the worde. For when men set up a devised worship, they set up also a devised God." *A Warning against the Idolatrie of the Last Times* (Cambridge, 1601), p. 15.

42. *Mystagogus Poeticus or the Muses Interpreter*, 3d ed. (1653): "*Pomponius* writes that this temple [of Hercules, commemorating Geryon's defeat] was consecrated by *Hercules* his bones; and *Lucian* shewes that the Thebans kept as a relique the bones of *Geryon*, and Memphis the hairs of *Isis*, which they shewed to strangers; From this we may perceive, whence the Church of *Rome* hath borrowed her practice in consecrating the bones of dead men, and proposing the sight of such reliques to pilgrims and strangers" (p. 137).

43. Osgood, Variorum ed., 254, says, "There is no more realistic episode in the whole poem." This is an instance of "surrealistic isolation," the peculiarly realistic quality of allegorical events; see Angus Fletcher, *Allegory: The Theory of a Symbolic Mode* (Ithaca: Cornell University Press, 1964), 100–108.

44. Note Una and Belge both in the wilderness; Arthur's shield defeating Orgoglio and Gerioneo; the battle watched by Una with her people, and by Belge with hers (11.15); the initial yielding of ground by both Arthur and Red Cross; the monster Error or the Dragon and Gerioneo's monster; the identification of both Gerioneo's and Duessa's monsters with the Lernean Hydra (11.32).

45. No one has proposed the diplomat Sir Sergis as an anagram of *gris* or Grey, stressing the Lord Deputy's role as wise statesman, revealed, e.g., in his dealing with the peaceful Irish (12.10). Hamilton glosses Sergis as from "sergeant" (at law) and "service" (p. 608).

46. Variorum ed., p. 263.

47. Trans. anon., in *Whether It Be Mortall Sinne to Transgresse Civil Lawes* (1566), 24.

48. *Mirror and Veil*, 158.

49. David Cannandine, rev. of William Gaunt, *Court Painting in England from Tudor to Victorian Times* (London: Constable, 1981), *TLS*, 13 March 1981, p. 294. Roy Strong also concedes that Renaissance court fetes were "extravagant assertions of a mirage of power," belonging to that branch of history that studies "what might have been." *Spendour at Court: Renaissance Spectacle and Illusion* (London: Weidenfeld and Nicolson, 1973), 247–48. Cf. Stephen Orgel, *The Illusion of Power: Political Theater in the English Renaissance* (Berkeley and Los Angeles: University of California Press, 1975), 88–89.

50. E.g., Joel Hurstfield, *The Illusion of Power in Tudor Politics:* "Shakespeare displays over and over again in his works, in his drama as well as in his histories, what Spenser does not, the central dilemma of kingship. If Spenser looks to the venerable traditions of the king's two bodies, and ignores the circumstances of the sixteenth century, it is in Shakespeare's drama that these issues are enlarged and explored" (p. 27). I would say that, as we come to know Book V better than we have, the difference between Spenser and Shakespeare on this point will diminish.

51. On the social bandit see Fletcher, *The Prophetic Moment*, pp. 146–64.

52. *Chronicles of England, Scotland, and Ireland*. 6 vols. (London, 1807), 2:483–84 (Year 1280). Both the year and the meaning of the event are given differently by modern historians, e.g., Helen M. Cam, "The Quo Warranto Proceedings under Edward I," *Liberties and Communities in Medieval England* (New York: Barnes and Noble, 1963), 173–82. Cf. *DNB*, s.n. Warenne.

53. Commendatory sonnet to Gaspar Contarini, *The Commonwealth and Government of Venice*, trans. Lewis Lewkenor (1599). On English interest in Venice as the model of mixed government, see Zera S. Fink, *The Classical Republicans: An Essay in the Recovery of a Pattern of Thought in Seventeenth Century England*. Northwestern University Studies in Humanities, no. 9 (Evanston, Ill., 1945), 28–51, and David McPherson's forthcoming book from the University of Delaware Press.

54. Richard H. Perkinson, "*Volpone* and the Reputation of Venetian Justice," *MLR* 35 (1940): 11–18 (n. 1), suggests the sonnet was written in 1595 or 1596, when Book V was published. Two of Spenser's other three commendatory sonnets appeared during these two years.

Chapter 4. Shakespeare: Liberty and Idol Ceremony

1. *New Readings vs. Old Plays: Recent Trends in the Reinterpretation of English Renaissance Drama* (Chicago: University of Chicago Press, 1979), 159, 146–66, 150. Much of what I am saying is also related to pp. 11–77.

2. Hugh M. Richmond, *Shakespeare's Political Plans* (New York: Random House, 1967), 203, makes this point about both plays.

3. Sanders, *The Dramatist and the Received Idea* (Cambridge: Cambridge University Press, 1968), 149.

4. Richard Palmer, *Hermeneutics*, 24. Note also his comment that "teachers of literature need to become experts in 'translation' more than 'analysis'; their task is to bring what is strange, unfamiliar, and obscure in its meaning into something meaningful that 'speaks our language.' This does not mean 'souping up' the classics and dressing Chaucer in twentieth-century English; it means recognizing the problem of a conflict of horizons and taking steps to deal with it, rather than sweeping it under the rug and concentrating on analytical games" (p. 29).

5. *Shakespeare's Historical Plays* (London: Oxford University Press, 1964), pp. 18, 19.

6. "Rabbits, Ducks, and *Henry V*," *SQ* 28 (1977): 279–96 (p. 287); revised in *Shakespeare and the Problem of Meaning* (Chicago: University of Chicago Press, 1981), 33–62 (p. 47).

7. "Julius Caesar: The Politics of the Hardened Heart," *ShakS* 2 (1966): 11–33.

8. Graham Holderness, *Shakespeare's History* (Dublin: Gill and Macmillan, 1985), 42. The discussion that follows has benefitted from this book as well as Calvin G. Thayer, *Shakespearean Politics: Government and Misgovernment in the Great Histories* (Athens: Ohio University Press, 1983).

9. George W. Keeton, *Shakespeare's Legal and Political Background* (London: Sir Isaac Pitman and Sons, 1967), 278–79.

10. In this respect Sanders (p. 188) notes the speech on God's angels, II.2.60.

11. See the long note on this line in the Arden ed. by Peter Ure (London: Methuen, 1961), p. 166, which typifies the editor's assumption of the Lily B. Campbell approach to kingship in this play (the line is said to be "normal Tudor doctrine").

12. The favorable treatment of York is one of the few blind spots in Wilbur Sanders' reading of this play. Sanders is forced to dismiss the York of the second half as "like an unfinished sketch" (p. 185).

13. E.g., Keeton, *Background*, 265; Ure, ed. *Richard II*, lxvi.

14. Richmond, *Shakespeare's Political Plays*, 128.

15. Matthew Black, Pelican ed., note at I.2.37.

16. For this reason one may question the staging, in the BBC's televised RSC production, of I.4 with a towel-draped Richard and his favorites in a sort of massage parlor. It simply reinforces Bolingbroke's version of Richard, which is not warranted by the text. The director also conveniently eliminates the scene in which the favorites console the queen. By contrast, in the 1986 RSC Stratford production Bolingbroke was a "brutal philistine" in a "single-minded reading" of the play: see Nicholas Shrimpton, "Shakespeare Performances," *Shakespeare Survey* 40 (1988): 180–81.

17. LaGuardia, "Ceremony and History"; James L. Calderwood, *Metadrama in Shakespeare's Henriad: Richard II to Henry V* (Berkeley and Los Angeles: University of California Press, 1979). Calderwood and I would seem to disagree with LaGuardia's view that "the simplest statement of the basic conflict in the play is that there is a continual counterpoint in the equation of word and object, and the separation of word and object" (p. 78). I believe the play works relentlessly toward "the separation of word [or symbol] and object"—ultimately the separation of crown from king.

18. Nevo, *Tragic Form*, 75.

19. M. M. Reese, *The Cease of Majesty: A Study of Shakespeare's History Plays* (London: Edward Arnold, 1971), 112.

20. See Michael Platt, "*The Rape of Lucrece* and the Republic for Which It Stands," *Centennial Review*, 19 (1975): 59–79, for an excellent study of personal and political violation in Shakespeare's poem.

21. *Killing the King*, Yale Studies in English 180 (New Haven, 1973): 27.

22. Tillyard, *Shakespeare's History Plays* (London: Chatto and Windus, 1944), 251. For a balanced critical appraisal of the anti-Tillyard school, see Robert P. Merrix, "Shakespeare's Histories and the New Bardolaters," *SEL* 19 (1979): 179–96.

23. "Rabbits, Ducks, and Henry V," 287.

24. Arguing against the consistency of Hal is William Babula, "Whatever Happened to Prince Hal? An Essay on 'Henry V,'" *SS* 30 (1977): 47–59; arguing for it, Carol Marks Sicherman, "King Hal: The Integrity of Shakespeare's Portrait," *TSLL* 21 (1979): 503–21, largely on the evidence of Hal's canniness throughout his plays.

25. *The Temper of Shakespeare's Thought* (New Haven: Yale University Press, 1974), 53.

26. Emrys Jones, *The Origins of Shakespeare* (Oxford: Clarendon Press, 1977), 13.

27. See, e.g., Kenneth Muir, "Shakespeare among the Commonplaces," *RES* 10 (1959): 283–89 (on *Adagia* in *R2*); Thelma N. Greenfield, "*A Midsummer Night's Dream* and *The Praise of Folly*," *CL* 20 (1968): 236–44; G. R. Hibbard, "Erasmus and More in the Age of Shakespeare," *Erasmus in English* 12 (1983): 2–10; L. T. Woodbridge, "Shakespeare's Use of Two Erasmian Colloquies," *N&Q* 30 (1983): 122–23. Attention to Erasmus and Shakespeare's fools begins with Enid Welsford, *The Fool* (London: Faber and Faber, 1935).

28. Jurgen Schafer, "Falstaff's Voice," *N&Q* 214 (1969): 135–36.

29. Born trans. *Education*, 225.

30. Jones, *Origins of Shakespeare*, 278–82, citing "Tragicus Rex" (*LB* 2:574).

31. *King Henry V*, Arden ed. (London: Methuen, 1954), xvi–xviii. See also Roy Battenhouse, "*Henry V* in the Light of Erasmus," *ShakS* 17 (1985): 77–88.

32. " 'Henry V' and the Bees' Commonwealth," *Shakespeare Survey* 30 (1977): 61–72. On the tradition of the bee-kingdom see below, p. 148.

33. E.g., "Such is the history of kingly power, from the beginning to the end of the world;—with this difference, that the object of war formerly, when the people adhered to their allegiance, was to depose kings; the object latterly, since the people swerved from their allegiances, has been to restore kings, and to make common cause against mankind." Everyman's Library ed. (London, 1906), 157. Hazlitt's continuing malign influence on productions of the play is noted by Gary Taylor, ed., *Henry V* (New York: Oxford University Press, 1984), 58. Taylor's introduction, probably the most valuable criticism on the play yet written, differs from my interpretation in emphasizing the king's responsibility for the deaths in the play.

34. Reese, *Cease of Majesty*, 317.

35. Levin, *New Readings*, 138, though some form of "two audience" approach is inevitable, e.g., to allow for theatrical irony. In his *Multiple Plot in English Renaissance Drama* (Chicago: University of Chicago Press, 1971), 116–19, Levin uses the evidence of plot structure to defend a pro-Henry reading of the play. Levin's argument is augmented in Brownell Salomon, "Thematic Contraries and the Dramaturgy of *Henry V*," *SQ* 31 (1980): 343–56.

36. Stoll, "Henry V," in *Poets and Playwrights* (Minneapolis: University of Minnesota Press, 1930); Wilson, ed., *Henry V*, New Cambridge Shakespeare (Cambridge, 1947); Gould, "A New Reading of *Henry V*," *English Review* 29 (1919): 42–55; Goddard, *The Meaning of Shakespeare* (Chicago: University of Chicago Press, 1951); Edwin Wilson, ed., *Shaw on Shakespeare* (New York: Dutton, 1961); Van Doren, *Shakespeare* (1939; rpt. Garden City: Doubleday, n.d.), 143–52; Zdenek Stribrny, "*Henry V* and History," in *Shakespeare in a Changing World*, ed. Arnold Kettle (New York: International Publishers, 1964), 84–101; Reese, *Cease of Majesty*; Jorgensen, "A Formative Shakespearean Legacy"; Calderwood, *Metadrama in Shakespeare's Henriad*; Thayer, *Shakespearean Politics*.

37. Rabkin, "Rabbits." For a related view of *1H4*, that it "confirms the Machiavellian hypothesis of the fraud even as it draws its audience irresistibly toward the celebration of that power," see Stephen Greenblatt, "Invisible Bullets: Renaissance Authority and Its Subversion," *Glyph* 8 (1981): 40–61 (p. 57). In the various incarnations of this essay Henry V gets short shrift, though the latest version improves slightly: see Greenblatt, *Shakespearean Negotiations* (Berkeley and Los Angeles: University of California Press, 1988), 12–65.

38. LaGuardia, "Ceremony," 71; see above, n. 17. Gunter Walch, " 'Henry V' as a Working-House of Ideology," *Shakespeare Survey* 40 (1988): 63–68, finds the play ambiguous in the disparity between what the Chorus says and what happens. He is right about the resulting complexity, but the truth about history is more accessible in this than in most of the other history plays.

39. Edward I. Berry, " 'True Things and Mock'ries': Epic and History in *Henry V*," *JEGP* 78 (1979): 1–16 (p. 8). The ceremony speech is also virtually unnoticed in Moody E. Prior, *The Drama of Power* (Evanston: Northwestern University Press, 1973), and in Greenblatt and Battenhouse.

40. "Shakespeare's *Henry V*: Another Part of the Critical Forest," *JHI* 37 (1976): 3–26.

41. *The Temper of Shakespeare's Thought*, 41.

42. Richard C. McCoy, " 'Thou Idol Ceremony': Elizabeth I, *The Henriad*, and the Rites of English Monarchy," in *Urban Life in the Renaissance*, eds. Susan Zimmerman and Ronald Weissman (Newark: University of Delaware Press, 1989), pp. 240–66, shows that Elizabeth herself contributed to the desacralizing of kingship reflected in *Henry V.*

43. See above, p. 63.

44. *De Republica Anglorum: A Discourse on the Commonwealth of England* (1853), ed. L. Alston (Cambridge University Press, 1906), pp. 59–60.

45. Contrast Calderwood, *Metadrama:* "Harry's speech on Ceremony and his prayer to the God of battles have no effect upon the English, who of course remain united as before" (p. 153).

46. *A Speech of John White* (1641), fol. 4I3, quoted in J. Sears McGee, *The Godly Man in Stuart England* (New Haven: Yale University Press, 1976), 87. Also cf. Spenser's use of "idol pomp," above, p. 106.

47. J. Strype, *Cranmer* (1848), I, 2, p. 206, quoted in Janet L. Nelson, "Inauguration Rituals," in *Early Medieval Kingship,* eds. P. H. Sawyer and I. N. Wood (Leeds: University of Leeds, 1977), 50.

48. *Reports,* Pt. VII (IV, 10a), quoted in Kantorowicz, p. 317.

49. Cf. Edward Symons, Essex royalist minister, addressing a neighboring Puritan minister: "First (Sir,) let me minde you: of what you yielded, namely, that the *King* is *King* before his *Coronation;* indeed his Crowne is but a note or ensigne of his Kingly dignity." *A Loyall Subjects Beliefe* (Oxford, 1643), 41.

50. *Adagia,* "Aut fatuum aut regem nasci oportere," p. 41.

51. Robert P. Merrix, "The Alexandrian Allusion in Shakespeare's *Henry V,*" *ELR* 2 (1972): 321–33, uses this passage to support an anti-Henrician reading, though it seems to me more germane to the opposite interpretation.

52. Stanley Wells and Gary Taylor, *Modernizing Shakespeare's Spelling, with Three Studies in the Text of Henry V* (Oxford: Clarendon Press, 1979), 92.

53. Cf. Reese, *Cease of Majesty,* 111.

54. See Walter, Arden ed., xxxiv.

55. See Drayton, *The Battaile of Agincourt,* lines 785–808, for a realistic account of civilian suffering during the artillery bombardment in the siege; Holinshed, ed. cit., 3:73–74, reports the pillaging after Henry enters Harfleur.

56. A. C. Bradley, *Oxford Lectures on Poetry* (1909; rpt. London: Macmillan, 1955), 257, was perhaps the first to note that, although Henry does not acknowledge it, he must know the bishops' true intentions.

57. *Education,* trans. Born, 255. Cf. *Complaint of Peace* in *Essential Erasmus,* trans. Dolan: "Yet priests dedicated to God as well as monks, who should be even more holy, now inflame men to murder. . . . Bishops leave their dioceses to perform the business of war" (pp. 190–91). In *2H4,* IV.2.5–30, the Archbishop of York also receives his share of such criticism.

58. *Obedience of a Christian Man,* 185, 206–7.

59. Drayton, *Barons Wars,* I.6; Holinshed also follows Hall here: see Walters, Arden ed., p. 160.

60. Reese, *Cease of Majesty,* 332.

61. Kelly, *Divine Providence,* 235.

62. Contrast Gurr: "Henry's intense fury at the rebels' disloyalty shows that he has more than a touch of his father's insecurity" (p. 67).

63. Harold S. Wilson, *On the Design of Shakespearean Tragedy* (Toronto: University of Toronto Press, 1957), 96, 210–12.

64. Sherman Hawkins, "Virtue and Kingship in Shakespeare's *Henry IV,*"

ELR 5 (1975): 314–42 (p. 342).

65. S. C. Sen Gupta, *Shakespeare's Historical Plays*, 146.

66. E.g., I.2.23, 263, 291; II.2.140–42.

67. Robert P. Adams, "Transformations in the Late Elizabethan Tragic Sense of Life: New Critical Approaches," *MLQ* 35 (1974): 353–63. Boris proposes that the appearance of James I's *The Trew Law of Free Monarchies* (1598) may have moved Shakespeare "to specify the importance of law, parliament, and council to a king in the proper government of England" (p. 229).

68. Smith, *De Republica Anglorum*, p. 21.

69. Boris, *Shakespeare's English Kings*, 35. On the "mystery" of monarchy in France, see Roland Mousnier, *The Assassination of Henry IV*, trans. Joan Spencer (London: Faber and Faber, 1973), 240–50.

70. Twysden, *Certaine Considerations upon the Government of England*, ed. John Mitchell Kemble. Camden Soc., vol. 45 (London, 1849), 18; Smith, *De Republica Anglorum*, 16 (Smith's reference to Louis XII may originate in Hotman, suggests the editor, p. xlii); Erasmus, "Spartam nactus es hanc orna," *Adagia*, 103.

71. Thomas Gainsford, *The Glory of England* (1618), 307; in France, "as for the Country-man, hee is called a Pesant, disparaged in his drudgery and servile toylsomnesse, liveth poore and beastly, is treacherous at advantage, and yet afraid of his owne shadow" (p. 241). Hall (fol. 110v) thought that during Henry VI's times the French towns went over to the French king because of their "abhoring theenglish libertie, and aspiring to the French bondage and native servitude."

72. Isaiah 32:10–20, noted by Walter, Arden ed., 143.

73. Adams, *Better Part of Valor*, 35–36, 69, 79–81, etc.

74. *CWE*, 5:18.

75. *CWE*, 5:378–79; cf. *Education*, trans. Born, 200–201, 203.

76. Gayle Greene, " 'The Power of Speech / To Stir Men's Blood': The Language of Tragedy in Shakespeare's *Julius Caesar*," *RenD* 11 (1980): 67–93 (p. 70). Greene remarks of trends in criticism, "Whereas traditional readings of the play concentrated on its political meaning, attempting to establish Shakespeare's sympathies as republican or monarchical, recent critics have found the ambiguity to be deliberate concluding that Shakespeare intentionally obscured the political issues in order to emphasize the problem of knowledge" (p. 70). True enough, but surely the "problem of knowledge" has grave political consequences in this play, which arouse emotions more immediately.

77. Ruth M. Levitsky, " 'The Elements Were So Mix'd,' *PMLA* 88 (1973): 240–45 (p. 242).

78. *Unity in Shakespearean Tragedy: The Interplay of Theme and Character* (New York: Columbia University Press, 1956), 40–54; rpt. *Shakespeare: Modern Essays in Criticism*, ed. Leonard F. Dean (New York: Oxford University Press, 1961), 205–15. Cf. Ernest Schanzer, "The Tragedy of Brutus," in *Shakespeare's Problem Plays* (London: Routledge and Kegan Paul, 1963).

79. Robert Hapgood, "Speak Hands for Me: Gesture and Language in *Julius Caesar*," *Drama Survey* 5 (1966): 162–70 (p. 164).

80. III.116–44, in *Elizabeth Minor Epics*, ed. Elizabeth S. Donno (New York: Columbia University Press, 1963). On Stoicism in *JC*, see two articles by Marvin Vawter: "*Julius Caesar*: Rupture in the Bond," *JEGP* 72 (1973): 311–328; and " 'Division 'tween Our Souls': Shakespeare's Stoic Brutus," *ShakS* 7 (1974): 173–95 (p. 192).

81. Mildred E. Hartsock, "The Complexity of 'Julius Caesar'," *PMLA* 81

(1966): 56–62 (p. 61).

82. *A Modest and Reasonable Examination* (1604), 66. On this point, strangely enough, Calvin could be used against the Puritans (*Inst.* VI.10.14). Cf. Bishop Thomas Morton, *Defense of the Innocencie of the Three Ceremonies* (1618), 88, which cites Calvin in just this way.

83. Anon., *An Apologie or Defence of . . . Brownists* (1604), 76.

84. *The Life of Our Blessed Lord and Savior Jesus Christ*, in *The Whole Works*, ed. R. Heber, rev. and corr. C. P. Eden (London: Longmans, Green et al., 1881), 2:133 (part I, sec. 5, par. 8–9).

85. *Vindiciae*, ed. Laski, 126. La Boétie's work (also called *Contr' un*) was written ca. 1550 and published in 1576; quoted in Shirley, *Richard Hooker*, 142, where it is also mentioned that *La reveille-matin* borrows the Colossus image, p. 190.

86. Cf. Vawter, "Rupture in the Bond,": Pindarus "represents the moral touchstone of the play on killing to escape bondage. Only by denying his own 'will' can he be a 'freeman'—an agent of free will" (pp. 313–14). This suggests that the play contains an extended pun on bond as desirable union and bond as in "bondslave"—developing the ancient paradox of freedom and responsibility.

87. *Shakespeare and the Common Understanding* (New York: Free Press, 1967), 112.

88. Nevo, *Tragic Form*, 124. For a penetrating discussion of this problem in the play, see William O. Scott, "The Speculative Eye: Problematic Self-Knowledge in 'Julius Caesar,' " *SS* 40 (1988): 77–89; see also Pierre Spriet, "Amour et Politique: Le Discours de l'Autre dans *Julius Caesar*," *Coriolan: Theatre et Politique*, Travaux de l'Universite de Toulouse-Le Mirail, ser. B, vol. 5 (1984), 227–39.

89. For the important point that the paganism of Brutus's world makes true self-recognition impossible, see J. L. Simmons, *Shakespeare's Pagan World: The Roman Tragedies* (Charlottesville: University Press of Virginia, 1973), 7–12, 14, 65–108; Spriet (p. 228) says it enhances the moral uncertainty of the play. Robert S. Miola, *Shakespeare's Rome* (Cambridge: Cambridge University Press, 1983), pp. 76–115, also discusses the play as a demythologizing of Caesar (p. 82) in which the characters are helpless to prevent Rome's slide into disaster.

90. *The Abridgement of That Book Which the Ministers of the Lincolnshire Diocese Delivered to His Majesty upon the First of December 1605* (1617), 44.

91. This instance of clothes-imagery is pointed out by L. C. Knights, "Personality and Politics in *Julius Caesar*," in Julius Caesar, *A Casebook*, ed. Peter Ure (London: Macmillan, 1969), 125.

Chapter 5. Milton and Civil Idolatry

1. Corrective to the purely secular viewpoint, with a helpful discussion of the historians' debates, is Finlayson, *Historians, Puritanism and the English Revolution*, esp. 67–76. See also Nicholas Tyacke, *Anti-Calvinism: The Rise of English Arminianism* (Oxford: Clarendon Press, 1987).

2. See John F. H. New, *Anglican and Puritan* (London: A. and C. Black), 15–18; William Bradshaw, *A Treatise of Divine Worship* (1604) rpt. in his *Several Treatises* (1660), fol. B4v; William Covell, *A Modest and Reasonable Examination* (1604), 180.

3. Millenary Petition in Henry Gee and W. J. Hardy, eds., *Documents Illustrative of English Church History* (London and New York: Macmillan, 1896), 508–11; William Barlow reports the king's speech in *The Summe and Substance of*

the Conference (1604), rpt. in Edward Cardwell, *A History of the Conferences and Other Proceedings Connected with the Revision of the Book of Common Prayer* (1849; rpt. Ridgewood, N.J.: Gregg Press, 1966), 203. On the conference see Tyacke, *Anti-Calvinists*, 9–28; Patrick Collinson, "The Jacobean Religious Settlement: The Hampton Court Conferences," in *Before the English Civil War*, ed. Howard Tomlinson (London: Macmillan, 1983), 27–51; William M. Lamont, *Godly Rule: Politics and Religion, 1603–60* (London: Macmillan, 1969) 28–30. Speech to Parliament, 21 March 1610, from *The Stuart Constitution: Documents and Commentary,*, ed. J. P. Kenyon (Cambridge: Cambridge University Press, 1966), 13. Taylor quoted in Christopher Hill, *Collected Essays* (Amherst: University of Massachusetts Press, 1986), 2:58.

4. *Eikonoklastes* (1649), ed. M. Y. Hughes in Milton, *Complete Prose Works* (New Haven: Yale University Press, 1962), 3:404, abbreviated throughout this chapter as *CPW*.

5. Milton's earlier poetry does show the influence of the liturgy. See William B. Hunter, Jr., "The Liturgical Context of *Comus*," *ELN* 10 (1972): 11–15, and Joseph A. Wittreich on *Lycidas* in *Visionary Poetics: Milton's Tradition and His Legacy* (San Marino: Huntington Library Press, 1979), 98–99. Too much of what is called "rite" in Thomas B. Stroup, *Religious Rite and Ceremony in Milton* (Lexington: University of Kentucky Press, 1968) is simply prayer (e.g., pp. 3, 16), and most of these prayers originate in the source for the Prayer Book texts, the Psalms. On Milton and the Psalms, see Mary Ann Radzinowicz, *Milton's Epics and the Book of Psalms* (Princeton: Princeton University Press, 1989).

6. Cf. *Paradise Lost*, VIII.589–94.

7. M. M. Ross's attempt to convert Milton into a sacramental poet in *Poetry and Dogma* (New Brunswick: Rutgers University Press, 1954) is amply refuted by Madsen (see below, n. 10), e.g., in that renouncing images in worship does not constitute doing so in poetry (p. 172). Ross still has his partisans, e.g., Boyd M. Berry, *Process of Speech: Puritan Religious Writing and* Paradise Lost (Baltimore: Johns Hopkins University Press, 1976), 9.

8. Victor Turner, *Dramas, Fields, and Metaphors* (Ithaca: Cornell University Press, 1974), 45–47.

9. *CPW*, 3:504–6; 6:670. The last passage continues: "So it is clear that the church has no need of a liturgy: those who prompt and assist our prayers are divine helpers, not human."

10. William G. Madsen, *From Shadowy Types to Truth* (New Haven: Yale University Press, 1968), 181.

11. Madsen, p. 108, referring to *Reason of Church Government*.

12. *Eikonoklastes*, *CPW*, 3:343; see above, p. 15.

13. *CPW*, 1:444. Entries under "Idolatry" were apparently made in the lost religious commonplace book (*CPW*, 1:365, second n. 1).

14. James Holly Hanford, "The Chronology of Milton's Private Studies," *PMLA* 36 (1921): rpt. in his *John Milton, Poet and Humanist* (Cleveland: Press of Western Reserve University, 1966) 109.

15. Michael Fixler, *Milton and the Kingdoms of God* (London: Faber and Faber, 1964), 208. Sir Robert Filmer, in his *Observations concerning the Originall of Government* (1652), had rightly criticized Milton's vagueness in defining "the people," in the sense of the origin of governmental authority, especially since Milton will allow only the "better part" of men a voice in government: "how shall we know, or who shall judge who they be?" (p. 14).

16. William Riley Parker, *Milton: A Biography* (Oxford: Clarendon Press,

1968), 1:361. An expressed reluctance to attack the late king, like that which begins *Eikonoklastes*, also opens *Eikon Alethine* (1649), fol. B1. For the argument that Milton displaces Charles with himself as idol, see Richard Helgerson, "Milton Reads the King's Book: Print, Performance, and the Making of a Bourgeois Idol," *Criticism* 29 (1987): 1–25.

17. Warren H. Lowenhaupt, "The Writing of Milton's *Eikonoklastes*," *SP* 20 (1923): 29–51, notes a parallel in the verse preface of *Eikon Alethine*, addressed "To the Doctor": "Impious Aegyptian . . . / To kill thy Apis, make thy God thy food" (i.e., exploit Charles for personal profit) (p. 38).

18. *Education*, trans. Born, 166.

19. Lowenhaupt demonstrates that *Eikonoklastes* was influenced by this tract.

20. I suggest this attribution because this rather well-turned poem is signed "Philaretes," the name Wither used in his earlier poems, *Faire-virtue, the Mistresse of Philarete* (1622). The author of *Eikon Alethine* gives evidence of having an education in common law, like Wither (e.g., p. 34).

21. *Eikon Alethine*, 83. In *Tetrachordon* (1645) Milton speaks of the "rashnesse of common textuaries who abolish lawes, as the rable demolish images, in the zeale of their hammers often violating the Sepulchers of good men" (*CPW*, 2:640). In *Eikonoklastes* he wished "not to justifie what enormities the Vulgar may committ in the rudeness of their zeal" in referring to Charles's complaints over the "pulling down of Crosses" (3:535).

22. See the long n. 91 in *CPW*, 4:366–67 on Milton's political doctrine as inferred from the later prose works.

23. Griffith, *The Fear of God and the King* (1660), 12. Although Milton's pamphlet addresses the title theme, the bulk of Griffith's sermon has to do with the latter part of his text: "My Son, fear God and the King, and meddle not with them that be seditious, or desirous of change" (Prv. 24:21).

24. *Censure* (1660), rpt. in William Riley Parker, *Milton's Contemporary Reputation* (Columbus: Ohio State University Press, 1940), 13. See Parker, *Milton*, 1:557, on the error of assuming that the *Way* is Milton's final, considered theory of the state.

25. *Eikonoklastes*, *CPW*, 3:367; for Milton in the Old Testament this phrase denoted apostasy to idolatry (n. 59).

26. Moloch is not always given the prominence he receives in Milton's hell. Alexander Ross, *Pansebeia* (1655), puts Beelzebub, Peor, and Baal as the chief demon-deities of Syria, with Moloch near the end of the list (pp. 65–67). As noted in the preface, this part of my book resembles and, I hope, augments Stevie Davies' valuable *Images of Kingship in* Paradise Lost.

27. Jason P. Rosenblatt, " 'Audacious Neighborhood': Idolatry in *Paradise Lost*, Book I," *PQ* 54 (1975): 553–68, approaches the Moloch-Solomon pair from a strictly theological direction: "The description of every idol is characterized by an alternation of emphasis from the demonic to the holy" (p. 562). This is true, my point being that this first idol pertains to what even Erasmus recognized as the most important realm of earthly existence, the political. Earlier commentators on Moloch have too quickly dismissed him as merely a militarist, e.g., J. B. Broadbent, *Some Graver Subject: An Essay on Paradise Lost* (New York: Barnes and Noble, 1960), 115. Patrick Cullen is closer to the point in identifying Moloch with the "devil" of the world-flesh-devil triad, "wishing to use 'Satanic strength' as a means to the godhead" (*Infernal Triad*, 101).

28. John M. Steadman, *Milton's Epic Characters: Image and Idol* (Chapel Hill: University of North Carolina Press, 1968), 253.

29. *A Critique of* Paradise Lost (London: Longmans, 1960), 43.

30. *A Perswasive*, 24.

31. On the bee simile, see James A. Freeman, *Milton and the Martial Muse* (Princeton: Princeton University Press, 1980), pp. 186–99.

32. Bennett, "God, Satan, and King Charles: Milton's Royal Portraits," *PMLA* 92 (1977): 441–57, revised as pp. 33–58 in her *Reviving Liberty;* Hill, *Milton and the English Revolution* (London: Faber and Faber, 1977), pp. 365–77. The seminal treatment of Satan as king is Merritt Y. Hughes, "Satan and the 'Myth' of the Tyrant," in *Essays in English Literature from the Renaissance to the Victorian Age,* eds. Miller MacLure and F. W. Watt (Toronto: University of Toronto Press, 1964), 125–48. Acknowledging both the oriental and Stuart qualities in Satan's portrayal, Hughes says that "Charles and the sultans were alike ectypes of the Satanic archetype in Milton's mythology" (p. 310). This essay refutes Malcolm Ross's argument of Milton's crypto-royalism in *Milton's Royalism* (Ithaca: Cornell University Press, 1943).

33. *Milton and the Renaissance Hero* (Oxford: Clarendon Press, 1967), 90.

34. Harrison, *Plain Dealing* (1649); the "imprimatur" is dated 2 May.

35. Davies, *Images of Kingship,* 49; see also my "Milton's Nimrod," *Milton Quarterly* 22 (1988): 38–44.

36. Luther, *Misuse of the Mass,* tr. Frederick Ahrens, *Luther's Works* (Philadelphia: Muhlenberg Press, 1955), 36, 227–28.

37. Steadman, *Milton and the Renaissance Hero,* 90–93; John R. Knott, Jr., *Milton's Pastoral Vision: An Approach to* Paradise Lost (Chicago: University of Chicago Press, 1971), pp. 150–58. On Nimrod, see above, pp. 17–18.

38. The "violent Lords" are also the Giants of XI.642 ff., although the narrative seems directed against a certain kind of aristocracy (note the Erasmus-like swipes at chivalry in XI.584 and 652) rather than the monarchy. On exploitative aristocracy cf. Steadman, *Milton's Epic Characters,* 178–79, and Milton's *Tenure* on titles of honor as "empty and vain" (*CPW,* 3:220).

39. Robert Crosman, *Reading* Paradise Lost (Bloomington: Indiana University Press, 1980), 234; cf. Steadman, *Milton and the Renaissance Hero,* 92.

40. *Surprised by Sin,* 103.

41. On the Puritan requirement for "filial familiarity, not servile fear" in man's relation to God, see Horton Davies, *Worship and Theology in England,* 3:213. The technical name for this fear was (from Greek) *deisidaimonia,* glossed by Edward Leigh as "Superstitio" or (quoting a pun in Cicero) "Timor dei inanis." *Critica Sacra* (1639), 138.

42. See especially the paragraph in *CPW,* 1:230–31.

43. My knowledge of Filmer and patriarchalism is indebted to Gordon J. Schochet, *Patriarchalism in Political Thought* (Oxford: Basil Blackwell, 1975). Page numbers in parentheses in the next paragraph refer to Schochet.

44. *CPW,* 4:236–37; the editor, n. 9, p. 327, calls this "Salmasius' analogy," though it is properly seen as a long-established pretext for monarchy. Cf. Milton's accusing Salmasius later of believing that the "absolute power of Kings" is inferred from "the ancient rights of a pater familias" (p. 472).

45. *Observations concerning the Originall of Government* (1652), p. 19.

46. Gerald J. Schiffhorst, "Patience and the Humbly Exalted Heroism of Milton's Messiah," *MS* 16 (1982): 97–113. Milton also suggests that even David was vulnerable to the temptations of tyranny: see David Quint, "David's Census: Milton's Politics and *Paradise Regained,"* in *Re-membering Milton,* ed. Mary Nyquist (New York: Methuen, 1987), 128–47.

47. Nancy Y. Hoffman, "Samson's Other Father: The Character of Manoa in *Samson Agonistes,"* *MS* 2 (1970): 194–210 (p. 205).

48. Broadbent, *Some Graver Subject*, 111.

49. Arnold Stein, *Heroic Knowledge* (Minneapolis: University of Minnesota Press, 1957), 48.

50. See, e.g., Zera S. Fink on the concept of "dictator" (I.113), *The Classical Republicans*, 195–96.

51. Wallace, *Destiny His Choice: The Loyalism of Andrew Marvell* (Cambridge: Cambridge University Press, 1968), 22–30. For Richard Baxter's later "horror" of James I's conquest theory in *The Trew Law of Free Monarchies*, see *Politics, Religion and Literature*, ed. Lamont and Oldfield, pp. 5–7. Stevie Davies also treats this subject in *Images of Kingship*, 40–41.

52. Hunton, *Treatise of Monarchy* (1643), 22; Bramhall, *The Serpent Salve* (1643), 8, quoted in Wallace, *Destiny*, 23, 25.

53. Christopher Hill, *Puritanism and Revolution* (1958; rpt. London: Panther, 1969), 58–125. Norman Yoke and Nimrodic Conquest are discussed in J. G. A. Pocock, *The Ancient Constitution and the Feudal Law: A Reissue with a Retrospect* (Cambridge: Cambridge University Press, 1987), 282–88, 318–19.

54. *Heroic Knowledge*, 88. Edward Tayler explores Satan's vs. Christ's time in *Paradise Regained* in *Milton's Poetry: Its Development in Time* (Pittsburgh: Duquesne University Press, 1979), 148–84.

55. 1 Corinthians 1:27, quoted by Walter MacKellar, *A Variorum Commentary on the Poems of John Milton*, vol. 4 (New York: Columbia University Press, 1975), 70.

56. Barbara Kiefer Lewalski, *Milton's Brief Epic: The Genre, Meaning, and Art of Paradise Regained* (Providence: Brown University Press, 1966), 162.

57. Hughes ed., *Complete Poems*, 487, cites Xenophon's remark that it is more divine than human to govern men who freely consent.—earlier noted as an important idea in Erasmus (above, p. 78). *Variorum Milton* (p. 77) compares *Reason of Church Government:* "Persuasion certainly is a more winning, and more manlike way to keepe men in obedience then feare" (Columbia ed., 3:181). Here "manlike" elevates the human to the level of what Xenophon called "divine."

58. *Variorum Milton*, 153.

59. Lewalski, *Milton's Brief Epic*, 188; *Variorum Milton*, 64.

60. *Variorum Milton*, 127 (on *PR*, II.324).

61. *The Priviledges of the People* (1649), 1.

62. Austin Woolrych, Introduction, *CPW*, 7:50, 53.

63. My view of the private-public structure roughly resembles the more finely attuned analysis in Lewalski, *Milton's Brief Epic*. It is also consistent with the subtle psychological structure outlined by Stein, *Heroic Knowledge*, which proceeds from the view that "Milton's political theory is based on his moral theory, on the individual state of man," so that the "real political arena is the self, where duty must be understood and managed" (p. 65). In the poem Christ's youth appears bent on redefining public good in terms of a wisdom that rejects force for persuasion (pp. 104–5).

64. Lewalski, *Milton's Brief Epic*, 219. The point is demonstrated on pp. 219–55.

65. Allan H. Gilbert, "The Temptation in *Paradise Regained*," *JEGP* 15 (1916): 599–611.

66. On the pomp of Cromwell's court see C. H. Firth, "The Court of Oliver Cromwell," *Cornhill Magazine* (September 1897): 349–64. On Milton's eventual disaffection with Cromwell see Woolrych, *CPW*, 7:86–87.

67. Lewalski has the Roman scene ending the kingdom sequence that began

with the banquet temptation (p. 274), but it seems to me that the temptation of learning continues that sequence, analyzing the philosophical grounds of kingship. Northrop Frye, *The Return of Eden* (1965; rpt. Toronto: University of Toronto Press, 1975), like many commentators on this poem, makes a much sharper discrimination than Lewalski (and I) between the episodes of the second temptation: Parthia is false power, Rome is false justice, Athens, false wisdom (p. 130), though he would perhaps allow that all three are different symptoms of the same disease. Still, I disagree that in rejecting Athens for the wisdom of Scripture Christ is being "a peevish obscurantist" (p. 134). What can this mean?

68. Frye, *Return of Eden*, 141.

69. See William J. Grace, "Milton's Views on Church and State in 1659," Appendix B in *CPW*, 7:522–30.

70. Quoted by Woolrych, *CPW*, 7:202.

71. *Return of Eden*, 111. John T. Shawcross, Paradise Regain'd: *Worthy t'Have not Remain'd So Long Unsung* (Pittsburgh: Duquesne University Press, 1988), shows how the problem of power in the poem is resolved in that "the creature can take on him an aspect of the power of the creator by exercise of the godliness within him" (p. 128).

72. Samuel Johnson, "Life of Milton," in *A Johnson Reader*, eds. E. L. McAdams and George Milne (New York: Pantheon Books, 1964), 398. See Ralph W. Condee, "Milton's Dialogue with the Epic: *Paradise Regained* and the Tradition," *YR* 59 (1970): 357–75.

73. *Milton and the Kingdoms of God*, 109.

74. On Christ and the kingdom of God, see Michael Grant, *Jesus: An Historian's Review of the Gospels* (New York: Scribner's, 1977), especially 7–29.

75. *Toward* Samson Agonistes, 150.

76. For a summary of criticism on the Chorus, see Radzinowicz, p. 62, n. 12. In support of her view that the final speeches show that the Chorus has progressed toward truth, she cites Jon S. Lawry, *The Shadow of Heaven* (Ithaca: Cornell University Press, 1968), and Anthony Low, *The Blaze of Noon* (New York: Columbia University Press, 1974). Bennett, *Reviving Liberty*, 126, says that the Chorus, in its "carnal vision," embodies the defects Milton saw in his fellow Christians.

77. Commonplace Book, *CPW* 1:491.

78. See Owen Barfield, *Saving the Appearances: A Study in Idolatry* (New York: Harcourt, Brace and World, 1965); Ong, below, note 79. Among applications of Barfield's ideas to Milton are John C. Ulreich, "The Typological Structure of Milton's Imagery," *MS* 5 (1973): 67–85, and Paul Piehler, "Milton's Iconoclasm," in *The Evolution of Consciousness*, ed. Shirley Sugerman (Middletown, Conn.: Wesleyan University Press, 1976), 121–35.

79. Ong, *Interfaces of the Word: Studies in the Evolution of Consciousness and Culture* (Ithaca: Cornell University Press, 1977), 207. I would agree with Radzinowicz (*Toward* Samson, 351) that Milton "demythologized the role of the poet." She thus questions William Kerrigan's concept of a vatic Milton in *The Prophetic Milton* (Charlottesville: University Press of Virginia, 1974).

80. Cf. John Goodwin, *Theomachia* (1644): because the Athenians worshipped the true God, but did so in ignorance, they "were Idolaters notwithstanding." "God regards no mans *zeale* without *knowledge*, though it should pitch and fasten upon things never so agreeable unto his Will." William A. Haller, ed., *Tracts on Liberty in the Puritan Revolution* (New York: Columbia University Press, 1933–41, 3:18, 19 (orig. pag.).

Epilogue: No Ceremony No Bishop, No Bishop No King

1. Gerard Reedy, S. J., "Mystical Politics: The Imagery of Charles II's Coronation," in *Studies in Change and Revolution: Aspects of English Intellectual History 1640–1800*, ed. Paul Korshin (Menston, Yorks.: Scolar Press, 1972), 19–42 (especially 30–33), citing Heath, *The Glorious and Magnificent Triumphs* (1661), 2; Morley, *A Sermon Preached at the Magnificent Coronation* (1661), intro. and pp. 57–60.

2. *A Sermon Preached at the Coronation of William III and Mary II* (1689), 5.

3. See *The Memoirs of Sir John Reresby*, ed. James J. Cartwright (London: Longmans, Green, 1875): "The procession to the Abbey of Westminster was very regular, but not attended by so many of the nobility as when the two last kings were crowned. The House of Commons were taken great care of in this solemnity, had a side of Westminster Hall prepared for them to see it, another place in the Abbey to see their Majesties crowned, and several tables prepared and covered with all sorts of meat, where they dined by themselves" (p. 454).

4. Thomas Rogers, *Lux Occidentalis: or Providence Display'd* (1689), 16.

5. David Ogg, *William III* (London: Collins, 1956), 59.

6. Martyn P. Thompson, "The Idea of Conquest in Controversies over the 1688 Revolution," *JHI* 38 (1977): 33–46.

7. Henry and Barbara van der Zee, *William and Mary* (London: Macmillan, 1973), 279.

8. *Twelve Generall Arguments* (1605), fol. C7v.

9. Elton, *Tudor Constitution*, 18; Loades, *Tudor court*, 192. Cf. Louis A. Knafla's point that James I's "speeches on the idea of kingship brought the 'mystery' of state out into the public marketplace and prompted the more self-seeking members of society to commend and advance it orally and in the press." *Law and Politics in Jacobean England* (Cambridge: Cambridge University Press, 1977), 65.

10. *History of the Rebellion*, ed. W. D. Macray (Oxford: Clarendon Press, 1888), 1:404 (IV.38).

11. Cranmer, "Of Ceremonies," in Book of Common Prayer, Everyman's Library ed., p. 325; Milton, *Of Reformation, CPW*, 1:523.

12. *A Sermon Preached before the Kings Majestie* (Cambridge, 1627), 25. I see no evidence that Griffith was influenced by this sermon despite the identical theme. Cf. Knafla's point, above, n. 9.

13. *Golden Remains*, 157.

14. *The Priviledges of the People*, 11.

15. *The Reformation of Images* (Berkeley and Los Angeles: University of Calif. Press, 1973), 202–3.

16. Natalie Zemon Davis criticizes the biases of historians for whom the "ritual method of living" is "shallow in regard to meaning and morality." See "Some Tasks and Themes in the Study of Popular Religion," in *The Pursuit of Holiness in Late Medieval and Renaissance Religion*, ed. Charles Trinkhaus and Heiko Oberman. Studies in Reformation Thought, vol. 10 (Leiden: E. J. Brill, 1974), 307–36 (p. 311).

17. Herman Schmidt, S. J., "Liturgy and Modern Society: Analysis of the Current Situation," in his ed., *Liturgy in Transition* (New York: Herder and Herder, 1971), 19.

18. Jean-Baptiste Molin and Protais Mutembe, *Le rituel du mariage en France du XIIe au XVIe siècle. Theologie Historique*, no. 26 (Paris: Beauchesne, 1974), 269.

19. See the collection on this subject, *A Discussion of Ritualization of Behaviour in Animals and Man*, in the series *Philosophical Transactions of the Royal Society of London*, Series B, Biological Series, 251 (1966).

20. *TLS*, 6 June 1975, 616.

21. *A Gathered Church: The Literature of the English Dissenting Interest, 1700–1930* (London: Routledge and Kegan Paul, 1978), 97.

22. Williams, *The Embodiment of Knowledge*, ed. Ron Loewinsohn (New York: New Directions, 1974), 28: "Can't men see, not plays, in Shakespeare, but observation. Poetry. It happens, not is made. Can't they see that the decay of the monarch all through his work is one of the most important documents in evidence. It came in big chunks. Now it is varnished down. We look through democratic varnish."

Bibliography

The Abridgement of That Book Which the Ministers of the Lincolnshire Diocese Delivered to His Majesty upon the First of December 1605. 1617.

Adams, Robert P. *The Better Part of Valor: More, Erasmus, Colet, and Vives on Humanism, War, and Peace, 1496–1535.* Seattle: University of Washington Press, 1962.

———. "Transformations in the Late Elizabethan Tragic Sense of Life: New Critical Approaches." *Modern Language Quarterly* 35 (1974): 353–63.

Allen, J. W. *A History of Political Thought in the Sixteenth Century.* 1928. Revised reprint. London: Methuen, 1957.

Anson, John. "*Julius Caesar:* The Politics of the Hardened Heart." *Shakespeare Studies* 2 (1966): 11–33.

An Apologie or Defence of . . . Brownists. 1604.

Arquillière, N. X. *L'Augustinisme politique: Essai sur la formation des théories politiques du Moyen-Age.* 2d ed. Paris: J. Vrin, 1955.

Augustine. *City of God.* Edited by David Knowles. Harmondsworth: Penguin, 1984.

Axton, Marie. *The Queen's Two Bodies: Drama and the Elizabethan Succession.* London: Royal Historical Society, 1977.

Babula, William. "Whatever Happened to Prince Hal? An Essay on 'Henry V.'" *Shakespeare Survey* 30 (1977): 47–59.

Bagehot, Walter. *The English Constitution.* 1867. Reprint. London: C. A. Watts, 1964.

Bainton, Roland H. "Erasmus and the Persecuted." In *Scrinium Erasmianum,* edited by J. Coppens. Leyden: Brill, 1969.

Baker, David J. "'Some Quirk, Some Subtle Evasion': Legal Subversion in Spenser's *A Vewe of the Present State of Ireland.*" *Spenser Studies* 6 (1985): 147–63.

Barfield, Owen. *Saving the Appearances. A Study in Idolatry.* New York: Harcourt, Brace and World, 1965.

Barlow, William. *The Summe and Substance of the Conference.* 1604. In Edward Cardwell, *A History of the Conferences and Other Proceedings Connected with the Revision of the Book of Common Pryaer.* 1849. Reprint. Ridgewood, N.J.: Gregg Press, 1966.

Baron, Hans. "Franciscan Poverty and Civic Wealth as Factors in the Rise of Humanistic Thought." *Speculum* 13 (1938): 1–37.

Battenhouse, Roy. "*Henry V* in the Light of Erasmus." *Shakespeare Studies* 17 (1985): 77–88.

Baumann, Uwe. "Thomas More and the Classical Tyrant." In *Thomas More and the Classics.* Edited by Ralph Keen and Daniel Kinney. *Moreana* 86 (1985): 108–27.

Baumer, Franklin L. *The Early Tudor Theory of Kingship.* New Haven: Yale University Press, 1940.

Bennett, Joan S. "God, Satan, and King Charles: Milton's Royal Portraits." *PMLA* 92 (1977): 441–57.

———. *Reviving Liberty: Radical Christian Humanism in Milton's Great Poems.* Cambridge: Harvard University Press, 1989.

Bergeron, David. Review of Roy Strong, *Art and Power: Renaissance Festivals 1450–1650. Renaissance Quarterly* 39 (1986): 788–91.

Berry, Boyd M. *Process of Speech: Puritan Religious Writing and* Paradise Lost. Baltimore: Johns Hopkins University Press, 1976.

Berry, Edward I. " 'True Things and Mock'ries': Epic and History in *Henry V.*" *Journal of English and Germanic Philology* 78 (1979): 1–16.

Bevington, David, ed. *Medieval Drama.* Boston: Houghton Mifflin, 1975.

Bible, 6 vols. Lyons, 1508 [1520].

Bible. *The Geneva Bible.* Introduced by Lloyd Berry. Madison: University of Wisconsin Press, 1969.

Bindoff, S. T. *Tudor England.* 1950. Reprint. Harmondsworth: Penguin, 1966.

Bland, D. S. "The Chester 'Navitivy': One Play or Two?" *Notes and Queries* 208 (1963): 134–35.

Blumler, J. G., et al. "Attitudes to the Monarchy: Their Structure and Development during a Ceremonial Occasion." *Political Studies* 19 (1971): 149–71.

Blythe, James M. "The Mixed Constitution and the Distinction between Regal and Political Power in the Works of Thomas Aquinas." *Journal of the History of Ideas* 47 (1986): 547–65.

Boff, Leonardo. *Jesus Christ Liberator.* Translated by Patrick Hughes. New York: Orbis, 1978.

Bond, Ronald. "Supplantation in the Elizabethan Court: The Theme of Spenser's February Eclogue." *Spenser Studies* 2 (1981): 55–65.

Boris, Edna Zwick. *Shakespeare's English Kings, the People, and the Law: A Study in the Relationship between the Tudor Constitution and the English History Plays.* Rutherford, N.J.: Farleigh Dickinson University Press, 1978.

Bousset, W. *The Antichrist Legend: A Chapter in Christian and Jewish Folklore.* Translated by A. H. Keane. London: Hutchinson, 1896.

Bradley, A. C. *Oxford Lectures on Poetry.* 1909. Reprint. London: Macmillan, 1955.

Bradshaw, Brendan. "The Elizabethans and the Irish: A Muddled Model." *Studies* 20 (1981): 233–44.

Bradshaw, William. *A Treatise of Divine Worship.* 1604. Reprint in his *Several Treatises.* 1660.

———. *Twelve Generall Arguments.* 1605.

Brady, Ciaran. "Spenser's Irish Crisis." *Past and Present* 111 (1986): 17–49.

Broadbent, J. B. *Some Graver Subject: An Essay on Paradise Lost.* New York: Barnes and Noble, 1960.

Buchanan, George. *The Powers of the Crown in Scotland.* Translated by Charles F. Arrowood. Austin: University of Texas Press, 1949.

Burnet, Gilbert. *A Sermon Preached at the Coronation of William III and Mary II.* 1689.

Calderwood, James L. *Metadrama in Shakespeare's Henriad: Richard II to Henry V.* Berkeley and Los Angeles: University of California Press, 1979.

Cam, Helen. *Liberties and Communities in Medieval England.* New York: Barnes and Noble, 1963.

"The Cambridge Prologue." *Non-Cycle Plays and Fragments.* Edited by Norman Davis. EETS Supplem. Ser. 1. London, 1970.

Cannadine, David. Review of William Gaunt, *Court Painting in England from Tudor to Victorian Times. Times Literary Supplement,* 13 March 1981, p. 294.

Canny, Nicholas. "Edmund Spenser and the Development of an Anglo-Irish Identity." *Yearbook of English Studies* 12 (1983): 1–19.

Cavanagh, Sheila. " 'Such was Irena's Countenance': Ireland in Spenser's Prose and Poetry." *Texas Studies in Literature and Language* 28 (1986): 24–50.

Cawdry, Daniel. *Superstitio Superstes: or The Reliques of Superstition Newly Revived.* 1644.

Censure of the Rota. 1660. Reprint. *Milton's Contemporary Reputation.* Edited by William Riley Parker. Columbus: Ohio State University Press, 1940.

The Chester Mystery Cycle. Edited by R. M. Lumiansky and David Mills. EETS, Supplem. Ser. 3. 1974.

Cicero. *De Officiis.* Translated by Harry G. Edinger. Indianapolis: Bobbs Merrill, 1974.

Clarendon, Edward Hyde, Earl of. *History of the Rebellion.* Edited by W. D. Macray. 6 vols. Oxford: Clarendon Press, 1888/

Clopper, Lawrence M. "The History and Development of the Chester Cycle." *Modern Philology* 75 (1978): 219–46.

Collinson, Patrick. "The Jacobean Religious Settlement: The Hampton Court Conference." In *Before the English Civil War,* edited by Howard Tomlinson. London: Macmillan, 1983.

Comes, Natalis. *Mythologiae.* 1567. Reprint. New York: Garland, 1976.

Condee, Ralph W. "Milton's Dialogue with the Epic: *Paradise Regained* and the Tradition." *Yale Review* 59 (1970): 357–75.

Contarini, Gasparo. *The Commonwealth and Government of Venice.* Translated by Lewis Lewkenor. 1599.

Coursen, Herbert. *Christian Ritual and the World of Shakespeare's Tragedies.* Lewisburg, Pa.: Bucknell University Press, 1976.

Covell, William. *A Modest and Reasonable Examination.* 1604.

Cranmer, Thomas. "Of Ceremonies." In Book of Common Prayer. Everyman's Library. London, 1932.

Creighton, Mandell. *Queen Elizabeth.* London: Longmans Green, 1899.

Crossman, Robert. *Reading Paradise Lost.* Bloomington: Indiana University Press, 1980.

Cross, Claire. *The Royal Supremacy in the Elizabethan Church.* London: George Allen Unwin, 1969.

Cullen, Patrick. *Infernal Triad: The Flesh, the World, and the Devil in Spenser and Milton.* Princeton: Princeton University Press, 1974.

Cursor Mundi. Edited by Richard Morris. *EETS,* o.s. 57. London, 1874.

Cyprian. "On the Vanity of Idols." In *Writings of Cyprian.* Translated by Robert Ernest Wallis. Ante-Nicene Christian Library 8. Edinburgh, 1876.

Daniélou, Jean. *The Origins of Latin Christianity.* Vol. 3. *A History of the Early Christian Doctrine before the Council of Nicaea.* Translated by David Smith and John Austin Baker. London: Darton, Longman and Todd, 1977.

Davenport, W. A. *Fifteenth Century English Drama.* Cambridge, Eng.: D. S. Brewer, 1982.

Davidson, Clifford. "The Digby *Mary Magdalene* and the Magdalene Cult of the Middle Ages." *Annuale Medievale* 13 (1972): 70–87.

Davie, Donald. *A Gathered Church: The Literature of the English Dissenting Interest, 1700–1930.* London: Routledge and Kegan Paul, 1978.

Davies, Horton. *Worship and Theology in England.* Vol. 2. Princeton: Princeton University Press, 1975.

Davies, Stevie. *Images of Kingship in* Paradise Lost: *Milton's Politics and Christian Liberty.* Columbia: University of Missouri Press, 1983.

Davis, Natalie Zeemon. "Some Tasks and Themes in the Study of Popular Religion." In *The Pursuit of Holiness in Late Medieval and Renaissance Religion,* edited by Charles Trinkhaus and Heiko Oberman. Studies in Medieval and Reformation Thought, vol. 10. Leiden: E. J. Brill, 1974.

Desmaizeaux, Pierre. *A Historical and Critical Account of the Life and Writings of the Ever-Memorable Mr. John Hales.* London, 1719.

A Discussion of Ritualization of Behaviour in Animals and Man. In *Philosophical Transactions of the Royal Society of London,* Series B, Biological Series, 251. 1966.

Donno, Elizabeth S. *Elizabeth Minor Epics.* New York: Columbia University Press, 1963.

Drayton, Michael. *Works.* Edited by J. William Hebel et al. Oxford: Blackwell, 1931–41.

Dunseath, T. K. *Spenser's Allegory of Justice in the* Faerie Queene V. Princeton: Princeton University Press, 1968.

Eccleshall, Robert. *Order and Reason in Politics: Theories of Absolute and Limited Monarchy in Early Modern England.* Oxford: Oxford University Press, 1978.

Edwards, Philip. *Threshold of a Nation: A Study in English and Irish Drama.* Cambridge: Cambridge University Press, 1979.

Eikon Alethine. 1649.

Eire, Carlos M., *War against the Idols: The Reformation of Worship from Erasmus to Calvin.* Cambridge: Cambridge University Press, 1986.

Eliade, Mircea. *Myths, Dreams and Mysteries.* Translated by Philip Mairet. 1960. Reprint. London: Fontana, 1974.

Ellis-Fermor, Una. *The Frontiers of Drama.* London: Methuen, 1945.

Elton, G. R. *Reform and Reformation: England, 1509–1558.* Cambridge: Harvard University Press, 1977.

———. *Studies in Tudor and Stuart Politics and Government.* 3 vols. Cambridge: Cambridge University Press, 1974–81.

———. *The Tudor Constitution: Documents and Commentary.* 2d ed. Cambridge: Cambridge University Press, 1982.

Erasmus, Desiderius. *Collected Works.* Edited by Craig R. Thompson et al. Toronto: University of Toronto Press, 1974–. *("CWE")*

———. *The Colloquies of Erasmus.* Translated by Craig R. Thompson. Chicago: University of Chicago Press, 1965.

————. *The Education of a Christian Prince.* Translated by Lester K. Born. New York: Columbia University Press, 1936.

————. *Erasmi Epistolae.* Edited by P. S. Allen. 12 vols. Oxford: Oxford University Press. ("Allen").

————. *Erasmi Opera Omnia.* Amsterdam: North Holland, 1969– ("OO").

————. *Erasmus on His Times: A Shortened Version of the Adages of Erasmus.* Translated by Margaret Mann Phillips. Cambridge: Cambridge University Press, 1967. ("Adagia").

————. *The Essential Erasmus.* Translated by John P. Dolan. New York: Mentor, 1964.

————. *Opera Omnia.* Edited by Jean Leclerc. 10 vols. Leyden, 1703. ("LB")

Evans, Arthur. *On Four Modern Humanists.* Princeton: Princeton University Press, 1970.

Evans, Maurice. *Spenser's Anatomy of Heroism.* Cambridge: Cambridge University Press, 1970.

Fernandez, Jose A. "Erasmus on the Just War." *Journal of the History of Ideas* 34 (1973): 209–26.

Filmer, Sir Robert. *Observations concerning the Originall of Government.* 1652.

"A Fine Fellow Erasmus." *Times Literary Supplement,* 3 June 1965, p. 454.

Fink, Zera S. *The Classical Republicans: An Essay in the Recovery of a Pattern of Thought in Seventeenth Century England.* Northwestern University Studies in Humanities 9. Evanston, Ill., 1945.

Finlayson, Michael G. *Historians, Puritanism, and the English Revolution.* Toronto: University of Toronto Press, 1983.

Firth, C. H. "The Court of Oliver Cromwell." *Cornhill Magazine,* September 1897, pp. 349–64.

Fish, Stanley. *Surprised by Sin.* New York: St. Martin's Press, 1967.

Fixler, Michael. *Milton and the Kingdoms of God.* London: Faber and Faber, 1964.

Fletcher, Angus. *Allegory: The Theory of a Symbolic Mode.* Ithaca: Cornell University Press, 1964.

————. *The Prophetic Moment: An Essay on Spenser.* Chicago: University of Chicago Press, 1971.

Fox, Alistair. *Thomas More: History and Providence.* New Haven: Yale University Press, 1983.

Franklin, Julian H., ed. and trans. *Constitutionalism and Resistance in the Sixteenth Century: Three Treatises by Hotman, Beza, and Mornay.* New York: Pegasus, 1969.

Freeman, James A. *Milton and the Martial Muse.* Princeton: Princeton University Press, 1980.

Frye, Northrop. *The Return of Eden.* Toronto: University of Toronto Press, 1965.

Fulgentius. *Sancti Fulgentii Episcopi Ruspensis Opera.* Edited by J. Fraipont. Corpus Christianorum Series Latina 91. Turnholdt, 1968.

Gainsford, Thomas. *The Glory of England.* 1618.

Gauchet, Marcel. *Le desenchantement du monde.* Paris: Gallimard, 1985.

Geldner, Ferdinand. *Die Staatsauffassung und Fürstenlehre des Erasmus von Rotterdam.* Berlin: E. Ebering, 1930.

Gilbert, Allan. *Machiavelli's "Prince" and Its Forerunners.* Durham, N.C.: Duke University Press, 1948.

———. "The Temptation in *Paradise Regained.*" *Journal of English and Germanic Philology* 15 (1916): 599–611.

Goddard, Harold. *The Meaning of Shakespeare.* Chicago: University of Chicago Press, 1951.

The Golden Legend. Translated by Granger Ryan and Helmut Ripperger. 2 vols. London: Longmans, 1941.

Goodin, Robert E. "Rites of Rulers." *British Journal of Sociology* 29 (1978): 281–99.

Goodman, Christopher. *How Superior Powers Oght to be Obeyd.* 1558. Reprint. New York: Facsimile Text Society, 1931.

Goodwin, John. *Theomachia.* 1644.

Gould, Gerald. "A New Reading of *Henry V.*" *English Review* 29 (1919): 42–55.

Grainger, J. H. "The Activity of Monarchy." *Cambridge Quarterly* 7 (1977): 297–313.

Grant, Michael. *Jesus: An Historian's Review of the Gospels.* New York: Scribner's, 1977.

Graziani, René. "Elizabeth at Isis Church." *PMLA* 79 (1964): 376–89.

Greaves, Richard L. "The Nature and Intellectual Milieu of the Political Principles in the Geneva Bible Marginalia." *Journal of Church and State* 22 (1980): 233–49.

Greenblatt, Stephen. "Invisible Bullets: Renaissance Authority and Its Subversion." *Glyph* 8 (1981): 40–61.

———. *Renaissance Self-Fashioning from More to Shakespeare.* Chicago: University of Chicago Press, 1980.

———. *Shakespeare Negotiations.* Berkeley and Los Angeles: University of California Press, 1988.

Greene, Gayle. " 'The Power of Speech / To Stir Men's Blood': The Language of Tragedy in Shakespeare's *Julius Caesar.*" *Renaissance Drana* 11 (1980): 67–93.

Greenfield, Thelma N. "*A Midsummer Night's Dream* and *The Praise of Folly.*" *Comparative Literature* 20 (1968): 236–44.

Greg, W. W., ed. *The Play of Antichrist from the Chester Cycle.* Oxford: Clarendon Press, 1935.

Gregory the Great. *Pastoral Care.* Translated by Henry Sweet. EETS, o.s. 45. London, 1897.

Griffith, Matthew. *The Fear of God and the King.* 1660.

Gross, Kenneth. *Spenserian Poetics: Idolatry, Iconoclasm, and Magic.* Ithaca: Cornell University Press, 1985.

Gurr, Andrew. " 'Henry V' and the Bees' Commonwealth." *Shakespeare Survey* 30 (1977): 61–72.

Hales, John. *Golden Remains.* 1673.

Halkin, Leon. "Erasme et la politique des rois." In *Die Humanisten in ihrer politischen und sozialen Umwelt*, edited by Otto Herding and Robert Stupperich. Boppard: Boldt, 1976.

Hall, Edward. *The Union of the Famelies of Lancastre and Yorke.* 1548.

Haller, William A., ed. *Tracts on Liberty in the Puritan Revolution.* 3 vols. New York: Columbia University Press, 1933–34.

Hanford, James Holly. *John Milton, Poet and Humanist.* Cleveland: Press of Western Reserve University, 1966.

Hapgood, Robert. "Speak Hands for Me: Gesture and Language in *Julius Caesar.*" *Drama Survey* 5 (1966): 162–70.

Hardin, Richard F. "Milton's Nimrod." *Milton Quarterly* 22 (1988): 38–44.

———. "The Resolved Debate of Spenser's 'October.'" *Modern Philology* 73 (1976): 257–63.

Harrison, Edward. *Plain Dealing.* 1649.

Hartsock, Mildred E. "The Complexity of 'Julius Caesar.'" *PMLA* 81 (1966): 56–62.

Hawkins, Sherman. "Virtue and Kingship in Shakespeare's *Henry IV.*" *English Literary Renaissance* 5 (1975): 314–42.

Hazlitt, William. *Characters of Shakespear's Plays.* Everyman's Library. London, 1906.

Helgerson, Richard. "Milton Reads the King's Book: Print, Performance, and the Making of a Bourgeois Idol." *Criticism* 29 (1987): 1–25.

Helterman, Jeffrey. *Symbolic Action in the Plays of the Wakefield Master.* Athens: University of Georgia Press, 1981.

Hemingway, Samuel B., ed. *The English Nativity Plays.* 1909. Reprint. New York: Russell and Russell, 1964.

Herding, Otto. "Isokrates, Erasmus, und die Institutio principis christiani." In *Dauer und Wandel der Geschichte: Aspekte Europäische Vergangenheit. Festgabe für Kurt von Raumer,* edited by Rudolf Vierhaus and Manfred Botzenhart. Munster: Verlag Aschendorff, 1966.

Hexter, J. H. *The Vision of Politics on the Eve of the Reformation.* New York: Basic Books, 1973.

Hibbard, G. R. "Erasmus and More in the Age of Shakespeare." *Erasmus in English* 12 (1983): 2–10.

Hill, Christopher. *Collected Essays.* 3 vols. Amherst: University of Massachusetts Press, 1986.

———. *Milton and the English Revolution.* London: Faber and Faber, 1977.

———. *Puritanism and Revolution.* 1958. Reprint. London: Panther, 1969.

Hobbes, Thomas. *Leviathan Parts I and II.* Edited by Michael Oakeshott. Oxford: Basil Blackwell, 1957.

Hoffman, Nancy Y. "Samson's Other Father: The Character of Manoa in *Samson Agonistes.*" *Milton Studies* 2 (1970): 195–210.

Holderness, Graham. *Shakespeare's History.* Dublin: Gill and Macmillan, 1985.

Holdsworth, R. V., et al. "Shakespeare." *Year's Work in English Studies* 65 (1984): 184–236.

Holdsworth, Sir William. *A History of English Law.* Vol. 5. London: Methuen, Sweet and Maxwell, 1924.

Holinshed, Raphael. *Chronicles of England, Scotland, and Ireland.* 6 vols. London, 1807.

Hooker, Richard. *The Folger Library Edition of the Works of Richard Hooker.* Edited by W. Speed Hill et al. 4 vols. Cambridge: Harvard University Press, 1977–82.

———. *Hooker's Ecclesiastical Polity Book VIII.* Edited by Raymond Aaron Houk. New York: Columbia University Press, 1931.

Hough, Graham. *A Preface to* The Faerie Queene. New York: Norton, 1963.

Hughes, Merritt Y. "Satan and the 'Myth' of the Tyrant." In *Essays in English Literature from the Renaissance to the Victorian Age*, edited by Miller MacLure and F. W. Watt. Toronto: University of Toronto Press, 1964.

Huizinga, Johan. *Erasmus and the Age of the Reformation.* Translated by F. Hopman. 1924. Reprint. New York: Harper and Row, 1957.

Hunter, William B., Jr. "The Liturgical Context of *Comus.*" *English Language Notes* 10 (1972): 11–15.

Hurstfield, Joel. *The Illusion of Power in Tudor Politics.* London: Athlone Press, 1979.

Hyma, Albert. "Erasmus and the Reformation in Germany." *Medievalia et Humanistica* 8 (1954): 99–104.

———. "Erasmus and the Sacrament of Matrimony." *Archiv für Reformationsgeschichte* 48 (1957): 145–64.

The Institucion of a Gentleman. 1555.

Isidore of Seville. *Allegoriae Quaedam Scripturae Sacrae.* MPL. 83.

Isocrates. *Isocrates.* Translated by George Norlin. Loeb Library. 1928. Reprint. London: Heinemann, 1966.

James I. Speech to Parliament, 21 March 1610. In *The Stuart Constitution: Documents and Commentary,* edited by J. P. Kenyon. Cambridge: Cambridge University Press, 1966.

James, Mervyn. *Society, Politics and Culture: Studies in Early Modern England.* Cambridge: Cambridge University Press, 1986.

Jameson, Frederic. "Religion and Ideology: A Political Reading of *Paradise Lost.*" In *Literature, Politics and Theory,* edited by Francis Barker et al. London: Methuen, 1986.

Jarrott, Catherine A. L. "Erasmus's Annotations and Colet's Commentaries on Paul: A Comparison of Some Theological Themes." In *Essays on the Works oif Erasmus,* edited by Richard L. DeMolen. New Haven: Yale University Press, 1978.

Jewel, John. *Reply to Harding's Answer.* Cambridge: Parker Society, 1847.

Johnson, Samuel. "Life of Milton." In *A Johnson Reader,* edited by E. L. McAdams and George Milne. New York: Pantheon Books, 1964.

Jones, Emrys. *The Origins of Shakespeare.* Oxford: Clarendon Press, 1977.

Jones, H. S. V. "Spenser's Defense of Lord Grey." *University of Illinois Studies in Language and Literature* 5 (1919): 151–219.

Jorgensen, Paul. "A Formative Shakespearean Legacy: Elizabethan Views of God, Fortune, and War." *PMLA* 90 (1975): 222–33.

Josephus. *The Works of Flavius Josephus.* Translated by E. Thompson and W. C. Price. 2 vols. London, 1777.

Kantorowicz, Ernst H. *The King's Two Bodies: A Study in Mediaeval Political Theology.* Princeton: Princeton University Press, 1957.

———. "Mysteries of State: An Absolutist Concept and its Late Mediaeval Origins." *Harvard Theological Review* 48 (1955): 65–91.

Keane, Ruth M. "Kingship in the Chester Nativity Play." *Leeds Studies in English* 13 (1982): 74–84.

Keeton, George W. *Shakespeare's Legal and Political Background.* London: Sir Isaac Pitman and Sons, 1967.

Keir, Sir David Lindsay. *The Constitutional History of Modern Britain, Since 1485.* 8th ed. London: A. and C. Black, 1966.

Kelly, Henry A. *Divine Providence in the England of Shakespeare's Histories.* Cambridge: Harvard University Press, 1970.

Kermode, Frank. "'The Faerie Queene', I and V." *Shakespeare, Spenser, Donne.* London: Routledge and kegan Paul, 1971.

———. *The Sense of an Ending.* Oxford: Oxford University Press, 1966.

Kerrigan, William. *The Prophetic Milton.* Charlottesville: University Press of Virginia, 1974.

King, John N. "Was Spenser a Puritan?" *Spenser Studies* 6 (1985): 1–31.

Knafla, Louis A. *Law and Politics in Jacobean England: The Tracts of Lord Ellesmere.* Cambridge: Cambridge University Press, 1977.

Knight, W. Nicholas. "The Narrative Unity of Book V of *The Faerie Queene:* 'That Part of Justice Which Is Equity.'" *Review of English Studies* 21 (1970): 267–94.

Knights, L. C. "Personality and Politics in *Julius Caesar.*" In *Julius Caesar, A Casebook,* edited by Peter Ure. London: Macmillan, 1969.

Knott, John R., Jr., *Milton's Pastoral Vision: An Approach to* Paradise Lost. Chicago: University of Chicago Press, 1971.

Koebner, Richard. "'The Imperial Crown of This Realm': Henry VIII, Constantine the Great and Polydore Vergil." *Bulletin of the Institute of Historical Research* 26, no. 73 (1953): 29–52.

Koerber, Eberhard von. *Die Staatstheorie des Erasmus von Rotterdam.* Berlin: Duncker & Humbolt, 1967.

Kogan, Stephen. *The Hieroglyphic King: Wisdom and Idolatry in the Seventeenth-Century Masque.* Rutherford, N.J.: Fairleigh Dickinson University Press, 1986.

Kolve, V. A. *The Play Called Corpus Christi.* Stanford: Stanford University Press, 1966.

Kristeller, Paul Oskar. *Renaissance Thought II: Papers on Humanism and the Arts.* New York: Harper and Row, 1965.

LaGuardia, Eric. "Ceremony and History: The Problem of Symbol from *Richard II* to *Henry V.*" In *Pacific Coast Studies in Shakespeare,* edited by Waldo F. McNeir and Thelma N. Greenfield. Eugene: University of Oregon Books, 1966.

Lamont, William M. *Godly Rule: Politics and Religion, 1603–60.* London: Macmillan, 1969.

Lamont, William, and Sybil Oldfield, eds., *Politics, Religion and Literature in the Seventeenth Century.* London: Dent, 1975.

Landino, Cristoforo. *Publii Virgilii Maronis Opera* [Commentary]. Strasbourg, 1502.

LaPiana, George. "Theology of History." In *The Interpretation of History,* edited by Joseph Strayer. 1943. Reprint. New York: Peter Smith, 1950.

Lease, Gary. "The Origins of National Socialism: Some Fruits of Religion and Nationalism." In *Religion and Politics in the Modern World,* edited by Peter H. Merkl and Ninian Smart. New York: New York University Press, 1983.

Leigh, Edward. *Critica Sacra.* 1639.

Leslie, Michael. *Spenser's "Fierce Warres and Faithfull Loves".* Cambridge, Eng.: D. S. Brewer, 1983.

Levin, Richard L. *The Multiple Plot in English Renaissance Drama.* Chicago: University of Chicago Press, 1971.

———. *New Readings vs. Old Plays: Recent Trends in the Reinterpretation of English Renaissance Drama.* Chicago: University of Chicago Press, 1979.

Levitsky, Ruth M. " 'The Elements Were So Mix'd.' " *PMLA* 88 (1973): 240–45.

Lewalski, Barbara Kiefer. *Milton's Brief Epic: The Genre, Meaning, and Art of Paradise Regained.* Providence, R.I.: Brown University Press, 1966.

Lloyd, Howell A. *The Rouen Campaign 1590–1592.* Oxford: Clarendon Press, 1973.

Loades, David M. *The Tudor Court.* London: B. T. Batsford, 1986.

Locher, G. W. "Zwingli and Erasmus." Translated by Isbell, Shaw, and Rummel. *Erasmus in English* 10 (1979–80): 2–11.

Lowenhaupt, Warren H. "The Writing of Milton's *Eikonoklastes.*" *Studies in Philology* 20 (1923): 29–51.

Ludus Coventriae, edited by K. S. Block. EETS, e.s. 120. London: 1922.

Lumiansky, R. M., and David Mills. *The Chester Mystery Cycle: Essays and Documents.* Chapel Hill: University of North Carolina Press, 1983.

Luther, Martin. *The Misuse of the Mass,* translated by Frederick Ahrens. *Luther's Works.* Vol. 36. Philadelphia: Muhlenberg Press, 1955.

Lydgate, John. *Fall of Princes.* Edited by Henry Bergen. EETS, e.s. 121–24. London, 1923–27.

MacKellar, Walter. *A Variorum Commentary on the Poems of John Milton.* Vol. 4. New York: Columbia University Press, 1975.

Maclachlan, Hugh. "In the Person of Prince Arthur: Spenserian *Magnificence* and the Ciceronian tradition." *University of Toronto Quarterly* 46 (1976–77): 125–46.

McConica, James Kelsey. *English Humanists and Reformation Politics under Henry VIII and Edward VI.* Oxford: Clarendon Press, 1965.

McCoy, Richard C. *The Rites of Knighthood: The Literature and Politics of Elizabethan Chivalry.* Berkeley: University of California Press, 1989.

McGee, J. Sears. *The Godly Man in Stuart England.* New Haven: Yale University Press, 1976.

Mack, Maynard, Jr. *Killing the King.* Yale Studies in English 180. New Haven, 1973.

Madsen, William G. *From Shadowy Types to Truth.* New Haven: Yale University Press, 1968.

Mansbach, S. A. "Pieter Brueghel's Towers of Babel." *Zeitschrift für Kunstgeschichte* 45 (1982): 43–56.

Mansfield, Bruce. "Erasmus in the Nineteenth Century: The Liberal Tradition." *Studies in the Renaissance* 15 (1968): 193–219.

———. *Phoenix of His Age: Interpretations of Erasmus ca. 1550–1750.* Toronto: University of Toronto Press, 1979.

Marius, Richard. *Thomas More: A Biography.* New York: Knopf, 1984.

Martines, Lauro. *Society and History in English Renaissance Verse.* Oxford: Basil Blackwell, 1985.

May, Stephen. "Good Kings and Tyrants: A Re-Assessment of the Regal Figure on the Medieval Stage." *Medieval English Theatre* 5 (1983): 87–102.

Mayer, Thomas F. "Faction and Ideology: Thomas Starkey's *Dialogue.*" *Historical Journal* 28 (1985): 1–25.

———. "Thomas Starkey: An Unknown Conciliarist at the Court of Henry VIII." *Journal of the History of Ideas* (1988): 207–27.

Melanchthon, Philip. *Whether It Be Mortall Sinne to Transgresse Civil Lawes.* 1566.

Merrix, Robert P. "The Alexandrian Allusion in Shakespeare's *Henry V.*" *English Literary Renaissance* 2 (1972): 321–33.

———. "Shakespeare's Histories and the New Bardolaters." *Studies in English Literature* 19 (1979): 179–96.

Mesnard, Pierre. *L'essor de la philosophie politique au XVIe siècle.* 3rd ed. *De Pétrarque à Descartes* 19. 1969.

"Millenary Petition." In *Documents Illustrative of English Church History,* edited by Henry Gee and W. J. Hardy. London and New York: Macmillan, 1896.

Miller, David Lee. *The Poem's Two Bodies: The Poetics of the 1590* Faerie Queene. Princeton: Princeton University Press, 1988.

Milton, John. *Complete Poems and Major Prose.* Edited by Merritt Y. Hughes. Indianapolis: Odyssey, 1957.

———. *Complete Prose Works of John Milton.* Edited by Don M. Wolfe. 8 vols. in 10. New Haven: Yale University Press, 1953–82 ("*CPW*").

Minkowski, Helmut. *Aus dem Nebel der Vergangenheit steigt der Turm zu Babel.* Berlin: Rembrandt Verlag, 1960.

Miola, Robert S. *Shakespeare's Rome.* Cambridge: Cambridge University Press, 1983.

The Mirroure of Mans Salvacionne. Roxburghe Club 118. London, 1888.

Le Mistere du Viel Testament. Edited by Baron James de Rothschild. Société des Anciennes Textes Francais 13. Reprint, 1966.

Mohl, Ruth. *Studies in Spenser, Milton, and the Theory of Monarchy.* New York: Frederick Ungar, 1962.

Molin, Jean Baptiste, and Protais Mutembe. *Le rituel du mariage en France du XIIe au XIV siècle.* Théologie Historique 26. Paris: Beauchesne, 1974.

Montaigne, Michel de. *Complete Essays.* Translated by Donald M. Frame. Stanford: Stanford University Press, 1958.

Montrose, Louis Adrian. "Interpreting Spenser's February Eclogue: Some Contexts and Implications." *Spenser Studies* 2 (1981): 67–74.

More, Thomas. *Complete Works of St. Thomas More.* Edited by Richard Sylvester et al. New Haven: Yale University Press, 1963–. ("*CWM*").

———. *The Correspondence of Sir .Thomas More.* Edited by Elizabeth F. Rogers. Princeton: Princeton University Press, 1947.

———. *Epigrammata.* Basel, 1518.

———. *History of King Richard III and Selections from the English and Latin Poems.* Edited by R. S. Sylvester. Translated by L. Bradner and C. A. Lynch. New Haven: Yale University Press, 1976.

———. *Selected Letters.* Edited and translated by Elizabeth F. Rogers. New Haven: Yale University Press, 1961.

———. *Utopia.* Translated by Robert M. Adams. New York: Norton, 1975.

Moretti, Franco. " 'A Huge Eclipse': Tragic Form and the Deconsecration of Sovereignty." Translated by D. A. Miller. *Genre* 15 (1982): 7–40.

Morley, George. *A Sermon Preached at the Magnificent Coronation.* 1661.

Morris, Christopher. *Political Thought in England: Tyndale to Hooker.* London: Oxford University Press, 1953.

Morton, Thomas. *Christus Dei, The Lords Anoynted.* Oxford, 1643.

———. *Defence of the Innocencie of the Three Ceremonies.* 1618.

Mosse, George L. *The Struggle for Sovereignty in England.* East Lansing: Michigan State College Press, 1950.

Mousnier, Roland. *The Assassination of Henry IV.* Translated by Joan Spencer. London: Faber and Faber, 1973.

Muir, Kenneth. "Shakespeare among the Commonplaces." *Review of English Studies* 10 (1959): 283–89.

Mulryan, John. "Erasmus and War." *Moreana* 23 (1986): 15–28.

Nédoncelle, M. "L'Humour d'Erasme et l'humour de Thomas More." *Scrinium Erasmianum,* edited by J. Coppens, vol. 2. Leyden: Brill, 1969.

Nelson, Janet L. "Inauguration Rituals." In *Early Medieval Kingship,* edited by P. H. Sawyer and I. N. Wood. Leeds: University of Leeds, 1977.

Nelson, William. "Queen Elizabeth, Spenser's Mercilla, and a Rusty Sword." *Renaissance News* 18 (1965): 113–17.

Nevo, Ruth. *Tragic Form in Shakespeare.* Princeton: Princeton University Press, 1972.

New, John F. H. *Anglican and Puritan.* London: A. and C. Black, 1964.

Nohrnberg, James. *The Analogy of* The Faerie Queene. Princeton: Princeton University Press, 1976.

Norbrook, David. *Poetry and Politics in the English Renaissance.* London: Routledge and Kegan Paul, 1984.

Northrop, Douglas A. "Mercilla's Court as Parliament. *Huntington Library Quarterly* 36 (1973): 153–58.

O'Connell, Michael. *Mirror and Veil: The Historical Dimension of Spenser's* Faerie Queene. Chapel Hill: University of North Carolina Press, 1977.

Oelrich, Karl Heinz. *Der späte Erasmus und die Reformation.* Reformationsgeschichtliche Studien und Texte, 86. Münster/Westfallen, 1961.

Ogg, David. *William III.* London: Collins, 1956.

Olin, John C. "The Pacifism of Erasmus." *Thought* 50 (1975): 418–31.

Ong, Walter. *Interfaces of the Word: Studies in the Evolution of Consciousness and Culture.* Ithaca: Cornell University Press, 1977.

Orgel, Stephen. *The Illusion of Power: Political Theater in the English Renaissance.* Berkeley and Los Angeles: University of California Press, 1975.

Ornstein, Robert. *A Kingdom for a Stage: The Achievement of Shakespeare's History Plays.* Cambridge: Harvard University Press, 1972.

Orru, Marco. "Anomy and Reason in the English Renaissance." *Journal of the History of Ideas* 47 (1986): 177–96.

Osborne, Francis. *A Perswasive to Mutuall Compliance under the Present Government.* Oxford, 1652.

Otto, Rudolf. *The Idea of the Holy.* Translated by John W. Harvey. London: Oxford University Press, 1923.

Ozment, Steven E. *The Reformation in the Cities: The Appeal of Protestantism to*

Sixteenth-Century Germany and Switzerland. New Haven: Yale University Press, 1975.

Palmer, John. *Political Characters of Shakespeare.* 1945. Reprint. London: Macmillan, 1961.

Palmer, Richard E. *Hermeneutics.* Evanston: Northwestern University Press, 1969.

Parker, William Riley. *Milton: A Biography.* Oxford: Clarendon Press, 1968.

Payne, John B. "Erasmus: Interpreter of Romans." In *Sixteenth Century Essays and Studies,* edited by Carl S. Meyer. St. Louis: Foundation for Reformation Research, 1971.

Perkins, William. *A Warning against the Idolatrie of the Last Times.* Cambridge, 1601.

Perkinson, Richard H. "*Volpone* and the Reputation of Venetian Justice." *MLR* 35 (1940): 11–18.

Peter, John. *A Critique of* Paradise Lost. London: Longmans, 1960.

Peter Chrysologus. *Sermones.* MPL. 52.

Peter Comestor. *Historia Scholastica.* MPL. 198.

Phillips, James. *The Reformation of Images.* Berkeley and Los Angeles: University of California Press, 1973.

Phillips, Margaret Mann. *Erasmus and the Northern Renaissance.* New York: Macmillan, 1950.

Piehler, Paul. "Milton's Iconoclasm." In *The Evolution of Consciousness,* edited by Shirley Sugerman. Middletown, Conn.: Wesleyan University Press, 1976.

Platt, Michael. "*The Rape of Lucrece* and the Republic for Which It Stands." *Centennial Review* 19 (1975): 59–79.

The Play of Antichrist. Translated by John Wright. Toronto: Pontifical Institute of Mediaeval Studies, 1967.

Porter, H. C. "Hooker, the Tudor Constitution and the *Via Media.*" In *Studies in Richard Hooker,* edited by W. Speed Hill, 77–116. Cleveland: Case Western Reserve, 1972.

Porter, H. C., ed. *Puritanism in Tudor England.* London: Macmillan, 1971.

Potter, Robert. *The English Morality Play: Origins, History, and Influence of a Dramatic Tradition.* London: Routledge and Kegan Paul, 1975.

Price, S. R. F. *Rituals and Power: The Roman Imperial Cult in Asia Minor.* Cambridge: Cambridge University Press, 1984.

Prior, Moody E. *The Drama of Power: Studies in Shakespeare's History Plays.* Evanston, Ill.: Northwestern University Press, 1973.

Prosser, Eleanor. *Drama and Religion in the English Mystery Play.* Stanford: Stanford University Press, 1961.

Quint, David. "David's Cenus: Milton's Politics and *Paradise Regained.*" In *Remembering Milton: Essays on the Texts and Traditions.* Edited by Mary Nyquist and Margaret W. Ferguson. New York: Methuen, 1987.

Rabanus Maurus. Commentary on Matthew. MPL. 107.

Rabkin, Norman. "Rabbits, Ducks, and *Henry V.*" *Shakespeare Quarterly* 28 (1977): 279–96.

———. *Shakespeare and the Common Understanding.* New York: Free Press, 1967.

———. *Shakespeare and the Problem of Meaning.* Chicago: University of Chicago Press, 1981.

Radzinowicz, Mary Ann. *Milton's Epics and the Book of Psalms*. Princeton: Princeton University Press, 1989.

———. *Toward Samson Agonistes: The Growth of Milton's Mind*. Princeton: Princeton University Press, 1978.

Reedy, Gerald, S.J. "Mystical Politics: The Imagery of Charles II's Coronation." In *Studies in Change and Revolution: Aspects of English Intellectual History 1640–1800*, edited by Paul Korshin. Menston, Yorks. Scolar Press: 1972.

Reese, M. M. *The Cease of Majesty: A Study of Shakespeare's History Plays*. London: Edward Arnold, 1961.

Renaudet, Augustin. "Erasme économiste." In *Mélanges offerts à M. Abel Lefranc*, n. ed., 130–41. Paris: E. Droz, 1936.

———. *Etudes Erasmiennes*. Paris: E. Droz, 1939.

Reresby, Sir John. *The Memoirs of Sir John Reresby*. Edited by James J. Cartwright. London: Longmans, Green, 1875.

Rhodes, J. T. "Erasmus and English Readers of the 1530's," *Durham University Journal* n.s. 40 (1978): 17–25.

Richmond, Hugh M. *Shakespeare's Political Plays*. New York: Random House, 1967.

Rogers, Thomas. *Lux Occidentalis: or Providence Display'd*. 1689.

Rosenblatt, Jason P. " 'Audacious Neighborhood': Idolatry in *Paradise Lost*, Book I." *Philological Quarterly* 54 (1975): 553–68.

Rosenthal, Joel, ed. *Kings and Kingship*. Acta 11. Binghamton, N.Y.: Center for Medieval and Early Renaissance Studies, 1986.

Ross, Alexander. *Mystagogus Poeticus or the Muses Interpreter*. 3d ed. 1653.

———. *Pansebeia*. 1655.

Ross, M. M. *Milton's Royalism*. Ithaca: Cornell University Press, 1943.

———. *Poetry and Dogma*. New Brunswick, N.J.: Rutgers University Press, 1954.

Salomon, Albert. "Democracy and Religion in the Works of Erasmus." *Review of Religion* 14 (1950): 227–49.

Salomon, Brownell. "Thematic Contraries and the Dramaturgy of *Henry V*." *Shakespeare Quarterly* 31 (1980): 343–56.

Salter, F. M. *Medieval Drama in Chester*. Toronto: University of Toronto Press, 1955.

Sanders, Wilbur. *The Dramatist and the Received Idea*. Cambridge: Cambridge University Press, 1968.

Sandler, Florence. "*The Faerie Queene*: An Elizabethan Apocalypse." In *The Apocalypse in English Renaissance Thought and Literature*. Edited by C. A. Patrides and Joseph Wittreich. Ithaca: Cornell University Press, 1984.

Sandys, Edwin. *Sermons*. Cambridge: Parker Society, 1841.

Scarisbrick, J. J. *Henry VIII*. 1968. Reprint. Harmondsworth: Penguin, 1972.

Schafer, Jurgen. "Falstaff's Voice." *Notes and Queries* 214 (1969): 135–36.

Schanzer, Ernest. *Shakespeare's Problem Plays*. London: Routledge and Kegan Paul, 1963.

Schell, Edgar T., and J. D. Schuchter, eds. *English Morality Plays and Moral Interludes*. New York: Holt, Rinehart, 1969.

Schiffhorst, Gerald J. "Patience and the Humbly Exalted Heroism of Milton's Messiah." *Milton Studies* 16 (1982): 97–113.

Schmidt, Herman, S.J. "Liturgy and Modern Society: Analysis of the Current Situation." In his ed., *Liturgy in Transition*. New York: Herder and Herder, 1971.

Schneidau, Herbert N. *Sacred Discontent: The Bible and Western Tradition*. Baton Rouge: Louisiana State University Press, 1976.

Schochet, Gordon J. *Patriarchalism in Political Thought*. Oxford: Basil Blackwell, 1975.

Scott, William O. "The Speculative Eye: Problematic Self-Knowledge in 'Julius Caesar'." *Shakespeare Survey* 40 (1988): 77–89.

Sellin, Paul. "The Hidden God: Reformation Awe in Renaissance English Literature." *The Darker Vision of the Renaissance: Beyond the Fields of Reason*. Edited by Robert S. Kinsman. UCLA Center for Medieval and Renaissance Studies Contributions 6. 1974.

Sen Gupta, S. C. *Shakespeare's Historical Plays*. London: Oxford University Press, 1964.

Servius. *Servii Grammatici . . . Commentarii*. Edited by G. Thilo. Leipzig: Teubner, 1887.

Shakespeare, William. *Complete Works: The Pelican Text Revised*. Edited by Alfred Harbage. New York: Viking, 1969.

———. *King Henry V.* Edited by J. H. Walter. New Arden ed. London: Methuen, 1954.

———. *King Henry V.* Edited by John Dover Wilson. New Cambridge Shakespeare. Cambridge, 1947.

———. *King Richard II.* Edited by Peter Ure. New Arden ed. London: Methuen, 1961.

Shaw, George Bernard. *Shaw on Shakespeare*. Edited by Edwin Wilson. New York: Dutton, 1961.

Shawcross, John T. Paradise Regain'd: *Worthy t'Have not Remain'd So Long Unsung*. Pittsburgh: Duquesne University Press, 1988.

Shirley, F. J. *Richard Hooker and Contemporary Political Ideas*. London: SPCK, 1949.

Shrimpton, Nicholas. "Shakespeare Performances . . . 1985–6." *Shakespeare Survey* 40 (1988): 169–83.

Sicherman, Carol Marks. " 'King Hal': The Integrity of Shakespeare's Portrait." *Texas Studies in Literature and Language* 21 (1979): 503–21.

Simmons, J. L. *Shakespeare's Pagan World: The Roman Tragedies*. Charlottesville: University Press of Virginia, 1973.

Simon, Joan. *Education and Society in Tudor England*. Cambridge: Cambridge University Press, 1966.

Sinfield, Alan, and Jonathan Dollimore, eds. *Political Shakespeare*. Ithaca: Cornell University Press, 1985.

Skelton, John. *The Complete Poems of John Skelton Laureate*. Edited by Philip Henderson. London: J. M. Dent & Sons, 1959.

Skey, Miriam Anne. "Herod the Great in Medieval European Drama." *Comparative Drama* 13 (1979): 330–61.

Skinner, Quentin. *The Foundations of Modern Political Thought*. 2 vols. Cambridge: Cambridge University Press, 1978.

Smith, Gordon Ross. "A Rabble of Princes: Considerations Touching Shakespeare's Political Orthodoxy in the Second Tetralogy." *Journal of the History of Ideas* 41 (1980): 29–48.

Smith, Sir Thomas. *De Republica Anglorum: A Discourse on the Commonwealth of England* (1583). Edited by L. Alston. Cambridge: Cambridge University Press, 1906.

Sobel, Eli. Review of Otto Herding and Robert Stupperich, eds., *Die Humanisten in ihrer politischen und sozialen Umwelt.* Boppard: Boldt, 1976. *Renaissance Quarterly* 31 (1978): 196–98.

Spenser, Edmund. *The Faerie Queene.* Edited by A. C. Hamilton. London: Longman, 1977.

———. *The Works of Edmund Spenser: A Variorum Edition.* Edited by E. A. Greenlaw et al. 10 vols. Baltimore: Johns Hopkins University Press, 1932–49.

Spriet, Pierre. "Amour et Politique: Le Discours de l'Autre dans *Julius Caesar,*" *Coriolan: Theatre et Politique.* Travaux del'Universite de Toulouse-Le Mirail, ser. B, vol. 5 (1984): 227–39.

Staines, David. "To Out-Herod Herod: The Development of a Dramatic Character." *Comparative Drama* 10 (1976): 29–53.

Starkey, Thomas. *A Dialogue between Pole and Lupset.* Edited by T. F. Mayer. Camden Society, ser. 4, vol. 37. London, 1989.

Stauffer, Ethelbert. *Christ and the Caesars.* London: SCM Press, 1955.

Steadman, John M. *Milton and the Renaissance Hero.* Oxford: Clarendon Press, 1967.

———. *Milton's Epic Characters: Image and Idol.* Chapel Hill: University of North Carolina Press, 1968.

Stein, Arnold. *Heroic Knowledge.* Minneapolis: University of Minnesota Press, 1957.

Stevens, Martin. *Four Middle English Mystery Cycles.* Princeton: Princeton University Press, 1987.

Stirling, Brents. *Unity in Shakespearean Tragedy: The Interplay of Theme and Character.* New York: Columbia University Press, 1956.

Stoll, Elmer Edgar. *Poets and Playwrights.* Minneapolis: University of Minnesota Press, 1930.

Storr, Anthony. Rev. of Patrick Roberts, *The Psychology of Tragic Drama. TLS,* 6 June 1975, p. 616.

Stribrny, Zdenek. "*Henry V* and History." In *Shakespeare in a Changing World,* edited by Arnold Kettle. New York: International Publishers, 1964.

Strong, Roy. *Splendour at Court: Renaissance Spectacle and Illusion.* London: Weidenfeld and Nicolson, 1973.

Stroup, Thomas B. *Religious Rite and Ceremony in Milton's Poetry.* Lexington: University of Kentucky Press, 1968.

Stump, Donald V. "Isis versus Mercilla: The Allegorical Shrines in Spenser's Legend of Justice." *Spenser Studies* 3 (1982): 87–98.

Symons, Edward. *A Loyall Subjects Beliefe.* Oxford, 1643.

Tayler, Edward. *Milton's Poetry: Its Development in Time.* Pittsburgh: Duquesne University Press, 1979.

Taylor, Gary. Introduction to Shakespeare, *Henry V.* The Oxford Shakespeare. New York: Oxford University Press, 1984.

Taylor, Jeremy. *The Life of Our Blessed Lord and Savior Jesus Christ.* In *The Whole Works.* Edited by R. Heber. Revised and corrected by C. P. Eden. London: Longmans, Green, 1881.

Tertullian. *On Idolatry.* Translated by S. Thelwall. Ante-Nicene Christian Library 11. Edinburgh: T. & T. Clark, 1869.

Thayer, Calvin G. *Shakespearean Politics: Government and Misgovernment in the Great Histories.* Athens: Ohio University Press, 1983.

Thomas Aquinas. *Summa Theologiae.* Vols. 40 and 41. New York and London: McGraw Hill and Eyre and Spottiswoode, 1964.

Thompson, Martyn P. "The Idea of Conquest in Controversies over the 1688 Revolution." *Journal of the History of Ideas* 38 (1977): 33–46.

Tillyard, E. M. W. *Shakespeare's History Plays.* London: Chatto and Windus, 1944.

The Towneley Plays. Edited by George England and Alfred W. Pollard. EETS, e.s. 71. London, 1897.

Tracy, James. *Erasmus: The Growth of a Mind. Travaux d'humanisme et Renaissance* 121. Geneva, 1972.

———. *The Politics of Erasmus: A Pacifist Intellectual and His Political Milieu.* Toronto: University of Toronto Press, 1978.

Travis, Peter W. *Dramatic Design in the Chester Cycle.* Chicago: University of Chicago Press, 1982.

Trevor-Roper, Hugh. *Catholics, Anglicans and Puritans: Seventeenth-Century Essays.* Chicago: University of Chicago Press, 1988.

Tudor Interludes. Edited by Peter Happé. Harmondsworth: Penguin, 1972.

Turner, Victor. *Dramas, Fields and Metaphors.* Ithaca: Cornell University Press, 1974.

Twysden, Roger. *Certaine Considerations upon the Government of England.* Edited by John Mitchell Kemble. Camden Society. Vol. 45. London, 1849.

Tyacke, Nicholas. *Anti-Calvinists: The Rise of English Arminianism.* Oxford: Clarendon Press, 1987.

Tyndale, William. *An Answer to Sir Thomas More's Dialogue, The Supper of the Lord.* Cambridge: Parker Society, 1850.

———. *Doctrinal Treatises.* Cambridge, Eng.: Parker Society, 1848.

Ulreich, John C. "The Typological Structure of Milton's Imagery." *Milton Studies* 5 (1973): 67–85.

Van der Noot, Jan. *Theatre for Worldlings.* 1569. Reprint. New York: Scholars' Facsimiles, 1939.

Van der Zee, Henry and Barbara. *William and Mary.* London: Macmillan, 1973.

Van Doren, Mark. *Shakespeare.* 1939. Reprint. Garden City: Doubleday, n.d.

Vawter, Marvin. " 'Division 'tween Our Souls': Shakespeare's Stoic Brutus." *Shakespeare Studies* 7 (1974): 173–95.

———. "*Julius Caesar:* Rupture in the Bond." *Journal of English and Germanic Philology* 72 (1973): 311–28.

Verba, Sidney. "The Kennedy Assassination and the Nature of Political Commitment." In *The Kennedy Assassination and the American Public,* edited by Bradley S. Greenberg and Edwin B. Parker. Stanford: Stanford University Press, 1965.

Vickers, Brian. *Francis Bacon and Renaissance Prose.* Cambridge: Cambridge University Press, 1968.

Vindiciae contra Tyrannos. Edited by Harold J. Laski, as *A Defence of Liberty against Tyrants.* New York: Harcourt Brace, 1924.

Walch, Gunter. " 'Henry V' as a Working-House of Ideology." *Shakespeare Survey* 40 (1988): 63–68.

Wallace, John M. *Destiny His Choice: The Loyalism of Andrew Marvell.* Cambridge: Cambridge University Press, 1968.

Ware, John. *The Priviledges of the People.* 1649.

Waters, D. Douglas. *Duessa As Theological Satire.* Columbia: University of Missouri Press, 1970.

———. "Spenser and the 'Mas' at the Temple of Isis." *Studies in English Literature* 19 (1979): 43–53.

Wells, Robin Headlam. *Spenser's* Faerie Queene *and the Cult of Elizabeth.* London: Croom Helm, 1983.

Wells, Stanley, and Gary Taylor. *Modernizing Shakespeare's Spelling, with Three Studies in the Text of Henry V.* Oxford: Clarendon Press, 1979.

Welsford, Enid. *The Fool.* London: Faber and Faber, 1935.

Williams, C. H. *William Tyndale.* London: Thomas Nelson, 1969.

Williams, William Carlos. *The Embodiment of Knowledge.* Edited by Ron Loewinsohn. New York: New Directions, 1974.

Williams, Penry. *The Tudor Regime.* Oxford: Clarendon Press, 1979.

Wilson, Harold S. *On the Design of Shakespearean Tragedy.* Toronto: University of Toronto Press, 1957.

Wittreich, Joseph A. *Visionary Poetics: Milton's Tradition and His Legacy.* San Marino: Huntington Library Press, 1979.

Wollman, David H. "The Biblical Justification for Resistance to Authority in Ponet's and Goodman's Polemics." *Sixteenth Century Journal* 13 (1982): 29–41.

Woodbridge, L. T. "Shakespeare's Use of Two Erasmian Colloquies." *Notes and Queries* 30 (1983): 122–23.

Woolf, Rosemary. *The English Mystery Plays.* London: Routledge and Kegan Paul, 1972.

Wootton, David, ed. *Divine Right and Democracy: An Anthology of Political Writing in Stuart England.* Harmondsworth: Penguin, 1986.

Wren, Matthew. *A Sermon Preched before the Kings Majestie.* Cambridge, 1627.

Yamaguchi Masao. "Kingship as a System of Myth: An Essay in Synthesis." Translated by Simon Pleasance. *Diogenes* 77 (1972): 43–70.

Yates, Frances A. *Astraea: The Imperial Theme in the Sixteenth Century.* London: Routledge, 1975.

The York Plays. Edited by Lucy Toulmin Smith. 1885. Reprint. New York: Russell and Russell, 1963.

Young, Karl. *The Drama of the Medieval Church.* 2 vols. Oxford: Clarendon Press, 1933.

Zeeveld, W. Gordon. *The Temper of Shakespeare's Thought*. New Haven: Yale University Press, 1974.

Zimbardo, Rose A. "Comic Mockery of the Sacred: *The Frogs* and *The Second Shepherds' Play*." *Educational Theatre Journal* 30 (1978): 398–406.

Index

Adams, Robert M., 19
Adso, 53–54
Antichrist, 53–54. *See also* Chester plays; Tegernsee
Aquinas, Thomas: *latria* in, 21–22, 79–80; *De Regimine Principum*, 73
Augustine of Hippo, 16–17; on *latria*, 21

Babel, Tower of, 122–23
Bacon, Francis, 162
Bagehot, Walter, 30
Bancroft, Bishop Richard, 204
Benediktbeuern Passion Play, 44
Bennett, Joan S., 11, 176
Beza, Theodore, 34
Blackwood, Andrew, 34
Blount, Charles, 203–4
Boccaccio, Giovanni, *De Casibus*, 19, 48, 73
Bodin, Jean, 34–35
Boétie, Etienne de la, 160
Bracton, Henry de, 23–24
Bradshaw, William, 33–34, 204
Broadbent, J. B., 189
Brueghel, Peter, "Tower of Babel," 49
Buchanan, George, 34, 38, 69–70
Budé, Guillaume, 73
Burnet, Bishop Gilbert, 202–3

Calvin, Jean, 37, 236
Cartwright, Thomas, 38
Censure of the Rota, The, 173
Chapman, George, 158
Charles I, King, 21, 119, 165, 170–72, 176, 186
Charles II, King, 202–3
Charles V, Emperor, 65, 73, 76
Chester plays: *Annunciation and Nativity*, 47, 49–52; *Antichrist*, 54–56, 215–16

Chrysaor, 113
Cicero: *De Officiis*, 19, 148; "father of his country," 182
Cinthio, G. B. Giraldi, 116
Civil idolatry: defined, 15, 39, 209
Clarendon, Edward Lord, 205
Cohn, Norman, 51
Colet, John, 66
Conquest theory, 94–95, 190–91
Constantine, 16
Contarini, Gasparo, 122
Cook, John, 49
Cooper, Bishop Thomas, 33
Coronation ceremony, 142, 202–4, 242
Corpus Christi, feast of, 44
Coursen, Herbert, 133
Covell, William, 159
Cox, John D., 11
Cranmer, Archbishop Thomas, 205
Creighton, Mandell, 31
Cromwell, Oliver, 49, 240
Cursor Mundi, 48
Cyprian, 16

Daniel, Samuel, 38
Daniélou, Jean, 16
Davies, Stevie, 10–11, 178
De Regimine Principum (Aegidius Romanus, Hoccleve), 72–73
Desacralizing, 28–34, 210, 213
Divine Right of Kings, The (Figgis), 31, 189
Dollimore, Jonathan, 10
Dorp, Martin, 72
Drayton, Michael, 132, 234
Dudley, Edmund, 60
dulia. See latria

Eccleshall, Robert, 62
Education of a Christian Prince, The (Erasmus), 20, 65, 72–81; aphorisms in, 73–75; critics of, 75–76; genre of,